# THE LONDON T TYPES

# THE LONDON T TYPES

KEN BLACKER

Capital Transport

First published 2015

ISBN 978-1-85414-395-2

Published by Capital Transport Publishing Ltd
www.capitaltransport.com

Printed by 1010 Printing International Ltd

# CONTENTS

# INTRODUCTION

This volume marks, in effect, the completion of a trilogy devoted to the buses and coaches bought by the London General Omnibus Company and its associates in the final years of its independent existence. The LT class six-wheelers, and their four-wheeled double deck ST counterparts, dominated the London bus scene during the later days of the LGOC and retained a significant foothold for two decades before the last remnants finally drifted away in 1953. The T class was different. Although clearly in the same general mould as the LT and ST, its impact on the LGOC itself was not so great, although the phenomenal growth and expansion of the Green Line network could not have been achieved without it. The big difference, however, is that the T class continued to grow, right through the tenure of the London Passenger Transport Board and into the early days of post-war nationalisation. Newer members of the class continued in service for several years after the LTs and STs had all gone, and as a result, remain fresher in the memory.

Even at its maximum, the T class was much smaller than the other two, and there was never a time when all of the vehicles that comprised it were in stock together. Having been built over a period of almost two decades, and further augmented by the miscellany of acquisitions from other oper-

ators in its earlier years, it was infinitely more varied than the LTs and STs, and for this reason it has not been possible to record the history of the class as an ongoing narrative as I did with the earlier volumes. Instead each sub-type is dealt with from start to finish in individual chapters, which I hope will not impair the enjoyment of reading about this most fascinating class of vehicles.

The onset of obsolescence meant that elements of the T class began to fade from the scene as early as 1937, long before I could possibly have any recollection of them, so I have had to rely mainly on contemporary records and photographs to get a 'feel' of what these early exiles from the fleet were like. My own personal experience of the Ts stretches from a schoolboy perspective in the later war years onwards, through to my early days working for London Transport during which they were an interesting, albeit diminishing, part of the scene. During those hectic years the T class was best known for the grip it held – through the highly successful 10T10 coaches – on the Green Line network where it predominated. I am a little ashamed to say that I cannot remember ever travelling on a 10T10 on the Green Line. My own local route was worked by Q-types, and on the rare occasions when I could afford the premium fares to take a joy ride on the Green Line, I always chose the TFs which seemed to offer a far more exhilarating run. It is a sad reflection on the deteriorating condition of many of the Ts that my best remembered journey on one was a miserable trip on a 9T9 between Guildford and Dorking on a pouring wet day when the windows were heavily steamed up and rain was seeping into the saloon in several places.

Events occur in life that can set you off on an unexpected course, and one such defining moment for me came when a group of friends (mostly now deceased) and myself decided in 1956 to buy T 31 from London Transport with the aim of saving a little bit of London bus history that was about to be lost for ever. To say that all didn't go well with our pioneering preservation effort would be an understatement, but from a personal perspective it started me off on a line of interest which I have pursued ever since and which fired the imagination of others so that, in seemingly no time at all, a huge bus preservation movement was created which still thrives today. Fortunately more competent and better financed people than ourselves later took T 31 under their wing, but I am proud that my little effort all those years ago helped towards its survival today.

This volume has been compiled using the vast amount of information, official and otherwise, that I have collected on the T class over a long number of years. I have tapped every possible source that I can find but obviously, after such a huge lapse of time, there are bound to be gaps in the accumulated knowledge, and even after the most ardent double-checking, odd inaccuracies may have crept in either in interpretation or even in the source material from which information is taken. Once again, I have done my best with the information available, and I hope it makes interesting reading.

As always, I would like to express my grateful thanks to everyone who has helped me over the years by supplying information, memories or photographs without which this history would have been nowhere near as complete. Special

thanks go, as they did with the LT and ST books, to my friend Alan Nightingale who has made great efforts to unearth photographs and additional information, and who kindly took on the unenviable task of reading and checking the draft of the text. Many of those whose help I freely acknowledge are no longer with us, and the list of absent friends has grown even longer since the ST book was published. Friends from the past who have contributed posthumously to this volume have included the late Peter Aldridge, Frank Davis, John Gillham, Ken Glazier, Bill Haynes, Don Jones, Vic Jones, Ron Lunn, Prince Marshall, George Robbins, Don Thompson and Reg Westgate. To John Aldridge, Tony Beard, Alan Cross, Les Hampton, Alan Pearce, Anthony Roscoss, Hugh Taylor and Mick Webber I must say a big Thank You for all your help.

Ken Blacker

# 1 THE FIRST OF THE T TYPES

## T 1-37, 39-50, 156

On Thursday 5th December 1929 a small contingent of new single deck buses entered service in London's far eastern suburbs unannounced and totally without any form of publicity. The new vehicles, T 1-10, were the London General Omnibus Company's first AEC Regals and their arrival completed the implementation of the very first stage in the Company's scheme for the wholesale renewal of its fleet using the very latest products to emerge from AEC's modern factory at Southall. The LGOC board had sanctioned the purchase of buses of three different models to cater for a variety of operating conditions; Renown three-axle double and single deckers (LT and LTL classes), Regent two-axle double deckers (ST), and the Regal single deckers comprising the T class with which this volume deals. These modern vehicles were urgently needed to enable General to extricate itself, just in time, from the danger of falling behind its competitors who were already exploiting the Company's weakness by pitting the likes of the ultra-modern Leyland Titan against the latter's standard offering, the slow and cumbersome NS. The comprehensive new range from the AEC stable was the work of G J Rackham who had been employed by AEC in July 1928 to revive its fortunes, and an early reward was a public announcement by the LGOC in August 1929 of its intention to purchase no fewer than 270 new chassis comprising 50 Regals, 120 Regents and 100 Renowns.

Early examples of the two double deck models had, in fact,

been received and placed into service before the first Regals arrived. LT 1 had started work with a great blaze of publicity on 6th August 1929, followed by ST 1 on 1st November. No public fanfare had greeted ST 1, but it was paraded at Chiswick for the trade press and other interested parties to photograph and admire. In total contrast, the LGOC shunned publicity entirely for its new Ts, and even omitted the customary photo session which normally preceded the introduction of new models until T 41 was, slightly belatedly, returned to Chiswick for this purpose on 9th January 1930. On the other hand, almost all of the initial batch of 50 Ts had successfully been placed into service before any of the production runs of LTs or STs were ready to take to the road, giving the Regal the honour of being the first of the three modern AEC models to make its presence really felt on the London scene. Though not outstandingly innovative in appearance, the new vehicles looked fresh and bright in a new albeit short-lived livery of red and cream.

In outward appearance the new T class Regals were functional and businesslike. T 27 was photographed in its first summer of operation working from Nunhead garage on the frying-pan style circular route 621 which habitually encountered heavy loadings on its short 28 minute round trip from Lord Hill, Peckham. After just 10 months in service, T 27 was the vehicle selected as the guinea pig for the pioneer conversion to front entrance layout. *W Noel Jackson © A B Cross*

Before looking at the new bus in detail, it is interesting to note how widespread its use was across the LGOC's territory right from the earliest days. The first garage to receive Ts was Romford for routes G1 (Collier Row–Cranham), G5 (Romford–Hornchurch) and 187 (Chadwell Heath–Harold Wood), although they were officially allocated to Seven Kings which was where major maintenance on them was carried out. In common with a number of small outlying garages, Romford had no vehicle allocation of its own but was provisioned from its most convenient large neighbour, in this case Seven Kings. Cricklewood garage placed Ts into service a week after Romford, on 12th December 1929, on route 104 (Golders Green–Burnt Oak). A really big day was 30th December with three introductions taking place: Nunhead on route 621 (Peckham circular), Holloway on route 110 (Finsbury Park–Golders Green) and Crayford on route 99C (Erith–Dartford). As in the case of Romford, the small Crayford garage had no vehicles of its own and its three Ts were officially based at Plumstead. With the programme now almost completed, a few vehicles were left unallocated and these started work, mostly between 2nd and 7th January 1930, at Sutton on route 113 (Banstead–Kingston).

The LGOC's purchase of new vehicles was authorised using sanction numbers, and the initial order for 50 Regals (T 1-50) was made against sanction no. 953, ahead of the first batch of double deck Renowns (LT 1-50), the first single deck Renowns (LT 1001-1050), and the first Regents after the initial prototype (ST 2-301), which were sanctions 977 to 979 respectively. At the time of placing the chassis orders, the Company's internal body numbers were allocated which, in the case of the first 50 Ts, were 10228-10277. AEC's chassis number for the 50 Regals, 662028-662077, indicated that they were amongst the earliest orders received, and in fact only one other operator – Plymouth Corporation – managed to get Regals into regular service ahead of the LGOC.

The model 662 was typical of the complete new range of passenger chassis that G J Rackham had designed for AEC which incorporated practically nothing from previous AEC models. It was built to a 17ft wheelbase to accommodate a body length of either 26ft, as required by the Public Carriage Office for buses licensed for service in London, or 27ft for wider use. The front end was particularly neat and compact with the handsome new radiator placed right at the front of the chassis frame, while behind it the engine, single plate clutch and gearbox were combined into one complete unit. The gearbox, designated D119 by AEC, gave four forward speeds with sliding mesh engagement of all indirect ratios. The front axle was a new design, and a Marles cam and roller steering box was used. To achieve a low floor line the worm drive differential unit was offset to the nearside, and the rear axle was also a new design, of the semi-floating type. Servo-assisted braking was provided on all four wheels using the single servo system current at the time.

The only unit on the Regal chassis – albeit a very important one – of which the LGOC had had previous experience was the A140 6.1 litre 6-cylinder overhead camshaft engine which, with 100mm bore and 130mm stroke, gave a rated power of 95bhp. This marked a 60% increase over the output of the 4-cylinder side-valve engines upon which the LGOC had previously placed such great store, and it benefited from the provision of pressure lubrication to the main bearings and big ends. Rackham had produced this engine very early in his time with AEC, and it had been rushed into service in the autumn of 1928 in the model 660 Reliance, which was in effect a re-working of the existing and now outdated ADC 426 chassis with a modern engine installed. The Reliance was used to bridge the gap until the new Regal, Regent and Renown models got into production, and the LGOC purchased 34 of these in 1929 with a mixture of bus and coach bodywork. A further five were bought in 1930, after the first Regals had come on the scene, which were fitted with second hand coach bodies.

Licensed for service at Nunhead on 31st December 1929, T 41 was already showing traces of a week's winter operation on its wheels and mudflaps when it returned to Chiswick for an appointment with the official photographer on a drab 9th January 1930. The uninspiring rear profile harked back to design trends of earlier times, especially in the use of boards rather than roller blinds for displaying route number and destination details, and the unpopular offside seat facing its open doorway left occupants susceptible to draughts and dust. *London Transport Museum*

The bodies for the 50 Ts were built at Chiswick, where they were stockpiled until new chassis began to arrive from Southall from 25th November 1929 onwards, and no attempt was made to keep the body numbers in sequence with the chassis and fleet numbers. Nor was a spare body provided to act as an overhaul float, which was the LGOC's normal practice with a fleet as large as 50, and though one was subsequently sanctioned it was never built. Of typical Chiswick construction, the bodies were framed mainly in seasoned English ash with steel flitches to give added strength, but unlike the contemporary LT and ST double deckers they contained no real elements of design innovation and could be described as evolutionary rather than revolutionary. Built as 30-seaters to a very conventional styling with open rear platform, they bore a marked similarity to a batch of bodies built on Reliance chassis in June 1929 for services worked on the LGOC's behalf by National in the Watford area. These had pioneered the use of a roller blind destination box at the front of the vehicle which now became a standard fitment, but the Ts marked a further step forward in having a fully enclosed driver's cab except for the permanently open doorway aperture. The fitment of a windscreen and glazed side panels was done as part of a May 1929 concession by the Metropolitan Police to the LGOC allowing 100 new buses to be equipped in this way on an experimental basis, the 50 Regals being selected for this purpose along with 49 LTs and one ST. At a modest unladen weight of 5 tons 1 cwt the completed vehicle clearly carried no surplus weight and would have been both lively and economical to operate.

Internally the new T type buses were comfortably furnished with deep sprung seats covered back and front in an attractive fawn moquette. None of the customary polished wood was evident in the internal décor; instead there was extensive use of grey-green 'scratchproof' rexine to cover the side panels as well as the window, ceiling and other mouldings, while the ceiling centre panels were covered in white rexine. There was an ample supply of half-drop windows, three on each side, of a new type with catches located at each corner of the top rail for lowering them, closure being achieved by pushing the frame upwards against the ratchet. Another new feature was the prominent raised ventilator panel on the front bulkhead which was a practical if not particularly attractive feature containing a sliding grid operated by the conductor. Pneumatic bells with untarnishable plungers were used in place of the traditional bell cord. But perhaps the most striking feature – which was also to be found on early LTs and STs – was the modernistic use of concealed lighting with the bulbs hidden behind translucent curved ceiling panels made of a non-flammable material called 'Acetaloid' but often referred to as 'Pearlite'. This arrangement was designed to give out a diffused and warm glow after dark whilst reducing clutter to a minimum and it was certainly effective in this respect though sometimes complained about as being difficult to read by.

At some stage between the placing of the contract and the commencement of deliveries the decision was taken to divert one of the new chassis from its original purpose and to body it instead as a coach for short distance limited stop work. The chassis eventually set aside for this was that of T 38 when it arrived at Chiswick from Southall on 19th December 1929. It was fitted almost immediately with the new coach body that had already been constructed, and it never became part of the recognised bus fleet. Its subsequent history as a Green Line coach is reviewed in chapter 2. Meanwhile newly built

bus body 10277 was left unused for a few months while an order (sanction no. 1003) for a single replacement chassis was processed. This was delivered from Southall as 662330 on 22nd May 1930 and given the next fleet number vacant at the time, T 156. Identical in every way to its predecessors but immediately recognisable by its GF registration number in place of the familiar UU, T 156 entered service at Nunhead on 4th July. An interesting note made at the time was that an experimental dust curtain was fitted to its rear entrance, but no records survive to show how this was fixed or what material it was made from.

One other vehicle stood apart from the main batch. This was T 43 which was delivered slightly later than the others and was fitted with an experimental 8-cylinder engine. It was, in fact, the first of five buses to be similarly equipped from new, the others being LTs 35 and 41 and STs 8 and 84. The LGOC's Development Engineer, Owen Watson, was particularly interested in exploiting the potential of the 8-cylinder in-line engine, having witnessed its smooth running in high class cars such as the Hillman, Lanchester and Wolseley, and he obtained permission to commission AEC to construct five such engines at Southall to the LGOC's specification. The engines are believed to have been a modification of the standard A140 overhead camshaft unit with a reduction from the usual 100mm bore down to 87mm to theoretically achieve the same swept volume. Being, obviously, longer than the normal engine, a large bonnet was required to accommodate it. In the case of the two double deck classes this was achieved simply by getting permission from the Metropolitan Police to project the radiator forwards by a few inches, but this course was not taken with T 43 even though to have done so would not have infringed the national maximum permitted length of 27ft. Instead the chassis frame was shortened behind the rear axle by 6 inches, and although the standard 17ft wheelbase was retained the overall body length was reduced to 25ft 6ins. Whilst the rear bay, which contained the entrance steps, retained its normal length, the one ahead of it and partly situated over the rear wheelarch was shortened and the difference could be clearly seen from outside the vehicle.

T 43 started work at Sutton on 16th January 1930, moving on to Holloway on 9th April and Nunhead on 2nd June, presumably as part of an ongoing test of its performance against standard vehicles in differing operating locations. It is not totally clear what level of refinement the Development Department was seeking to achieve as the standard 6-cylinder engine ran as smoothly as anyone could wish for within a public service vehicle, and in the event the results on all five vehicles proved disappointing. The 8-cylinder engine actually produced a rated bhp of only 85, a reduction of 10bph because mixture distribution proved to be less satisfactory than anticipated using a single carburettor on such a long engine, and vehicle by vehicle the experiment was discontinued. One of the last was T 43 which received a standard 6-cylinder engine on its first overhaul at Chiswick in January 1931.

*Right* Ts 28 and 29 were amongst the first contingent received at Kingston in May 1931 by which time they had undergone their first overhaul and were in the revised livery of red and grey which incorporated a greater spread of red below the windows. Both front and rear aspects of the body design can be seen in this view taken in Bridge Street, Staines, with T 29 facing the camera and T 28 further away. Even from a distance it can be clearly seen that the rear registration plate of the latter vehicle has been lowered from its original location on the waistrail. *J F Higham © A B Cross*

The driver of T 43 appears to be deep in discussion with a colleague, perhaps about the merits or otherwise of the 8-cylinder engine fitted to this particular vehicle, as evidenced by the forward projection of the radiator and the snout-like effect which it has produced. Clearly visible is the penultimate bay in the bodywork which was the one that was shortened to produce a 6 inch reduction in the overall length of the body. T 43 was on its second assignment when photographed, having been used at Holloway garage to serve route 110 between Finsbury Park and Golders Green from 9th April to 1st June 1930 inclusive.
*W Noel Jackson © A B Cross*

Green was the colour which predominated over the interior décor, not only on the side panels and on the window and ceiling mouldings, but also on the coverings of the deeply sprung and very comfortable seats. The widespread use of rexine coverings meant that the overall effect was not as sumptuous as if polished wooden mouldings had been fitted, but the system of hidden lighting was undoubtedly ultra-modern for its time. The gentle diffused glow which it gave can be seen in the night-time photograph looking towards the front of T 41, where the new and somewhat ugly type of raised ventilator panel stands out prominently above the mirror and the fareboard holder. Also of note are the two plungers for the pneumatic bell system which are placed where they could prove hard to reach when the seats below them are fully occupied. The half-drop windows initially had pinch grips at each end, but these were replaced a few years later by the type with a single central push-down lever widely used on the LTs and STs.
*London Transport Museum*

The first overhaul cycle, which commenced with T 1 on 10th October 1930 and went on into early January 1931, with T 156 following in July, saw each vehicle dealt with as an individual unit with no body or other identity changes taking place. A modification to the external livery saw the original cream relief replaced by the LGOC's standard grey (which more closely resembled off-white), and at the same time the area of red was increased to incorporate the raised panels below the windows. At the same time the opportunity was taken to correct a number of shortcomings which had become evident during the first year's operation and which had been put right during July on T 43 using this vehicle as a guinea pig. Foremost amongst the tasks was a strengthening of the main body structure above the cab and canopy where it is probable that the initial design had not taken sufficient account of the weight imposed by the destination box and its associated blind winding gear. Evidence that the work had been carried out was provided by a thickening of the black band which was now deeper at the front end than elsewhere on the vehicle. To improve passenger acceptability the ceiling mounted handrails at the rear of the saloon were lowered by 2 inches and a footrest was provided over the rear differential. At the front of the saloon the first nearside seat was reduced from a double to a single, bringing the seating total for each vehicle down to 29. Above everyone's head, the diffused lighting panels were replaced by conventional exposed bulbs, no doubt to the relief of garage staff who no longer faced the rigmarole of unscrewing items of bodywork each time a faulty bulb needed changing.

At the same time a far greater transformation was taking place on T 27 which had gone into Chiswick for overhaul from Nunhead on 30th October. The open rear entrance had always been unpopular on single deckers because the dust and dirt drawn in through it by suction were not pleasant for passengers seated at the rear, but it was a feature that had been insisted upon for all large omnibuses by the Metropolitan Police. The Police had now rescinded this rule, and the LGOC was anxious to adopt a front entrance design for its new fleet of LT six-wheeled single deckers which was about to go into production. A suitable design had been drawn up, but the Company wished to test the concept before launching into full-scale production, and T 27 was earmarked as the test bed for this. The result was a workmanlike-looking body with open front entrance doorway and a central emergency door in the rear wall. Seats were provided for 30 arranged in transverse rows at the front, four on the nearside and five on the offside, with long inward-facing seats for six on each side at the back. In its rebuilt form T 27 increased in weight from the original 5ton 1cwt 0qr to 5tons 7cwt 1qr, and it presented an attractive styling which rapidly became familiar once the new LTs began pouring into service from April 1931 onwards. T 27 resumed work at Nunhead in its new form on 4th December 1930, but it would not be until the very final days of the LGOC's existence in 1933 that more of the batch would be similarly converted.

T 17 arrived at Enfield garage in September 1931. Having undergone its second overhaul by the time it was photographed at the Angel, Edmonton, on its way from Golders Green to Chingford, it now carries the body formerly on T 16 as it was destined to do for the rest of its long working life which lasted through to January 1953. Strengthening work carried out at the front end of the bodywork is indicated by the thicker profile of the black band above the cab area and canopy. *J F Higham © A B Cross*

The original allocation of Ts to garages remained fairly steady throughout 1930 although, with new LT 'Scooter' single deckers in the offing, big changes lay ahead. On 9th April 1930 a schedule alteration resulted in some of Cricklewood's Ts transferring to Edgware (although their official allocation was Hendon because Edgware had no fleet of its own at the time). This was followed on 22nd October 1930 by the theoretical transfer of the three Ts from Plumstead to Sidcup, although in fact no visible change was apparent as the vehicles concerned were those operating from Crayford garage and the reallocation merely reflected an alteration in administrative arrangements. However a really big event impacted on the small Crayford garage on 1st April 1931 when control of it was transferred to the East Surrey Traction Company along with the services and rolling stock that went with it. On the day before the reorganisation came into effect, 31st March, the three Ts that had been at Crayford from the start – T 15, 21, 26 – were handed over to East Surrey, and two more were transferred in from other LGOC garages to meet East Surrey's future requirements, these being T 25 from Cricklewood and T 35 from Holloway. From that moment onwards the fate of these five vehicles swung off in a totally different direction from that of the main batch, and their subsequent history is picked up in chapter 4.

Once the many Scooter LTs came on stream the allocation of Ts underwent an almost complete change, leaving Romford as the only one of the original garages to retain these vehicles throughout 1931 and beyond. In subsequent years it gained an official vehicle allocation of its own instead of being reliant upon Seven Kings, and was renamed Hornchurch to avoid confusion with the two Green Line garages based in the town. The litany of T losses in the face of incoming LTs began with Holloway in April 1931 followed by Nunhead in May and Sutton, Edgware and Cricklewood in June. Temporary re-allocations of Ts to Tottenham and Leyton met the same fate in October as did some at Elmers End in December. Two recipients of Ts during the year that were destined to keep them for a much longer period were Kingston (and its Weybridge outstation) in April and West Green in June, while Enfield and Harrow Weald were recipients destined to retain them for longer than the next twelve months.

An upheaval overtook the Ts with the commencement of their second overhaul cycle in October 1931. Without having any spare bodies or chassis available, the authorities at Chiswick nevertheless decided to overhaul 44 of the 45 remaining vehicles (front entrance T 27 was excluded) on the flow system used for larger classes, which could only be done by causing two vehicles to 'disappear' from the scene to create floats for the duration of the programme. The first two to arrive for overhaul, T 10 and T 20, were the ones that were 'lost' for three months after which all the remainder (except for T 156 which, being newer, was overhauled later), changed their identities. The last to be overhauled was the non-standard T 43 whose body and chassis clearly could not be intermixed with the remainder, but seemingly unaware of this, the staff at Chiswick promptly reallocated its fleet number to another vehicle. At the completion of its overhaul in January 1932, the only identity still available was T 10, so this is what it became for the rest of its career. This method of overhauling was never again used on this batch of Ts and no further body or chassis changes were ever carried out on them.

During overhaul the steering on all vehicles was changed to the worm and nut type favoured by the LGOC over the original Marles arrangement, but between overhauls ten of the batch were selected for the installation of an improved servo assisted Lockheed hydraulic braking system, five each at Kingston and Romford. Installed during May and June 1931, these were originally T 2, 5, 7, 9, 10, 33, 34, 37, 40 and 42 but these identities were lost during overhaul later in the year and the final ten were T 1, 2, 6, 7, 13, 28, 33, 34, 39 and 40. These retained their Lockheed systems thereafter but from 1933 onwards were intermixed indiscriminately with the remainder and no further attempt was made to keep them at specific garages.

Allocations to garages continued to change according to scheduling and other requirements with little stability for the class other than at Romford, Kingston/Weybridge and West Green. At the formation of the London Passenger Transport Board on 1st July 1933 the fleet disposition was as follows:

| | |
|---|---|
| Seven Kings (for Romford) | 12 |
| Kingston and Weybridge | 9 |
| West Green | 6 |
| Twickenham | 6 |
| Hendon (for Edgware) | 4 |
| Hounslow (for Uxbridge) | 4 |
| Elmers End | 4 |

Apart from the frequently changing allocations, this was a time of flux for this group of vehicles in other ways too. A small scale experiment using 3-speed constant mesh gear-boxes commenced in March 1933 (and possibly even as early as October 1932) which is thought to have eventually embraced T 9, 11, 16 and 37. It was tried out at Elmers End and Romford garages and later also at Uxbridge, but is believed to have been discontinued by about November 1934. In November 1932 five vehicles had more powerful A145 115mm engines installed, presumably for comparison purposes, which were tried out initially at Kingston/ Weybridge, Romford, West Green and Harrow Weald garages (the latter lost its Ts in April 1933). Two more were installed a year later and thereafter there were always a number of higher powered vehicles within the batch although specific vehicles varied from time to time according to engine availability.

Right from the very start, a common complaint from conductors concerned the relative inaccessibility of the front destination box winding gear which could be reached only by clambering on the front nearside dumbiron, and even then presented a problem for conductors of short stature. In about April 1933 a most unusual remedy was produced. The obvious solution to the problem would have been to relocate the winding handle into the driver's cab but instead a totally different approach was adopted whereby the existing external winding handle was removed from its spindle and replaced by a cream-painted contraption which could be operated from ground level. In order to do this the conductor was armed with a long metal rod-like device with a winding handle on its lower end and a cup on the upper to locate over the blind winding apparatus. The same arrangement was fitted to the Scooter LT fleet, but it is doubtful if the new gadgetry had been in use for even a year before a sense of practicality dawned and the unavoidable decision was taken to transfer the blind winding gear into the cab for the driver to operate. This was carried out from January 1935 onwards, and possibly even a little earlier.

T 156 was always the odd man out by virtue of its high fleet number and GF registration. Seen outside Kingston garage in sparkling condition just after being overhauled in March 1935, it now carries the full range of modifications to which this batch of vehicles were subjected during their first half-decade of service. When viewed from the offside, they were virtually indistinguishable in front entrance format from the appearance they had presented in their rear entrance days. *J F Higham © A B Cross*

Inter-garage transfers occurred frequently, and after the previous photograph was taken of T 17 (page 12) it spent time at Elmers End and Romford before finally arriving on the semi-rural services operated by Kingston and Weybridge garages. Converted to front entrance whilst at Romford in November 1933, it still carries the GENERAL name though not for much longer. Photographed just after route 62 had been renumbered 219 upon abandonment of the Bassom numbering system in October 1934, it gained LONDON TRANSPORT fleet names at its next overhaul in December of that year. During its previous overhaul the tester's seat and leather strap were removed but the fixed starting handle was left in place; this will be removed on its next visit to Chiswick. The white-painted and short-lived blind winding contraption located under the canopy will also be dispensed with and the operating handle re-located inside the cab. *Getty Images*

The final major act under LGOC auspices was the commencement of a programme for rebuilding the whole batch into the front entrance format already carried by T 27. The rebuilding was done on overhaul starting in March 1933, when the opportunity was also taken to reposition the destination winding gear inside the driver's cab, and it may well be that replacement of the pneumatic bell system by an electric one was also carried out then. The extensive work that had to be done on each vehicle meant that there was not the capacity to tackle all of them within a single overhauling cycle. Although seven had already been dealt with by the time of the London Transport takeover, almost two more years were to elapse before the programme was complete during which time it was commonplace to find front and rear entrance Ts mixed together on the same service. The last rear entrance one of all was T 8 which went to Chiswick for rebuilding from Kingston garage on 11th February 1935.

The LPTB era ushered in very little outward change to start with except for the obvious updating of the legal ownership wording on each vehicle, and the GENERAL fleet name was retained through to May 1934 when the famous LONDON TRANSPORT one came into general use. However the last week of September 1933 saw a rapid programme introduced of fitting vehicles to carry offside route stencil letters which, in the case of the Ts, was placed at the foot of the window in

the fourth bay. The latter part of 1933 saw the start of the removal of the tester's tip-up seat from above the autovac tank which had formerly been a Public Carriage Office requirement for half-cab buses along with the leather strap below the canopy for the tester to cling on to. A programme was also commenced for removing the fixed starting handles which were replaced by a detachable sprung type carried in a wooden block in the cab just to the right of the footbrake. From about July 1934, rear corner bumpers, which had been fitted to most if not all of the batch in 1931, were removed and replaced by a couple of raised mouldings at the foot of the rear panels just adequate for cyclists and others to bump up against.

Somewhat belatedly, London Transport decided in March 1936 to record photographically the conversion of the 1T1s to front entrance layout, and chose West Green-based T 30 for this purpose as it happened to be conveniently on hand in Chiswick Works at the time, where its sixth overhaul had just been completed. The half-bulkhead behind the doorway with its conveniently-placed electric bell push can be clearly seen, and the former mirror space now earns revenue as an advertisement panel. Leather hanging straps are a helpful feature for passengers occupying the inward facing seats, and the new grey 'lozenge' pattern moquette matches the interior décor where a rather drab grey has replaced the original green. *London Transport Museum*

In March 1934 London Transport introduced a new coding system for all its major classes of vehicle under which the vehicles in this batch received the basic classification 1T1. (The whole process is described in more detail in chapter 11). There were, however, sub-types created in the coding within the 45 vehicles to cover differences in their mechanical specification, the outcome being as follows:

1T1 The basic vehicle with A140 engine and single servo brakes: T 4, 5, 9-12, 14, 17, 18, 20, 22-24, 29-32, 37, 41, 42, 44, 46-48, 50, 156

1/1T1 Vehicles with A140 engine and Lockheed brakes: T 1, 2, 6, 7, 28, 33, 34, 39, 40

2/1T1 Vehicles with A145 engine and single servo brakes: T 3, 8, 16, 19, 27, 36, 45, 49

3/1T1 Vehicle with A145 engine and Lockheed brakes: T 13

A completely separate code, 2T2, was allocated to the shortened vehicle, but this was applied erroneously to T 43 (its original identity up to 1932) and not to the correct vehicle, T 10. This came about through a defect in the usually impeccable recording system employed at Chiswick, and the strange thing is that no-one there seems to have noticed the error, which was perpetuated throughout the life of both vehicles, raising a question as to how useful the coding system really was in respect of a class such as the Ts. Towards the end of the 1930s a slow start was made on replacing the single servo arrangement on the non-Lockheed vehicles with a more positive triple servo system, but the coding system was never amended in recognition of this.

Barely a year passed between 1933 and the outbreak of war without a garage somewhere in the fleet either gaining or losing all of its T allocation, and the position was made more complex by a growing tendency to use these vehicles as replacements for LTs when the latter became unavailable. Twickenham garage, for example, which had found itself in receipt of six Ts on 21st June 1933, lost them all in January 1934, whilst Elmers End and Hendon (Edgware), where Ts had made a come-back in November 1932 (Elmers End) and March 1933 (Hendon), lost them all again in October and

January 1934 respectively. Cricklewood returned to the fold in January 1934 and Chalk Farm amassed twelve from August 1934 onwards and saw them all depart in March and April 1936 under an onslaught of new Q types. Croydon had an allocation of a few from March 1936 to March 1939, while Enfield re-entered the scene in March 1936 and Catford gained some in August 1937 but saw them move to Bromley a year later. The decade ended with West Green losing its Ts in June 1938 while Sidcup regained them in January 1939 and Old Kent Road got its first-time allocation in June of that year. After all these changes, the position at the outbreak of war on 3rd September 1939 was:

| | |
|---|---|
| Hornchurch | 14 |
| Sidcup | 7 |
| Cricklewood | 6 |
| Uxbridge | 5 |
| Enfield | 4 |
| Bromley | 4 |
| Kingston/Weybridge | 2 |
| Old Kent Road | 2 |
| Hounslow | 1 |

Throughout 1938 and 1939 a series of contingency plans was drawn up in anticipation of war being declared, and one result of this forward planning was that larger bus operators were instructed to keep a number of vehicles on stand-by for the army to call upon at short notice. Two days before war was officially declared, many London Transport vehicles were released for military work together with a number of volunteer drivers, and though the great majority of those selected were double deckers in view of their higher carrying capacity, some single deckers were also conscripted from 1st September including six 1T1s. The Ts involved were posted to army locations in the London area and came from two garages with Cricklewood supplying T 18, 22, 48 and Bromley T 37, 41, 44. They were mostly used on short journeys between various barracks or for carrying troops to the rifle ranges at Rainham and Purfleet, and T 22 was the only one to venture any distance outside London when it travelled to Gosport on 20th September. All were handed back to London Transport to resume their normal duties on 21st September.

When viewed from the back, the 1T1s looked almost identical to many of the 'Scooter' LTs, employing the same combination of wooden destination board below a metal route number stencil, both attached to the frame of the emergency door. Catford garage's T 37 was one of four such vehicles received on 4th August 1937 for the inauguration of new route 232 between Beckenham Junction and Hayes which was designed to serve the rapidly expanding housing developments along its path. It was photographed against a background of the opulent new homes of the Coney Hall estate which had earlier been served by a private bus provided by the developer. *Charles F Klapper © Omnibus Society*

At its final pre-war overhaul in December 1938 Enfield's T 23 has received the now-standard simplified livery eliminating black paintwork from the window frames of the driver's cab and along the window ledges. It has also been modified by the insertion of an extra offside opening window complete with glass louvre above it, the latter being a surprising feature as a tentative start was being made at about the same time on replacing the glass fittings with solid metal rainshields. Close examination of what is visible of the inside of the window pillars shows that the saloon interior has been brightened up with an STL-style two-tone brown and cream décor that was also applied to a number of LT double deckers at the time in replacement for the usual drab grey. *D Evans © Omnibus Society*

In common with the rest of the London Transport fleet blackout conditions were imposed with the outbreak of war which required extensive lamp masking and the white painting of mudguard edges and other areas of bodywork to assist recognition after dark. The silver roofs of buses were repainted matt grey and, from December 1941 onwards, brown. After the blitz of 1940 anti-shatter mesh was widely applied on windows not fitted with safety glass. Three vehicles in this batch – T 16, 19 and 36 – were repainted in the temporary brown and cream livery at Chiswick tram depot in early 1943 when pigments for standard paint were in short supply. By and large this was an unsettled era for the 1T1 family which suffered an average of four garage reallocations apiece during the course of the war whilst 19 of them spent various lengths of time unlicensed. At the other extreme T 4, 40 and 156 at Uxbridge and T 3 and 39 at Hornchurch presented an acme of stability by serving at these locations uninterrupted throughout the six years of war.

With the war at its height, T 1 waits to depart from the Royal Forest Hotel terminus at Chingford on a short working to Sewardstone Road while working from Enfield garage, to which it was allocated for almost the whole duration of the conflict. Masked headlamps and white-painted mudguard and doorway markings were typical wartime features as was the anti-shatter netting on the windows which, again typically, has been removed from two of the nearside ones, possibly by disgruntled passengers. As a wartime measure the nearside route number stencil holder was re-located on the whole batch to the top of the first window necessitating removal of the glass louvre to accommodate it. *W J Haynes*

Various factors relating to wartime service cuts and time-table modifications resulted in some major reallocations during 1940 beginning on 6th March when all of Sidcup's Ts, which by that time numbered ten, were displaced by 5Q5s formerly at Kingston. Most of the Ts moved to Holloway for a short stay which lasted only until 15th April. On 1st September all of Cricklewood's Ts were replaced by LTs and moved across to bolster the number in stock at Enfield. Two double deckings came next: Hornchurch's route 253 on 20th November 1940 (whereupon it was renumbered 165) and Bromley's 232 a week later (which became 138). With no work available for them within the Central Bus department, nine of the deposed Ts were sent out on loan to Country Buses where they ran from time to time at a variety of garages, the extent of which can be judged by the following summary of the buses concerned (all dates inclusive):

T 6    Windsor 20/11/40-3/12/40; Amersham 4/12/40-29/4/41
T 13   High Wycombe 30/11/40-7/10/41; Hertford 8/10/41-28/6/42
T 24   Windsor 20/11/40-3/12/40; Amersham 4/12/40-29/4/41
T 31   High Wycombe 30/11/40-7/10/41; Amersham 8/10/41-31/12/41
T 32   Hertford 20/11/40-3/12/40; Hemel Hempstead 4/12/40-1/4/41; Leavesden Road 2/4/41-30/4/43
T 37   Hertford 20/11/40-8/12/40; Hemel Hempstead 9/12/40-1/4/41; Leavesden Road 2/4/41-31/1/43
T 41   High Wycombe 30/11/40-7/10/41; Amersham 8/10/41-31/12/41
T 43   Hertford 20/11/40-3/12/40; Hemel Hempstead 4/12/40-1/4/41: Leavesden Road 2/4/41-4/1/42
T 44   High Wycombe 30/11/40-7/10/41; Hertford 8/10/41-28/6/42

Most were still actively employed on country service when, after a lapse of more than a year, they were supplemented by six more:

T 11   Hertford 1/3/42-29/9/42
T 45   Amersham 1/3/42-31/5/42; Hemel Hempstead 1/6/42-19/1/43; Luton 20/1/43-22/1/43; Leavesden Road 23/1/43-31/5/43
T 46   Hertford 1/3/42-29/9/42
T 47   Leavesden Road 3/1/42-22/2/42; Luton 23/2/42-31/5/43
T 48   Hertford 1/3/42-31/10/42
T 50   Hertford 1/3/42-31/10/42

In August 1941 the Minister of War Transport issued a significant new directive via the Regional Transport Commissioners that henceforth single deck buses could be modified to carry the same number of standing passengers as there were seats in the vehicle up to a maximum of 30 standing passengers. This was to be achieved by installing perimeter instead of transverse seating and could be used where it was necessary to relieve pressure on specified services. London Transport was quick to make use of this new facility, though only to the extent that 20 standing passengers would be allowed per vehicle, which was probably the maximum that could be negotiated with the Trade Union. Board approval was speedily given to spend £6,580 on converting no fewer than 188 T, LT and Q single deckers. In the case of the 1T1s it was found possible to accommodate 29 seated passengers, a loss of one over the conventional arrangement, and the conversion was simpler to carry out than on some other types of vehicle because so many seats at the rear of the saloon already faced inwards.

The conversion necessitated the provision of a number of white painted stanchions and rows of ceiling mounted leather straps on each side to support the standees. The vehicle weight was increased by almost 3cwt to 5tons 11cwt due largely to the extra amount of woodwork needed to support the seats in their new position. A number of single deckers of various classes, including a variety of T-types, were gathered at Chiswick in November 1941 to enable trial conversions to be carried out on them. In most cases a single vehicle of each sort was chosen, but in the case of the 1T1s both T 17 and T 27 were used as guinea pigs which, after gaining formal approval, re-entered service at Kingston in their revised form on 14th and 28th November respectively. Between 30th December 1941 and the end of February 1942 a further 22 were dealt with based at Enfield (9), Kingston (8), Uxbridge (3) and Leavesden Road (2). Later in 1942 the need arose for more high capacity single deckers and six more 1T1s were converted between the 6th and the 29th August, two each at Enfield and Hertford and single ones at Hemel Hempstead and Luton. Altogether 30 had been converted to standee format comprising T 1, 2, 4-9, 12, 16, 17, 19, 23, 27-29, 31-34, 36, 37, 40, 43, 45, 47-50, 156.

Fortunately, in spite of working in some vulnerable areas, the 1T1s suffered no wartime casualties through enemy action. However one vehicle, T 34, emerged from the war with a different appearance from the remainder, although the prosaic reason for this was an accident incurred in July 1941. It emerged on 1st October completely repanelled from the waistline downwards with flush panels relieved by a moulding a few inches below the waistrail. At the front, a standard round cab as used on LTs and STs was now fitted with the result that, on approaching, the vehicle could easily be mistaken for a Scooter LT. On a few others a start had been made in the late nineteen-thirties – as on the Scooters – in replacing glass window louvres with metal rain strips, but this had not progressed far before war intervened. A few more were dealt with during the war, but the majority retained their glass louvres into the post-war period albeit in an increasingly dilapidated state. With glass in short supply the replacement of broken non-essential items would have ranked at the very bottom of the priority list.

In the middle of the war, when the need for relatively low capacity petrol engined single deckers had subsided, four unlicensed 1T1s were converted to snow ploughs in anticipation of bad weather conditions during the winter of 1942/43, the vehicles concerned being T 24, 37, 41 and 42. It was intended that they would serve the same purpose during the following winter too, but an upsurge in demand required their return to service and the ploughs were removed during late November 1943, their place as snow ploughs being taken by other, obsolete T class vehicles. T 24 and T 42 were placed back into service at Merton on 1st December, while T 37 and T 41 were resuscitated at Uxbridge and Sidcup respectively on 1st January 1944. Once again the use of the 1T1s had become widespread, including short term placements at locations as varied as Muswell Hill, Dalston, Leyton, Hanwell and Loughton, the latter being an association that would last well into the post-war era. At the end of the war two out of the 45 vehicles were delicensed, but the remainder were now more widely spread than ever amongst eleven garages:

| Enfield | 10 | Dalston | 2 |
|---|---|---|---|
| Uxbridge | 7 | Elmers End | 2 |
| Kingston | 6 | Cricklewood | 1 |
| Hornchurch | 5 | Old Kent Road | 1 |
| Sidcup | 5 | West Green | 1 |
| Loughton | 3 | | |

This interior view of T 9 shows the seating rearrangement carried out to bring the total carrying capacity, including standees, to 49. White-painted grab rails are a useful new feature and exactly the right number of leather straps has been provided to enable the 20 standing passengers to be carried safely. In this instance – and untypically for a T type vehicle at that time - the recently reupholstered seats are covered in a style of moquette which was still comparatively unfamiliar then but which would become ubiquitous after the war, its browns, reds and greens sitting uncomfortably against the standard grey of the T-type interior. Wartime lamp masks are in evidence, and the wording on the paper labels pasted on the boarded-up windows stating "The fabric on the windows is for your protection – please do not interfere with it" relates to the mesh on the accompanying glass panes. *London Transport Museum*

T 27 stands at Staines GWR station towards the end of the war. Despite the provision of internal stanchions in connection with its conversion to standee status, T 27's roof demonstrates the pronounced sag towards the centre which developed on most of these vehicles. Full-length metal rainshields have replaced the separate window louvres, and were probably fitted either when the vehicle was overhauled at Alperton garage in March 1942 or when it visited there again in March 1944. Despite wartime supply problems, the wheels of this and all other 1T1s were changed from the original deeply-dished type carrying low pressure tyres to the more normal variety as found on LTs, STs and STLs on which high pressure tyres were fitted. *W J Haynes*

With hostilities at an end, it was theoretically time to revert the standee buses back to a conventional seating layout but instead, in a surprise move, two more were converted – T 46 and T 18 in September and October 1945 respectively – apparently to provide greater capacity on certain journeys at Sidcup garage. The first reversion to normal layout was Kingston's T 5 during its overhaul in November 1945. However such was the pressure on the overhaul programme that progress was very slow and the last conversion back to normal seating layout did not take place until January 1950. In fact ten vehicles were never dealt with, and T 6-8, 18, 19, 43, 47-50 retained their perimeter seating right up to the time of their withdrawal even though their maximum permitted standing capacity reverted to eight once the war had ended.

For some years the 1T1s had been the oldest operational single deckers in the fleet and their age was beginning to show through sagging roof lines and various body distortions. The strengthening brackets provided at the doorway when they were converted to front entrance layout had proved inadequate and a further cure was evolved which required a substantial strengthener of about ⅜ inch steel to encase the top of the doorway. The legs of the strengthener extended down the pillar on each side of the doorway, the vertical section being much deeper on the pillar behind the doorway – here it reached right down to the waistrail – than on the bulkhead side. On some vehicles, where the weight of the front canopy and destination box was causing the unsupported structure on the nearside to sag, a curved bracing piece was inserted below the canopy to give better support. No heavy overhauling was carried out on them in the years immediately after the war; in fact some were never overhauled after 1945. On those that were, the chassis and mechanical units received the greatest attention, but the bodies were repainted inside and out, and the internal renovations made a big difference where the drab grey paint,

which had long ago covered all the rexine, was replaced by brown, surmounted by a pale green band above the windows and the seat backs were also painted green. Some were even reupholstered in the post-war standard moquette which was becoming very familiar through the spread of the new RT class. In February 1947 another round cab oddity was created in the form of T 45, although it differed from T 34 in that it was only the driver's cab that was altered while all the other panelling retained its typical LGOC styling.

Operationally the 1T1s were intermixed with the twelve strong class of Ts inherited from Thomas Tilling along with remnants of the 1/7T7/1 former Green Line coaches, some of the latter still carrying green livery well into the post-war era. Certain services were scheduled to be covered by these vehicles in their entirety, but over and above this the three classes of petrol Regals could be found on occasion almost anywhere deputising for other classes of single decker and, not infrequently, even helping out on double deck services during an era of desperate vehicle shortage when, for the first time, they could be viewed at work right in the heart of the City of London and the West End. By the start of the winter programme on 9th October 1946, and in the face of new T types being delivered in the shape of the 14T12s (see chapter 17), the only operations scheduled exclusively by petrol engined Ts were:

| ENFIELD (E) | | Mon-Fri | Sat | Sun |
|---|---|---|---|---|
| 205 | Chingford–Hammond Street | 6 | 6 | 4 |
| 242 | Epping Forest–Potters Bar | 8 | 9 | 8 |
| HORNCHURCH (RD) | | | | |
| 248 | Cranham–Upminster | 1 | 1 | 1 |
| 250 | Romford–Epping | 4 | 4 | 5 |
| KINGSTON (K) | | | | |
| 218 | Kingston–Staines | 14 | 14 | 22* |

*includes route 215

The ending of hostilities saw the prompt removal of most of the wartime markings from London's buses except for the white disc at the rear, but a few exceptions such as T 49 retained their white door posts until they were called into Chiswick for overhaul. In the case of T 49 its next and final overhaul was in July 1947. By this time the 1T1s had far exceeded their planned life span and the deterioration in the bodywork of many of them was becoming very evident, as witnessed on T 49 by the severe distortion over the doorway and the drooping towards the nearside of the front canopy. At overhaul, it was not considered worthwhile converting T 49 back to its normal internal layout and its perimeter seating was retained right through to its withdrawal for scrap in January 1949. *Alan B Cross*

On some 1T1s an attempt was made to correct the sinking front canopy by inserting a curved bracing piece as exhibited by T 44. Evidence of further restructuring, carried out on this vehicle in May and June 1947, is the repositioning of the front opening window into the third bay along with the replacement of the glass louvres, and the fitting of a new black band above the windows which has a common depth throughout its length. The use of single deckers on central area services occurred quite frequently in the early post-war years, and T 44 has been borrowed from Edgware by Cricklewood garage to help out on route 16 alongside its regular STLs such as the one standing behind it in Victoria bus station. The schoolboy enthusiast seems more interested in taking notes of the new RTL on route 29 rather than in these two elderly gems.
*D A Jones*

In addition Sidcup garage had a long standing scheduled allocation of these vehicles, theoretically to supplement the Q type on route 241 (Sidcup–Welling) to the extent of 10 Ts on Mondays to Fridays and 6 on Saturdays, but in practice they could just as frequently be found on route 228 (Eltham–Chislehurst).

With a huge combined fleet of LT, ST and T vehicles all of about the same age and several years past their projected replacement date, it was inevitable as early as 1946 that odd cases would come to light of vehicles so badly deteriorated that nothing could be done to save them short of an almost total body rebuild, which was not feasible at the time. Although double deckers had been going away to outside contractors – principally Mann Egerton at Norwich – in considerable numbers no facilities could be found to carry out similar work on the single deck fleet. T 19 at Enfield was the first to totally succumb to advanced decrepitude and was delicensed on 1st January 1947. Kingston's T 29 was condemned a month later while at Chiswick where it had been sent for overhaul. Both were dismantled in May 1947. Later in the same year, out of the blue, London Transport received an approach in September 1947 from Kent & Sussex Woodcraft Ltd of Ashford, Kent offering its services in rebuilding coachwork on single deckers, their factory having insufficient height to take double deckers. Trading as Kenex, they were already carrying out 'wear and tear' repairs on single deckers for the East Kent Road Car Company.

London Transport arranged to send two single deckers to Kenex on a trial basis and dispatched T 1 and LT 1043 to Ashford on 17th December 1947. Although Kenex managed to complete its work on LT 1043 fairly promptly this was not the case with T 1 which did not return to London until 28th July 1948. Prior to this, London Transport had been approached by Marshall's Flying School Ltd of Cambridge, an altogether bigger concern than Kenex with its own well-equipped body building and repair department, offering to work on both double and single deckers. As a result of this, a tentative plan had been drawn up to send 80 LTs to Marshall's for rebuilding and 40 Ts to Kenex. However the delay in returning T 1 brought London Transport to the conclusion that Kenex had over-assessed its capacity and informed them that no more renovation work would be coming their way. Fortunately for Kenex this did not mark the complete end of London Transport's connection with them, and starting in June 1948 they began a successful programme of building new bodies on redundant STL chassis redeployed as store lorries and tower wagons.

The initial programme drawn up with Marshall's was to rebuild 120 vehicles, including 24 Ts. In theory it would have been more cost effective to concentrate resources solely on higher capacity LTs, but London Transport needed to ensure a supply of rolling stock capable of crossing the bridge at Walton-on-Thames which had been subjected to a 7 tons gross weight limit since being damaged during an air raid in 1940, and the 1T1s were the only 30-seaters in the fleet which complied with the weight requirements when fully laden. The construction of a temporary replacement bridge had been mooted but meanwhile it was necessary to ensure at least four more years of working life for some of the 1T1s. Later, after reassessing its single deck needs, London Transport reduced the rebuilding programme to 78 (18 T types and 60 LT).

The two vehicles with LT/ST style rounded cabs were well-known odd-men-out amongst the 1T1 fleet in post-war years. When approaching they could easily be mistaken for a 'Scooter' LT and were virtually undistinguishable from each other, but from other angles they could easily be told apart. T 34 was a pre-war rebuild with flush side panelling and full-length rainshields, whereas T 45 was a later conversion and retained much of its original styling. Both appeared at a variety of garages in post-war times, with T 34 having been photographed at Romford station while doing a stint at Hornchurch garage in the second half of 1949. T 45 migrated to Kingston after receiving bodywork attention at Chiswick in February 1950. *D A Jones/Denis Battams*

The Olympic Games held in London in 2012 were marked by the huge fleet of brand new double deckers amassed to fulfill the demanding transport requirements of this prestige event. Things were very different on the previous occasion when the Olympics were staged here between 29th July and 14th August 1948. Nicknamed the Austerity Games to reflect the straitened early post-war times in which they were held, they coincided with the chronic vehicle shortage afflicting London Transport, leaving athletes and officials to be transported between their lodgings and Wembley Stadium in whatever happened to be available. Scruffiness was no bar to a vehicle's use on Olympic duties as witnessed by T 16. Mechanically up to scratch, having received a chassis overhaul two months earlier, no attempt was made to spruce up the bodywork to suit the occasion. Officially allocated to Muswell Hill, it ran on loan to Putney Bridge garage for the duration of the games and was photographed in the yard behind the garage alongside a diminutive CR 20-seater also on Olympic duty. *Dave Jones collection*

At the start of the post-war era the use of a full complement of rear-end destination equipment – route boards and number stencils – was still maintained in all garages running 1T1s and 'Scooter' LTs, but the practice gradually fell away and by the time that T 36 was photographed running on route 228 from Sidcup garage in the summer of 1948 it had become comparatively rare to find a full display still in use. This was T 36's last year of operation in its old form; in November 1948 it was delicensed prior to travelling to Cambridge to become one of the earliest Marshall rebuilds. *F G Reynolds*

The authorities at Chiswick had decided that in the case of the 17 to 19 year old single deckers a much more thorough renovation was needed than on LT and ST double deckers with their shorter projected life span, and Marshall's was contracted to recondition each single deck body to what was termed 'as new' standard. Technically these would be rebuilds because items such as windows, windscreens, seats, bulkhead ventilators, light fittings and destination gear would be salvaged. However all the main structure, including the body shell and underframe, plus virtually all of the panelling, would be brand new. In the case of the Ts it was obviously imperative that there should be no material increase in unladen weight as a result of all this work, and in fact Marshall's managed to actually shave 2cwt off the original weight with no detrimental effect, probably through widespread use of aluminium panelling instead of steel.

A sample LT was sent to Cambridge on 15th March 1948 and work on it was sufficiently advanced for a production line to be set up four months later. Meanwhile a start had been made on overhauling the chassis of the vehicles selected for rebuilding after which they were stored at Aldenham until required in Cambridge. The first of the production batch, a pair of LTs, left Aldenham for Marshall's on 23rd July 1948, slightly ahead of the first four-wheelers, T 32 and T 42, which went on 9th August. The first of these to arrive back at Chiswick was T 42 on 4th March 1949 and it was evident, just by looking at it, that a major transformation had taken place. Although retention of the original outline had been achieved out of necessity to accommodate the re-use of as many old

fittings as possible, the new external rear, side and cab panelling was flush sided in contemporary style. A very slight modernisation had been achieved at the square-looking rear end by giving a radius to the top of the last window on each side and by removing the rounded corners from the bottoms of the back windows on either side of the emergency exit. One detailed change was that the nearside route number plate holder was now built into the bodywork above the doorway instead of being displayed in the first side window. The sweeping away of the old image was completed by the adoption of the latest livery usually applied to more modern single deckers – all-over red with thin cream moulding.

The transformation inside the body was huge. Marshall's had made a very plausible attempt to emulate the style and ambiance of the current RT design by changing the colour of the window pillars half way up, the yellow at the top being separated from the brown below by RT style polished bracelets. A typical RT feature was the cream moulding with red central insert that ran all the way around the vehicle above the windows. The green backed seats were upholstered in the now standard moquette, although the overall attempt to achieve modernity was marred a little because the seats themselves, though very comfortable, were clearly from a bygone age. The traditional grab handles were gone from them, and in their place full height stanchions were now installed. The light fittings, too, looked out of place for the modern image, but far more incongruous was retention of the prominent and rather ugly front ventilator which had looked outdated even when first installed back in 1930.

Although regular overhauling had ceased, attempts were still made to keep members of the class looking smart through body repaints, although these were spasmodic and unco-ordinated, with some vehicles inevitably missing out and displaying a very unkempt appearance as a result. Croydon's T 33, however, looks very smart in the summer of 1949 as it cruises along the tram tracks in Streatham deputising for a double decker on route 133. Work on the body of this vehicle, carried out in June 1947, has resulted in the removal of the radiused upper corners from almost all windows, but passengers are still carried on wartime style perimeter seating. Quite remarkably, although it was never again overhauled, T 33 remained in service – latterly at Kingston – until as late as November 1952. *F W Ivey*

The rebuilt Ts drifted back from Marshall's to Chiswick over the course of 1949, the last one to be received being T 2 on 6th October. In their revised form the bodies were reclassified T1/1. Perhaps surprisingly, no effort appears to have been made at their final overhaul to bring the chassis up to a common standard with regard to their engine and brake fittings with the result that the 18 converted vehicles were variously coded as 1T1/1, 1/1T1/1 and 2/1T1/1. However many of these codings are known to have been incorrect as they failed to reflect changes made on individual vehicles in later years. The full list of Marshall rebuilds is T 2, 9, 14, 16, 17, 22-24, 27, 28, 32, 36, 37, 40-42, 44, 46.

While the rebuilding programme was in progress less fortunate 1T1s were reaching the end of the line, and abruptly so in many cases when PSV71 notices were slapped upon them. No fewer than seventeen were written off books during the course of 1949 including T 10, the short length oddity which finished its working days at Elmers End in May 1949. Their sudden loss was not so greatly felt as it would have been a year earlier thanks to the significant delivery from October 1948 onwards of 100 new TD class Mann Egerton bodied Leyland PS1s. The 1T1s were driven from their last full-time haunts at Enfield and Hornchurch in February 1949 leaving route 218 at Kingston as the only one still reliant on them. Those that were not earmarked for withdrawal were increasingly deployed as temporary replacements for LTs away at Marshall's for rebuilding. This brought them to a number of garages where they had not been present for quite some time, if at all, such as Croydon, Elmers End, Hounslow, Leyton, Muswell Hill, Sutton and Tottenham. Between July 1949 and January 1950 Hornchurch enjoyed a 1T1 revival to cover its LTs on route 247 as these gradually drifted away. Once their usefulness ceased, the 1T1s departed from all the garages at which they had latterly worked, Sidcup being the last, and from 18th March 1950 all those that survived, whether rebuilt or unrebuilt, could be found only at Kingston.

Although the Marshall rebuilds were created solely with future use at Kingston in mind, a few of them were initially allocated elsewhere, but all had been gathered up at Kingston

as early as May 1949 with the sole exception of T 17 which stayed at Sutton through to early July. Many months later, to much surprise, a further vehicle arrived at Kingston which had been rebuilt in the Marshall style, not at Cambridge but at Chiswick. The last T had only just come back from Marshall's two days earlier when, on 8th October 1949, T 30 was taken out of service at Hornchurch and sent to Chiswick where its stripping-down commenced. The result of the four months long exercise became clear when T 30 arrived at Kingston on 23rd February 1950 looking very much like a Marshall product, both inside and out, apart from a few minor tell-tale differences such as the omission of a route stencil holder from above the doorway and a slightly longer rainshield on the offside which covered the driver's small window as well as the passengers' ones. Only at the back end, where the original window contours were retained, was any major variation apparent, although a glance at the unladen weight panel revealed that it was 2cwt heavier. In the absence of any confirming paperwork, it can only be assumed that the body parts used in T 30's reconstruction were left over from the Marshall contract, perhaps as a result of its partial curtailment, and the authorities at Chiswick thought that they were too good to waste! Despite the extensive alterations to the bodywork, T 30 was not re-coded and remained officially a 1T1.

Apart from the rebuilt vehicles, seven others remained at Kingston still in recognisably original condition and retaining the old red and white livery with brown roof. These were T 1 (the Kenex rebuild), and T 11, 31, 33, 34, 45 and 156. It will be noted that the two round cab vehicles, T 34 and T 45, were among them. Ample rolling stock was on hand for route 218, which required 16 vehicles on Mondays to Fridays on the through service from Kingston to Staines (3 others, which ran only between Kingston and Walton-on-Thames town, did not need to be 1T1s). With 25 vehicles available it was possible to introduce new route 264 (Sunbury–Hersham Green via Walton bridge) on 3rd May 1950 using four 1T1s, and to extend it from Sunbury to Kingston on 27th June 1951 at the cost of two more.

The only beneficiary within the T class from the aborted scheme to place 40 vehicles with Kenex for major body overhauling was T 1, which retained most of its original features, along with the traditional red and white livery, when it finally emerged from the Ashford workshops in August 1948. After an initial post-reconstruction spell of work at Kingston, T 1 served at Sidcup for six months from September 1949 onwards and was photographed at the Well Hall station terminus of route 228 on which it could usually be found. The use of black-painted radiators on older members of the fleet was quite common at the time, being an acceptable alternative to scrapping aluminium shells which could no longer be buffed-up to a satisfactory standard.
*F W Ivey*

Although some regretted the loss of certain original styling features and felt that the application of a modern livery on such old vehicles was inappropriate, there is no doubt that Marshall's of Cambridge made a good job of combining old with new. Admittedly there was no disguising, even from the most unobservant passenger, that beneath the shining exterior lay a very old vehicle, but it was heartening to see 1T1s in such good condition after years of comparative decrepitude. T 28, seen just after re-entering service on 7th September 1949, demonstrates that the fitment of flush side panels extended even to the cab area, while T 37, reinstated a few months earlier on 30th March, shows the revised location for the route number stencil above the saloon entrance. *A M Wright/Alan Nightingale collection*

It seems unfortunate that, although the rebuilding by Marshall's resulted in virtually new body structures, no attempt was made to instal route or destination equipment at the rear during rebuilding. Passengers are seen boarding T 32, the first of the class to be given the Marshall treatment, at North Cheam with one of Sutton's distinctive fleet of post-war Daimlers making a right turn in the distance. In a slight attempt at modernisation, Marshall's have omitted the curves from the lower corners of the back windows. *Alan B Cross*

The Marshall rebuilding programme was in full swing when, in June 1949, a scheme was developed for the conversion of almost all remaining petrol engined buses to oil using reconditioned engines retrieved from scrapped vehicles. The only exclusions would be the Leyland Cubs used on the Inter Station service and the Commer half-deck vehicles operated on behalf of the Airways Corporations for which no suitable oil engines were thought to be available. The main target of the programme was the remaining fleet of 99 single deck LTs, but 8 lowbridge STs and the 24 LTC private hire coaches were also included along with 32 Ts. The latter figure represented the number of buses initially thought necessary to cover all existing and projected operations over the bridge at Walton, the conversion of which was thought to be worthwhile at a cost of £57 per bus – a total of £1,824 – given an expected saving of £365 per vehicle per annum in operating costs. The programme was later trimmed to 26 Ts.

All the petrol to oil conversions were carried out at Chiswick using A173 engines with 105mm bore removed from scrapped STLs which were expected to give a similar performance to that of the 110mm petrol engines and should show an improvement over the 100mm engines with which the majority of the Ts were fitted. The rear axle ratio of 5¾:1 used in all of them in their later days was retained. No physical alteration to the appearance of the vehicle was needed except for the removal of the external autovac tank. The 26 Ts were dealt with over a five month period starting with T 42 on 17th January 1950, so for a while it was possible to compare the performance and sound of the melodious petrol engine (and its periodical backfires!) with the more raucous sound of the familiar AEC 7.7. The last vehicle to be converted was T 31 on 15th June 1950.

Interior views of T 28 show the slightly uneasy combination of RT-style décor and seat covering with outdated lamp, ventilator and bell push fittings. Although the former grab handles have been removed from the backs of the seats, the vertical poles at the front end of the body provide a more than satisfactory alternative, but whereas on the LT-class rebuilds leather straps hanging from the ceiling were provided to assist passengers at the rear of the saloon, handrails suspended from above were considered adequate on the Ts. The object stuffed into the front ventilator is the conductor's time card! *John C Gillham © Tony Peters*

Easily confused with one of the rebuilds from Cambridge, T 30 marked Chiswick's sole attempt at rebuilding a 1T1 in Marshall fashion. A keen eye was needed to observe the slight differences which, on the offside, were the continuation of the rainshield to cover the short window on the driver's cab, and the omission of a radiused upper corner from the rearmost side window. Still very shiny, T 30 was photographed on 4th March 1950, nine days after returning to service in its new form. Whereas all the Marshall rebuilds were reclassified as 1T1/1, T 30 retained its original 1T1 designation. *Alan B Cross*

New route 264 was inaugurated on 3rd May 1950 between Sunbury and Hersham Green, and for its first two years was scheduled to be worked from Kingston garage. A subsequent extension in June 1951 brought the 264 into Kingston itself where T 11 is seen outside the Southern Region station alongside Weymann-bodied RT 2354, the latter still carrying its original livery and restricted blind display. T 11 went on to become one of the lucky unrebuilt 1T1s to last in service right through to 1952. *Alan B Cross*

T 44 was one of the Marshall rebuilds transferred into the new Norbiton garage on its opening day, 14th May 1952. It remained there until withdrawal in January 1953 and was photographed shortly before its demise under the overhead wires in Kingston with not a trolleybus in sight but closely followed by RT 313, with Kingston's T 14 on route 218 trailing along behind. The era of diesel engines has now fully arrived, a condition to which T 44 was converted in May 1950, hence the removal of the Autovac tank from its prominent position on the front panel. The wordy bulkhead slipboard refers to the 5d minimum fare aimed at discouraging local journeys between Kingston and Hampton Church. *LCC Tramway Trust collection*

On 14th May 1952 the splendid new garage at Norbiton opened for business together with its separate engineering unit in well-equipped premises just off the London Road, and it brought long overdue relief to the grossly overstretched garage in the centre of Kingston. The intricacies of scheduling and staff rostering meant that the 264 was one of the services for which Norbiton took responsibility, and as a result seven 1T1s were transferred across from Kingston to cover the six scheduled workings. Only Marshall rebuilds were ever allocated to Norbiton which meant that, from then onwards, Ts in the old red and white colours ceased to appear on route 264.

Even before Norbiton opened, the availability of 1T1s for service had begun to wane as unrebuilt members of the class became unfit for further use. T 1 was the first casualty in July 1951 with both of the round cab vehicles, T 34 and T 45, following suit on different dates in December of the same

year. When T 156 was withdrawn in August 1952 its chassis was re-used under the body of T 30 whose own chassis had become defective, retaining the identity of the latter vehicle. The last of all to survive in the old red and white colours was T 33 which succumbed on 22nd November 1952. By the end of that year only twelve vehicles remained available for service which was an insufficient number to cover all the scheduled workings on routes 218 and 264, and London Transport had to resort to using 4Q4s and post-war 14T12s with a limit placed on the number of passengers carried across Walton bridge to avoid infringing the weight limit. Middlesex County Council had arranged for the construction of a replacement bridge which, though a temporary structure, was free of any weight restriction but this could not open until later in 1953 and final replacement of the 1T1s could not wait until then. The last ones were withdrawn from Norbiton on 16th January 1953, leaving six (T 17, 22, 27, 32, 40, 42) to

The end of an era, not just for the 1T1s but also for Kingston bus station which has resonated to their comings and goings for so many years but will soon do so no longer. Accompanied on this occasion by green and cream liveried Q 15 and a Putney Bridge based RT2, T 33 was photographed on 12th April 1952 and subsequently became the last of the class to run in service in unrebuilt condition. It was withdrawn on 25th November of the same year. Standing alongside red liveried Q 21 is T 32, which shared the honour with five other Marshall rebuilds of being serviceable right up to the very last day of operation, 31st January 1953. The bodywork has suffered a few scuffs, but by and large it still presents a reasonable image to the world even in its final days. *Alan B Cross/D W K Jones*

soldier on at Kingston for a couple of weeks longer. These were withdrawn on 1st February 1953 which, coincidentally, was the same day that the last few LTs ceased running at Dalston, bringing a whole generation of London single deckers to an end almost a full decade later than anyone would have expected them to last at the time they were built.

All had been sold to dealers by July 1953 with one very notable exception, the nowadays famous T 31. Early in October 1951 it had been taken into Chiswick where the exterior of the bodywork was fully repainted, not in the all-red scheme that had been universally applied since August 1950 but resplendently in the old red and white style with brown roof. It was the last vehicle in the regular bus fleet ever to be repainted in this way. If the intention was to return it to service at Kingston, this did not happen and instead it was delicensed on 16th October and placed in store, first of all at Mortlake garage and later in the regular storage yard at Forest Road, Walthamstow. Revived on 1st July 1952, T 31 entered the final stage of its working life as a replacement for former Tilling T 317 at Chiswick Works where it found mixed use as a part time staff bus and also as an occasional driver trainer. It was officially based at Hounslow garage for maintenance purposes although seldom found there, transferring to Norbiton in November 1955. In this twilight role the vehicle became famous for outliving all the rest of the 1T1s by more than three years, and at some time during this period it gained a unique but drab livery of almost all-over red except for a black cantrail band and brown roof. Finally declared redundant and delicensed on 1st June 1956, T 31 was sold on 18th October to become the initial privately-sponsored bus preservation project from which the whole of today's massive bus preservation movement has since sprung. Nowadays it is back in its original 1930 condition and can be viewed in the London Bus Museum at Brooklands.

Parked up inside the grounds of Chiswick Works on 11th October 1951 and looking incredibly smart after receiving a fresh coat of paint, T 31 looks ready to be relicensed for another stint of public service. However looks can be deceptive and beneath the shiny paintwork all is so far from well that it would be impossible for T 31 to gain even a short duration Certificate of Fitness. However, though its service days may be over, great things lay ahead for T 31, and after spending a few twilight years on miscellaneous work at Chiswick, it still survives today in preservation.
*John C Gillham © Tony Peters*

# 2 THE FIRST GREEN LINES
## T 38, 51-149, 155, 157-206

In chapter 1 it was noted that the chassis for T 38 was diverted upon arrival at Chiswick from its intended purpose as a service bus and was used instead as a test bed for a new type of coach body. The T class had, in fact, arrived on the scene at an appropriate time, right in the middle of one of the most interesting and cut-throat episodes in the development of London's transport network. With expansion of profitable local operations denied to them by the oppressive but very necessary Restricted Streets legislation, budding entrepreneurs had turned to the development of what were sometimes termed "London suburban coach" services, linking the centre with towns lying around the periphery of the capital beyond the boundary of the Metropolitan Police area. Running on a limited stop basis, usually at very affordable fares and mostly on attractive headways, these were classed as stage carriages but were only controlled by the Metropolitan Police insofar as they conformed to dimension and weight regulations. Despite their limited stop nature they were beginning to have a serious impact on local bus and tram operations, leaving the Underground group with no option other than to use its considerable muscle to tackle the problem head on. Lord Ashfield made the position very clear to shareholders, leaving them in no doubt that it would only be a matter of time before the Company inaugurated coach services of its own to most major towns lying within a 30 mile radius of London.

The LGOC had already dipped an initial toe in the water on 2nd October 1929 when it began a coach service between Watford and Golders Green where passengers could change

to the Underground for a quick run into central London. The AEC Reliance all-weather coaches needed to operate the service were freed-up from the private hire fleet whose excursions and tours commitment had diminished with the ending of the summer season and, fortuitously, a closed but fully equipped company-owned garage was available in Leavesden Road, Watford, from which to operate them. Despite intense competition from Bucks Expresses, Hewitt's Premier Omnibus Company and Mack's Safety Coaches – all of whom offered the advantage of through journeys into central London – the LGOC persevered, and on 18th December 1929 introduced a second service from Watford right through to Charing Cross.

With this experience to fall back on, the LGOC plotted an expansion of its local coach operations which would be on a vast scale, using Easter 1930 as a springboard from which to

Photographs of T 38 are notable by their absence, the only known ones being two almost identical views of it taken at Golders Green as late as 1936 by which time it was in its final condition and carrying standard country area two-tone green livery. The LGOC and its successor, London Transport, both failed to photograph the vehicle despite its importance in the history of the development of Green Line, and amateur photographers seem to have missed it too, perhaps because of its somewhat peripatetic existence. Even in the instance shown here, it appears to have been pressed into service at short notice judging by the lack of route boards and running numbers, and the use of a paper sticker where a destination blind should have been. *J F Higham © A B Cross*

gain as much advantage as possible from the expected buoyancy of the summer traffic. In order to do so it needed to purchase a very large number of new vehicles. Its first move, however, was to produce the specification for a coach suited to this particular type of operation which would fall midway between the luxury vehicles which the Company used for touring and its standard service bus. A new body was designed with this purpose in mind, and T 38 was the chassis on which it was to be trialled.

Construction of T 38's new body, away from the main production line, was probably well under way when its future chassis was taken into stock on 19th December 1929. Surprisingly little is known about it, the LGOC having been uncharacteristically reticent to publicise its latest creation either during or after manufacture. No official photographs appear to have been taken and no paperwork survives, so although T 38 subsequently ran in service for eight years, not very much about it has been recorded. The body was constructed to the same six-bay layout as the standard bus bodies for T 1-50, but it was considerably taller in order to accommodate a higher floor line with all of its 28 seats facing forwards. A rounded cab, topped by a well-rounded canopy incorporating a single line destination screen, ensured that its frontal profile was quite unlike that of the conventional bus body. The entrance remained at the rear, but was enclosed by a conductor-worked swing door which opened out on to the pavement, while the emergency door was situated at the back and was glazed although the panels on either side of it were not, giving a rather gloomy appearance to the rear end of the vehicle. A fixed roof was fitted as were bus-type half-drop windows. The livery, which consisted of standard LGOC red with black lining-out below the waistline, with black above, and a silver roof, was intended to be the standard for future coach deliveries. Oddly, T 38 was issued body number 8822 in the series normally reserved for miscellaneous service vehicles. The only record about its construction which seems to have survived is its cost which amounted to a quite hefty £739 13s 5d, considerably in excess of the £346 172 0d incurred on each of the bus bodies for T 1-150 but not exorbitant for an experimental one-off.

Operation of the two Watford services was the responsibility of the Company's private hire department, and when T 38 was licensed on 25th March 1930 it went initially to the department's main garage at Brixton. Transferred to Leavesden Road on 1st April to work on the Watford–Golders Green service, it lasted for only two months before being transferred back on to private hire contract work, based initially at Merton and later at Sutton, until March 1931 when it returned to Chiswick for its first overhaul.

Without waiting for the results of T 38's trial operation General placed two orders in quick succession for new Regal chassis, the first for 100 for delivery between April and June 1930 to be followed by a second batch of 50 in August and September. As regards the bodywork for them, events appear to point towards a divergence of opinion within the LGOC's upper management over the suitability of the body on T 38 for the work it was to perform, for even while it was under construction an alternative version was being created on the drawing board from which a prototype was quickly constructed.

The new design was destined to form the basis for the future fleet and arrangements were put in hand for construction to be undertaken as soon as the chassis were delivered. With its own factory at Chiswick unable to undertake the construction of more than 50 for the first contract and none at all for the second, space was booked at two outside manufacturers to provide the balance. Short Brothers (Rochester) Ltd and Hall Lewis & Company Ltd of Park Royal were each contracted to build 25 bodies for the first batch followed by a further 25 for the second.

AEC was asked to supply one chassis for the first contract ahead of the others for the prototype body to be mounted on. This arrived at Chiswick on 12th March 1930 as 662299 and was united with its new body on the same day. Even though, at this stage, no fleet number had been assigned to the new vehicle, it was paraded on the very next day for an extensive range of official photographs to be taken, in total contrast to the apparent indifference with which T 38 – which had still not yet entered service – was being treated.

Following receipt of the first chassis the remainder, 662353-451, were allocated fleet numbers T 51-149. Body numbers for the entire batch of 100 were 11004-11053 (LGOC), 11054-11078 (Short) and 11079-11103 (Hall Lewis), but the products of all three were completely jumbled up within the T 51-149 batch. While construction was going on the Hall Lewis company (then in liquidation) was re-formed as Park Royal Coachworks Ltd on 12th April 1930 but the vehicles in this batch built after the changeover date continued to be referred to as Hall Lewis products. Eventually the prototype coach based on chassis 662299 was given the fleet number T 155, the intervening numbers T 150-154 having been taken by a batch of private hire Regals – see chapter 5.

The chassis supplied under the initial contract for 100 were fairly typical examples of AEC's output of the time with 17ft wheelbase to accommodate an overall body length of 26ft, but they differed from normal practice – and indeed from T 1-50 – in having nearside fuel tanks. Powered by the same A140 6-cylinder 37.2hp 100x130m engines as T 1-50, developing 95bhp at 2000rpm, they had standard four speed crash gearboxes, Marles steering, Dewandre single servo brakes and semi-floating rear axles.

The new coach body was an interesting combination of standard Chiswick design features mixed with elements of appearance and comfort already adopted by the LGOC's competitors specifically to attract passengers to coach travel. The exterior lines were softened compared with the contemporary bus body by gently curving the pillars from the waist line upwards, and a seven-bay layout was adopted which enabled each row of seats to have good outward visibility unobstructed by pillars. Thick sprung seats were provided which, though reasonably high backed for comfort, were low enough not to impede forward vision. All seats faced forwards, those above the wheelarches being raised by a few inches. Total seating capacity was 27, a single seat being placed at the rear with luggage space beside it. The emergency door was located at the front of the saloon on the right hand side. Although the overall height of the body was some 2 inches less than on T 38, it still had a higher waist line than many contemporary coaches and required two steps to reach the main saloon floor from the entrance platform which was situated at the back where a wide door aperture occupied a substantial part of the 6ft 10ins rear overhang. The unsatisfactory kerbside slam-door arrangement on T 38 was not perpetuated; instead a pair of recessed hinged doors which did not block the pavement was installed inside the entrance at the top of the second step. Under the control of the conductor, they were pushed outwards when open.

With a saloon heater mounted in a boxed arrangement on the front bulkhead, a clock, a mirror, luggage racks and gold-coloured curtains on chromium plated rods, plus ample lighting through neat jellymould lamps, the mainly fawn and brown interior gave an unfussy but fairly sumptuous air well-suited to the competitive market which the new vehicles were about to enter.

Externally the new coach was painted in the same GENERAL red and black livery as T 38. This was enhanced by chromium plated surrounds to all the driver's cab windows. An unusual feature was a narrow subsidiary window above the windscreen (which in later life was panelled over, probably to reduce glare). Arrangements were made to put the new coach into production without further modification apart from the addition of a rear view mirror for the driver, and while the future T 155 was still un-numbered it was made available for examination at Chiswick by representatives from Short's and Hall Lewis whose contract was to build exactly identical bodies, both in shape and quality, for which they were duly provided with the appropriate plans and patterns. The only known deviation was that Hall Lewis was permitted to panel the rear roof dome and window surrounds

as separate units with a dividing moulding clearly separating the two, whereas on the other bodies a single sheet of metal was employed, panel beaten into shape, a time consuming and expensive business which appears to have been incompatible with Hall Lewis's manufacturing process.

The first of the new Regals entered service between Charing Cross and Windsor via Colnbrook and Slough on Easter Sunday 20th April 1930 and, like the Watford services, they ran under the auspices of the LGOC's private hire department. Rented garage premises were obtained in Alpha Street, Slough, and the first seven new vehicles were licensed there on the 17th. These were T 51, 60, 62, 63, 69, 71 and 74. Others joined them, including the prototype T 155, as the service built up. The first few were all Chiswick-bodied, but on 26th April the first Hall Lewis example, T 57, made an appearance although none of the Short Brothers vehicles had yet come off the production line. By the end of June, 23 red Ts were running from Alpha Street garage. After only a few had been built the frontal design was enhanced by the addition of an illuminated sign above the destination screen carrying the operator's name and most, but perhaps not all, of the very early ones were later brought into line.

One of the earliest LGOC coaches into service was T 59 which, though not available for the Windsor run on the opening day 17th April 1930, was licensed to start service from the Alpha Street garage a week later. The white coated crew are standing beside it at the London terminus on the Victoria Embankment outside Charing Cross Underground station. Only a few of the early Chiswick-built coaches, T 59 included, entered service without an illuminated fleet name at the front above the destination aperture, and though most of these were later provided with this equipment it is thought that not all of them were. *W Noel Jackson © A B Cross*

*Opposite* On 13th March 1930 the official photographer was summoned to Chiswick Works to photograph the body shop's latest creation, an urban coach of great importance to the LGOC. Resting upon its success were the Company's grand aspirations for a rapid and dominating entry to a fast expanding new market. Unusually, no fleet number was allocated at this stage and the vehicle was known simply by its registration number GF 525. Bearing little resemblance to the LGOC's current bus designs, the new coach looked particularly smart in its red and black livery, embellished by further black lining-out on the red panels, a silver roof, chromium plated windscreen pillars and white walled tyres. A particularly nice touch was the displaying of intermediate points for a proposed London-Windsor service in gold signwritten letters on the glass window louvres. Although the saloon was enclosed by folding doors in the traditional manner, these were inset within the bodywork and avoided the awkward obstruction of the pavement common to so many coaches of the time. In due course the vehicle received fleet number T 155 prior to being licensed for service almost a month after the photographs were taken. *London Transport Museum*

Black and white photography cannot do justice to the internal appearance of the new coach with its combination of green floor and upholstery, brown polished mouldings and gold curtains. There was a plentiful provision of lamps with neat jellymould covers, and the only jarring feature was the crude bus-style ventilator placed on the front bulkhead above the clock. The forward-facing view was taken inside T 155 while the view looking towards the back was recorded two months later on T 89. *London Transport Museum*

The black lining-out used to embellish T 155 was not perpetuated on production vehicles, but otherwise the livery remained initially unchanged as demonstrated by red and black T 116 licensed with East Surrey fleet names on 2nd June 1930 ready to start work four days later. The place names displayed on the window louvres inflexibly tied the coach to the London-Dorking service. Despite the heavy uniforms worn by the East Surrey crew the photograph was clearly taken on a very hot day as all the saloon windows, including the half-drop placed – somewhat unusually – in the emergency exit, are fully open. *W Noel Jackson © A B Cross*

Nine red Ts eventually joined the Autocar fleet with numbers ranging between T 65 and T 112, and carrying bodywork by all three manufacturers. Hall Lewis built the body for T 65 which was photographed at its inner London terminus located in Regent Street close to Oxford Circus. Several weeks have elapsed since the vehicle was new and the original arrangement of painting place names on the window louvres has been replaced by the use of more informative and practical wooden side route boards listing six intermediate points on the route between London and Tunbridge Wells. *Charles F Klapper © Omnibus Society*

The next batch to enter service consisted of eleven vehicles placed at Leavesden Road garage between 8th May and 13th June to release older vehicles from the Watford operations. Service expansion by the LGOC under its own account had now temporarily come to a halt, but plans were afoot to start further coaching operations using two of its subsidiary companies as agents. Inaugural day was 6th June 1930 when the East Surrey Traction Company began running from Oxford Circus to Dorking via Epsom, to Reigate via Sutton, and to Redhill via Croydon, while Autocar Services started in head-on competition with its main rival, Redcar, between its base at Tunbridge Wells and Oxford Circus.

In both cases the fleets were expanded to meet their new commitments through the receipt of new T-types which were registered in their names but remained the property of the LGOC. For East Surrey this arrangement was nothing new,

a substantial part of its existing bus and coach fleet being LGOC-owned, but Autocar – which was actually a fully-owned subsidiary of East Surrey – had previously owned all of its rolling stock outright. In preparation for the starting day, eleven new Regals were dispatched to Reigate between 2nd and 4th June while Autocar received five from 31st May onwards. All vehicles carried exactly the same red and black livery as those already in service with the LGOC but carried their respective operating company's fleet name and legal details. Included within the vehicles supplied to both fleets were the first examples with Short Brothers' bodywork. Additional coaches were drafted in to enable both operators' services to be doubled from hourly to half-hourly headways on 24th June at which time four East Surrey vehicles were reallocated to Leatherhead garage for the London–Dorking service.

Meanwhile events were unfolding at Underground group headquarters where it had been decided that a corporate identity was needed to take forward and market the expanding coach operation as a single unit instead of on the piecemeal basis that had been adopted so far. It has been stated that Lord Ashfield himself suggested the name 'Green Line' for this operation, and on 9th July 1930 Green Line Coaches Ltd was established with its registered office at 55 Broadway. A new corporate livery was devised with a base colour of green broken by a deep black band under the windows with a narrower one on the rubbing strake below and also on the mudguards, with a silver roof and orange wheels, and during June 1930 T 119 was painted in this livery. When it was demonstrated for board members' approval at 55 Broadway it carried the Green Line name in an elliptical arrangement giving a suggestion of the group's bullseye motif, but this clearly did not find approval and a plain block capital arrangement was adopted as standard instead. Before long the Green Line name would become synonymous with London suburban coach services, but in the meantime a few more red coaches were destined to take the road.

The last batch of red coaches was licensed on 1st July 1930 with the objective of starting a new service between Charing Cross and Windsor via Hounslow and Staines on the 10th of that month. Operated by General, the operation was based at a newly-acquired Company-owned premises in London Road, Staines, where a temporary, prefabricated building formerly used at Potters Bar had been erected in May to house the new fleet. A total of 65 red-liveried Ts was now in service distributed as follows:

| General | T 51, 53-64, 69, 71, 74, 78-80, 83, 84, 87, 89, 94-97, 99, 101, 104, 105, 107, 108, 111, 114, 115, 120, 129, 155 |
|---|---|
| East Surrey | T 52, 66, 72, 73, 81, 82, 85, 90, 91, 100, 102, 103, 110, 113, 116-118 |
| Autocar | T 65, 70, 77, 86, 88, 98, 106, 109, 112 |

Just a week after the Staines-based operation commenced, on 17th July 1930, Green Line made its debut in direct competition with the established Skylark operation to Guildford, starting from a London terminal at Charing Cross and travelling via Barnes, the Kingston-by-pass and Ripley. Nine coaches were provided initially (T 67, 76, 93, 130, 134, 137, 138, 144, 145) operated from rented space in the yard of Rice & Harper Ltd in London Road, Guildford, which remained in use until a permanent location in the town was opened on 8th April 1932. On 31st July two more coaches were added, bringing the Guildford allocation to its maximum of eleven. Meanwhile the Green Line name had also made its name felt north of the capital when, between 19th and 21st July 1930, the whole of the Leavesden Road fleet of red coaches was usurped by newcomers in green livery.

The first coach to be painted in Green Line colours was T 119, and Lord Ashfield himself was amongst the senior officials who gathered to inspect the vehicle outside the Underground group's head office at 55 Broadway. It was still unlicensed and running on trade plates at the time. Their seal of approval apparently did not extend as far as the stylised form of fleet name which was not applied to any other vehicles and was presumably removed before T 119 entered service. Although it carried wording for the London–Windsor service, T 119 actually started work at Metcalfe's garage in Romford on the Brentwood run.

Two of the coaches used to inaugurate the very first Green Line service on 17th July 1930 are seen at their Guildford operating base on 10th October undergoing mechanical attention. With no garage of its own in the town, Green Line was forced to find temporary parking and fuelling facilities which, in this instance, were at Rice & Harper's, a motor car garage and local Daimler agent. Servicing was carried out by East Surrey engineers, and the vehicle closest to the camera with the mechanic seated on the front mudguard is T 144. Tucked into a corner behind it is T 76; both carry Short Brothers bodywork. *London Transport Museum*

July 23rd 1930 was the next big day when two new operations were scheduled to begin, both in head-on competition with existing private operators. To the east, a service between Charing Cross and Brentwood was based in the Lincoln Works of coachbuilders Metcalfe (London) Ltd on Eastern Avenue, Romford, while to the west the existing LGOC premises at Staines housed coaches for a new Charing Cross to Sunningdale service via Hounslow, Staines and Egham. The Brentwood operation opened under the Green Line banner with twelve new coaches in green livery, but the Sunningdale run was controlled by General using red coaches displaced from Leavesden Road which, from 1st September, also reached Ascot by diverting every other Sunningdale journey. Ascot was the final expansion under General auspices, but prior to this a Charing Cross–Maidenhead operation had begun on 2nd August using coaches transferred from Slough garage and now housed in an open-sided barn adjacent to Maidenhead station. This garaging arrangement quickly proved unsatisfactory and on 22nd October the coaches were transferred back to Slough. The Metcalfe premises were also later vacated, probably on 2nd March 1931, in favour of a one-time farmyard in Hare Street, Gidea Park.

The Brentwood service used up the last available coaches from the initial delivery of 100 and it was now time for the follow-on series of 50 to roll off the production lines. The replacement service bus for T 38 had now occupied fleet number T 156, so the new batch was numbered on from this as T 157-206. With chassis numbers 662503-552, they were a slightly updated version of the first batch with triple servo Dewandre braking and the LGOC's now standard worm and nut steering arrangement. The Short Brothers bodies for these were numbered 11285-11309 and the Hall Lewis ones were 11310-11334 and, as far as is known, there was no difference between these and the earlier batch.

The first 100 new coaches had opened up a vast amount of new coaching territory in a very short time, an amazing feat of organisation and administration, not least of all because under the nineteenth-century Town Police Clauses Acts still in force individual licences had to be obtained for each coach operating through country districts which had exercised their licensing powers in addition to the regular Metropolitan Police District licence. The Brentwood route, for example, required licences from Romford Rural, Romford Urban, Hornchurch and Brentwood District Councils. Overall, the coaches themselves had performed quite well, but dissatisfaction with their braking power had led to trials on certain vehicles using alternative gear supplied by Westinghouse, and a sense that the vehicles were underpowered had also led to experimentation with the fitting of higher ratio 5:1 back axles in place of the regular 6¼:1 on a fairly substantial number of vehicles and on all new ones numbered between T 127 and 149. The braking system was improved by the use of a triple servo from T 157 upwards, but the second delivery reverted to the 6¼:1 axle ratio and the question of improving performance was left in abeyance until an order for further new chassis was placed. On the bodywork, the displaying of intermediate points in gold lettering on the glass window louvres proved ineffective as well as operationally restrictive, and in July 1930 brackets for prominent side boards were fitted to all vehicles, becoming a regular feature of Green Line operation for many years to come.

From 1st September 1930 the first vehicles in the second batch began to be licensed for operation and plans were well under way for six more new services to commence during the next couple of months. It might have been expected that the formation of Green Line Coaches Ltd would have seen a simplification of the administrative arrangements for the group's coach operations, but instead a complex structure prevailed. From 13th September the Reigate service was officially transferred to Green Line Coaches' control using brand new vehicles licensed on the 11th, although for a few days these carried labels stating that they were 'Operated by the East Surrey Traction Company'. In the days that followed the red coaches on the Dorking and Redhill services appeared with stickers stating 'This is a Green Line Service' as did the Autocar coaches at Tunbridge Wells, although the vehicles themselves remained registered to the operating companies. On 29th September all nine Ts at Tunbridge Wells were replaced by Autocar's own all-weather Regal coaches which had become available with the ending of the summer touring season. These received Green Line labelling a couple of months later. The displaced Ts, which remained officially part of the Autocar fleet, promptly reappeared on East Surrey services surprisingly still carrying their Autocar legal ownership details. On 1st October the Guildford based fleet was transferred from Green Line control to East Surrey who were now its managing agents, although the vehicles themselves remained Green Line property.

Also on 1st October 1930 the services formerly vested in the LGOC were transferred to Green Line, and from the same day the fleets based at Slough, Staines and Maidenhead appeared with Green Line paper labels covering the GENERAL fleet name. A start was also made with repainting the red vehicles into green livery. Although operational control of the services changed hands overnight this did not apply, as might have been expected, to ownership of the vehicles. Instead the change from LGOC to Green Line ownership was carried out piecemeal, vehicle by vehicle, as each individual coach went into Chiswick to be repainted into green livery, after which it was subsequently presented to the police authorities to regularise the ownership change. The initial emphasis of the repainting programme was focused mainly on Staines garage, and a snapshot of the situation on 16th October found it to be as follows:

| | |
|---|---|
| Staines | LGOC ownership (red) T 79, 97, 104, 120, 129 |
| | Green Line ownership (green) T 64, 83, 87, 99, 101, 105, 108, 111, 115 |
| Slough | LGOC ownership (red) T 51, 54, 55, 59-63, 69, 74, 78, 89, 96, 155 |
| | Green Line ownership (green) T 53, 56, 57, 107 |
| Maidenhead | LGOC ownership (red) T 58, 71, 84, 114 |

Three former Staines vehicles (T 80, 94, 95) were now at Reigate under Green Line ownership but East Surrey management.

The 50 Ts comprising the second batch were all placed into service within a period of seven weeks, the last three being licensed on 15th October 1930. By now they were already regarded officially as outdated and a new, improved version was on the stocks to emerge at the very end of the year as T 207-306. The first reasonably sized allocation of the latest batch consisted of nine vehicles licensed at Leavesden Road between 2nd and 5th September ready for the start on the 8th of a service between Charing Cross and Tring. These were followed into service on 20th September by the same number of coaches running between Charing Cross and Harpenden via Elstree and St Albans. Directly operated and owned by Green Line, they were based at the Luton Road, Harpenden premises of A P Morgan's Comfy Cars, one of the most lucrative and best run of the St Albans area independent bus operators and a theoretical threat to the LGOC's commercial interests in Hertfordshire which at the time were safeguarded by its agent, the National Omnibus & Transport Company. Comfy Cars provided parking, washing and fuelling facilities to Green Line in an arrangement that worked so satisfactorily that it lasted into London Passenger Transport Board days and was not finally terminated until December 1933.

National itself became a 'managing agent' for Green Line who were glad to avail themselves of the former's services when expanding further in Hertfordshire and north Essex, and some 20 Ts ultimately came under National's wing and were treated almost as part of its own fleet. All maintenance on them was carried out by the Company and most overhauls, when they became due, were undertaken in its works at Watford High Street garage although occasional ones were done at Chiswick. The Company also developed a system whereby, if vehicles were scheduled for their annual licensing inspection but were not due for overhaul, they would go to its Ware garage for a major docking and touching-up of the paintwork before being presented to the Metropolitan Police the next day.

A sample vehicle, and the first one of the second batch to be licensed, was T 161 which was sent to Watford High Street garage on 1st September 1930 for National to inspect. Six more were licensed on 12th September ready for the start of a new Charing Cross–Welwyn Garden City service on the 17th. Initially housed with motor engineers Jenner-Parson Ltd in Welwyn Garden City, they had moved by mid-November to the premises of the large Welwyn Stores in Bridge Road before ending up in H E Prime's garage in Queen Street, Hitchin to which town the operation was extended on 14th January 1931. Nine Ts which inaugurated a Charing Cross–Bishops Stortford service via Loughton and Epping on 1st October were housed from the start in National's premises at Bishops Stortford.

East Surrey acted as the agent for a new Oxford Circus to Godstone via Croydon and Whyteleafe run commenced on 29th September 1930 and worked from Godstone garage by a mixture of brand new Ts and older ones newly repainted from red to green. Subsequent openings under East Surrey auspices – Oxford Circus to Great Bookham on 1st October, Oxford Circus to Westerham on 8th October, and Oxford Circus to Oxted on 22nd October depended partly on re-allocated T-types and also on the availability of older private hire vehicles in green livery, the Oxted run being covered totally by these vehicles which were subsequently repainted into Green Line's darker green shade. The last new Ts in the batch to be earmarked for a service inauguration were a group of seven licensed on 9th and 10th October 1930 to start work on the 11th between Charing Cross and Chertsey via Kingston and Weybridge. Weymann's coachbuilding works in the latter town served as their operating base in the first instance. Rather unusually, this operation was initially run by the LGOC as agent until February 1931 when responsibility for the Addlestone outpost, along with the former LGOC ones at Staines and Slough, was transferred to East Surrey.

An interesting event occurred on 26th January 1931 when five Ts began working for the Amersham & District Motor Bus & Haulage Company on a new express service between Amersham (Oakfield Corner) and Oxford Circus via Uxbridge. Though not a part of the Green Line operation it was worked in conjunction with it, Amersham & District being 50% owned by the LGOC through a nominee company. The original plan had, in fact, been to operate beyond Amersham to Chesham, but delays in obtaining approval from Chesham Council in the very last days of local authority licensing meant that the opening had to go ahead without this extension. The delay cost the company dearly, for when the go-ahead was finally received allowing through operation to commence on 15th February, this was six days after a Ministry of Transport deadline imposed on the introduction of new services prior to the introduction of the Road Traffic Act. Under the terms of the Act, the Chesham projection was subsequently refused by the Traffic Commissioners and had to be withdrawn on 22nd June 1931.

Nothing visibly distinguished the fifty coaches in the T 157-206 batch from earlier deliveries although a number of mechanical improvements were incorporated within them. A typical example, seen laying-over on the Embankment along with coaches on various other Green Line services, is Short Brothers bodied T 186, one of those which inaugurated the Bishops Stortford run on 1st October 1930. It was operated on Green Line's behalf by National from its Bishops Stortford garage, and it is interesting to note that, unlike the LGOC associate companies, National did not trouble to remove the 'Regal' insignia from the radiator before placing the vehicle into service. *E G P Masterman*

Seen negotiating Red Lion Street, Chesham, in the service of Amersham & District shortly after coaches from Oxford Circus had reached the town on 15th February 1931 is T 96. At the time this coach was still in its original red and black colours from the days when it worked on General's coach operation from Slough, although the new owner's fleet names have been applied and A &D initials are displayed at the front. T 96 was repainted into green Amersham & District livery shortly afterwards.

On 13th January 1931 the Commissioner of Police was notified that nine coaches were to be transferred to Amersham & District ownership. Six of these were currently owned by Green Line (T 55, 56, 69, 89, 99, 185) while the other three were the very last red ones still in the ownership of the LGOC (T 71, 96, 104). Five of these vehicles (T 55, 69, 71, 96, 104) were transferred to Amersham on 14th January ready to inaugurate the new service on the 23rd while the remainder were received on the 20th and licensed on the 29th. This number of vehicles was well in excess of what the service required and almost immediately, on 30th January, T 55, 56, 99 and 185 were dispatched back to Chiswick. A strong rumour going the rounds at the time was that the Amersham company intended to commence a second express service from High Wycombe but had been deterred from doing so by the coming of the Road Traffic Act, and this could explain why an excessive number of vehicles was obtained in the first place. The Company did subsequently formally apply for a road service licence for a High Wycombe express service but withdrew it when, having seen how many applications the Metropolitan Traffic Commissioner was refusing, it acknowledged the hopelessness of its case.

The five remaining coaches (T 69, 71, 89, 96, 104) were formally sold to Amersham & District during February using funds supplied for this purpose by the LGOC. They paid £1,169 8s 0d per coach compared with the £1,320 0s 0d that each one had cost when new little more than six months earlier. Between March and May 1931 they were repainted at Chiswick into full Amersham & District livery which was a more cheerful shade of green than used by Green Line, relieved by a cream waistband, silver roof and buff wheels, a simple but effective combination which, along with the handsome scroll fleetname, made the coaches look more attractive than they did in Green Line livery. Instead of being numbered within the Amersham & District fleet the five coaches retained their original T numbers for identification purposes and, unusually, record cards continued to be kept on them by the Green Line organisation as they did with other non-owned vehicles in the East Surrey and Autocar fleets. Under the Road Traffic Act the five coaches were licensed in the East Midland Traffic Area and not the Metropolitan, and so their Metropolitan Stage Carriage plates were surrendered.

T 69 arrived with Amersham & District in January 1931 carrying Green Line colours but was repainted at Chiswick into the new owner's livery early in April. Amersham & District's lighter green and cream gave an unusual and refreshingly cheerful appearance to the now familiar body style, and the boldly written fleet name was a further welcome embellishment. The side route board has been crudely amended to comply with the road service licence, cutting out Chesham and the former pick-up point in Denham, both of which had been disallowed by the South Eastern Traffic Commissioner. *D W K Jones*

A concerted effort was now made to repaint the 26 coaches which retained their original red livery and were still licensed to the East Surrey and Autocar fleets, with the result that all of them appeared in Green Line livery and under Green Line ownership between 20th February and 28th March 1931. The Autocar ones were dealt with first, and although record keeping surviving from that time is incomplete it appears that they finished their days in red livery dispersed among a variety of East Surrey locations including Addlestone, Crawley, Guildford and Reigate itself. None of them had returned to their home base at Tunbridge Wells after leaving there in September 1930.

T 38 was also now repainted into green livery and transferred into Green Line ownership under which it started work at the end of March 1931 between the Company's new central London coach station at Poland Street, near Oxford Circus, and Uxbridge. This service, which commenced on 7th February 1931, was worked principally by new Regal coaches from the next (T 207-306) batch, garaging space for which was rented at the back of the AEC works in Southall. This fortuitous arrangement meant that AEC engineers were on hand to deal with experimental features which certain of these vehicles carried, and it is believed that T 38 was equipped with an experimental engine during the time it was based at Southall, although details of it are not known. T 38's stay there lasted until its next overhaul was due on 3rd March 1932 at which time the experimental engine was probably removed and it returned to Leavesden Road to renew its

acquaintance with the Watford–Golders Green service which it had worked briefly when new.

With the T 207-306 batch entering service between December 1930 and February 1931 (see chapter 3) the spotlight fell away from the earlier vehicles although their spheres of operation widened in some cases with the linking-up of various Green Line services to form cross-London operations, and from 21st February 1931 all Green Line routes were lettered, although the letters were shown only on the side route boards not on the destination blinds. Between about October 1930 and January 1931 many were enhanced by the fitting of sprung bumpers on the rear corners, while in March 1931 Staines-based T 175 is believed to have been the first to demonstrate Green Line's attempt to make its vehicles look brighter and more attractive by replacing the original rather sombre main colour with a more cheerful shade of sage green.

Hall Lewis bodied T 101 awaits passengers at Watford in early London Transport days prior to departing on route I to Crawley. Gone are the chromium plated surrounds to the driver's cab windows and the curtains from the saloon, but a new addition is the enamelled triangular Green Line insignia on the radiator introduced early in the Board's days. The name on the side has been reduced to an insignificant size on the black waist band, and a similar transfer on the driver's dash merely duplicates the name above. *J F Higham © A B Cross*

By the end of 1931 big organisational changes were afoot, and at a board meeting of the East Surrey company at 55 Broadway on 14th December 1931 it was decided to absorb within it all the services in the northern country district currently run on the LGOC's behalf by National. An Extraordinary General Meeting followed on 20th January 1932 at which it was resolved to change the Company's name – which would be inappropriate under the revised circumstances – to London General Country Services Ltd. The name change became effective just over a week later on the 28th, and on 1st March 1932 the National operations were transferred to London General Country Services. This left Green Line Coaches Ltd as owners of the Green Line rolling stock with LGCS as operating agent at most of its locations although there were exceptions such as the Comfy Car base and, notably, Autocar which remained as a separate entity and was not absorbed into LGCS. This all changed on 29th July 1932 when the whole Green Line operation was taken into the ownership of London General Country Services, reducing the Green Line name to the status of a trade mark. Overall responsibility for the vehicles passed from Chiswick to the LGCS's headquarters at Reigate. From a historian's point of view this was unfortunate for the latter's record keeping was nowhere near as comprehensive as Chiswick's, leaving large gaps in our knowledge of what transpired during the next three years.

The Reigate era persisted beyond the formation of the London Passenger Transport Board on 1st July 1933, on which date all the assets of London General Country Services passed to the new undertaking, which meant that all 150 of the Green Line Regals, along with T 38, passed into the Board's ownership with the exception of the five Amersham & District vehicles. These remained outside the London Transport orbit until 29th November 1933 when the Company's assets were finally acquired, uniting all the vehicles under a common ownership for the first time.

Under the Reigate regime overhauls and major repairs were carried out in the extensive and well-equipped new premises which had opened there in January 1932 alongside the old garage. This situation persisted up to 25th February 1935 when control of the vehicles passed back to Chiswick which now became the central overhauling point for the whole fleet, and as part of the same reorganisation the address quoted on the legal ownership panel of each vehicle was changed from Bell Street Reigate to 55 Broadway. Prior to this, in an attempt to standardise operations between the central and country departments, the latter had started to fix stencil holders for garage code letters and running numbers on to the sides of vehicles. These came into use on a gradual basis towards the end of 1934 starting with the frequent Romford services where they were of most value, and were introduced more generally in the early part of 1935. The recommencement of overhauling at Chiswick also saw the adoption of a revised livery for country area vehicles, including Green Line coaches, where the heavy-looking black bands were removed and window surrounds began to be painted in a light, apple shade of green which combined well with darker green lower panels.

Acquisition by the LPTB of the former Batten's and Tilbury Coach Services express coach operations eastwards from London, together with local bus services in the Grays area, took the Board into territory which the Underground group had not formerly penetrated. The situation familiar in the early days of Green Line was repeated whereby temporary operating premises had to be sought, and the yard of Seabrook's Brewery in Grays was used until London Transport's own garage opened on 25th February 1935. T 83 stands in these unprepossessing surrounds along with a Gilford coach, showing the type of rear route board then in use on the 7T7s and the small rear corner bumpers with which the Regal coaches were equipped from late 1930 until 1934/35. The moulding above the rear window denotes a Hall Lewis body and presents an enigma. T 83 carried an LGOC body when new, and the assumption must be that at some time in the Reigate era an exchange of bodies or of vehicle identity has taken place. *London Transport Museum*

Although all the Ts had been issued with body numbers when new, these fell out of use during LGCS days and appear to have got 'lost' somewhere in the system. Replacement numbers were issued as the vehicles went through their first Chiswick overhaul, but as they were dealt with a vehicle at a time over a period of more than a year and were intermingled with all the other vehicles then being overhauled as well as new ones, the resultant range of body numbers was spread widely between 15344 and 16829. Also on overhaul, the coding system introduced for Central Bus vehicles in March 1934 was applied to the Green Line Ts, albeit not with any degree of sophistication. Irrespective of their various braking systems or other differences, all of the vehicles described in this chapter, even T 38, were classified 7T7.

An event which pre-dated the London Transport era – and probably occurred in the latter part of 1932 – was the removal of all the curtains from inside the coaches. Together with their retaining rails and bars, they quickly disappeared, and accompanying their departure went much of the coaching ambience that they had formerly evoked. Rumour has it that their removal was brought about by a fear of fire from lighted cigarettes, but the opportunity to achieve a major cost saving would no doubt also have influenced the decision. Once overhauling commenced at Chiswick other features disappeared too such as the rear corner bumpers (where fitted), the testers' tip-up seat and strap from under the canopy, and fixed starting handles. At the same time the autovac tanks were raised to a higher level to improve their effectiveness, with the side light now mounted on the front of them.

Having seen five years' continuous service, many of the coaches were beginning to look a little jaded despite regular overhauling, and in March 1935 Frank Pick decreed that any of them which were not reasonably satisfactory in respect of upholstery or equipment should be brought up to standard at a cost of not more than £80 per vehicle, with the proviso that such expenditure should only be made on vehicles known to have an effective life of more than three years ahead of them. Towards the end of 1935 a system was introduced to distinguish buses from coaches in the country fleet by the use of a small letter B (for Bus) or C (Coach) placed after the fleet number. Useful, more than anything, for administrative purposes, these letters were quickly applied as a suffix to the fleet numbers of all vehicles, and as those described in this chapter were still employed exclusively on coach work they all received the C suffix.

By early 1935 the use of LGOC style garage plates and running numbers had been adopted throughout the country fleet and adorn the old traditional Green Line livery of green and black on Leavesden Road's T 162. On this vehicle, the new LONDON TRANSPORT name has been applied and its Green Line identity has been almost completely extinguished except from above the front destination box. T 162 will wear these colours only until October 1935 when the now fashionable livery of two-tone green will be applied to it. Seen in the deep south of Green Line's territory outside The George in Crawley, T 162 demonstrates that it has lost its tester's tip-up seat but that its fixed starting handle remains in position, temporarily at least. A new and quite stylish side route board is now in evidence.

The start of 1936 found the Regal coaches well spread out throughout the country fleet, with their presence felt at 23 out of the 31 garages. Some Green Line services were operated by 7T7s exclusively, while on others they shared work with the later batch of 1/7T7/1 Regals. The number of vehicles per garage on 1st January 1936 was:

| | |
|---|---|
| Romford, London Road | 30 |
| Grays | 12 |
| Guildford | 12 |
| Epping | 11 |
| Addlestone | 9 |
| Hitchin | 8 |
| Leatherhead | 7 |
| Amersham | 7 |
| Watford, Leavesden Road | 6 |
| Chelsham | 5 |
| Dorking | 5 |
| Hertford | 5 |
| High Wycombe | 5 |
| Tring | 5 |
| St Albans | 4 |
| Tunbridge Wells | 4 |
| Dunton Green | 3 |
| East Grinstead | 3 |
| Hatfield | 2 |
| Hemel Hempstead | 2 |
| Swanley | 2 |
| Windsor | 2 |
| Reigate | 1 |

T 38 is not included in the above figures. This vehicle was allocated to Watford High Street garage, which played a minor role in Green Line work at the time, and it was transferred to nearby Leavesden Road when this ceased on 18th March 1936. It remained there only until 12th June after which it spent short spells at Luton, Romford (London Road), Romford (North Street), Windsor and Staines before being finally withdrawn from service on 1st September 1938.

Mid-way through 1936 the first significant attempt to update the Green Line fleet got under way with the purchase of 50 new Regals (the 9T9 class) and 50 new AEC Q-types (6Q6), and the entry into service of these flowed fairly constantly between June 1936 and January 1937. The 7T7s were not the prime target at this stage, the priority being to dispose of the sizeable fleet of Gilford coaches still in service on Green Line. This inevitably meant a good deal of reshuffling of allocations in which the 7T7s were quite heavily involved. In particular it was urgent to tackle the very large fleet of Gilfords still resident at Romford, London Road garage, which resulted in no fewer than 61 7T7s being transferred into there during the last three months of 1936 plus a further five in January 1937.

1937 was a fairly quiet year for the 7T7s, but this was the lull before the storm. The contracts for a total of 266 new 10T10 coaches were being negotiated which would inevitably see the end of the 7T7s during 1938, and not before time because developments in coach design during the decade had been so rapid as to render them obsolete despite their comparative youthfulness. A few were redeployed in the country area as buses, but this was probably regarded only as a temporary arrangement as the vehicles concerned never lost their official classification as coaches or their C suffixes, and it is not known exactly which or how many vehicles were used in this way. The great majority soldiered on as coaches, and until T 158 was abruptly withdrawn on 29th November 1937, probably after of an accident, the whole 7T7 class remained intact.

A few more stragglers were withdrawn early in 1938, but the new 10T10s began entering service in June and this was when the blitz on the 7T7s started in earnest. Just beforehand, on 21st May 1938, Romford (North Street) garage had closed and its fleet, which latterly included five 7T7s, was transferred to the London Road premises to join the huge contingent already gathered there. Withdrawals came thick and fast; 26 in June, 24 in July, 22 in August, 16 in September, 33 in October and, finally, the last 20 on 1st November 1938. Of these, 15 had latterly been at Romford on Green Line work, while three at Addlestone and one each at Guildford and Windsor are all believed to have finished their days on bus duties.

Eccleston Bridge at Victoria, long synonymous with Green Line operations, is the setting in December 1936 for Hemel Hempstead based T 118 midway on its journey on route F between its home town and Edenbridge. The vehicle is in its final Green Line condition wearing the two-tone green livery now employed universally throughout the Country Bus & Coach fleet. Gone, now, is the distinctive Green Line radiator badge in favour of the standard green bullseye motif.
*London Transport Museum*

No time was lost in placing the redundant vehicles on the market, but with the likelihood of war looming and bringing with it a growing sense of urgency to conserve resources, sales ceased in March 1939 by which time 110 (including T 38) had been sold. In having Regal chassis that were still comparatively modern, it was inevitable that very many of these would be rapidly snapped up by other operators, and before long ex-London Transport Ts began to reappear in service in many parts of the country, often with modern new coach bodies masking their true age.

The premonition that the onset of war would cause some of the 7T7s to be required in service once again was quickly fulfilled when, on 2nd September 1939 and only one day before the declaration of hostilities, 14 of them were abruptly relicensed for service as buses, five each at Swanley and Watford High Street, two at Tring and one each at Hertford and Luton. A number of 9T9 service buses had been withdrawn for conversion into ambulances and the 7T7s were probably intended to cover this shortfall, although they were all withdrawn again on 26th September as things settled down. Four of the Swanley ones were put in store at Guildford garage and the remainder were all locked away in the temporarily closed Green Line garage at Hitchin until they were needed again. The 7T7s that had not been temporarily revived in September 1939 were all held in open storage along with many other vehicles in the old AEC works at

Forest Road, Walthamstow, from which 17 were removed and taken to Chiswick from February 1940 onwards. Having been earmarked for other duties, their bodies were scrapped and they joined the service vehicle fleet fitted with various types of lorry body. All of those selected were from the second, T 157-206 delivery to take advantage of their triple servo braking systems, the actual vehicles being T 160, 163-165, 167, 169, 171, 172, 174-176, 181, 199, 203, 206.

In addition to the 17 vehicles converted into lorries during 1940, there was T 120 which was later to become renowned for its longevity in being the only one of the 7T7 batch to survive with London Transport after the war. Withdrawn from passenger service at Romford on 1st November 1938, T 120 subsequently joined all the others in store at Walthamstow. October 1940 found it at Chiswick being modified to become part of London Transport's internal ambulance fleet in which it was numbered 456W and replaced a 1/7T7/1 originally converted for this purpose but destroyed by enemy action. To suit T 120 for its new role as an ambulance much more work was required than had been the case with the 1/7T7/1s. A doorway had to be cut in the back to accommodate stretchers, while the original rear entrance and steps were removed and the aperture panelled and glazed to match the rest of the nearside. The transformation was completed by inserting a new passenger entrance at the front enclosed by a simple pair of jack-knife doors.

It will probably never be known how many 7T7s were diverted temporarily for use as buses towards the end of their operational careers. T 191, photographed in East Grinstead on a 434 service to Horsham (with a Southdown Leyland Tiger standing behind), was probably ejected from coach operation on 1st June 1938 upon the arrival at East Grinstead of a fleet of new 10T10s. With its Green Line names painted out, it would not have served as a bus for very long as it was finally withdrawn from use on the last day of the same month and sold later in the same year. T 101, based at Windsor, was given a slightly more professional treatment for its short career as a bus with provision for a route number plate to be inserted in front of where the Green Line insignia had once been. It was photographed in Slough and is believed to have worked from Windsor garage in this guise throughout the months of May and June 1938. *Andrew N Porter/ J F Higham © A B Cross*

A major resumption of Green Line operation on 4th November 1940, augmented by yet more services on the 18th, put the Country Bus department's single deck fleet under considerable pressure, and from the 11th of that month the remaining 7T7s began to be activated once again starting with two each at Amersham, Dorking, Hertford, Luton and Windsor. Others followed, the biggest single contingent comprising six at Dunton Green on 1st December, until eventually 19 were back in use. Although often to be found covering a variety of local bus duties, they could also commonly be seen back on Green Line work. They sometimes covered scheduled duties, especially on route 35 (Aylesbury–Victoria) from Amersham garage, but more often worked the many duplicates that had to be run to meet the burgeoning demand for travel, notably on routes 26/26A (Windsor/Farnham Common–Victoria) from Windsor garage and 45 (Luton–Victoria) from Luton and St Albans garages. The latter garage was not actually scheduled for Green Line work but was frequently called on to help out, as was Dunton Green which often provided 7T7s as duplicates on Tunbridge Wells' extremely busy route 5 (Tunbridge Wells–Victoria). The full list of garages officially allocated 7T7s during this wartime period comprised Addlestone, Amersham, Dorking, Dunton Green, Hertford, Luton, Reigate, St Albans and Windsor, but inter-garage loaning was commonplace and even the tiny Tunbridge Wells garage's TW plates could be seen on the side of 7T7s from time to time.

None of the class had been overhauled since the middle or latter part of 1937 and even then they had only received what were described as "light" overhauls in anticipation of their early withdrawal from service. This omission was rectified, mostly between October and December 1941, when they were given body overhauls and were repainted, for the first time, into the 1940 Lincoln green and off-white livery.

Double-decking of various Green Line services gradually eased the availability of single deck rolling stock, allowing a start to be made in November 1941 on finally withdrawing the 7T7s from service, and one by one the various garages relinquished their holdings of these vehicles. By government decree, the Green Line network was discontinued for a second time on Wednesday 30th September 1942, this time for the remaining duration of the war, and reallocation of rolling stock consequent upon this spelt the end for the last four 7T7s remaining in service, T 94, 113, 121 at Amersham and T 109 at Dorking.

Even then the story had not quite ended for the last 19 7T7s (T 120 excluded). During the winter months of 1943/44 and again in 1944/45 they were fitted out as snow ploughs and stationed at various strategic locations in case they were required for use. The very end came during the first few days of May 1945 – just before the war in Europe drew to a close – when they were all sold to the War Department for use by the Allied Control Commission in war-ravaged continental Europe.

This left just T 120, which continued to perform its role as ambulance 456W until it was released from these duties on 15th November 1945, whereupon it regained its original bus identity. An exchange of body with T 305 found it reclassified as a 1/7T7/1 in which form it returned to passenger service at Luton on 1st January 1946. As recorded in the next chapter, T 120 transferred to central area work in November 1946 where it ran from Norwood, Cricklewood, Hornchurch and Sidcup garages, still in green livery, until its deteriorating condition brought about its final withdrawal in April 1949.

*Below left* The war brought a totally unexpected reprieve to a few 7T7s and it is unfortunate that only poor photographs are known to exist of these vehicles in the very twilight of their career. With an inspector proudly standing by, T 94 waits in Sevenoaks bus station while operating on route 454. It worked at Dunton Green garage during December 1940 and subsequently right through to January 1942 before being transferred for use elsewhere. After the photograph was taken in November 1941 it received a body overhaul at which it adopted wartime green and white livery. *J G S Smith collection*

The sole survivor of the 7T7 era to continue in service after the war was T 120, now regarded officially as a 1/7T7/1 and carrying the 1931 Weymann front entrance body formerly on T 305. It ran in this form right through to April 1949 and was photographed in Epping on 29th September 1948. Allocated at the time to Hornchurch garage, it was still in green livery and was looking somewhat uncared for, which was hardly surprising as the paintwork on it dated back to November 1945. *Alan B Cross collection*

# 3 THE SECOND GREEN LINE BATCH

## T 207-306

The acquisition of the next batch of Green Line coaches was a remarkably well organised operation carried out in record time against a strict deadline. With the implementation of the Road Traffic Act looming on the near horizon, operators were given preliminary notice that only services already in operation on 1st March 1931 would be considered eligible for a Road Service Licence when these were brought into effect under the terms of the Act. The LGOC, acting on behalf of Green Line, had to move fast to place orders in the autumn of 1930 for 100 chassis and bodies which it could realistically rely upon being built and commissioned for service within the short time span available.

As AEC was a fellow member of the Underground organisation, it was presumably reasonably easy to ensure that its resources were geared to the production of 100 Regal chassis within the required timescale even at the expense of deferring other contracts. In fact the first few were delivered in the closing days of October 1930 and all had been received by the end of January 1931. The acquisition of bodies was more problematic especially as the LGOC had no spare capacity within its own resources at Chiswick to construct any of them. Tender documents were distributed to a number of likely bodywork suppliers in the full knowledge that no individual one would have the capacity to produce all 100 bodies within the envisaged timescale and that the order would have

to be split. Such was the haste that tenders submitted during the last week of September were turned into firm orders on 1st October with construction being split three ways. The largest share went to Duple Motors & Bodies Ltd who were contracted to build 50 at the rate of eight per week commencing eight weeks from receipt of the final drawings and patterns; the remainder were allocated 25 apiece to Weymann Motor Bodies (1925) Ltd at Addlestone and Ransomes, Sims & Jefferies Ltd at Ipswich. As in the case of the 7T7s, all three manufacturers were required to follow the original drawings so closely that it would be impossible to tell which factory individual bodies had been built at.

Although the T 207-306 batch of Green Line Regals bore several notable differences from their predecessors, there was no denying the overall family resemblance. T 208 demonstrates the characteristic nearside lines of these coaches, including the front entrance with sliding door, as it stands outside the Weymann works in Station Road, Addlestone, which provided the initial accommodation for coaches on the Chertsey service when it commenced in December 1930. T 208 started work on it shortly afterwards, having been licensed on 1st January 1931. Very appropriately it carries a Weymann-built body, but being brand new when photographed it had not yet received its Green Line radiator triangle. The board on the side incorporates the route letter C, slightly ahead of the official introduction of route lettering to Green Line services on 21st February. *London Transport Museum*

The only one out of the three bodywork contractors with whom the LGOC had previously done business was Ransomes who had successfully fulfilled a number of contracts in the past, most recently the provision of 60 double deck bodies on AEC Regent chassis for operation by East Surrey and Autocar. Sadly, this was to be their last. The Weymann bodies were of interest because they were the first ever built at the Addlestone works using the conventional composite model of construction combining a jointed timber framework with pillars flitched with steel and bracketed at vulnerable points to give added srength. Prior to this the Company had specialised in its own patented design of flexible construction devoid of joints and held together by bolted metal plates, with panelling of fabric (or, in the case of later psv bodies, fabric-covered aluminium). The order for Green Line bodies pointed a new way ahead for Weymann which, following the introduction of metal-framed bodies in 1932, marked a decline for the Weymann patented bodies although a few orders were taken from provincial operators until as late as 1939. The large contract placed with Duple – which never became a regular contractor for the LGOC or its successor London Transport – raises the question as to whether the Company actually had the capability of building as many as eight bodies a week in its admittedly modern factory at Hendon or whether, as Duple was known to do at other times of pressure, some of the work was outsourced. Either way, the LGOC's commandeering of so much coachbuilding capacity went down badly with a number of smaller operators who viewed it, rightly or wrongly, as a deliberate ploy by the Combine to deny them opportunities to obtain new vehicles of their own prior to the March 1931 deadline, and there were undoubtedly some independent proprietors who suffered through their inability to source bodies on time.

The Regal chassis for T 207-306 (662703-802) incorporated some of the design improvements introduced during the 7T7 production run such as worm and nut type steering and triple service brakes (although these were now by Westinghouse and not Dewandre), but some further differences were introduced too. Foremost was the adoption of AEC's new and more powerful A145 110mm bore engine rated at 110bhp with which a new 5.2:1 axle ratio was specified. The earlier batch had been fitted with 22 inch wheels to take 38x8¼ tyres, but smaller 20 inch wheels were now fitted with 38x9 low pressure tyres. Because a front entrance with sliding door was now specified, the 35 gallon fuel tank was moved to the offside.

Although bearing a marked family resemblance and built to exactly the same box dimensions (9ft 3ins height and 26ft 0ins length), the bodies on T 207-306 marked an improvement over the previous series in a number of respects. They were immediately distinguishable because the illuminated GREEN LINE panel at the front was mounted below the destination aperture resulting in a distinctive and instantly recognisable frontal profile. More strategically important, though, was the relocation of the entrance doorway which was now placed at the front where a sliding door could be installed. The emergency exit was now located in the centre at the back, and these rearrangements allowed seven equal-sized bays to be employed, terminating in a rear that was rather more curved than what had gone before. Although the lower panels and side windows were the same depth as on the 7T7s, the cantrail was placed a little higher, resulting in a slightly more shallow roof to keep the vehicle within the same overall height. The shallower roof produced an equivalently taller offside window to the driver's cab, and the auxiliary window above the windscreen – a feature inherited from the previous batch – was also larger than before but was now fitted with darkened glass to reduce glare. However its value, if it ever had any, was reduced because much of it was obscured by the downward projection of the GREEN LINE panel and, in any case, as on the 7T7s these windows were soon panelled over.

Early in its working career, Chelsham-based T 239 is seen operating between the new Poland Street coach station near Oxford Circus (which opened on Christmas day 1930) and Edenbridge, a destination which was reached only 2-hourly although short-working journeys were available every 30 minutes as far as Chelsham. The service became J under the lettering scheme then about to be introduced. T 239 was one of 32 new Ts distributed by East Surrey amongst its various garages to displace less suitable rolling stock from Green Line work. *Charles F Klapper © Omnibus Society*

Once on board the passenger had only two steps to climb instead of three to reach the saloon floor and, as before, all the seats were forward facing. These were exactly the same as used previously, but in order to accommodate 30 passengers they were placed slightly closer together. No floor space was available on these vehicles for passengers' luggage so much larger and more substantial racks were employed above the seats. The main lamps were now located under the luggage racks instead of in the main roof, which made reading conditions much better at night, although a single row of lights was also placed along the centre of the ceiling to light the gangway.

With an unladen weight of 5tons 19cwt 2qr T 207-306 were more than 8cwt heavier than the earlier batch, but this certainly did not hinder their progress. The combination of a large engine with a 5.2 axle ratio meant that they were fast, and extremely so. It was said at the time that, under the right circumstances, they were capable of reaching 60mph, which would be a remarkable achievement for coaches whose legally permitted top speed had only been raised to 30mph as recently as 1st January 1931. Whatever the truth of their exalted achievements, they were certainly involved in a number of speeding prosecutions in their early days, and before long steps were taken to slow them down. Every vehicle had its axle ratio lowered to 6¼ while the majority were also re-engined with the smaller A140 unit to ensure that no speed records were ever broken again.

Experimental features were incorporated on a number of chassis. The Lockheed hydraulic braking system was tried out on T 220 for which purpose the chassis following on from the end of the main production block, 662803, was specially equipped from new. This took the place of T 220's booked chassis, 662716, which went instead as a service bus to East Surrey. Twenty-four chassis at the end of the batch – those on T 282-304, 306 – were supplied with the novel "thermo-economic" system of water temperature management employing thermostatically controlled radiators which could be readily recognised by a series of prominent vertical tubes in place of the normal grille. The same system was later tried out on experimental Green Line double deck coach LT 1137 and also on a number of otherwise standard LT service buses, but in most instances it was not retained for long and presumably proved less useful than had been hoped.

It was when viewed from the back that the new Ts were seen to differ most substantially from the earlier batch through having a central emergency door. They were also provided from new with the three-layered corner bumpers favoured by management at the time. Spruced up with white walled tyres especially for the photographic session on 10th February 1931, T 302 is as yet unregistered and still in prime condition as delivered from the Weymann factory which obviously also supplied the roof-mounted route boards ready-painted in preparation for the appropriate lettering to be added at Chiswick.
*London Transport Museum*

From the viewpoint of styling and décor, the interior bore few surprises, being mainly a follow-on from what had gone before as demonstrated by T 302. The idea of raising the seats in the rearward half of the body was perpetuated, offering a good view of the passing scenery. The large luggage racks, though rather bulky in appearance, were obviously very sturdy and could accommodate quite large suitcases, while there were plenty of lights below the racks to provide a good standard of night-time illumination. An area of criticism which subsequently emerged was the relative paucity of handrails at the entrance, the only ones being on the left of the passenger when boarding with nothing substantial on the right to hold on to, which many passengers found inconvenient especially when loaded-down with items of luggage. *London Transport Museum*

The most promising and most talked-about development within the industry at the time was the development of the compression ignition engine powered by heavy oil, usually then referred to as the 'oil' engine. In October 1930 AEC announced the availability of its new A155 6-cylinder overhead indirect injection oil engine employing the German Acro air-cell combustion system, and the LGOC was quick to avail itself of some of these for trial use under a variety of operating conditions. A small batch was ordered by the LGOC for use in double deckers, the first three of which entered service in December 1930 powering new STs followed from February 1931 onwards by nine in larger LT six-wheelers. The same engine was obtained for use in a few Green Line coaches in order to gain experience of their performance on a different type of work, and vehicles fitted with them entered service on 6th February 1931 numbered T 216, 274 and 305. With bore and stroke of 110mm and 142mm respectively, the A155 engine had a swept volume of 8.1 litres and a rated power output of 95bhp at 2,400rpm which, fortuitously was exactly the same as that of the A145 petrol engine making performance comparisons particularly meaningful. Being longer than the equivalent petrol engine, the A155 caused the radiator to be projected forward by almost 5 inches while the bonnet and radiator were both set at a slightly inclined angle, making the three oil engined coaches immediately recognisable even when silent. For a short period between about February 1932 and some time in 1934 the three vehicles were equipped with experimental fully floating back axles, but the purpose and subsequent conclusions of this trial are not known.

It has already been well recorded in companion volumes on the LT and ST classes that the A155 oil engine was not successful; in fact its performance bordered on disastrous. The pronounced diesel knock that had been anticipated was not, in fact, as bad as had been feared but in most other respects, including fuel consumption, the new engines fell well short of what had been expected. They were extremely smoky, emitting objectionable exhaust fumes which were at their worst when the engines were cold and giving rise to numerous public complaints, and they quickly proved highly prone to costly bearing and camshaft failures. An odd feature of AEC's design was that the A155 was ungoverned as to its maximum speed, and it may be that runaways contributed to some of the serious mechanical failures that occurred. To their credit, AEC took hardly any time at all to get to grips with the problem, calling upon the expertise of Ricardo &

Company Ltd of Shoreham to come up with a major redesign. The A161 engine which emerged had a completely new design of block and head, the latter employing what was known as the Ricardo 'Comet' rotary swirl combustion chamber. With a bore now increased to 115mm, power rating was raised to 130bhp, and with a swept volume of 8.850 litres the engine commonly known as the AEC 8.8 was born. The three T-type oilers are thought to have been given new A161 engines early in 1932, and though T 216 was later converted to petrol, probably in 1936, the other two retained their oil engines for the whole of their working lives in London.

The new vehicles began to arrive at Chiswick from the coachbuilders in mid-December 1930, the exact dates being unknown except in the case of Ransomes whose first one was received on the 17th. The first four entered service at Slough on 23rd December to augment the existing fleet there; these were Weymann-bodied T 214 and Duple-bodied T 218, 224, 225. All three bodybuilders had adhered to their production promises by delivering on time, and the first from the Ransomes stable to enter service – T 209, 212 – did so less than a fortnight later on 5th January 1931. Time was now of the essence if new services were to be started, operators having now been informed that instead of the 1st March deadline that they had expected for new start-ups, the final date had now been fixed as Monday 9th February 1931. Any service commenced after this would have to be withdrawn by 31st March otherwise prosecutions would ensue. However before the new Ts could inaugurate further services there was some catching-up to do. After the last of the earlier batch had been delivered further new Green Line operations had commenced using an ad-hoc mixture of rolling stock, including private hire vehicles and coaches released for the winter months from excursion and tour work, most of which had slam doors and were deficient in luggage space etc.

To rectify this problem, no fewer than 32 new coaches were sent to East Surrey at Reigate. Although the vehicles themselves now all belonged officially to Green Line Coaches Ltd, other associated companies – East Surrey, National and Autocar – still operated some services as agents with East Surrey by far the most important of these. The latter kept no specific record to show which of its garages the Green Line coaches were distributed to although it is known that they were spread between Chelsham, Crawley, Dunton Green, East Grinstead, Godstone, Guildford, Leatherhead and Swanley, as well as Reigate itself. The services now provided with proper Green Line rolling stock were autumn 1930

Removal of the curtains on safety grounds left the Ts looking rather more spartan and less coach-like than before, even when viewed from the outside as demonstrated by T 216 which was photographed inside Reigate garage. Taken in early LPTB days, albeit still wearing original livery, the fact that this was one of the three oil-engined members of the class can be seen from the unusual length of its bonnet. The fully-floating rear axle carried by the three oilers for a short period in their lives is also in evidence. *Snook & Son*

start-ups linking Oxford Circus with Godstone Green, East Grinstead, Oxted and Westerham. National needed new coaches too, to cover an existing service from Charing Cross to Hertford which had started on 22nd November 1930, and these were garaged in its premises at Ware. Finally among the catch-ups was the Tunbridge Wells service which Autocar had run using its own vehicles since the previous batch of Ts had been withdrawn from there; ten new ones were supplied in the first few days of February 1931.

A number of new operations commenced on 14th January 1931 for which, fortunately, enough new vehicles were available. Leavesden Road supplemented its earlier batch of Ts with new ones to cover an extension of the Redhill–Charing Cross service to Bushey, while a projection of the Welwyn Garden City service to Hitchin on the same day saw two new vehicles joining earlier Ts which were now housed in Prime's garage at Hitchin (which later became London Transport's permanent premises in the town). At 55 miles from end to end, the Reigate–Hitchin service was now one of the longest of its kind anywhere in the country. The next important date was 31st January when new Ts were sent to join earlier ones at Weymann's factory in Addlestone to work a service between the Company's new coach station at Poland Street near Oxford Circus, which had opened on Christmas Day 1930, to West Byfleet, while another temporary garaging premises was opened in a former foundry in Hanworth Road, Sunbury to provide a base for six new Ts inaugurating a service from Poland Street to Sunbury Common. A new service from Poland Street to Rickmansworth via Harrow and Pinner brought yet more Ts to Leavesden Road's allocation which now stood at 31 including engineering spares. At Leavesden Road, and increasingly at other garages too, it became quite usual to see both types of T, rear and front entrance, mixed together on the same service.

With the 9th February deadline looming, the next service started just in time when new Ts began running between Poland Street and Uxbridge via Ealing on the 7th. Allegedly the original intention had been to run as far as Beaconsfield but insufficient vehicles were available to allow this to happen. Interestingly the six new Ts provided to cover the four scheduled workings were garaged inside the AEC works at Southall in an area at the back later used for railcar production. These included the three oilers which, in running alongside three standard petrol models, gave both AEC's and the LGOC's engineers an excellent opportunity to compare results, and also meant that skilled staff from the manufacturer were at hand to deal with problems which might occur on the oilers, as they often did.

Like some of its competitors, Green Line decided to chance its luck by beginning new services after the 9th February deadline. The first of these was an extension of the Godstone Green–Tring operation northwards to Aylesbury for which space was rented in the old Cubitt car factory at Aylesbury to house four coaches overnight. No specific vehicles were allocated there, provision being made from within Leavesden Road's allocation. On 21st February a new service opened between Charing Cross and Upminster via Barking for which additional new coaches were allocated to Metcalfe's works in Romford (moving on 3rd March to alternative premises in Gidea Park). Very quickly the Company began to doubt the wisdom of these introductions, and no doubt anxious not to get on the wrong side of the new Traffic Commissioners, withdrew both the Aylesbury and Upminster operations on 1st April 1931.

This photographic record taken by the LGOC's laboratory at Chiswick on 21st December 1931 shows the severe accident damage sustained by oil-engined T 305 while working between London and Uxbridge on route Q, which inevitably resulted in its body being written off. At this early stage in its life it still had its original semi-floating back axle. The sheer scale of destruction shows graphically the weakness of wooden framed bodywork when subjected to severe impact. In the background, on what appears to be a foggy day, are four brand new LTs – both double and single deck – still awaiting licensing, and a newly-overhauled DS class 2½ ton Dennis formerly with the London Public Omnibus Company.

Most of the new coaches only operated in the original shade of green for less than a year. Overhauling of them commenced in August 1931 from which they emerged freshly repainted in the new, brighter shade introduced earlier in the year. The overhauling arrangements were interesting in being spread amongst a number of workshops. The heaviest load fell on the East Surrey facility at Reigate which dealt not only with the coaches directly operated by the Company as an agent for Green Line, but also those based at Addlestone and Sunbury as well as the ones housed with Autocar at Tunbridge Wells. A few were dealt with at Chiswick and the remainder were overhauled at the two Watford garages. The coaches operated by National were dealt with at its premises in Watford High Street while Leavesden Road garage – which had been extended and modernised in 1931 – handled its own vehicles and also those used on the Brentwood service and the small fleet kept in the AEC works at Southall. By February 1932 all were running in the new colours.

During their time in London very few of the Green Line Regals exchanged bodies, there being no mass alterations to identity occurring on overhaul as was the case in the LGOC fleet. However an early isolated instance of body changing was set in motion in December 1931 when oil-engined T 305 was involved in a serious accident. Taken into Chiswick on 16th December, its Ransomes bodywork was diagnosed as beyond worthwhile repair and was removed for scrap later in the same month. At an unknown date, but probably soon afterwards, Addlestone based T 268 joined it at Chiswick, also unfit for service. Generally regarded as having been involved in an accident, it is thought in fact to have suffered serious engine failure, leaving its Weymann body intact. The latter was transferred to the chassis of T 305 – the date for this being recorded as 15th March 1932 – and six days later it resumed work at its Southall base. The chassis of T 268 was duly scrapped and the vehicle was written off books when only 15 months old.

The London General Country Services era had now arrived and the Company had taken overall responsibility for all Green Line operations. The services formerly worked by National on the LGOC's behalf had passed to LGCS on 1st March 1932, and on 29th July 1932 all the assets of Green Line Coaches Ltd were absorbed into LGCS. Control of the whole Green Line operation was now firmly vested at Reigate, which even appeared to possess a fair degree of autonomy when it came to vehicle purchasing policy. Its influence clearly held sway in 1933 when it came to sourcing a new body for accident damaged T 232.

LGCS's record keeping being what it was, the process by which T 232's body was designed and ordered is not known, and nor are any specific dates relevant to it. The Reigate management appears to have enjoyed a mutually beneficial rapport with the Weymann coachbuilding concern at Addlestone, the main outcome of which was the batch of twelve lowbridge 'Godstone' STLs (1044-1055). These proved to be excellent vehicles in which Chiswick influence, if any, was minimal, their great strength lying in the MCW patented metal framework using tubular steel pillars of flanged box section which formed the basis of their construction. The same metal framework was used for T 232 which emerged in April 1933, a year ahead of the STLs, as only the second metal body to be built at Addlestone. The result was a long, low streamlined coach far more modern in appearance than anything yet seen on Green Line.

The LGCS's Chief Engineer, W A C Snook was closely associated in the development of the new body and in the negotiations for its purchase, but certain features such as the shape of the bulge below the windscreen point to actual design work having been carried out in the drawing office at Addlestone. The curved rear end with central emergency door was particularly attractive, and the designer's solution to raising the rear windows to match the higher seating at the back of the saloon whilst retaining the continuity of line of both the waistrail and cantrail, was particularly neat. Great thought had obviously gone into the display of destination information, this being the only vehicle in the Green Line fleet to display the route letters (which had been introduced in February 1931) at front and back rather than relying

purely on boards carried along the side. The boards themselves were dispensed with, to be replaced by four glass fronted apertures on each side displaying illuminated stencils giving details of the line of route, though this might not have been such a good idea as the stencil plates may well have been inclined to rattle as the vehicle went along and their location, behind the luggage racks, would have made them difficult to get at. Although the standard 17ft wheelbase was retained, the new body had a 6 inches longer overhang at the rear bringing it to 26ft 6ins, and with the bottom rail quite low built, grounding may well have been a problem with this vehicle.

The saloon was enclosed by a G D Peters vacuum operated door through which the passenger reached a pleasant interior with 30 seats all facing forwards. The seats were covered front and back in an attractive green moquette which also lined the side panels. Although new to the Company at the time, this was later used to good effect on the 'Godstone' STLs, and it contrasted well with the brown hide trimming and the highly polished window surrounds to give a very welcoming look. A particularly nice feature was the use of handsome lamp shades mounted vertically on each pillar. One drawback in the design, however, was that the comparatively shallow ceiling left no room for luggage racks over the last three rows of seats. Despite its solid appearance, the rebodied T 232 tipped the scales at only 5ton 14cwt unladen which was more than a quarter of a ton less than the vehicle had weighed in its original form.

The years 1932 and 1933 marked an interesting phase during which the LGOC negotiated the acquisition of a number of competing express services which it integrated into the Green Line network. Green Line Ts were often called upon to deputise for acquired coaches, often to allow the latter to be given a much-needed overhaul. Such was the case when operation of J S Ray's Regent Motor Services run between Oxford Circus and Hertford was taken over on 27th February 1932 and Ts, such as Duple bodied T 262, were drafted in to replace Regent's four Gilfords. Pending granting of the licence and formal transfer of ownership – which occurred on 8th April – the Ts displayed the Regent name on the fronts of their otherwise full Green Line livery, and they continued to do so for a while afterwards, remaining on the ex-Regent workings which became known as Green Line route CF. *J F Higham © A B Cross*

The new metal-framed body which T 232 carried when it emerged from the Weymann factory in April 1933 was well ahead of its time in styling and quite unlike anything seen on Green Line up to that time. Particular attention had obviously been paid to the display of route information although, surprisingly, different sized boxes were provided at front and rear. The side route stencils, carried behind glass, were eye-catchingly different from the wooden boards normally used. For the first time on a Green Line T, the driver's compartment was provided with a door, albeit only of half height. T 232's first sphere of operation in its new form was on route R between Reigate and Hitchin and when photographed in service at the former terminus it lacked any sign of a fleet number on the nearside. *E G P Masterman/John Aldridge collection*

With their separate polished top rails, the lightweight seats on T 232 looked rather bus-like, but thanks to the use of colourful fabrics for the seats and side lining panels, together with very attractive lamps, the overall effect was pleasant and modern. A big drawback, however, was the paucity of luggage accommodation brought about by the low ceiling. *John Aldridge collection*

The formation of the London Passenger Transport Board on 1st July 1933 and the various events affecting the Green Line Regals during the years 1933-35 have been described in the previous chapter and apply to this batch too. The issuing of new body numbers upon overhaul resulted in T 207-306's bodies being numbered anywhere between 15345 (T 264) and 16831 (T 224); the unique T 232 was 15856. Under the 1934 coding system the majority of vehicles became 1/7T7/1, exceptions being the three oilers which were 2/7T7/1 and T 232 which was 1/7T7/2.

Under London Transport's auspices the use of miscellaneous rented premises for the garaging of coaches was ended as soon as practicable. The Comfy Cars garage in Harpenden, for example, was not needed after Boxing Day 1933 since the Board now had its own premises in St Albans taken over from St Albans & District. Of particular interest was the closure of the operation from AEC's Southall works on 3rd January 1934 where the three oil engine Ts had been based. Although the operations were taken over by Amersham and High Wycombe garages these three vehicles were sent to Reigate, being kept together there until 1936 when they began to be dispersed to other garages. The use of diesel engines had now become widespread and, despite the non-standard nature of their 8.8 litre engines within the Country Bus & Coach fleet, it was presumably no longer seen as necessary to keep them together. It was probably round about this time that one of the three, T 216, was converted from oil to petrol.

By the start of 1936 the 1/7T7/1s were just as widely spread across the fleet as were the 7T7s, claiming a presence at 24 out of the department's 31 garages. Both types were heavily intermingled, the only garages with 1/7T7/1s but no 7T7s being Crawley, Godstone and Luton whilst, conversely, only Grays and St Albans had 7T7s but no 1/7T7/1s. In addition there were various ex-independent Regals, Leyland Titans and Tigers, and Gilfords scattered around the Green Line fleet, the current emphasis being on eliminating the Gilfords from it as quickly as possible. No garages had really

large holdings of 1/7T7/1s, the disposition of which on 1st January 1936 was:

| | | | |
|---|---|---|---|
| Epping | 14 | Amersham | 2 |
| Luton | 13 | Hatfield | 2 |
| Hertford | 10 | High Wycombe | 2 |
| Dunton Green | 8 | Hitchin | 2 |
| East Grinstead | 6 | Romford, London Rd | 2 |
| Windsor | 6 | Swanley | 2 |
| Chelsham | 4 | Tunbridge Wells | 2 |
| Dorking | 4 | Watford, Leavesden Rd | 2 |
| Reigate | 4 | Guildford | 1 |
| Addlestone | 3 | Hemel Hempstead | 1 |
| Crawley | 3 | Leatherhead | 1 |
| Godstone | 3 | Tring | 1 |

The three oilers were at Reigate, and excluded from the figures above is T 232 which at the time was allocated to Guildford. This vehicle appears not to have been very popular, being on the move every few months and transferring to Godstone in September 1936, Dunton Green in May 1937, Epping in October 1937 and Reigate in February 1938. Other chapters describe the fleet renewal process from 1936 onwards, but it was not until 1938 that redundancy first hit vehicles in the T 207-306 batch and the first one of all to go was odd man out T 232, which was delicensed on 25th March 1938.

More than a year into the London Transport era, in September 1934, Addlestone based T 255 is seen in Upper Regent Street on route from Hertford to Guildford on route M. The brackets over certain place names on the side route display were provided so that slip boards could be inserted to give the flexibility of also running on routes AM and BM. The vehicle is still recognisably in almost original condition although the chrome work around the cab has been painted over and the subsidiary window above the windscreen blanked out. In order to accommodate the LONDON TRANSPORT name on the main side panels, the GREEN LINE legend has been relegated to small letters on the black waist band. *London Transport Museum*

Hertford bus station with Green Line Regals T 300 (nearest the camera) and T 282 in attendance along with former Penn Bus Company Gilford GF 191 and nearly-new Leyland Cub C 16 both working on local services. All four vehicles carry the two-tone green livery introduced in 1935 while the Ts demonstrate that the single rear route board formerly carried on the rear dome has now been replaced by three smaller and easier to reach ones at waist rail level. *Alan B Cross*

Prior to this, progress in eliminating the Gilfords led to an influx of 1/7T7/1s into Grays from October 1936 followed by Romford (North Street) and St Albans in December. January 1937 found a small allocation at Northfleet with a new input of Green Line work there. Meanwhile a decision had to be taken about what to do with the 1/7T7/1s when they became surplus to requirements and by early 1938 a three-pronged course of action had been decided on. Some would be converted to diesel and fitted with three years old Weymann bodies removed from AEC Reliances, others would be converted as

they stood for use as service buses in the Country Bus fleet, whilst a further group would be given various types of lorry body for use in the service vehicle fleet. Only those not required for any of these purposes would be sold.

In a sense, those in the first category were the most important as they were the ones with the longest life expectancy, and the chassis of T 232 was used as the prototype for these, its modern body having meanwhile been scrapped. The remaining vehicles destined for the same fate were taken out of service between September and December 1938, 26 in all being set aside for this purpose. Reclassified as 11T11, they were destined to remain on front line work until 1952 and are thus still reasonably well remembered. In all, there were 31 11T11s, some others having been converted from former independent Regals taken over in 1933, and they are all described as a group in chapter 16. For the record, the vehicles from the T 207-306 batch converted to 11T11s were T 208, 212-216, 223, 226, 232, 234, 236, 237, 253, 255, 261, 266, 267, 271, 275, 276, 280, 283, 285, 296, 298.

In August 1935 T 232 received the latest two-tone green livery and, carrying LONDON TRANSPORT as its fleet name, was based at Guildford garage for the M group of services which ran from Guilford, Byfleet or Esher to a common northern terminus at Hertford. The rear bumpers have been removed and the once-polished side mouldings have now been painted over. The following overhaul, which occupied three weeks in August and September 1936, resulted in the disappearance of the side route boxes and their substitution by conventional roof-mounted route boards, as well as the removal of the route letter aperture from the front of the vehicle. It ran in this form from Dunton Green on route D between May and October 1937.

During the mid-nineteen thirties attempts were made to brighten up the Green Line Ts which, after half a decade of hard work, were beginning in many cases to look quite jaded. This interior view of Chelsham based T 217 was taken as it emerged from overhaul in November 1935 showing a freshly painted ceiling, cream in the centre and a dark colour (probably black) over the luggage panels. Such treatment may have brightened the environment a little but was hardly in keeping with the semi-luxury ethos that Green Line was trying to promote. *London Transport Museum*

Twenty-two vehicles withdrawn in the latter part of 1938 were overhauled in readiness for rebodying as open lorries between May and July 1939, whereupon they were renumbered in the W series set aside for AEC Regals within the miscellaneous fleet. The vehicles selected for this purpose were T 210, 221, 227, 238, 241-243, 245, 246, 256, 257, 259, 260, 269, 278, 279, 282, 284, 294, 299, 303, 304. Shortly afterwards T 306 was rebodied as an overhead wire lubricator for the Tram & Trolleybus department. Further descriptions of these can be found in chapter 19.

The 24 vehicles set aside for conversion into buses would have been the ones which, upon inspection, were found to be both mechanically sound and – perhaps more importantly – carrying bodywork still with a fair degree of life left in it. The conversions were done at Chiswick and took place with relatively little external alteration to the existing body structure except for the construction of a front indicator display of London Transport's standard size for single deckers which projected in a box-like structure above the main roof line, at the same time reducing the depth of the downward projection of the canopy where it had formerly accommodated the GREEN LINE legend. Continuous rainshields replaced the glass window louvres and the brackets for the side boards were removed. Internally, the saloon heater was disconnected and the clock removed, and a full-height partition was erected behind the doorway which accommodated a used ticket box and supported handrails considered essential for the revised

type of work. Starting with T 291 in June 1938, the conversions continued through to January 1939, the vehicles selected for this treatment being T 207, 211, 217, 218, 230, 231, 233, 235, 239, 240, 244, 248, 251, 263, 272-274, 281, 286, 288, 291, 293, 295, 305. Prior to conversion into buses two of them had been given better bodies than their own; these were T 274 and T 281 which inherited the bodies from T 250 and T 298 when the latter were converted into 11T11s. In August 1939 one further body was converted to replace the previously converted one on T 244, which had presumably been involved in an accident while working as a bus from Hemel Hempstead garage. It received the body from T 287 when the latter was reduced to a trailer to carry emergency lighting.

No new designation was given to the bus conversions and their bodies continued to be classified as 1/7T7/1. The first to take up bus work was T 291 at Hertford on 1st June 1938, and from then until the start of January 1939 they steadily came into service at a whole host of garages spread far and wide across the Country Bus network. There appeared to be no clear plan for their redeployment and inter-garage transfers frequently occurred. The two remaining 8.8 litre oilers were amongst those converted and these appear to have been allocated to garages with blithe disregard for the sheer non-standard nature of their motive power. Both were relicensed in their new form on 1st January 1939 and T 274 went firstly to Dartford before transferring on 25th January to Grays where it remained until early in the war, while T 305 embarked on its bus career at Addlestone. Except perhaps for the first three or four to be converted, all carried the latest Country Bus livery of Lincoln green. Despite the very recent nature of their conversion, 8 out of the 24 were taken out of service and delicensed on 1st June 1939, five at Hertford and one each at Dartford, Guildford and Windsor. It is not known what, if any, future plans existed for these, but in any case fate intervened and they were pressed back into action at the start of the war.

1/7T7/1s destined to pursue radically different post-Green Line careers are seen at Eccleston Bridge. Duple bodied T 213, a Leatherhead vehicle, wears the earlier version of the two-tone green livery as applied to Green Line coaches with LONDON TRANSPORT fleet name on the side but with a GREEN LINE transfer still in place on the front dash. In this particular case the livery dates from its February 1936 overhaul, and the C suffix to the fleet number to denote its coach status was probably applied at the same time. Chelsham's T 217 on route F demonstrates the return of the GREEN LINE name to the main panels and its omission from the cab resulting from its overhaul in January 1937. The conductor on this vehicle is standing far enough back from the open entrance door to give an unobstructed view of the handrail which was later provided on all these vehicles to the right of the doorway to assist passenger movement. Also visible is the revised position of the autovac tank which has been raised to improve the gravity feed. Both vehicles were withdrawn from Green Line work in the latter part of 1938 when T 213 was rebodied and re-engined as an 11T11, while the Ransomes body on T 217 was modified to allow the vehicle to be demoted to bus operations. *D W K Jones/G H F Atkins*

Looking back at the late 'thirties Green Line scene, 22 garages managed to hold on to at least a few 1/7T7/1s during the 1938 summer season when they provided handy augmentation to the new 10T10 coaches then coming into service. From 25th September onwards they were steadily withdrawn, leaving Romford (London Road) as the only garage with any still in stock at the start of 1939. The situation there had been highly fluid for the whole of the 1938 summer with 1/7T7/1s being drafted in from all over the Green Line network to replace 7T7s, repeating the instability that had afflicted this garage a couple of years earlier when 7T7s arrived en masse to replace Gilfords. Between May and

December 1938 no fewer than 70 1/7T7/1s were received at Romford including all 13 from the Romford (North Street) allocation when this garage closed on 30th November 1938. Thirteen petrol Ts were expected to remain on Green Line service until the first batch of new TFs was licensed, and though one of these fell by the wayside and was duly scrapped, the remainder soldiered on up to and including their last day of operation which was 24th March 1939. Next day TF 15-26 introduced a fresh and almost ultra-modern look to Green Line travel and the last 12 of the old Ts were delicensed. Those in service up to the very end were T 209, 219, 229, 249, 258, 262, 265, 270, 277, 287, 301, 302.

By the outbreak of war on 3rd September 1939 the great majority of the T 207-306 batch still remained in London Transport ownership in one form or another; in fact only 10 out of the 99 inherited by London Transport had left its ownership. Two had been broken up at Chiswick and a further eight had been sold to dealers, a halt having been placed on sales after March 1939 to build up a strategic war reserve. The yard at Forest Road, Walthamstow was where the twelve coaches delicensed at Romford on 25th March were sent to join the others already in store there.

On 2nd September 1939, with the nation now in a state of high alert, the eight 1/7T7/1 buses that had been delicensed on 1st June were hurriedly placed back into service at Leatherhead (3), Hertford (2), and Dorking, Luton and Watford High Street (1 each), but few of their allocations remained very permanent thereafter. Fairly full use was made of all 24 vehicles over the course of the next three years and though the locations at which they made their greatest mark were Addlestone, Amersham, Hemel Hempstead, Hertford and Windsor, they could appear almost anywhere, often for short periods of time, to meet specific operating requirements. In November 1941 T 244 was used as a trial vehicle for conversion to perimeter seating still retaining its official capacity of 30 seats but with the capability of carrying a further 20 standing passengers. It entered service in this form at Addlestone on 20th December following which all except the two oilers were similarly converted between January and March 1942. This was intended to be only a temporary arrangement to last for the duration of the war, but in fact only two were destined to revert to a conventional seating layout after peace was resumed.

Back in 1939, preparations for war had been going on behind the scenes for many months prior its commencement, hence the stockpiling of withdrawn Ts. An example of these

preparations occurred on 1st August when T 301 was coaxed back into life at the Walthamstow storage yard. Its destination was Chiswick Works where it was to serve as the guinea pig for a small fleet of emergency ambulances that the Staff Welfare Department felt it would need in the event of aerial bombardments targeting the Board's key properties. T 301 was stripped out internally to accommodate stretchers, and tests found that the rear doorway would have to be widened – and the adjacent windows reduced in size accordingly – in order to let stretchers pass through easily. With the prototype conversion successfully completed and an inventory built up of the stocks of ready-machined woodwork etc. necessary to complete a further 15 vehicles, the remainder were brought into Chiswick between the 15th and 25th August and their conversions to ambulances were all successfully completed by the end of the month. Most of the vehicles concerned were those that had run at Romford until the very last day of Green Line operation by 1/7T7/1s and in all likelihood they were selected simply because they were the nearest to the gate at Walthamstow and therefore the easiest to extract in a hurry. It was decided that, for the duration of their service as staff ambulances, they would be counted as part of the miscellaneous vehicle fleet in whose green livery they were repainted. The vehicles converted, with their new W series fleet numbers, were as follows:

| 423W | T 301 | 427W | T 297 |
|------|-------|------|-------|
| 431W | T 209 | 435W | T 262 |
| 424W | T 252 | 428W | T 219 |
| 432W | T 292 | 436W | T 258 |
| 425W | T 264 | 429W | T 270 |
| 433W | T 265 | 437W | T 302 |
| 426W | T 290 | 430W | T 229 |
| 434W | T 277 | 438W | T 249 |

Having concluded its Green Line career at Romford on 1st December 1938, T 273 spent most of that month in Chiswick being overhauled and rebuilt for use as a service bus. Newly rechristened as T 273B, it officially re-entered service at Addlestone on 1st January 1939, but was photographed working a Redhill circular service from Reigate garage to which it was never officially allocated. A number of modifications have been made to the bodywork, but the one which stands out most is the radically re-profiled front destination box. The vehicle's main side panels are in the darker Lincoln green shade recently adopted as the new standard colour for the country fleet. *Alan B Cross*

T 286 was one of the 1/7T7/1 buses taken out of service on 1st June 1939 after only nine months of use in its revised condition. Like the others, it was hastily relicensed at the start of the war and was photographed in Sevenoaks bus station, along with one of the Weymann metal-bodied front entrance STLs whilst operating from Dunton Green garage between November 1939 and January 1940. An early type of blackout shield has been fitted to the nearside headlamp and the bulb removed from the offside one. T 286's wartime service as a bus lasted intermittently through to the start of May 1945 after which it was sold to the War Department for use abroad. *C Carter*

The converted Ts became fixtures at strategic locations throughout the London Transport system for the duration of the war. These included Underground depots at Acton, Golders Green, Morden and Neasden; the permanent way works at Lillie Bridge; Greenwich and Lots Road power stations; overhaul works at Chiswick, Charlton and Fulwell; and operational garages and depots at Battersea, Hammersmith, Hanwell, Nunhead, Putney Bridge and Streatham (tram). With the exception of T 258 (436W) all were stood down from their ambulance duties at the end of the war and were re-absorbed into the bus fleet. The former T 258, which had been damaged by bomb blast at Morden in November 1940, was subsequently rebodied as a lorry and remained as such for the remainder of its London service.

In August 1942 a directive was issued requiring all buses serving the strategic Vickers aircraft works in Weybridge to be camouflaged, and an immediate start was made in repainting most of the fleet at Addlestone garage, plus some at Leatherhead and Kingston, into all-over grey. Three 1/7T7/1s at Addlestone were included amongst these, although the only genuine member of the class to be included was T 244. The other two were former independent vehicles which had subsequently been reclassified as 1/7T7/1, namely one-time Watford & District T 369 and ex-Bucks Express T 391 (see chapters 13 and 7 respectively). The three ran in grey livery at Addlestone for less than a year, being delicensed on 1st June 1943 when more modern replacements became available.

In common with various other types of large single decker, the 1/7T7/1s were viewed as potential for conversion to perimeter seating and a trial run was carried out on T 244 which was allocated to Addlestone garage at the time. The existence of luggage racks meant that no additional ceiling handrails or straps needed to be provided, the only extra supports being three full-height stanchions on each side. The photographs were taken just after the conversion was completed, on 25th November 1941, and T 244 re-entered service with a carrying capacity of 50 on 20th December. Subsequently only two 1/7T7/1s were ever converted back to their original seating layout after the war and T 244 was one of them. *London Transport Museum*

On 30th September 1942 the two oil engined Ts were finally withdrawn from passenger service, T 274 having served latterly at Grays and T 305 at Epping. However they remained in stock, stored at Walthamstow along with other non-standard vehicles that London Transport was not allowed to dispose of under wartime restrictions. The great surprise is that they had remained in service for so long, and at so many different garages. They were the only vehicles in the country fleet with the obsolete and non-standard A161 engine which was not particularly efficient and still operated on the indirect injection system of combustion no longer favoured by London Transport. Unlike the bulk of the Board's AEC diesel engines the A161 was not capable of conversion to direct injection at reasonable cost, and the only other location at which they could be found within the London Transport organisation was Mortlake Central Bus garage on a few LTs.

At much the same time as the two oilers in the batch were being discarded because of their non-standard engines, two others were in the process of being converted to producer gas operation. When running on gas they towed two-wheeled trailers built by J Brockhouse & Son of West Bromwich and fitted out with hoppers, filters, coolers and other items necessary to produce gas from anthracite by the Bristol Tramways & Carriage Company. The full process of producer gas production and operation is described in the companion volume on the ST class and is not repeated here. The two vehicles concerned were part of a small, nine-strong single deck gas fleet operated by London Transport (the remaining vehicles were of type 5T4 and are described in chapter 8), and during their time under gas propulsion they were reclassified 12T7/2. Unfortunately no photographs are known to exist of any of these single deckers with their gas trailers.

Following small scale trials in 1939-41, London Transport embarked on an ambitious scheme to expend the use of gas propulsion as a means of conserving liquid fuel supplies by converting 20 vehicles at Grays garage. Gas operation began there in a small way in August 1942 with a couple of STs, and despite various setbacks, including the relatively poor performance of the vehicles, the conversion gradually gained pace. Most of this garage's work required double deckers, but Rainham local service 375 was operated by T types, and in October 1942 T 273 was converted to gas.

However its use on the 375 eventually proved impractical. Gas producer buses ideally needed to work on services which went past or at least near to their refuelling points and T 273 was at a disadvantage in having its nearest refuelling point several miles away in Grays. On 13th April it was transferred to Addlestone garage to start a new phase in its gas career.

Faced by a deteriorating supply of liquid fuels as a result of German submarine activity, the government had issued an edict in June 1942 requiring major bus operators to convert 10% of their licensed fleet to gas within a July 1943 deadline. Though completely unachievable in full, it forced London Transport to look well beyond its voluntary programme at Grays to determine other feasible areas of gas operation. Almost all of those identified required double deckers, the only exception being route 462 (Staines–Leatherhead) operated by Addlestone and Leatherhead garages, and T 273 was destined to form part of the rolling stock for this. However the scheduled starting date was not until 1st June 1943 which meant that T 273 was available until then for staff familiarisation work at Addlestone, and later at Leatherhead, where it remained. T 288 had now been similarly converted, and it stayed in storage for a while at Addlestone until the operations commenced. Route 462 then had a full allocation of gas buses for just over a year, until in August 1944 the Ministry of War Transport gave provisional authority for the withdrawal of gas producer fleets, the tide of war having now turned with fuel imports becoming much more reliable. According to official records T 288's gas producer trailer was removed on 29th August and T 273's a day later, leaving the vehicles to run on petrol with their engines still tuned for gas operation and their tow bars still attached, until such time as they could be dealt with properly. Both were altered back to their original condition early in December.

T 233 received green and white livery during its first wartime overhaul at Reigate in August 1940. Photographed working a route 462 journey to Fetcham on 3rd October 1942 it had just undergone its second wartime overhaul, again at Reigate, which was completed just three weeks earlier on 12th September. Presumably as a wartime economy, repainting extended only as far as the driver's cab, front mudguards and roof, leaving the main side panels for another time. The anti-shatter mesh on the windows disguised the fact that perimeter seating was in place inside the vehicle. *Frank Willis*

With the ending of all Green Line operations on 30th September 1942 for the duration of the war single deck bus availability for country services was greatly eased and along with other developments, notably the double decking of a number of services or parts of services in the 1943 summer programme, the need for 1/7T7/1s on bus services was significantly diminished. A major phase of delicensing took place, some on 1st May 1943 and others on 1st June, after which only six were left still operational, three at Windsor, one at Hertford, plus the two gas buses mentioned above. Thereafter others were relicensed, and later delicensed again, to meet certain short term requirements, but the next significant move came when seven (T 231, 239, 263, 272, 281, 293, 295) were hastily dragged out of storage on 19th July 1944 and sent to the Central Bus garage at Elmers End to provide short term cover from the 20th on route 227 (Penge–Chislehurst). A German V1 rocket had hit the garage on the evening of the 18th with disastrous consequences, completely destroying more than 40 vehicles and rendering many others inoperable until they could be repaired. The green Ts remained at Elmers End until 1st August when they were delicensed, some never to be used again.

In the later winters of the war years, 1943/44 and 1944/45, it was deemed advisable to have snow ploughs on hand at strategic locations, and various members of the T class were set aside for this purpose. Four of the T 207-306 batch were included – T 272, 274, 293 and 305 – including, notably, the two withdrawn oilers for which this was destined to be their final task while in London Transport ownership.

Fortunes had reached their lowest ebb by 1st January 1945 when the sole 1/7T7/1 still licensed for service was T 207 at Windsor, but things were about to change. Rolling stock shortage on Central Buses found grey liveried T 244 rushed into service at Kingston on 12th January, followed by T 217 at Loughton on 2nd February and T 231, 251, 281 and 286 at Enfield within the next few days. Not all proved to be perma-

nent; the Loughton vehicle was delicensed on 1st March, while T 281, 286 were needed back in the country area at St Albans and Hemel Hempstead respectively on the 7th of that month. However the clear intention was demonstrated to include at least a few 1/7T7/1s permanently within the Central Bus fleet by the fact that T 231 and T 251 had been repainted into red livery before taking up their new employment at Enfield, while Kingston received T 273 newly repainted red on 19th February and grey T 244, already resident there, was painted red in March.

The war was almost at an end when London Transport was put under pressure by the Ministry of War Transport to release single deck buses for use in war shattered parts of the European Continent by the Allied Control Commission. In addition to the 7T7s sold for this purpose, as recorded in the last chapter, the focus also turned to the delicensed 1/7T7/1s, sixteen of which departed in May 1945, most of them a few days before the war in Europe ended and a couple afterwards. The two withdrawn oilers were not wanted for this purpose and remained in store; otherwise the only ones still operational when the war ended were green T 207, 230 at Windsor, and red T 231, 251 at Enfield and T 244, 273 at Kingston. The two Kingston vehicles were restored to their original internal layout with transverse seating but the others retained their wartime standee arrangements until withdrawal well into the post-war era.

It was a great novelty, at first, to see 1/7T7/1s in red livery, and the fourth one to be so treated was Kingston's T 244 in March 1945. For Central Bus use the B suffix has been omitted from the fleet number. It is not known where the repainting was carried out, but it is presumed that the interior of the bodywork remained untouched, and it retained its perimeter seating layout at the time although it was removed later. With the war drawing to a close, upkeep of the window mesh was no longer regarded as necessary and blackout restrictions were relaxed. *J F Higham © A B Cross*

Soon after the war, the future of the two now-unused oilers T 274 and T 305 was reviewed and it was decided that, because of their non-standard engines, there was no further requirement for them within the fleet. They were sold in January 1946, but before they departed the body of T 305 was examined and deemed suitable for retention for further use. In November 1945 it was swapped with the body from T 120, which had latterly served as a staff ambulance, allowing T 120 to resume work from Luton garage on 1st January 1946, now classified as a 1/7T7/1 and to all intents and purposes completely interchangeable with any of the remaining members of the T 207-306 batch.

A revival of the fortunes for the 1/7T7/1s came shortly after the war's end when the future of the fifteen remaining ambulances came up for review. Two options were put forward in June 1945; one to convert them back into coaches and the other to break them down for spare parts. The decision was taken to convert them back for passenger service regaining their old fleet numbers, and this was no doubt influenced by the fact that, having run very little mileage for several years during which they were kept under cover in most instances, they were inevitably in better condition than their few remaining compatriots even though none had been subjected to a full overhaul since before the war. Official authorisation for this was given on 10th July 1945 and the task of returning

them to passenger use was given to the overhaul shop at Chiswick tram depot where they began to accumulate from 14th July onwards. Their seats were reinstalled and heaters removed, and the necessary handrails, fare board holders and used ticket boxes provided. At the front a simpler method of accommodating the standard destination display was employed than on the pre-war rebuilds by incorporating the new screen into the existing space without going to the trouble of providing new structural work or making any alterations to the existing roof line. As a result of this, the two types of 1/7T7/1 could be easily distinguished in post-war years when viewed from the front, and indeed also from the rear where the wider emergency door installed for ambulance purposes was retained.

In post-war years the remaining 1/7T7/1s fell into two visually different categories; those which still retained their original sloping indicator box profile at the front and those which did not. The former were in a slight majority and one of these, T 252, is seen at Uxbridge in the company of ST 435, one of the elderly Regents indigenous to the area at the time. Despite linking two major towns, Slough and Uxbridge, route 458 was notable for being monopolised by the oldest petrol single deckers in the country fleet, on which an exhilarating ride could be enjoyed on occasions. T 252 was unusual at the time for still retaining a full set of glass window louvres. *D A Thompson*

Operation of 1/7T7/1s by the Country Bus & Coach department came to a sudden halt in August 1949 with all vehicles running for the last time on the 28th. Photographed at Windsor Castle shortly before the final day, T 277 is working on short local route 445 which had been added to the itinerary for these vehicles when single-decked in May 1948. After a lifetime of country service, T 277 moved to Hounslow, Bromley, and finally Kingston where its big claim to fame was that it became – by the margin of a single day – the very last petrol-engined bus to be available for passenger service on London Transport. *Alan B Cross*

The relative smartness of paintwork on green T 230 was not a good indication of the true condition of the bodywork lying beneath it, and the fact that one of the offside pillars has required bracing was an indication that all was not well when the photograph was taken in Eltham on 2nd August 1948. The reason for the last windows on both sides of the saloon being boarded up is not known. It is evident that the standee seating layout has been retained on T 230, which soldiered on for another three months until it was declared to be unfit for further service at Sidcup garage on 18th November 1948. *Alan B Cross*

All fifteen were repainted into standard green and white bus livery and employed initially in the country area; in fact none of them were ever repainted red. The first to re-enter service was T 229 at Windsor on 3rd September 1945, and for the first time it was decided to work the 1/7T7/1s on specific routes of their own starting with Windsor's 458 (Uxbridge–Slough) and adding to this from 1st January 1946 routes 356 (Luton–Flamstead) and 376 (Luton–Kensworth) from Luton garage, all of these being services not approved at the time for operation by longer single deckers. The last three to re-enter service, on 6th March 1946, did so at Amersham on the 394 group of routes, but this proved short lived and they soon joined their compatriots at Windsor. From then on, Windsor and Luton remained the only two garages in the country area from which 1/7T7/1s could be seen in action, the Windsor remit being widened on 19th May 1948 to include route 445 (Windsor–Datchet Common) when the latter was converted to single deck operation. Red liveried T 244 strayed from Kingston to Luton in May 1946 and was repainted back into green livery five months later.

On 29th August 1949 the employment of these vehicles by Country Buses came to an abrupt halt when the last six at Windsor and the last five at Luton were all transferred to Central Buses.

T 207 was one of the green-liveried 1/7T7/1s that made an impact on double deck services out of Norwood garage from November 1946 onwards. It was photographed on route 3 in snowy conditions outside Crystal Palace High Level station during the extremely harsh winter of 1946/47, and it is no surprise that the saloon door has been closed. T 207 was later repainted red – in July 1948 – while working from Kingston garage. *D W K Jones*

On Central Buses the 1/7T7/1s found their niche in post-war years covering where nothing else was available, and generally beginning to look more and more decrepit as time went on. The post-war era started with them helping out on scheduled single deck operations at Enfield and Kingston, where they continued to feature for the remainder of the decade. A huge surprise ensued when six of them (T 120, 207, 230, 231, 249, 297) were diverted on to double deck work from 16th November 1946, all of them from Norwood garage and more often than not on route 3. This was the era when surplus single deckers – even tiny CR class 20-seaters – commonly appeared on the busiest of central area services to help alleviate the desperate shortage of serviceable double deckers. The six Ts stayed at Norwood all through the winter of 1946/47, with T 120 passing to Cricklewood and T 207 to Victoria – both on 3rd May 1947, for further central London

work. T 207 was painted red in July 1948 but no other livery changes took place after 1945 except that T 219, which was the last green one ever to receive a repaint, appeared in the Country Bus department's latest styling in green and cream at some time early in 1948 and was the only one to do so.

Right up to 1949, their last full year of operation, 1/7T7/1s could be seen from time to time helping out on various double deck services, and even as late as August 1949 Willesden garage received a short lived allocation of them. More commonly they could be found at a number of garages with scheduled single deck workings in addition to the original ones at Enfield and Kingston; these included official allocations from time to time at Bromley, Elmers End, Hornchurch, Hounslow, Muswell Hill, Sutton and Tottenham, though unofficial loans inevitably spread their remit even wider than this.

T 219 was unique in being the only one of its type ever to receive the green and cream livery applied to many country area vehicles from 1948 onwards. On this particular version of the livery, the green areas extended to the mudguards, roof, and the whole of the front and back bodywork, with cream being confined merely to the side window areas. Repainting of shabby bodywork was frequently carried out on older vehicles at the time, but in most cases no record was kept of where or when it was done, and this applies to T 219. Ejected from Windsor on 29th August 1949, T 219 subsequently ran from a succession of Central Bus garages and was on loan from Muswell Hill to Catford – a garage with no single deckers of its own – when photographed at West Croydon helping out on route 75. Today it is part of the valuable collection preserved by the London Transport Museum. *Denis Battams*

T 230 was taken from Sidcup to the repair shop at Aldenham where a team was on hand to evaluate the condition of vehicles referred to it and to repair them for a return to work whenever possible. Partly stripped down, it is seen in the company of an LT double decker undergoing a similar assessment. In the case of T 230, it was found not to be worth repairing and was scrapped in December 1948, becoming the first of the 1/7T7/1s which remained after the war to meet this fate. *D A Jones*

The first post-war withdrawal was T 230 in November 1948, and a further ten followed in 1949. However for old and obsolete petrol-engined single deckers they proved to be surprisingly resilient and no fewer than eleven were still active at the start of 1950 distributed amongst five garages: Hornchurch (T 207, 219, 273, 292), Hounslow (T 265, 270), Kingston (T 277, 297), Muswell Hill (T 262, 290) and Sidcup (T 244). While the last few petrol double deckers were fast fading away from the fleet – the final operational ones being withdrawn on 26th January 1950 – the few remaining 1/7T7/1s continued in service, though various of them inevitably fell by the wayside as the weeks passed by. With the maintenance of petrol supplies at garages becoming more

problematic and uneconomical, it became prudent to concentrate the final few in one garage which, from 1st May 1950 onwards, was Kingston. Only three then still survived of which T 292 was delicensed on 11th May, T 207 on 16th May, and last of all, T 277 on 18th May.

A solitary survivor, which exists to this day, is T 219. After seeing 1950 in at Hornchurch it was fairly promptly displaced by a new TD and moved on 16th January to Muswell Hill. A further transfer occurred on 25th January to Hounslow. On 30th March T 219 was inspected at Chiswick when the decision was taken to set it aside for preservation, and just under a year later it joined London Transport's museum fleet in their storage compound at Reigate.

The very last petrol-engined vehicles still employed on regular bus service were all based at Kingston garage, and it was on routes radiating from there that you had to travel to savour the sound of a sweet-running petrol engine – plus its occasional backfires! – for the last time. It was only dire need that kept petrol-engined 1T1s and 1/7T7/1s in service as late as May 1950, and T 207 typified the final days of an era when it was seen at the setting down point for route 218 in Cromwell Road, Kingston. The last red-liveried 1/7T7/1 in service, T 207 still looked quite smart when it went off to Daniels' scrapyard at Rainham on 16th May, having run for the last time on the previous day. *J H Aston*

# 4 REGAL BUSES ON COUNTRY SERVICE
## T 372-390

On 12th June 1929 the LGOC gained full control of the Reigate based East Surrey Traction Company Ltd and, with it, Autocar Services Ltd of Tunbridge Wells which had been an East Surrey subsidiary since 5th April 1928. As recorded in the companion volume on the ST class, the LGOC lost no time in sending AEC Regent demonstrator UU 6610 (the future ST 1139) to, firstly, East Surrey and then to Autocar to gain practical experience in operating the new family of buses from AEC to which, through common ownership, the LGOC was inextricably tied.

Although it had not been in service long UU 6610 was already showing great promise when a board meeting at 55 Broadway in October 1929 authorised a substantial order for new vehicles for the East Surrey and Autocar companies comprising 60 Regents and 39 Regals, anticipating that the first of both types would be ready for service in March 1930. The Regals were apportioned as 22 for East Surrey and 17 for Autocar, with the order further sub-divided into 21 30-seat buses (16 for East Surrey and 5 for Autocar) and 18 all-weather coaches (6 for East Surrey and 12 for Autocar). Tenders were issued to outside manufacturers for the supply of bodywork for all 99 vehicles, as a result of which Hall Lewis & Company Ltd of Park Royal was contracted to build all the single deckers.

The chassis numbers for the 39 Regals did not run consecutively but were interspersed with other orders received by AEC between 662124 and 662243. Buses and coaches within the contract were similarly interspersed but this was of no consequence as there were no mechanical differences between the two. The first bus to be licensed for service is believed to have been East Surrey's PG 7025 on 3rd March 1930, and all 22 buses were in use by the end of April. The all-weather coaches, which bore no similarity whatever to the buses either inside or out, are described in chapter 5.

The very first Regals delivered for country bus service were distinguishable by the ornate black lining-out which considerably enhanced their red and cream East Surrey livery. Presumably the cost implications of these embellishments were the reason for their abandonment on the majority of deliveries. Seen in this April 1930 line-up outside Leatherhead garage is one of the new Regals, its exact identity hidden by the starting handle, accompanied by new Ransomes bodied Regent PG 7728 (the future ST 1096) similarly adorned, though the Regent lacks the white walled tyres of the smaller vehicle. Also in view and looking very outdated is open-cabbed XW 9877, ex-LGOC K-type 24-seater K 1086 which was returned to its parent fleet in June 1931.

Apart from replacing a few small AEC 202-type 22 and 24-seaters of 1925 vintage, most of the 16 East Surrey buses were required for fleet augmentation. They were registered PG 6780-6785, 7025, 7503-7511 and were allocated fleet numbers 260-275. The latter were totally out of sequence with the registration numbers, but this was not apparent as they were not displayed on the vehicles, East Surrey having decided just about the time they were delivered to abandon the use of fleet numbers. Under a long-standing arrangement a substantial proportion of the East Surrey fleet was made up of LGOC-owned vehicles as part of a contractural agreement whereby the Reigate company operated certain services on the LGOC's behalf. Although there were no markings on the vehicles concerned to denote their real ownership, six of the Regals (PG 7506-7511) were LGOC property and for this reason body numbers 11135-11140 were allocated to them by the Chiswick licensing office. This, again, was purely a paper exercise as the numbers were never displayed on the vehicles and later fell into disuse. The five Regals for Autocar were KR 2921-2925 and they carried fleet numbers 107-111. All five were received in March 1930 and were the first single deck intake of any consequence by the Company since a large batch of Associated Daimler 416 types in 1927. They were wholly owned by Autocar, but apart from their fleet names and legal lettering they were identical to the East Surrey batch.

Taking pride of place at the entrance to Swanley garage is former Woking & District Thornycroft 29-seater OT 7822, but tucked away behind it is ex-LGOC T 21, one of the five Regals transferred to East Surrey on 1st April 1931 with the operations from Crayford garage. Crayford had only the most basic engineering facilities and T 21 has possibly come to Swanley for docking. The fleet name on the side of the Thornycroft denotes that the photograph was taken in LGCS days but the East Surrey name is still prominent above the garage door. *Dave Jones collection*

In external appearance there were few significant differences between the Hall Lewis bodies on these 21 Regals and the Chiswick bodies built for T 1-50; both body shops were clearly working to the same plans. The country vehicles lacked the radiused corners at the tops of the windows which seemed to give them a slightly more chunky appearance than the LGOC batch, and they were provided with a half-height driver's door in acknowledgement of the more exposed terrain that they would generally be working in. The side lights were raised to cantrail level, a feature also specified on the contemporary Regents. Inside, the type of seats and the seating layout remained the same as on T 1-50 but the unconventional translucent lighting panels had given way to conventional bulb holders, covered initially by attractive round jellymould globes but later left bare. The external livery was East Surrey's standard red on the lower panels with a yellowish-cream above, surmounted by a silver roof,

and on the first few vehicles delivered to East Surrey the red panels were picked out with ornate black markings although the use of these was soon abandoned, presumably on cost grounds. The five Autocar vehicles were also painted red and cream, and were the first new vehicles to abandon Autocar's traditional and attractive mauve livery. Probably under East Surrey influence, repaints into red had taken place since August 1929 and the last new vehicle to arrive in mauve had been Regent demonstrator UU 6610 in July 1929, although this too had been repainted red and cream in January 1930.

Their first overhaul found the Regals repainted into LGOC red and grey albeit still retaining East Surrey fleet names and operator's details. PG 7505 is seen again, but this time in a very different part of the Company's territory – Green Lane, New Eltham – heading for Orpington on route 422 shortly before the company became London General Country Services. *Alan Nightingale collection*

As outlined in chapter 1, East Surrey's small fleet of Regal buses increased by five with the takeover from the LGOC on Wednesday 1st April 1931 of Crayford garage and the services operated from it. Under the LGOC's auspices Crayford garage had no vehicle allocation of its own and had latterly been regarded as an outpost of Sidcup, but since the only T-types allocated to Sidcup at the time were purely used on Crayford operations it was inevitable that these would be transferred to East Surrey. An order went out from the Licensing Superintendent on 28th February to the Chiswick engineers to ensure that Sidcup's T 15, 21, 26 were "in thoroughly sound and clean condition and painted with the East Surrey Company's markings" in good time for the transfer to take place. In fact five Ts were needed for the revised operation so T 25 and T 35 from elsewhere in the LGOC fleet were also pinpointed for transfer. Henceforth the fate of these five Ts was set to parallel exactly that of East Surrey's own Regals which meant that they escaped the conversion to front entrance and other subsequent changes that befell the rest.

Unlike the NS double deckers that were transferred to East Surrey on the same day, it was not deemed necessary to give the five Ts a complete overhaul beforehand. They had, in fact, all been overhauled during the closing months of 1930 and carried the current version of the standard LGOC red and grey livery. They did not look out of place amongst East Surrey's own Regals which were currently in the process of adopting the same colours as they went through their first overhaul. The Autocar fleet also adopted red and grey as its standard colour scheme, although in the case of both companies their traditional style of fleet name was still retained.

1931 saw the addition of yet more new Regals to the East Surrey and Autocar fleets. The total number was less this time at 24 (13 for East Surrey and 11 for Autocar) and only five of these were ordered as buses. First to arrive, in March

Autocar's two Park Royal bodied Regals of March 1931 bore many similarities to the 1930 deliveries but the wide, doorless front entrance was an obvious innovation, and the extra body length was accommodated by inserting a narrow extra bay at the rear. The front canopy is braced, which suggests that a weakness in this area had been anticipated, and the glass window louvres were mounted above all side windows whether these opened or not, even the small ones at the back. KR 9919 was the first of the pair and was numbered 152 in the Autocar fleet. *Snook & Son*

1931, were Autocar's KR 9919/9920 (fleet numbers 152 and 153). These carried 30-seat Park Royal bodies which closely resembled the previous year's batch of Hall Lewis bodies, and naturally so since one builder was the successor to the other. There were, however, major differences brought about by important changes to the specification. For a start the vehicles were 1 foot longer at 27 feet, the difference in length being accommodated on the bodywork by an additional short bay at the rear. Surprisingly they reverted to the use of full-drop instead of half-drop windows to provide internal ventilation even though this arrangement was more complex to build whilst making the body framework weaker and more susceptible to deterioration through rain ingress. Glass rainshields were provided over the whole length of the saloon which made it impossible to determine from outside which windows could be opened and which could not. The vehicles were built to the front entrance specification now favoured by the Combine companies in preference to the former draughty and dusty open rear platform arrangement. In common with current LGOC practice, no door was provided at the front entrance which remained permanently open.

Rather more noteworthy were the three East Surrey buses, PL 6456-6458, which post-dated the Autocar vehicles by three months, being licensed between 31st May and 26th June 1931. Similar in mechanical specification to the Autocar duo, including increased length of 27ft, the main point of note lay in their Weymann-built bodies which bore almost no trace of LGOC influence in their design. The bodywork, which had a number of features in common with a batch of six Morris Commercial Viceroys built by Weymann for East Surrey as part of the same contract, is thought to have been designed at Addlestone with very little input from the operator. The sleek, low-roofed bodies were noteworthy for the very marked, curved up-sweep at the front of the roof to accommodate a standard-sized indicator box. These two also reverted to the use of full-drop windows marking a return to a design feature eschewed by the LGOC some years earlier. Internally, polished wood instead of rexine gave a distinctly provincial air to the general décor. Even the external livery was non-standard in that the roof was painted in the same grey as the window frames instead of the now-standard silver. As these three new Regals were officially LGOC owned, they were allocated body numbers 13055 (PL 6457) and 13084/85 (PL 6456/6458).

The latest East Surrey Regals had barely completed six months' service when the Company was renamed London General Country Services, with the new title beginning to

appear on vehicles from 27th February 1932 onwards. The same LGOC-inspired red and grey livery was retained and the fleet name adopted by the enlarged organisation was GENERAL written in bold letters on a rectangular silvery grey base with the smaller wording COUNTRY SERVICES below it. At the start, ownership of the vehicles remained divided as it had been in East Surrey days with part of the fleet owned by LGCS itself and the remainder by the LGOC. However the intention all along had been to consolidate ownership within a single company, and this was achieved on 7th April 1932 when all the LGOC-owned vehicles were formally sold to LGCS and this included, of course, the nine Regal buses. For all operational and engineering purposes the new organisation was now totally divorced from the LGOC, taking complete control of its own affairs from its headquarters at Bell Street, Reigate.

The identity change did not affect Autocar which, though now a subsidiary of LGCS, continued running unchanged. Its separate identity was retained in the prior knowledge that, under the terms of the London Passenger Transport Bill then making its way through Parliament, the outlying nature of its operating territory would place it almost wholly beyond the remit of the new authority. By retaining it as a separate entity, with its own clearly defined assets, it could easily be divorced from Reigate's control when the time came and transferred into different ownership.

The 27ft long bodies supplied by Weymann for East Surrey's PL 6456-58 followed the same layout as the two latest Autocar deliveries but managed to look entirely different. Virtually no trace of LGOC influence can be detected in their low and quite sleek lines, and a particularly notable feature was the way the front destination box swooped up from the metalwork of the front dome. At the rear there was more than a hint of curvature in contrast to the bolt upright design favoured by the LGOC. These two photographs show PL 6457 (the future T 381) in its early days. *Snook & Son*

The short-lived LGCS lasted less than eighteen months, during which time PG 7507 (later to become T 375) is seen at Windsor about to depart on trunk service 36 to Guildford. The LGOC-influenced red and grey colour scheme remains unchanged apart from having received the new fleet name, and the vehicle has been embellished with a silver-sprayed radiator grille. PG 7507 was one of the six Regals in this batch loaned to East Surrey, and later to LGCS, by the LGOC until ownership was formerly transferred to the LGCS in April 1932. Standing between it and the statuesque figure of Queen Victoria is a Morris Commercial on Frowen & Hill's Borough Bus Service, one of the many small bus enterprises which once flourished in and around Windsor.
*J F Higham © A B Cross*

The newest Regals in the East Surrey fleet, the distinctive Weymann-bodied trio, came under three different ownerships within a fraction over two years, but remained all the while under Reigate's control. Destined to be the only one which would last in London service into and through the war years was PL 6458 (the future T 382). It is seen in LGCS days at Dorking North station having just arrived on a route 22 journey from Holmbury St Mary.
*Charles F Klapper © Omnibus Society*

UU 6641 had been known as T 26 in LGOC days and would become so again under London Transport ownership. Seen on the stand in Westgate Street, Dartford, in the company of the LGOC's NS 1240, it still carries running number plate holders as a disused reminder of its former ownership. Under Reigate management, tinkering with the bodywork has already taken place resulting in the removal of its half-drop windows and their accompanying glass louvres, which must have made travelling inside it a stuffy proposition on hot days. These items were later reinstated, but their removal acted as a foretaste of the modifications that would be made on many of the country area Regals in years to come. *J F Higham © A B Cross*

The big split has taken place. The LPTB has been formed and Autocar is now controlled by Maidstone & District. KR 9919, which had been numbered 152 in former days, now displays fleet number 30 in typical Maidstone & District style enclosed within a circle. The new owner's livery of two shades of green and cream is carried, but the vehicle itself is unmodified and the traditional Autocar fleet name is still prominent. *J F Higham © A B Cross*

Meanwhile the Autocar fleet continued to be overhauled at Reigate where the impressive modern works were capable of dealing with 21 vehicles a week drawn from LGCS's very mixed stock, and also from the Green Line fleet which, in a separate reorganisation, was placed under LGCS control on 29th July 1932. If additional assistance was required for this overhaul programme it was available at the Watford High Street premises which had passed from National to LGCS control on 1st March 1932, though for the most part it was ex-National vehicles that were dealt with there.

Once it became well established, the Reigate maintenance regime appears to have thrived as an independent overhaul works with very little Chiswick influence or input, and it continued to do so into early London Passenger Transport Board days. The new organisation inherited East Surrey's disregard for fleet numbers (although, perversely, an exception to this was made in the case of the Green Line fleet), and it ignored the body numbers inherited with the vehicles formerly owned by the LGOC. The Chiswick production line

system based on a float of spare chassis and bodies was not replicated at Reigate, and nor could it have been with a fleet so mixed and for which no spare bodies were available anyway. In fact Reigate functioned in much the same traditional manner as did the central works of most provincial bus operators, resulting in each vehicle maintaining its own chassis and body integrity.

A distinct change of appearance became official policy when, from March 1933 onwards, the official livery for the LGCS bus fleet was changed from red to green. This was done to pre-empt the creation of the London Passenger Transport Board on 1st July 1933, the decision having already been taken that its country area buses would be green to distinguish them from the central area red. The actual livery chosen was a close copy of that already in use on Green Line coaches consisting of sage green panels enhanced by black horizontal reliefs and mudguards, silver roof and orange wheels. The earlier style of fleet name was replaced by the single word GENERAL in gold lettering.

Introduced right at the end of the LGCS era, the new green and black livery quickly spread throughout the whole of the LPTB's country fleet during 1933 and 1934, initially accompanied by the GENERAL fleet name but with the famous LONDON TRANSPORT insignia from May 1934 onwards. Captured in action early in 1935, after running number plates had come into use but before fleet numbers had been allocated to them, are PG 7509 (T 377) outside the typical rural post office in Chaldon and PG 7505 (T 389) *opposite* somewhere on the long trunk service between Watford and Windsor formerly worked by AEC Regals of the Lewis Omnibus Company. The conductor stands with his back to the front bulkhead while a camera-conscious passenger climbs aboard. *Charles F Klapper/London Transport Museum*

On 1st July 1933, the same day the LPTB came into being, ownership of Autocar passed to Maidstone & District Motor Services Ltd which inherited the seven Regal buses along with the rest of the undertaking, leaving only stage carriage operating rights for the section between Tonbridge and Sevenoaks to pass to the LPTB along with a small garage in Whitefield Road, Tunbridge Wells and the well-equipped coach stand in Lime Hill Road used as the terminus for the Green Line limited stop operation which the Board retained. The Autocar identity was initially retained under its new ownership, but the Regals received new fleet numbers 25-31 (KR 2921-2925, 9919, 9920) in the Maidstone & District series, and by November 1933 a start had been made in repainting the Autocar fleet into Maidstone & District's standard green and cream. On 1st May 1935 Autocar ceased to exist as a separate entity and its fleet was merged into that of the parent company. The seven Regal buses were destined for a long second career with Maidstone & District, but within the Company's coach fleet rather than as buses, for which their appearance was transformed through the provision of handsome and modern new Harrington 32-seat bodies in 1937/38. With the exception of no. 29 (KR 2925) which was requisitioned by the army in 1941 (but reappeared after the war in private ownership), they served M&D until 1952.

The former London General Country Services organisation formed the backbone of the Country Bus & Coach department of the new London Passenger Transport Board, and with the same administration in charge it was inevitable that in its early days the department bore striking organisational similarities to what had gone before. The LGCS system of managing without fleet numbers remained in force, and the former company's green and black livery with GENERAL fleet name quickly became commonplace, not only on ex-LGCS rolling stock but also on the incredible variety of makes and sizes of vehicle taken over from a host of operators absorbed under the Board's compulsory purchase powers. Control of all vehicle matters remained centralised at Reigate where the main overhauling facilities gradually became overwhelmed under the burden of the rapidly expanding and infinitely varied fleet.

It is known that considerable transferring of vehicles between garages took place to meet ever-changing operating requirements and to cover the absence of newly acquired vehicles while urgent overhauling work and repainting was carried out on them, but once again Reigate's less than meticulous keeping of records means that large gaps exist in our knowledge of exactly what occurred in the early days of London Transport.

The first outward sign of change came in May 1934 when use of the GENERAL fleet name was discontinued in favour of LONDON TRANSPORT which, within about a year, had become universal. For now the Country Bus & Coach department continued to plough its own distinctive furrow, but not for much longer. Signs that changes were afoot and that the country department was to be brought more in line with its Central Bus counterpart appeared towards the end of 1934 when vehicles began to be fitted with holders for garage plates and running number stencils. Code letters were allocated to garages (and in some cases subsequently modified when it was found that they clashed with ones already in use on Central Buses), and by the start of 1935 all were fully in use.

Other major changes were in the pipeline too. During the later months of 1934 complex plans were finalised for a total reorganisation of the engineering function which would bring the Country Bus & Coach department fully within the Chiswick orbit. The aim was to transfer control of the country fleet away from Reigate to Chiswick which, from 25th February 1935, would take over full responsibility for organising and implementing the overhaul programme for the entire London Transport fleet. Chiswick's sophisticated system of control required all vehicles to be identified by fleet numbers, and Reigate's method of recognition by registration number was incompatible with this. It was necessary, therefore, to allocate fleet numbers to all vehicles likely to remain in stock for any reasonable period of time which, of course, included all the Regals. The five one-time LGOC vehicles (T 15, 21, 25, 26, 35) thus regained their old identities and the remainder were numbered for the first time as follows:

| | |
|---|---|
| PG 6780-6782 | T 372-374 |
| PG 7507-7511 | T 375-379 |
| PL 6456-6458 | T 380-382 |
| PG 6783-6785 | T 383-385 |
| PG 7025 | T 386 |
| PG 7503-7506 | T 387-390 |

As with various other Chiswick-inspired numberings of the time, there appears to be no rhyme or reason as to why the batch of numbers T 372-390 was allotted in the sequence shown, which is neither in registration or chassis number order, and nor does it represent the order in which the vehicles first went to Chiswick for overhaul. Furthermore the three newest and conspicuously different Weymann-bodied vehicles, T 380-382, are not placed at the end of the sequence, which would have seemed logical, but right in the middle.

Working the Redhill circular, Reigate based T 387 shows off its newly acquired fleet number together with the B suffix denoting its status as a bus within the country fleet. A minor modification since its earlier days has been the substitution of an LGOC-type bulb horn behind a mesh cover in place of the less discreet type favoured by East Surrey which projected from the front of the bodywork. The green and black livery was quickly eliminated, and although it still looks quite smart T 387 is shortly to go for overhaul, in November 1935, after which it will emerge in two-tone green for service at Dartford. *J F Higham © A B Cross*

Addlestone's T 15 passes near its home base on its way to Guildford bearing the standard pre-war two-tone green colours which it gained in June 1935 in place of the old green and black. A modification carried out at the same time was the removal of its fixed starting handle. Typical of most of the country area Regal buses, T 15 moved around many times during the late nineteen-thirties. As well as being allocated to Addlestone (twice), it also ran from Hatfield, Amersham, Hertford, Staines, Windsor and Hemel Hempstead. *J F Higham © A B Cross*

The Chiswick system also required the use of body numbers. Although the five low-numbered Ts had carried these from new, albeit subsequently discarded during the East Surrey/LGCS era, they were not renewed even though they were still held on the record card for each individual vehicle. The same applied to the other one-time East Surrey vehicles which had initially been the property of the LGOC; their original body numbers were also still known, but instead new numbers were issued to all of them, but only as each vehicle went through overhaul. The resultant body numbers, which were not only mixed up with other overhauled vehicles of various types but also with batches of new vehicles, thus covered a wide range between 15341 and 16974. The chassis and body coding system was also extended to the country area vehicles, albeit somewhat imprecisely, as a result of which the five one-time LGOC vehicles were classified as 5/1T1/1 and the others 4/1T6, completely ignoring the difference in length and body style between T 380-382 and the remainder.

The first intake of Country Bus vehicles into Chiswick for overhaul took place in January 1935, a few weeks ahead of the official 25th February implementation date for the new arrangement, but the input was only tentative at first. Until at least the end of March some overhauls were carried out at Reigate, although in certain cases only the chassis were overhauled there and the bodies were dealt with at Chiswick. At the same time a new colour scheme was introduced which, at least when newly applied, gave a brighter and more cheerful appearance to the country fleet. Gone, now, was the use of black from the main panels, its use henceforth being confined to narrow horizontal mouldings and mudguards, and instead vehicles were painted in two shades of green with the darker colour on the lower panels and the lighter one around the windows. With overhauls still being carried out on an approximately annual basis at this time, it took only about a year for the former green and black livery to be eliminated entirely.

Under the grip of the Chiswick regime it was only a matter of time before comprehensive records were once again kept of vehicle allocations and other relevant matters. The 24 Regal buses, meanwhile, had wandered considerably from their East Surrey roots and by the spring of 1935 they were widely distributed around the Country Bus fleet. The following is believed to be an accurate statement of their disposition at the time that Reigate relinquished control over their movements. By then the only traditional East Surrey garages still with any in stock were Godstone and Leatherhead.

| | |
|---|---|
| Addlestone | T 375 |
| Amersham | T 377, 387 |
| Dartford | T 35, 386 |
| Godstone | T 372 |
| Guildford | T 376, 381, 389 |
| Hertford | T 25 |
| High Wycombe | T 373, 374, 378, 382, 383, 390 |
| Leatherhead | T 379, 385, 388 |
| Slough (Bath Road) | T 15, 21, 26 |
| Windsor | T 380, 384 |

Because of the hilly terrain, the one-time Amersham & District garage at High Wycombe was recognised as being a testing one from which to operate Regals in their standard form, and by 1935 it had become policy to convert any that were based there to a 7 axle ratio instead of the regular 6¼. This brought some stability to a few units of the fleet, although many others seemed to be almost constantly on the move. Between 1936 and 1938 a host of inter-garage transfers resulted in them appearing at an ever-widening range of locations including Dunton Green, Hemel Hempstead, Staines, Swanley, Tring and Watford (Leavesden Road).

Rather surprisingly, in view of the short life span which officially lay ahead of them, a programme was instituted in 1936 of rebuilding the bodies on many of the former East Surrey Regal buses, including some of the ex-LGOC quintet acquired with the Crayford takeover, and in at least eight cases vehicles had their appearance changed by replacing the typical LGOC-style raised panels below the windows with flat panels and conventional mouldings. It is not known for certain that this work was carried out at Chiswick and there is the possibility that it was also done elsewhere, perhaps at Reigate. In many instances the glass louvres above the windows were dispensed with and replaced by metal strips, sometimes running the whole length of the body and in other cases covering only the opening windows. On some vehicles the new main lower panels were in one piece but in other cases they sported a horizontal dividing strip, the end result being that these once identical vehicles went through the latter part of the nineteen-thirties exhibiting a number of little differences that helped to distinguish them one from another. With the changes came increases in unladen weight, probably as a result of strengthening measures to add rigidity to the bodywork, with the result that few, if any, retained their original weight of 5tons 1cwt, ending up anywhere between five and nine hundredweight heavier than this.

Although their future life span was perceived to be limited, the bodywork on several of the country area Regals was rebuilt during the period 1936/37, an obvious result of which was the loss of the LGOC-inspired raised waistrail panels in favour of a more conventional arrangement. Typical of the vehicles treated in this way was T 26 which was dealt with in October and November 1936. These official photographs of the renovated vehicle were taken for record purposes in June 1937, at which time it was officially allocated to Hertford garage. The interior view shows the functional but somewhat spartan appearance of these vehicles in their later years which is not helped by the use of mundane and not very colourful 'lozenge' pattern moquette. *London Transport Museum*

Another rebuild was T 384 which was dealt with in May 1937 while based at Tring garage. It was reallocated to Hertford in October of that year and was photographed laying over in the town's bus station. In this instance the glass window lourvres have been replaced by metal strips, though this was not always done. The lower panels remain undivided on this vehicle although this was not the case on all the ex-East Surrey rebuilds. The side lights have been moved down to waistrail level, as they were on all vehicles in this batch whether rebuilt or not. *J F Higham © A B Cross*

The beginning of the end came on 1st June 1938 when T 390 was withdrawn from service at Hertford and sold a few weeks later. Its routine overhaul had become overdue and it was presumably decided that this was an expense not worth incurring since a predictable service life of no more than six months lay ahead for any of the batch. The influx of new T class Regals for Green Line service indirectly rendered all of the older members of the class redundant. In early August

1938 two out of the three Weymann bodied saloons were withdrawn – T 381 at Hertford and T 382 at Luton – and on the first day of each month from 1st September onwards a steady stream of withdrawals took place. The last day of operation was 31st December, the final six withdrawals on 1st January 1939 being T 15, 26, 379 at Hemel Hempstead, T 21 at Addlestone, T 372, 385 at Dartford and T 380 at Hertford, the latter being the last of the Weymann trio.

The final pre-war allocation of Weymann-bodied T 382 was to Luton garage, and it is seen at Park Square in the company of a Ransomes bodied ST which is just about to be overtaken by one of Luton Corporation's Daimler double deckers. T 382 was withdrawn from these duties on 1st August 1938. Distortion above the doorway is a clear sign of trouble with the timber body framework, despite which T 382 was revived at the start of the war and then operated spasmodically until September 1942 after which it served for a while as a snow plough. *D W K Jones*

Unrebuilt T 385, which by chance carried a matching registration number, was one of the lucky Regals which enjoyed a renewed lease of life because of the war. With wartime grey paint on its roof, white mudguard markings and headlamp masks, it is seen working from Reigate garage to which it was allocated between November 1940 and April 1941. *G J Robbins collection*

The withdrawn Ts were soon put up for sale and nine were disposed of to dealers between September 1938 and March 1939. In view of the comparative newness of their chassis it is hardly surprising that most (if not all) were quickly snapped up for further use, many of them as coaches with replacement bodies fitted. However, with the strong possibility of war now in the offing, disposals were then halted, and throughout the fateful spring and summer of 1939 14 remained in store, some at Chiswick tram depot and others in the old AEC works at Walthamstow, both of which were major storage locations for London Transport's redundant buses.

The call for service came on 2nd September 1939, the day before war officially broke out, when in a frenzy of activity at the Forest Road works in Walthamstow, seven out of the nine T-type saloons stored there were amongst the many vehicles brought hurriedly back into use. T 372, 373, 375 were dispatched to Dartford, T 376 to Hertford, T 382, 385 to Leatherhead and T 383 to Luton, their presence at these locations being needed to help mitigate the overnight conversion of many newer vehicles into ambulances. Their return to the active fleet was brief, and as things settled down it became

possible to delicense them again on 26th September after just 3½ weeks back in service. During October 1939 two of them (T 372 and T 373), along with T 379 and T 388 from Chiswick tram depot, were dismantled at Chiswick works, probably to provide an enhanced float of Regal spare parts to help alleviate a worsening supply position.

This left ten of the batch in stock, and this figure was reduced to eight in January 1940 when T 26 and T 375 passed to the Inspector of Supply Transport, Southern Area, for war work. On 8th March 1940 the only two still remaining in Chiswick tram depot were moved, along with many other unlicensed vehicles, to the old Thomas Tilling workshops at Bull Yard, Peckham to facilitate the tram depot's conversion into a body overhaul shop. T 15 was fatally damaged, along with many other buses and coaches stored in Bull Yard, by a direct bomb hit on the evening of 7th September 1940, but T 21 was found to be usable and was removed for storage elsewhere in case of further need.

All seven remaining vehicles were destined to enjoy one further spell in public service. On 23rd October 1940 the only one of the one-time LGOC quintet still remaining, T 21, was taken from storage in Hitchin garage along with T 376 and

The only one of the five 'Crayford' Regals still in London Transport ownership at the outbreak of war was T 21. After surviving the Bull Yard bombing it was repainted into the now standard green and white livery and undertook almost two years' further passenger service between October 1940 and September 1942 at Dorking, Reigate, Leatherhead and Staines. It was photographed at Redhill whilst working from Reigate garage in March 1941. *A N Porter*

T 383, and all three were relicensed at Dorking. Just over a week later, on 1st November, the remaining four were pulled from the yard at Walthamstow for renewed service at Reigate. Included amongst these were T 377 and T 384, neither of which had been used since the autumn of 1938, along with T 385 and T 382, the latter being the last surviving Weymann odd-man-out. By 4th December all seven could be found at Reigate, but further transfers saw six of them at Leatherhead from 2nd April 1941 whilst, from 9th June 1942, they were dispersed to a variety of locations. Between January and October 1941 all seven passed through the Reigate shops for a body overhaul from which most emerged in the standard wartime Country Bus livery of green and white with grey roof. The end came abruptly on 30th September 1942. This was the day decreed for the withdrawal of all Green Line operation for the remaining duration of the war, and with many far more modern vehicles suddenly available for local bus operation, no place remained for seven elderly and obsolete saloons. Their final allocations were Amersham (T 376, 384, 385), Dorking (T 382), Hertford (T 383), Leatherhead (T 377) and Staines (T 21).

Even now their usefulness was not wholly at an end. During the winter of 1943/44, and again in the winter of 1944/45, all seven were equipped as snow ploughs and stationed unlicensed at various strategic locations throughout the fleet. Much more interesting and surprising, though, was that T 383-385 were relicensed on 13th June 1944 for one further spell of passenger-carrying duty, the first two at Hackney Central Bus garage and T 385 at Epping (with T 383 moving to Windsor from 21st June). They were required – along with other elderly vehicles – to transport prisoners of war who were arriving in large numbers as a result of the D-Day offensive, an operation conducted from Hackney garage. After just a fortnight the three Ts were once again delicensed on 1st July 1944, and apart from their winter snow plough duties, this really was the end of their London career.

Between 1st and 4th May 1945, just a few days before the war in Europe came to an end, all seven joined 48 other redundant Ts sold to the Ministry of War Transport for use by the Allied Control Commission in occupied Germany.

The final, unglamorous task for several of the country area Ts was as snow ploughs, a very necessary task in the days when winters were harsher than they are now. In typical snowy conditions, and with its plough attached, is T 383 which served at Hertford garage during the winters of 1943/44 and 1944/45. Although overhauled in September 1941, this vehicle appears, unusually, to be in a coat of all-over Lincoln green (except for its grey roof) instead of the standard green and white. In contrast T 376, which was photographed out of use during the summer months, carries correct livery received on overhaul in January 1941. It spent both of its active snow plough winters at High Wycombe garage. *Alan B Cross collection/Frank Willis*

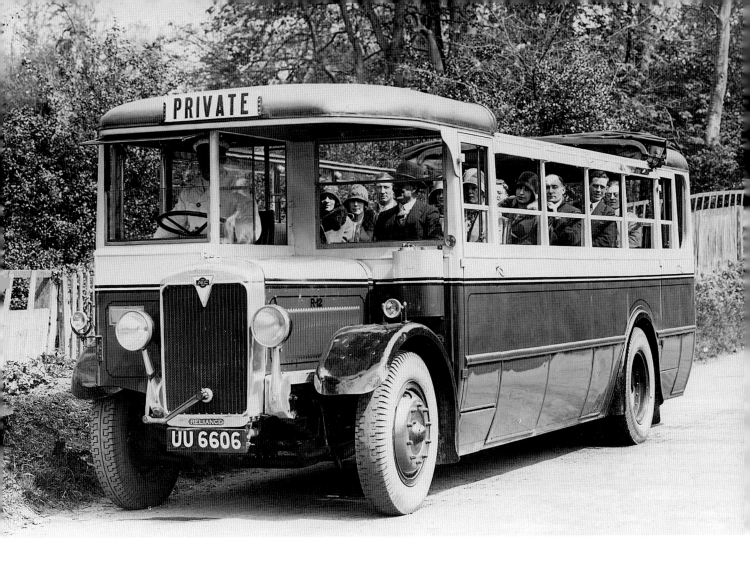

# 5 CAPE CART HOODS AND SUNSHINE ROOFS
**T 150-154 T 309-345**

A little remembered aspect of the T class is that 42 of them were ordered for service with various Combine operators as 'all-weather' coaches with roofs that opened wide to help passengers luxuriate in the warmth of the sun as they watched the scenery passing by. In these days of air-conditioned coaches it is easy to forget, or never even to experience, how pleasant it can be to travel in the fresh air at gentle speeds, but this facility was taken for granted by coach passengers taking excursions and tours in earlier decades. Even as late as the nineteen-thirties many coaches used on touring duties were supplied with roofs that could be opened. This was a decade when coach styling changed apace as streamlining took hold, with the result that vehicles which had represented the acme of modernity when they were new had begun to look decidedly outdated just a few years later, so it was no surprise that all 42 of the all-weather Ts of 1930/31 had disappeared from service by the time that the summer 1938 touring season got under way.

One particular feature that rapidly faded from fashion was the so-called 'cape cart' hood, a contraption of bowed canvas or leather on a sliding wooden or metal frame which was clumsy and difficult to operate swiftly and efficiently when showers threatened whilst, in the extreme, it was not unknown for violent gusts of wind to get under the hood and wrench the material from its supports. Most of the 42 T-types had canvas hoods and only a few were fitted with the much more practical sliding roof that quickly gained prominence.

No photographs are known to exist of T 150-154 in their original condition. However the previous year's deliveries, on AEC Reliance chassis, were very similar in general appearance and, apart from the obvious difference of the low-mounted Reliance radiator, this photograph of one of these gives a general impression of what the new Regals must have looked like. The vehicle shown here in green and cream private hire livery is R 12, posed with a full load of passengers and its cape cart hood has been pushed fully back to show the joys of coach travel. *Dave Jones collection*

Cape cart hoods were specified for T 150-154, five Regals that the LGOC ordered in readiness for the 1930 summer hiring season. Unusually for LGOC Regals of the time they were constructed to a length of 27 feet which precluded them from any form of bus or Green Line type operation, but they were not intended for this type of work anyway and the additional length allowed 32 passengers to be carried on very comfortable moquette covered seats. Typically for their time, they had a dual arrangement of hinged doors on the nearside, enabling passengers to get in and out at both ends of the vehicle. A third door was also available at the front on the offside, for use when the vehicle was parked on the wrong side of the road, and this incorporated a step below the doorway which hinged outwards when the door was opened. In later years this fell out of regular use and was designated purely as an emergency door.

The Regal chassis, which had standard 100x130 engines, 6¼ ratio axles and Dewandre braking systems, were dispatched to the Weybridge factory of the Hoyal Body Corporation (1928) Ltd between 14th March and 8th May 1930. Hoyal was not one of the LGOC's normal body suppliers, and though it became insolvent and was liquidated in August 1931 part of its factory site continued to be associated with London's transport history when the LPTB's new Addlestone garage was erected on it. The five Regals were finished in the LGOC's attractive green and cream private hire livery and were distributed to the Company's private hire garages at Harmood Street, Chalk Farm and the former Cambrian Landray depot in Waterworks Road, Brixton Hill; they entered service between 26th April (T 153) and 31st May (T 150).

A feature of the new coaches was the offside entrance with folding step as demonstrated by the bowler hatted gentleman who was probably a member of the design team at Chiswick. Again the vehicle is not one of the new Regals but Reliance R 6. *London Transport Museum*

This photograph of T 151, taken in London Transport days, shows how the Hoyal bodywork appeared once it had been repainted into the darker green and black of the standard Green Line livery. The frontal appearance of the vehicle was transformed when a Green Line style indicator display was fitted, including provision for a roller blind which was of doubtful value since the vehicles were only ever used on hire work and probably seldom displayed anything other than the word PRIVATE. *London Transport Museum*

The five were destined to last only a year in their original form. An internal reorganisation saw the transfer of the LGOC's private hire operations to the newly formed Green Line Coaches Ltd and, when existing contractual obligations were fulfilled, the five Regals were transferred into Green Line ownership on 23rd April 1931 (T151, 152) and 5th May 1931 (T 150, 153, 154). This turned out to be more than a paper exercise for their appearance was changed considerably under their new management. Starting with T 152, which had been modified in preparation for the changeover, they were repainted into full Green Line livery (even though they were never used on Green Line work) and were fitted with Green Line style destination boxes, which marked a distinct improvement over the brackets for a slip board that had been carried previously. This work was probably carried out in Strachans' factory in North Acton where a sizeable number of other canvas-topped vehicles had been similarly treated, but there is no confirmation of this.

Further managerial reorganisation came just over a year later, on 29th July 1932, when all of Green Line's assets were absorbed into London General Country Services Ltd and T 150-154 changed hands yet again. From an outside perspective there was no sign of change, but behind the scenes this was rather more than a mere paper exercise because control of the Green Line fleet, with all its associated records and documentation, moved from Chiswick to Reigate. The five private hire Regals continued to run from Brixton garage which was now the sole operational location for LGCS's private hire fleet.

The LGOC was not the only Combine operator to receive new coaching stock in 1930; the associated East Surrey and Autocar fleets were scheduled to receive new vehicles too. Coaching was more important to the two country operators than to General as both relied heavily in the summer months on income from their programmes of coastal and other excursion work. As recorded in chapter 4 an order was placed with AEC by the LGOC on behalf of its two subsidiaries for a total of 39 Regals of which 18 were to be bodied as coaches, six for East Surrey and twelve for Autocar. In the case of the six East Surrey coaches all were to be owned by the Company itself with no element of LGOC ownership involved; Autocar, of course, always owned its own vehicles outright. Although of generally similar mechanical specification to T 150-154, they differed in being 1ft shorter at 26ft with a correspondingly reduced seating capacity of 29. The bodywork contract for all 39 Regals, both buses and coaches, was awarded to Hall Lewis who built them at their Park Royal factory with the first coach rolling off the production line in March 1930.

PG 7681, the first of East Surrey's batch of six, has just been built and is posed for a press photograph outside the Hall Lewis factory in Park Royal. In fact the photo session was slightly premature as the finishing work on the body had not quite been completed, with gold lining-out still to be applied on the deep black panel below the windows. Three years later the vehicle would become T 309, and later T 393, in the London Transport fleet. It is interesting to note how the far right hand bay of the Hall Lewis factory building has been modified to accommodate covered-top double deckers. *J M Aldridge collection*

With its canvas hood rolled right back, light streams into the interior of PG 7683 on what is clearly a chilly day, helping to illuminate the smiling but overcoated and behatted passengers seated within camera range. They are happy to pose for the publicity shots essential to launch the Company's latest word in coach travel. The two-door layout of the bodywork can be clearly seen as can the popular seat ahead of the front doorway looking out over the curved bulkhead corner. *Snook & Son*

Fleet names were not carried on the sides of any of the 1930 Regal coaches when new. This view illustrates the offside lines of Autocar's KR 3031, the first of the new Regals to be licensed for service. In this instance the canvas roof is firmly shut. Although representing the latest in coach design at the time, the styling of the Hall Lewis bodies quickly became outdated and within a few years these vehicles were ready to be discarded as old fashioned. *Snook & Son*

The Hall Lewis bodies for both operators were identical in all respects right down to their livery which was East Surrey's standard coach scheme of brown (officially known as wine red) and black, and they were intermixed on the production line. Autocar's KR 3031 (fleet number 112) was the initial vehicle delivered in March 1930 and the remainder, which entered service in April and May, comprised Autocar KR 3237, 3238, 3561-3569 (114-124) and East Surrey PG 7681-7683, 7839-7841, The East Surrey vehicles carried no fleet numbers. The Company was in the process of abandoning the use of fleet numbers and the six Regals were the first new vehicles not to have them.

In outward appearance these 18 coaches bore very little resemblance to the LGOC quartet. They were constructed without a full width front canopy, and though the sharply sloping roof over the driver's cab precluded the use of a destination box there, a small one was fitted above the nearside bulkhead window. The half-canopy style was gaining in popularity at the time but in this instance the outcome was a rather inelegant appearance. Another styling feature popular at the time, which served no real purpose but weakened the structure of the body, was the insertion of a curved window on the nearside where the front corner pillar would normally be, behind which a forward facing 'observation' seat was located immediately ahead of the front doorway. As on the LGOC vehicles, dual hinged doors were provided on the nearside but these vehicles had no offside doorway. Most had canvas folding roofs, though these were confined only to the roof section itself, the curved outer panels being fixed, but at least two of the East Surrey vehicles (PG 7840, 7841) had rigid sliding roofs instead of canvas ones and it is possible that one or more of the Autocar vehicles were similarly equipped. At only 5tons 1cwt (compared with 5tons 9cwt on the LGOC batch) these were clearly quite lightly constructed vehicles and by all accounts this showed as they were reported as being quite rattly when in motion.

The typical interior of one of the 1930 Regals is demonstrated by PG 7681, and shows the sunshine roof in its fully rolled-back position. For cold weather motoring a substantial Clayton heater was provided on the front bulkhead. Curtains were not considered necessary, perhaps because they could have been an impediment to sightseeing, and there were no luggage racks. However there was ample lighting through rectangular-shaped jellymould covers and passengers were accommodated on 29 comfortable moquette-covered and leather-trimmed seats. *J M Aldridge collection*

Autocar ran an extensive programme of morning and afternoon country tours for which the new Regals were ideal, and many of these tours are listed on the boards adjacent to the main picking-up point in Tunbridge Wells. The rear aspect of the Hall Lewis body is demonstrated by KR 3237 as it loads up with passengers. This vehicle was subsequently allocated fleet number T 326 for use on Green Line services, one of the batch of numbers that remained unused in London Transport days.

As intended, the East Surrey coaches were based at Reigate and the Autocars at Tunbridge Wells, and in their early days they were used on coastal runs, country excursions and private hire. However the rapid expansion of short express coach operations increasingly called upon them to be used as duplicates and by the summer of 1931 the vehicles of both operators had been repainted into full Green Line livery. Unlike T 150-154, they were short enough at 26ft to be acceptable for Green Line work despite their paucity of destination equipment and their cumbersome swing doors, although their half-canopy layout precluded the fitment of Green Line style indicator boxes. They still, of course, had to

perform their normal duties too, and this brought an unexpected intervention from the newly appointed Traffic Commissioner who had been questioned by other operators about the legality of vehicles carrying the Green Line name appearing at coastal resorts and other places. Honour was duly satisfied when, in accepting the need for co-ordination and economy, the Traffic Commissioner decreed that Green Line coaches bearing the name of Trevor Davies (the Secretary of East Surrey and Autocar) could be used on such operations whilst those carrying the name of John Christopher Mitchell (ie the regular Green Line fleet) should be used only on Green Line services and on no other licensed operations.

More all-weather coaches joined the East Surrey and Autocar fleets in 1931. The Regals comprising the second Autocar batch could turn up in some surprising places at times. Three of them are seen here, along with an AEC Reliance, in the yard of the Bridge Garage at Ongar in April 1932. They are providing temporary cover for the 10-vehicle fleet of Gilfords and Leylands run by Associated Coaches (Ongar) Ltd while these were away being repainted. Their service to London had been acquired by the LGOC on 31st March and lettered AO in the Green Line series. The photograph was taken before Green Line fleet numbers in the T series were allocated to these coaches. *London Transport Museum*

March and April 1931 saw the entry into service of 19 more all-weather coaches, the composition on this occasion being 10 for East Surrey (which again the Company owned outright) and 9 for Autocar. The East Surrey vehicles were PL 6467-6476 and the Autocars were KR 9911-9918, 9921 (fleet numbers 154-162). The chassis specification was the same as for the 1930 deliveries except that triple servo brakes were now fitted, and once again the bodies were constructed on a single production line at Park Royal but now under the auspices of Park Royal Coachworks Ltd. Painted from new in Green Line livery these differed considerably from the previous batch in external appearance, notably in having conventional full-width front canopies with Green Line style indicator boxes, and rounded cabs. There was now only one nearside hinged door, situated near the front, but an offside emergency exit was provided behind the rear wheel. A luggage rack was fitted on the roof and provision was made for Green Line route boards to be carried along the roof on each side. To suit their conventional touring duties, deep moquette-covered seats continued to be specified as did folding canvas roofs (although PL 6470 and PL 6476 had rigid sliding roofs and a few others may also have done so).

The ten latest coaches running under East Surrey auspices did so for less than a year before the renaming to London General Country Services took place in January 1932.

However in the case of all sixteen former East Surrey Regal coaches this turned out to be only a temporary arrangement. On 11th May 1932 responsibility for them was transferred to Green Line Coaches, bringing them into the same ownership as T 150-154. This transfer was part of a wider scheme carried out on the same day under which Green Line took over the whole of the LGCS's coaching and private hire fleet which, in addition to the sixteen Regals, also consisted of 2 Guys, 2 Maudslays, 2 Morris Viceroys, 3 Thornycrofts, 6 Associated Daimlers and a solitary GMC.

Under Green Line management the Regals were issued with fleet numbers within the T class starting at T 309 and following on from a pair of vehicles inherited with the business of Bucks Expresses (Watford) Ltd which had become T 307 and 308, themselves a continuation of the standard

Despite having opening roofs, slam doors, roof luggage racks and other coach-like accoutrements, the 1931 intake could be easily mistaken at a quick glance for standard Green Line luxury coaches because of their livery, front indicator displays and route boards. With one more pillar per side, and rounded cabs, they appeared to have little in common with the coaches of a year earlier. Carrying its Green Line fleet number and showing Green Line Coaches Ltd as the legal owner, T 317 stands at Sunbury Common in May 1933 at the start of a journey on Green Line route S to Poland Street coach station. In 1935 this vehicle was renumbered T 401. *J F Higham © A B Cross*

PG 7681 proclaims its identity as T 309 on one of the typical small rectangular bonnet plates used by Green Line. It has carried full Green Line livery since 1931 but, as the legal ownership panel shows, this photograph dates from early London Transport days. It was taken on 15th December 1933, a year or more before the vehicle was officially renumbered T 393. Whereas, in earlier days, both nearside doors were intended for regular use, the rear one is now clearly marked 'Emergency Door Only'. *London Transport Museum*

Green Line fleet numbering which had ended at T 306. Thus PG 7681-7683, 7840, 7841 became T 309-314 and PL 6467-6476 became T 315-324, and these fleet numbers were displayed forthwith, using conventional transfers on the offside and embossed rectangular metal plates affixed to the top left hand corner of the bonnet side. Obviously, in allocating these fleet numbers, the Green Line management was oblivious to the fact that the LGOC had already set aside T 307-318 for a batch of twelve vehicles ordered for operation on its behalf by Thomas Tilling Ltd, the inevitable result being that when both sets of vehicles came together under the London Passenger Transport Board in 1933 their numbers clashed. Because, at the time, the Green Line fleet came under Chiswick control for all engineering matters and over-hauling, the sixteen Regal coaches were allocated body numbers 13403-13418, although not in sequence.

The 11th May arrangements took an interesting turn with regard to the Autocar fleet, which remained a separate legal entity. The Company's 21 Regals all carried Green Line colours but were only used part of the time on Green Line work according to requirements; for the remainder they fulfilled Autocar's own tours and private hire duties. Even though they remained in Autocar ownership, they gained fleet numbers in the Green Line series as well as their Autocar numbers, and as a result the 1930 batch became T 325-336 as well as being 112, 114-124 in the Autocar series, and the later vehicles became T 337-345 as well as 154-162. Body numbers were not allocated to them.

In September 1934 T 310 (renumbered T 394 soon afterwards) now carries the LONDON TRANSPORT fleet name and is seen actively employed on Green Line work from Ware garage, making a stop in Upper Regent Street while on its way to Esher. With no provision for the display of route information apart from its very basic front destination box, the only indication that T 310 is working on route M is a small plate to this effect mounted just above the autovac tank. *London Transport Museum*

Looking back, it seems incredible that just over two and a half months after the 11th May reorganisation another major upheaval occurred when, as already recorded in chapter 2, the whole of the Green Line operation was placed under London General Country Services' ownership, bringing back under the latter's control vehicles which had been removed from it such a short time beforehand. The big day was 29th July 1932 when all of Green Line's assets were officially sold to the LGCS which meant that responsibility for its rolling stock was transferred from Chiswick to Reigate, bringing massive changes to overhauling and stores administration procedures. It also meant that the records for the 16 all-weather Regals which had passed from Reigate to Chiswick in May now moved back again! This major reorganisation was no doubt carried out with the passage of the London Passenger Transport Bill in mind and setting up an organisation best suited to meet forthcoming requirements.

With the formation of the London Passenger Transport Board on 1st July 1933 the destiny of Autocar's 21 all-weather Regal coaches took a new turn when ownership of the company passed to Maidstone & District Motor Services who abandoned the Green Line fleet numbering but retained their original Autocar numbers. Their Green Line inspired fleet numbers T 325-345 were never used by London Transport.

Under Maidstone & District control the newer batch of Autocar Regal coaches left Tunbridge Wells on 1st May 1934 to enter the parent fleet, their places being taken by Tilling Stevens coaches now fitted with new bus bodies. The remainder became Maidstone & District stock exactly a year later when Autocar ceased to exist. The 1930 vehicles all received splendid new Harrington coach bodies in 1938 and

KR 3238 was rebodied once again in 1941 after its first Harrington body had been destroyed by enemy action. The later and more modern looking vehicles lasted basically unaltered through to the end of the war apart from being equipped with internal parcel racks and undergoing a certain amount of re-seating to improve their carrying capacity. In 1946 KR 9911, 9915 and 9916 were given new Harrington coach bodies and were the last of the former Autocar stock still active at the time they were finally withdrawn from service in 1953.

The vehicles inherited by London Transport led an uneventful existence. The former T 150-154, which had ceased to use their fleet numbers under LGCS ownership, continued in their role as private hire vehicles at Brixton, retaining Green Line colours but carrying the new LONDON TRANSPORT name on their side panels after it came into general use in May 1934. Later in that year strong consideration was given to providing them with more modern bodies, but this came to nothing. The restoration of fleet numbers after Chiswick took over responsibility for the Country Bus & Coach department's rolling stock, including the private hire fleet, in February 1935 saw the revival of the identities T 150-154 for these five vehicles but, strangely, in reverse order to what had applied before. This appears to have been done so as to bring the fleet numbers into numerical order with the registration numbers GF 479-483, in contrast to the LGOC who had numbered the five vehicles in reverse order to their registration starting with T 150 at GF 483 down to T 154 at GF 479. Thus the former T 150 now became known as T 154 and so on, leaving only the vehicle in the centre of the batch, T 152, to retrieve its original identity. Their use became seasonal and they were delicensed each winter

Looking smart and presentable for its final summer operating season is T 151, seen here in the company of various other members of the private hire fleet most of which will become redundant upon arrival of the new LTC class coaches. Delicensing on 1st October 1937 will mark the end of the road with London Transport for all five coaches in the T 150-154 batch, which will shortly be put up for sale and should prove attractive to future purchasers because of the low and largely summers-only mileage which they will have accumulated during their eight years of existence. Minor repositioning of the side lights and driver's mirror have been carried out in recent times on T 151, but the most significant change to it in latter days has been a renumbering from its former identity as T 153. *J F Higham © A B Cross*

Soon after receiving the latest two-tone green colours in April 1935, T 396 stands in the yard of the old St Albans garage awaiting its next call to duty, which may be on Green Line duplication work or even on a local bus service, where its heavy swing doors would be more of a hindrance than a help. Already looking obsolete and a prime candidate for early withdrawal, T 396 confounded everyone by being selected in 1938 as the prototype 11T11 conversion, securing a massive extension to its working life which lasted right through to 1952. *D W K Jones*

between October or November and the commencement of the next year's seasonal upturn in March or April. At their last overhaul, just before the start of the 1936 season, T 150-154 were repainted in the new standard country bus scheme of two-tone green. The 1937 season proved to be their last, and when they were delicensed on 1st October it proved to be the end of their London career. The beautiful new LTC class of AEC Renown coaches, with their thermostatically controlled heating systems, Marconi radios and wonderfully luxurious seating were due to come on stream within a few weeks to transform the private hire fleet out of all recognition.

The one-time East Surrey coaches found themselves dispersed around garages in the southern part of the country fleet to fill in on Green Line work when required with occasional forays on to ordinary bus work. At the end of 1934 six were at Tunbridge Wells, three at Dunton Green, two at Guildford, and one each at Addlestone, Chelsham, Dorking, East Grinstead and Godstone. By 1935 the decision had been taken to renumber some of them to eliminate duplication with the ex-Tilling vehicles T 307-318. The sensible thing to do to avoid splitting any batches would have been to renumber the Tilling vehicles, but the opposite course was chosen. Alternatively, numbers in the now-vacant series T 325-345 could have been used, but this option was not adopted either. Instead, in April 1935, all of the first series (T 309-314) and four of the second (T 315-318) were renumbered T 393-402 respectively (following on from former Bucks Express T 307 and 308 which had likewise been renumbered T 391 and 392).

Despite the drawback of having canvas hoods and swing doors, the sixteen Regals continued in service, latterly in two-tone green livery, though their appearances on Green Line

work diminished after March and April 1936 when eight of them were transferred to the private hire department garaged mainly at Brixton but now with an overflow at Old Kent Road. In common with T 150-154, these eight (T 319, 320, 322, 393, 395, 397, 401, 402) were all withdrawn from service on 1st October 1937. The remainder continued to make occasional appearances on Green Line duties from various garages for up to eight months longer, the final withdrawals occurring on 1st June 1938 in the form of T 321, 400 at Dunton Green, T 323 at Tunbridge Wells, T 393 at Epping, T 394 at Hatfield, and T 398 at Guildford. Three of the class were transferred to the Tram & Trolleybus department as service vehicle stock in March 1938, T 319 and T 393 as tramway conduit cleaners and T 320 as an overhead wire lubricator. With one exception, all the remainder were sold to dealers between March and August 1938, and before they departed, five of them had their lamps, speedometers, generators and dials removed, as did all of the T 150-154 batch, so that these units could be overhauled at Chiswick prior to being re-used on new AEC Mercury lorries. However the loss of these items did not prevent most from being re-sold by dealers for further use as coaches, often with new bodies fitted.

The sole exception was T 396 which, after withdrawal from service at Romford (North Street) on 1st January 1938, made its way to Chiswick to act as the guinea pig for the rebodying of 31 early Regals, along with the fitment of new oil engines, to become the handy and long-lived 11T11 class, the story of which is told in chapter 16. In this guise T 396 spent three times longer within the fleet than any of its contemporaries and continued to serve London Transport until 1952.

T 401 (formerly known as T 317 and shown as such in an earlier photograph) stands in the summer sunshine of 1937. With the centre section of its roof rolled right back, it is waiting to carry passengers on a private excursion to Windsor. Gone from its rather undistinguished-looking body are the glass window louvres, route board brackets and roof luggage rack which this small batch formerly carried. T 401 was withdrawn from service when the season finished on 1st October 1937. Perhaps more characterful and interesting is the vehicle standing behind, centre-entrance Dennis Lancet DT 9 inherited from the Penn Bus Company in August 1935. *J F Higham © A B Cross*

# 6 THE CHISWICK-BUILT CB CLASS
## T 1000-1002

Discretely numbered a considerable distance above their contemporaries in the T class, T 1000-1002 were not AEC Regals at all but something infinitely more unusual and – as time would subsequently show – considerably less satisfactory and vastly more expensive to build and operate. The decision to construct them can be traced back to a Board meeting of the LGOC on 17th January 1929 when funding was approved for the manufacture of twelve vehicles to the Company's own designs. Six of them would be two-axle single deckers designated the CB class and the balance would comprise six three-axle double deckers of class CC. It is presumed that the first 'C' in their designation denotes Chiswick which was where the designs originated. The absence of a CA class is explained by the fact that this was reserved for a future double deck version of the two-axle chassis which was never subsequently built. In view of the events that unfolded it is probable that a proposed further variant, the CD single decker in six wheeler form, never even got on to the drawing board.

Rumour has it that there were management elements inside the LGOC who favoured the in-house production of a fleet of vehicles based on its own designs rather than buying from AEC, and this was not an entirely fanciful proposition. The Company had amassed considerable experience of chassis construction through successfully assembling NS chassis at Chiswick for three years using units supplied by AEC, a policy forced upon it to relieve pressure on the latter's over-stretched works at Walthamstow. Going one stage further, the LGOC had designed and built for itself a small fleet of

eight 24-seat semi-forward control charabancs numbered AW 1-8 in June and July 1926, while another fleet of home-made products to emerge from Chiswick works between 1924 and 1928 were 50 Dorman-engined 1½ and 2 ton light trucks known as the V class.

The LGOC's January 1929 decision to design and construct its own vehicles, albeit limited to a mere twelve, might seem perverse in view of the Company's close link to AEC through common Underground group ownership, especially since AEC had recently acquired large modern manufacturing

*Above left* For reasons best known to itself, General appears to have studiously avoided taking photographs of the three CB class single deckers, suggesting that they did not feel any great sense of pride in what their engineers at Chiswick had created. A 'near miss' came early in July 1931 when double deck LT 512 was being photographed outside the licensing shop at Chiswick to record the latest style of body created for these vehicles. A peep inside the open doorway reveals that, waiting just inside ready to be licensed for service, are double deck LT 522 and single deck LT 1150 plus, more significantly, newly completed T 1000 which can be easily recognised by its distinctive radiator.

*Above right* The front end of the CB class, and their CC double deck equivalents, was ugly in the extreme, and it will always be a mystery why the designers adopted such an ungainly and pugnacious styling for the radiator. Even the 'GENERAL' casting at the top is applied without any sense of finesse. The two removable side covers below the 5ft long bonnet are apparent in this close-up view of T 1000 taken early in its operating days. *J F Higham © A B Cross*

facilities at Southall which could cope with all of the LGOC's requirements and, indeed, depended upon fulfilling them to ensure financial viability. However the situation at the time had to be viewed against the perspective of an AEC product range which had become outclassed by other manufacturers and had failed to keep up with modern design trends, a situation which would prove highly detrimental to the LGOC if left untackled. G J Rackham's installation as Chief Engineer at AEC in place of Charles Edwards, with an edict to rapidly turn things around, had only occurred relatively recently, and though specimens from his new range were beginning to appear, they were as yet untried. At the same time as approving construction of the twelve CB and CC vehicles, the LGOC board also authorised the purchase of two four-wheeled Regents and two six-wheeled Renowns from AEC's new range, but nevertheless their decision to pursue their own vehicle designs as well as AEC's was probably wise under the circumstances which prevailed at the time.

The twelve complete buses were nominally to be built under the auspices of the Union Construction & Finance Company Ltd, the Underground group's Feltham-based manufacturing concern which, in addition to constructing carriage stock for both tube and sub-surface Underground lines, also built the superb 'Feltham' trams as well as the bodies for the 60 'Diddler' trolleybuses. It is possible that the UCC was viewed as a device for channeling funds to the project, but it appears always to have been the intention that the actual chassis assembly would be carried out by the LGOC itself at Chiswick, whose coachworks were authorised to build the bodies for all twelve vehicles. The whole enterprise was driven by the LGOC's Research Engineer, Owen W J Watson, whose department had ultimate responsibility for the design, manufacture and in-service monitoring of the twelve CB and CC vehicles.

The decision to proceed with the project was not based solely on future plans and promises. In fact work had already been going on for several months on the initial CC chassis which had progressed from the drawing board to the mock-up stage at Chiswick during the course of 1928. Furthermore a power unit for it – one of two engine designs to emerge from the Chiswick team – had already been manufactured on the Company's behalf by Henry Meadows & Son Ltd at Wolverhampton. Although fate was subsequently to decree otherwise, at the time the future for the engine designs looked promising. Further background to this, and to other aspects of the project, can be referred to in the companion volume on the LT class.

By 1930 construction of two chassis was under way, but both were of the CC type and there was still no sign of the CB four-wheeled version. Progress was dilatory, partly – it is thought – through lack of strategic direction by Watson but also because of a tendency to make adjustments to the design, sometimes quite major ones, at short notice. The slow progress was in stark contrast to Rackham's achievements at AEC which saw the whole of his new passenger chassis range brought into full production while Chiswick was struggling to get its first vehicle on the road. This did not occur until 2nd August 1930 when the first CC-type double decker, numbered LT 1000, began work at Nunhead garage where its unreliability and mediocre performance were amply demonstrated, leading to hasty design changes being adopted for chassis still to be constructed, and delaying the introduction of any more vehicles into service until 1931.

It was not until 20th May 1931 that the first CB, T 1000,

was officially taken into stock, although a few more weeks were destined to elapse before it was finally approved by the Public Carriage Office and signed off as fit to enter public service. Viewed from the front, T 1000 was by no means an object of beauty, being distinguished by an unduly large and supremely ugly radiator which projected pugnaciously forward of the front wheels at the head of a bonnet which was a full 5 feet in length. Beneath the bonnet adequate space had been provided to accommodate an 8-cylinder in-line engine, which was another project Watson's Development Department wished to pursue. Events had overtaken it when an 8-cylinder engine was procured from AEC and installed in new T 43 in January 1930, so it was never necessary to produce an LGOC-designed equivalent to this configuration.

The Meadows-built engine was of the overhead valve type with all six cylinders in a single casting which was claimed to give rigidity to the engine as a whole, and an interesting feature was that the valves, which were of special steel alloy and located in the cylinder head, were operated by twin over-head camshafts with the sparking plugs arranged centrally in the spherical cylinder head. It was claimed that, although this entailed a more complicated design and a considerable increase in weight, it produced the ideal combustion chamber. The seven bearing crankshaft and all the journals were stated to be of exceptionally large diameter, while the four-blade fan was mechanically driven. All the auxiliaries, such as the water pump, lighting dynamo, carburettor, magneto and starting motor were arranged on the nearside. The 100mm bore and 130mm stroke engine gave a swept volume of 6.1 litres and, by chance, coincided exactly with G J Rackham's successful design for AEC. The engine was, unusually, accessed by two separate removable panels on the nearside and there was even a narrow detachable panel on the offside ahead of the driver's dash. A single plate clutch linked the engine to the gearbox which had only three forward speeds. The latter was separately mounted on the chassis, a conventional but now outdated arrangement which produced less positive and responsive gearchanging than when the gearbox was unit mounted with the engine and clutch as was the case with Rackham's designs for AEC.

At the front of the vehicle a Marles steering box was used, and the axles were purchased from Kirkstall. Those at the rear were of the fully floating type, and this was probably the only design feature on the whole chassis that might conceivably be considered an advance over the AEC Regal. Unlike the 1T1s, where an axle ratio of $6\frac{1}{4}$ :1 was specified, the ratio for T 1000 was 7 :1 even though the vehicle theoretically enjoyed a similar power output.

Body numbers 10484-10489 were allocated to the six single deckers at the time the project was authorised. These followed on immediately from the six CC bodies but, unlike the latter, construction did not start well in advance of the availability of the chassis, which turned out to be fortuitous. In the case of the double deckers five out of the six planned bodies were built fairly promptly, only for three of them to take up valuable storage space for several months because their chassis had not been constructed; eventually they were modified to fit on to standard AEC Renown chassis. When two more CC chassis finally became available these were fitted with later-style bodies diverted from the main LT construction programme and, at about the same time, construction of the fifth and sixth CC chassis was cancelled. The decision to reduce the scale of the experiment at this point, taken in about September 1931, also extended to the single deckers, resulting in only three out of the six seeing the light of day. Although no background documentation relating to the costs of this programme – which was now clearly floundering – have survived, it would be logical to surmise that the combination of delays and problems encountered up to this point would have resulted in a serious over-run of the original financial authorisation had the scope of the project not been curtailed.

Because of its unduly long bonnet the body length of T 1000 had to be reduced to bring the vehicle within the required 26 feet, resulting in one bay being shorter than the others. This was the same principle that had applied earlier to T 43 (see chapter 1) although in the case of T 1000 the bay selected for shortening was the very last one. The vehicle seated 29 and it was built to much the same front entrance styling as the LT single deckers of the time, with a destination box at the front but not at the rear. Internally it was fitted out with the then-standard square-backed, well-padded sprung seats using the same general décor as on the LTs. The one big difference was that the driver's cab was built directly on to the chassis and did not form part of the main bodywork, a practice common a few years earlier but by then seldom used. Being less wide than the main body, the cab had a correspondingly narrower windscreen above its rounded dash than was found on the LT. The cab design was a feature shared with the first two CC double deckers and the benefits

of adopting it are not immediately obvious against the draw-back of a seemingly cramped working environment for the driver.

T 1000 was licensed for service on 7th July 1931 and was allocated to Kingston garage, as were T 1001 and 1002 when they finally arrived, and though surviving details of their operations are sparse it is believed that they did not normally work on Kingston's own schedules. 'Home' for them was the small garage at Weybridge which had no vehicle allocation of its own to cover its four scheduled workings and was supplied from Kingston. From photographic evidence it would appear that T 1000 was employed firstly on route 79, an 86 minutes long country run between Kingston (Omnibus Station) and Woking (Albion Hotel) via Esher, Weybridge and Byfleet which became the 219 under the October 1934 renumbering. Weybridge garage had only one working on route 79, so when the other two arrived they would also have covered routes 61 (Kingston–Staines via Chertsey, later renumbered 217) and 62 (Kingston–Staines via Laleham, later 218).

The final months of 1931 witnessed a belated spurt to get the four remaining Chiswick-built vehicles into service, with the two outstanding double deckers being licensed just ahead of T 1001 and 1002. The construction of T 1001 was completed on 6th November and it was ready to start work on the 20th, the equivalent dates for T 1002 being 17th November and 7th December. The fundamental difference between these two and T 1000 was that the driver's cab was now constructed in the conventional way as part of the main bodywork. This meant that the offside of it was flush with the main bodywork and it featured the customary narrow window behind the driver's doorway. Even when viewed from the front the difference in cab construction was evidenced by the wider windscreen now fitted. T 1001 and 1002 also benefited by having a rear destination box, a feature which had been incorporated in new LT type single deckers since July 1931, while passengers may perhaps have noticed that they now sat on the latest type of curved back seats albeit inside an otherwise unchanged interior.

T 1001 displays the wider windscreen of the conventionally mounted cab on the second and third CB vehicles as it hurries through Byfleet late in LGOC days, carrying a destination blind display that is considerably more informative than the one in the previous photograph and with all its windows open to provide internal cooling on a hot day. The front end of its bodywork has now been reinforced as demonstrated by the greater depth of the black band in this area. *J F Higham © A B Cross*

The 'snout' effect caused by the 5ft long bonnet is very apparent when viewed from the offside, with the radiator projecting so far beyond the front of the cab structure that space is available to incorporate a small detachable panel to give access to the engine and fan. In fact, by the time that T 1000 was photographed in its later London Transport days, a conventional AEC engine was fitted which left much of the space below the bonnet unoccupied. *J F Higham © A B Cross*

The Chiswick-designed engines appear to have proved troublesome right from the start, though sadly no records now exist to show exactly where the defects lay. It is known that the six-wheelers were unable to run to time even on lightly loaded journeys, and this problem could have afflicted T 1000-1002 also. As early as November 1931 the Meadows-built engine was removed from one of the double deckers, LT 1051, and replaced by a Gardner 5LW oiler, and although this also proved to be a failure through being underpowered, it paved the way for the eventual removal of the original engines from all seven Chiswick-built chassis. LT 1051 was again in the news when a standard AEC 110mm petrol engine was installed during a prolonged overhaul lasting between July and September 1932, and the same treatment was meted out to T 1002 when it went for overhaul in December of the same year. In the case of the single decker, however, a 100mm engine was deemed adequate together with an axle ratio of 6½ :1, but a new feature common to both was the provision of an external autovac tank. AEC engines were fitted to the remainder during 1933; T 1000 was dealt with in August while T 1001 was the last of the seven to lose its Meadows engine during November.

Totally unconnected with their mechanical woes, the three single deckers suffered a bodywork problem which they shared with the 200-strong class of LT 'Scooters'. Within their first year of service it became clear that all was not well at the front end where the bulkheads began to break loose. The problem had to be tackled as a matter of urgency and as each bus went through its first overhaul the body was stripped down and strengthening brackets inserted at cantrail level (and probably also at floor level, though this has not been confirmed). Being quite substantial the new brackets would have protruded above the roof level black band and in order to hide them a new, deeper band was installed around the front of each vehicle. It was easy to tell when a body had been strengthened as the front end black band no longer matched up with the rest of the body.

Not much is known to have happened to T 1000-1002 during the early years of London Transport apart from a few modifications which affected all of the contemporary fleet and not just these three vehicles. These included the replace-

ment of the fixed starting handle by a removable one held in the cab, the removal of the tester's tip-up seat below the front canopy and its accompanying leather strap, and the replacement of the air bells by electrically-operated ones. No recorded details survive of the performance of these three vehicles during the mid-nineteen thirties although experiments with various axle ratios suggest that they still ran below par even with AEC engines fitted. They continued to operate on the same services until 6th October 1937 when a major revision saw the withdrawal of the 217, the cutting back of the 219 from Woking to Weybridge, and the introduction of a new 219A Weybridge local service. With the exception of the latter day 219A all their operations were very different in nature from the intensive start-stop work on which the CC six-wheelers were employed which must have given an interesting comparison of how the design concept coped under such vastly less demanding conditions. Then, apparently quite suddenly on 23rd February 1938, all three were delicensed and placed in temporary storage at Bromley garage, moving on 10th June to more permanent accommodation at Chiswick tram depot.

The three buses spent the second half of 1938 and the whole of 1939 in the tram depot without turning a wheel. They were reactivated on 8th March 1940, but only to send them to a new location for further storage. The space occupied by these and other unused vehicles was now required for conversion to a body overhaul shop, and the stored fleet was re-located to the former Tilling premises at Bull Yard, Peckham. The three CB vehicles finally came into focus at a management meeting on 9th July 1940 when their status was reviewed and it was recorded that, because of their non-standard parts, they were very costly to maintain, a position which had worsened with the advent of war because it was now almost impossible to procure spare parts for them. They had been considered for conversion into armoured vehicles but this idea was rejected because of the maintenance difficulties. Their disposal was agreed, although it could not be implemented until approval was received from the Railway Executive Committee, to which London Transport now reported. This was duly forthcoming, and in August 1940 they were sold to Henry Lane, a Chelsea garage proprietor.

The following month found them in the well-known west London fleet of Valliant Direct Coaches Ltd, and whilst hardly classifiable as coaches, they presumably helped to cover some of the war related contracts which this company amassed. Subsequent details are unclear, but T 1001 and 1002 are recorded as having been commandeered by the War Department for civil defence work in 1941, and possibly T 1000 went there too. Remarkably all three were still in existence at the end of the war, albeit disused, and licensing records show that T 1001 and T 1002 passed to H S North Ltd of Derby in May 1946. There is no further record of T 1002 being used in any capacity and it may be surmised that it was cannibalised to keep T 1001 going until its final licence expired in July 1947.

# 7 BUCKS EXPRESS

## T 307 & 308

The first second hand Regals to come within the LGOC's orbit were JH 32 and JH 33. They were the two newest items of rolling stock in the fleet of Bucks Expresses (Watford) Ltd which also included five Gilfords and three Maudslays, all of which came under the LGOC's control on Saturday 20th February 1932 when it purchased the full share capital of the Watford company.

The acquisition came as part of the LGOC's policy of buying-out as many of the London express operators as possible which was the only means of expansion left to it following the implementation of the Road Traffic Act. Some of the acquired undertakings were on their uppers and were glad to sell, but this was not the case with Bucks Express (the company's name was always shown in the singular on time-tables and other publicity) which was highly profitable and extracted a hefty purchase price. Up to now Bucks Express had always been one step ahead of the LGOC, having commenced its express service from Watford to London on 26th September 1929, a few days ahead of the LGOC's pioneering operation to Golders Green, and thereafter sustaining its leading position by offering the most superior level of service and regularity of all the competing coaches between the Hertfordshire town and the capital. Its proprietors were T E Greenwood, owner of the Enterprise 'pirate' buses in London, and S F St George whose garage at 67 The Parade in Watford High Street was the Company's operating centre and also its well-sited outer terminal point. The two business partners co-existed in a permanent state of animosity and it was thanks to Bucks Express's manager, the very competent H C Dinham, that the business survived and prospered, though its eventual sale was probably inevitable.

The LGOC was obliged to keep its new acquisition as a separate undertaking as any attempt to change its name or status through the traffic courts would inevitably have led to objections and possibly even loss or curtailment of the licence. It continued to run the business from Bucks' premises under Mr Dinham's control until 17th May 1932 after which the coaches were moved across town to Leavesden Road garage and run as part of the Green Line organisation. They were repainted into Green Line colours, though still bearing the 'Bucks' name, and the two Regals received fleet numbers T 307 and T 308 following on from the last of the vehicles specifically built to establish the Green Line network. They were allocated body numbers 13366/67 though these were never carried and were duly 'lost' under the London General Country Services regime when it took over ownership of all Green Line and associated operations on 29th July 1932.

The two Bucks Regals were based on standard chassis with A140 100mm engines and triple servo brakes, and they carried 30-seat front entrance Dodson bodies which looked quite striking in their brown, yellow and black livery. The most unusual thing about them was that they were a very close albeit slightly taller copy of the standard Green Line coach of the time. They had the same semi-rounded contours, an identical combined destination display and name panel, and even an LGOC style open driver's doorway which no other operators' vehicles emulated. The extra height below the windows was presumably inserted in order to raise the floor line so that the seats, which were all forward facing, cleared the rear wheel arches with only minimum intrusion, while the back four rows were raised on plinths to improve forward visibility. It meant that three shallow rather than two somewhat steeper steps had to be incorporated at the entrance to reach floor level. The two vehicles entered service on 3rd July 1931 to replace a pair of smaller and older Gilford CP6s and were the newest in the Bucks fleet.

The earliest photograph of a Bucks Express Regal known to still survive is this view of T 392, taken working from Watford High Street garage during the period between its overhaul into two-tone green livery in October 1935 and its transfer to the nearby Leavesden Road garage in March 1936. It is seen at Golders Green on the short Green Line service between there and Watford originally pioneered as an LGOC operation in October 1929. *J F Higham © A B Cross*

Bucks Expresses (Watford) Ltd was absorbed into the London Passenger Transport Board on vesting day, 1st July 1933, and the Watford–Oxford Circus service – lettered since takeover in the Green Line series as AW – was fully absorbed into the Green Line network. The two Regals remained on Green Line duties, although in the absence of any specific records the exact details of their employment during early London Transport days are not known. By the start of 1935 T 307 was based at High Wycombe and T 308 at Watford High Street. When the country area engineering records were transferred from Reigate to Chiswick on 25th February 1935 the duplication of fleet numbers with those of ex-Tilling Ts was realised, and T 307 and T 308 were renumbered T 391 and T 392 respectively. At overhaul in October of that year they were issued with body numbers 16020 and 16012 and at the same time the classification 2/8T8/4 that had been tentatively allocated to them was amended to 1/7T7/1 in recognition of their similarity to T 207-306, and this is the code that they always carried.

In common with the 'real' 1/7T7/1s, the two Bucks Regals were transferred between garages to suit operating requirements, but they came together again at St Albans in May 1937 and moved from there as a pair to Romford (North Street) in January 1938. This was to be their last posting as Green Line vehicles, and on 1st September of the same year they were delicensed and sent to Chiswick for conversion into buses. The same work was carried out on them as on the other 1/7T7/1s being converted at the same time, including the rebuilding of the front dome with angular bus-style destination boxes and the insertion of a full height partition behind the doorway which probably gave added strength to the structure as well as reducing draughts. On 1st October 1938 both began their new career as buses, T 391 at Hertford and T 392 at Swanley.

The war years saw the pair re-united once again at Hemel Hempstead from October 1939, moving to Windsor in December 1940. T 392 remained at the latter garage but T 391 was transferred to Addlestone in February 1942 where it was painted grey six months later. In December of the same year both were modified with perimeter seating to achieve a carrying capacity of 50 including 20 standees. They became redundant on 1st June 1943 and were delicensed, although T 392 was revived at Windsor from October 1943 until September 1944, and again for a short spell at Hemel Hempstead in February and March 1945. On 2nd May 1945 it was sold to the Ministry of War Transport.

With so many standard T-type vehicles being sold for use by the Allied Control Commission in the first few days of May 1945, including some with modern and much more substantial bodywork, it is little short of amazing that T 391 was retained for service well into the post-war era, the sole survivor of the many Dodson bodied vehicles that once ran in the London area in the service of a plethora of independent operators. It was saved as the result of a decision to relicense it for Central Bus service at Kingston on 16th January 1945 while still in grey livery, and is recorded as having been repainted red on 24th April. Almost a year later, on 15th April 1946, it was back at Chiswick for a routine overhaul which resulted in considerable reconstruction of the bodywork. The most noticeable outcome of this was the complete removal of the passenger door and the narrow recess inside the saloon into which it had formerly slid. Normal transverse seating was re-installed, and in its revised form T 391 became a regular performer on Kingston area services right through

*Top* Although officially classified as a 1/7T7/1, there was no mistaking T 391 in post-war years because of its very visual extra height, which was particularly noticeable in the vicinity of the cab with the unusually elevated positioning of its windscreen in relation to the filler cap. This view shows T 391 in a typical pose operating from Kingston garage on route 218 which was where it could normally be found. *Alan B Cross*

*Above* Both of the ex-Bucks Express vehicles were converted to buses in September 1938, and this view inside T 391 shows the full-height doorway partition inserted at the time along with the positioning of a fare chart holder where the heater used to be, and the used ticket box. Surprisingly the substantial luggage racks were retained as were the ash trays. This photograph, taken at the end of T 391's working life when the interior was looking somewhat careworn, shows how the first bay appeared after the sliding door was removed in 1946. *Alan B Cross*

to 1949. Its tall appearance compared with the usual 1/7T7/1s ensured that it stood out clearly from all the others, and in recognition that its high floor line might have proved an inconvenience to less mobile passengers, some of the more alert conductors could be heard warning those alighting that they had an extra step to negotiate.

The end came quickly in mid-1949. No longer required at Kingston, T 391 left there on 18th May and was transferred to Edgware. A move back south to Sutton on 1st June found it almost instantly condemned even though it looked very smart at the time, having received a full external repaint only about two months earlier. In the typical way that redundant vehicles were rapidly removed from London Transport premises at that time, T 391 made its final journey to Daniels' scrap yard at Rainham the very next day.

# 8 BLUE BELLE AND QUEEN LINE

## T 346-357

The year is 1932 and a sense of stability now reigns over the complex and extensive range of short distance express coach services radiating from London to towns throughout the Home Counties. The introduction of Road Service Licensing in May 1931 meant that cut-throat and often foolhardy competition to establish new footholds had become a thing of the past. The only way that expansion could now be achieved was through buying existing operations and the LGOC, through its Green Line subsidiary, had embarked on its next task of consolidating its position in the market by paying premium prices if necessary as an inducement to other operators to part with their businesses. In pursuance of this policy tentative approaches were made to a number of coach owners to ascertain their willingness to sell, one of which was Blue Belle Motors Ltd of 43-45 Acre Lane, Brixton which ran a well-patronised service between Paddington and East Grinstead.

Blue Belle was a substantial organisation registered in 1927 to carry on a business whose origins dated back to 1921. By 1932 its principal shareholder was Reginald Toms, and the Company was best known for its substantial range of seasonal services to coastal resorts all around the south-east of England. In 1929 it had built a substantial new coach station at 66-86 Clapham Road, Kennington, demolishing a private park known as The Shrubbery and some houses fronting Clapham Road in order to do so. The London Terminal Coach Station, as the new property was known, was a really splendid development consisting of a 650ft deep covered garage fronted by a 200ft deep and 100ft wide fore-court with buildings on each side containing refreshment and

waiting rooms, shops, a booking hall, and also refuelling facilities for coaches. It quickly became the terminal station for many other well-known operators of the time, and during 1931 it was recorded that the station was used for some 11,000 coach departures. Blue Belle's own mass departure at 10.00am each morning was a sight to behold as a stream of blue and black coaches departed for Littlehampton and Bognor Regis, Brighton and Worthing, Margate and Ramsgate, Eastbourne, Hastings, Folkestone, Portsmouth and Southsea, and Southend, and they were nearly all timed at arrive back in the evening at about 8.50.

A further development in 1930 was the purchase of a splendid new fleet of 30 AEC Regals to replace most of the former mixed fleet of Gilfords and Leylands. Registered GC 7407, 8568, GF 5124-5136, 8348, 8349, GJ 5365-5367, 8068-8074, 8390-8392, they were all bodied as 30-seaters by London Lorries at their Spring Place works in Kentish Town. Placed into service between February and June 1930, they were comfortable coaches typical of their time with deep

One of Blue Belle's large batch of Regals exudes a sturdy, workmanlike appearance as it stands outside London Lorries' premises in Kentish Town alongside the LMS railway line. Time was to prove that appearances could be deceptive and after a five year working life the bodies were worn out, but when new they represented the acme of modern coaching, and the deep leather seats certainly looked inviting enough. The photograph was taken before the vehicle was licensed and it is not known if this was one of those that subsequently passed into Green Line ownership. *Dave Jones collection*

leather seats, each individually numbered, a patented sunshine roof, and dual outward-swinging doors at front and rear. The opening roof was of particular interest and was called the 'Plein Azur' which, as its name suggests, was a French design for which London Lorries held the sole manufacturing and distribution rights throughout Great Britain and Ireland. It was of the sliding type, which was quite a new concept at the time, with a lightweight sliding section made of timber and steel and covered with waterproof fabric. It was attached to an endless roller chain which was wound from a geared handle in the roof of the driver's cab, so that that the driver could open or close the sunshine roof without leaving his seat, and London Lorries claimed that the roof could be fully opened or closed in 20 seconds. In March 1931 the 30 Regals were joined by ten more (GO 112-121), again London Lorries bodied and to the same general specification except that their windscreens were markedly more upright and the roofs more deeply domed.

Publicised as "Something Entirely New", five of the Regals inaugurated Blue Belle's venture into the realms of express coach operation on Wednesday 1st October 1930 with a pair of daily services sharing common territory between the RAF memorial on the Victoria Embankment and Godstone, diverging at that point to East Grinstead via Blindley Heath and Westerham via Oxted. Introduced to reduce the Company's heavy reliance on seasonal work, these soon needed augmenting, and major revisions in December 1930 found them extended across central London to a new terminus at Charles Rickards' office in Spring Street, Paddington, while the Westerham coaches were diverted away from their original routeing via Thornton Heath, Croydon Aerodrome and Purley to service instead Norwood, Crystal Palace, Beckenham and Bromley, with a later extension beyond Westerham to Edenbridge. This latter service later fell foul of the new Road Service Licensing procedure and ceased in December 1931, but the Paddington–East Grinstead run continued to work profitably, and it was the acquisition of this that the LGOC had in mind in January 1932 when it began negotiations with Blue Belle.

The Company indicated to the LGOC that, in principle, it was not averse to disposing of the service, but General's negotiators were unaware that, at the same time, Blue Belle's management was in the process of selling the whole business, including the East Grinstead operation, to the engineering and bodybuilding concern G Scammell & Nephew Ltd, who duly took over ownership in February 1932. The Blue Belle coach operation continued as before under the same manager, L A Mitchell, but the LGOC now had to re-open negotiations with the new owners, and it was not until 19th July 1932 that the sale agreement between Blue Belle and Green Line Coaches was signed, with Green Line taking over operation the next day.

Six Regals passed to Green Line on 20th July for which the latter paid £948 apiece. These were GF 5135 (Blue Belle 4), GF 5136 (3), GJ 8068 (27), GJ 8069 (29), GJ 8072 (22) and GJ 8073 (23), and in due course Green Line allocated them fleet numbers T 346-351 to follow on from the Autocar batch. It is

Already looking a little down at heel after suffering a few minor scrapes, GF 5125 is seen at work on the Paddington–East Grinstead run carrying informative side boards listing the main picking-up points on the way, notably Croydon aerodrome. An unusual design feature of the London Lorries bodies was the flare at the foot of two of the main offside panels, which contrasted with the tumble-home arrangement on the rest of the body and did not seem to serve any practical purpose. GF 5125 was not one of the coaches that subsequently passed to Green Line ownership. *N Hamshere*

Only the 'Green Line Coaches Ltd' legal lettering – plus removal of all the curtains from inside the saloon – gives away the fact that GF 5135 is no longer in Blue Belle ownership following the takeover on 20th July 1932. This vehicle carries no provision for side route boards, which probably indicates that it was not one of those regularly used on the East Grinstead service in Blue Belle days. It will soon be repainted green and receive its fleet number T 346. *J F Higham © A B Cross*

not known for sure how these six came to be selected from amongst Blue Belle's stock of 40 Regals, and they were not necessarily the same ones that had been employed on the East Grinstead service in its Blue Belle days. Under Green Line ownership they were regarded as 31 seaters, the additional seat probably being achieved simply my reclassifying the back seat to carry five instead of four without any physical alteration being made to the actual seating layout.

As a postscript to the Blue Belle story, although it could not be foreseen at the time, Scammell's had bought the undertaking at precisely the wrong moment. 1931 turned out to have been the high point in leisure coach travel after which a severe drop occurred, and this impacted particularly heavily on the Clapham Road coach station as, one by one, the coach operators that had used it went out of business. Blue Belle had itself suffered through forced cut-backs under the Road Service Licensing system, but the new owners worked hard to stimulate trade in increasingly difficult circumstances, including the innovative introduction in 1933 of ten new Regals with deck-and-a-half bodies incorporating rear observation saloons. In the same year the lease on the coach station, which had been operated by a subsidiary called Coach Travels Ltd, was put up for auction and was purchased by Red & White Services Ltd of Chepstow who subsequently bought the Blue Belle coach business itself in November 1936. The coach station, which closed at the start of the war, failed to re-open afterwards, and in June 1946 Blue Belle was sold to the United Service Transport Company. Older readers may recall the incongruous sight in early post-war years of the once proud Blue Belle name adorning elderly coaches in United's drab allover-green livery.

Six further Regals which passed to Green Line as T 352-357 are appropriate to include in this chapter because, by pure coincidence, not only did their paths cross with those of

ex-Blue Belle T 346-352 in independent days, but their fate under London Transport ownership – including modernisation with new bodywork – was identical. They came from Queen Line Coaches & Baldock Motor Transport Ltd which, as its lengthy and cumbersome title suggests, was an April 1930 amalgamation of two separate organisations under the common ownership of Johnson, Neal Ltd of 327-329 Harrow Road, Paddington. Johnson, Neal was the main agent for De Dion Bouton so, not unnaturally, both the Baldock and Queen Line fleets consisted entirely of De Dion coaches. The re-organisation was carried out to facilitate sale of the coaching activities which were henceforth owned by a number of finance houses with Peter Livesey, a director of the Mutual Finance Indemnity & Guarantee Corporation Ltd as Chairman. Livesey's company provided the new company with a headquarters organisation at its own address, 302-308 Regent Street, but the coaching base was moved from Paddington to Blue Belle's new London Terminal Coaching Station in Clapham Road.

Queen Line was the fleet name used by the new management on all its vehicles, which were used on two regular services. One was the frequent Baldock to London express service pioneered by Baldock Motor Transport back in October 1928, and the other was an ex-Queen Line long distance run from London to Llandudno via Shrewsbury and Chester. Wishing to update their image, the new owners decided to purchase ten new coaches, and an indication of the close co-operation enjoyed at the time with the Blue Belle management is that the latter actually placed the order on Queen Line's behalf. Ten new London Lorries bodied Regals were included in the same order as ten very similar vehicles for Blue Belle, which was probably a beneficial arrangement to both parties in bringing down the price per unit thanks to the bulk buying.

A black and white photograph cannot do justice to the attractive and unusual fawn and blue livery carried by the Queen Line Regals. The more upright frontal styling of the 1931 London Lorries bodywork is apparent when compared with the previous year's deliveries to Blue Belle. The patterned effect applied to the narrow waist rail adds to the ornateness of the vehicle's appearance, and the neat but narrow sliding rear door can be clearly seen. *Dave Jones collection*

Queen Line's new Regals were licensed in two batches, the first in January 1931 (GN 4414-4418) and the second in March (GN 8238-8242), and they looked very attractive in a livery of fawn and blue. In most respects they were identical to Blue Belle's final batch except that Queen Line specified only a single narrow door, of the sliding rather than the hinged type, which was placed at the rear and permitted a seating capacity of 32. They were more powerful than the Blue Belle vehicles, being fitted with the new A145 engine whose extra speed would have proved useful, particularly on the Llandudno run. The new Regals took over both of the Company's regular services, leaving a few remaining De Dions available for private hire and excursion work and to provide duplicates for the Regals when required.

The issuing of road service licences left Queen Line disadvantaged on its Baldock run which had to be cut back at its London end from 1st February 1932 and could now only run as far as Kings Cross coach station, depriving the Company of much of its London clientele, with further losses caused by a restriction placed on picking-up points within the Metropolitan area. Queen Line's operating centre now moved to 74 Park Hill, Clapham, which was probably a cheaper arrangement than could be obtained at the London Terminal Coaching Station, and this also became the registered office from 8th July 1932. By December 1932 Queen Line had approached the LGOC with an offer to sell the Baldock service and a draft agreement for sale was subsequently prepared in February 1933. As originally drawn up, the contract was between Queen Line and London General Country Services, but at the last moment the Combine changed the arrangements and it was Green Line whose name appeared as purchaser and who took over on Wednesday 26th April 1933.

Six Regals passed to Green Line to become T 352-357 (GN 4416, 8238-8242), leaving four with Queen Line for its Llandudno run along with a number of De Dions. On takeover the coaches, which had been in good condition when inspected at the beginning of the year, were found to have been somewhat neglected since then and were now dirty, had worn tyres, and in some cases were suffering from lack of greasing. After the takeover Queen Line (renamed Queen Line Coaches Ltd in March 1934) struggled through to May 1938 when, with its assets no longer adequate to meet its liabilities, a decision was taken to wind it up.

T 346-357 all duly appeared in Green Line livery and, in about December 1933, the ex-Queen Line vehicles were fitted with saloon heaters which they had not had previously. Although only four years old their London Lorries bodies were showing signs of fragility, which meant that expensive rebuilding would be necessary to keep them operational. It was decided that when the Certificates of Fitness expired on the six ex-Blue Belle vehicles they would be taken out of service pending a review of their future, and on 27th June 1934 T 346-349 (and probably also T 350 and T 351) were delicensed and left in storage at their last operational garage, Crawley. Not long afterwards the decision was taken to fit new bodywork to all 12 vehicles, and on 6th October 1934 T 346 was removed from Crawley and taken to Chiswick Works where it was stripped for examination along with AEC Reliance R 1 and un-numbered ADC 416-type UC 2265 to determine the scope and cost of any necessary conversion and modernisation work which needed to be carried out on them prior to rebodying.

Early in the London Transport era, GJ 8072 is seen in Kingsbury Square, Aylesbury, virtually unaltered from its Blue Belle days except that it now carries full Green Line livery as T 350. It is working service AT to London (Marble Arch) taken over from Red Rover on 30th November 1932. T 350 ran with its original body for only about a year under London Transport ownership. *J F Higham © A B Cross*

Meanwhile the allocation of chassis and body codes to the various acquired Regals resulted in T 346-351 receiving the code 5T4 while T 352-357 were 6T5, but in both instances these remained purely notional. The vehicles never passed through Chiswick Works in their original guise to receive these codes, and for the same reason their original London Lorries bodies were never given London Transport body numbers.

A total of 43 new 26ft long metal-framed bodies had been ordered from Metro-Cammell Weymann Motor Bodies Ltd for construction at the Weymann factory in Addlestone and T 346-357 were amongst the intended recipients of them. The design office at Chiswick had produced a workmanlike and attractive styling with which to update the Country Bus fleet at minimum cost, and it was intended that all 43 rebodied vehicles would be back in service by the middle of 1935. Built with well-rounded front and rear ends, the new bodies exhibited clear influences from the current styling used on STL double deckers including the use of rubber mudguard sections with streamlined extensions behind the wheels, and inconspicuous side lights hidden away inside the front panelling, in this case in the front dome. The relative ineffectiveness of these lamps at night, not to mention the difficulty of replacing faulty bulbs, led to a re-think soon afterwards and these remained the only single deckers to carry this design feature. Internally the new bodies initiated a new and ultra-modern appearance through the use of neat pressed metal window surrounds to eliminate all dirty corners and ledges. These were attractively rexine covered in contrasting shades of brown and pale green separated by polished metal bracelets, giving a really bright and welcoming appearance. The floor was merged into the side lining panels to eliminate any corners into which dirt and dust might be trapped.

The 43 bodies came in two distinct batches: 31 on Reliance chassis (including one earlier ADC), and the remaining very similar but not identical 12 on T 346-357. The bodies built for the Regals were approximately 2 inches taller than the others and had a flat, rather than sloping bottom edge to the driver's windscreen. Eventually the 31 also ended up on Regal chassis to become the well-remembered 11T11 class (see chapter 16).

Body numbers 15090-15120 were allocated to the Reliances and T 346-357 carried bodies 15121-15132 in numerical order. The 5T4 coding, which had previously applied only to the ex-Blue Belle vehicles, was now extended to the whole batch as they had all become identical, and the 6T5 code was allowed to lapse.

When the instructions went out on 28th January 1935 for all 43 vehicles covered by the rebodying programme to be brought into Chiswick only eleven were still in service, including all six of the ex-Queen Line Regals T 352-357 which were still active at Hitchin. It was originally anticipated that these six would arrive at Chiswick between 7th and 18th March, but the programme was running late and it proved helpful in easing the overall coach availability position to keep all six in service for a little longer. They were finally delicensed into Chiswick, one per working day in fleet number order, at the end of May with the last, T 357, arriving there on 4th June 1935.

Behind the scenes, a change of mind had occurred over what the rebodied Regals would be used for. Initially intended as service buses, the decision had been taken by March 1935 to divert them to the private hire fleet based at Brixton. The current strength of this very mixed fleet stood at 38 (consisting of 22 AEC, 8 Dennis, 4 Leyland, 2 Morris Commercial, 1 Albion and 1 Daimler) which was considered inadequate for the coming summer season to the extent of 12 coaches, which just happened to be the number of Regals being rebodied. Although lacking most typical coach fitments, it was arranged that the new bodies would seat only 26 to at least provide a fair degree of comfort and leg room, the seats themselves being of the very latest type with tubular aluminium frames and quickly removable cushions. This style of seat, which was to become the London Transport standard for many years to come, was already appearing on new trolleybuses but this was the first time it had been used on motor vehicles. A very bold and colourful moquette upholstery was used but it was destined not to be perpetuated on subsequent vehicles, the Board's subsequent policy being to avoid floral and other flamboyant patterns on the grounds that they were 'worrying' and destroyed the continuity of design.

Also photographed in early London Transport days, T 354 is seen at Baldock still working on its original Queen Line service which appears, at the time the photograph was taken, to have not yet received its route letters AK. T 354 still carries its rectangular Green Line bonnet plate fitted at the time of its takeover in April 1933. It is thought that all the ex-Queen Line Regals remained on the Baldock run until they were withdrawn for rebodying in 1935.
*J F Higham © A B Cross*

September 1934, and T 354 is seen in the little market town of Stevenage in the days long before its quaintness was lost as a result of the massive New Town development. London Transport has removed T 354's roof luggage rack, but has attached a route board to the back of the vehicle while, on the sides, holders for the future running number stencils have been provided but are not yet in use. The handsome, green panelled passenger shelters, built to several designs, emphasised the new corporate image and were a fine advertisement for London Transport until their disappearance in the early post-war years. *London Transport Museum*

Although the future of its London Lorries body has already been sealed, T 355 enjoys a short reprieve enabling it to carry on running from Hitchin garage on route AK until 1st June 1935. Unlike the Blue Belle vehicles, the ex-Queen Line Regals lasted in service long enough to carry garage and running number stencils for a few months. The drab Green Line livery is a far cry from the eye-catching colours carried by these vehicles in their early days. *D W K Jones*

Former Blue Belle T 351 shows off its modern contours to Green Line passengers soon after being rebodied in October 1935. On this occasion it is not working route J as intended but is heading south on the longer route I (Abbots Langley–Crawley). It is actually a Reigate-based vehicle but on this occasion is carrying WT (Watford, Leavesden Road) plates as a result of having 'slept out' at the latter garage on the previous evening, a common occurrence on many Green Line routes and also on certain country area bus services. *J F Higham © A B Cross*

Even after their demotion to bus duties, 5T4s could occasionally be called upon to cover Green Line duplication work, especially on summer Sundays and bank holidays when huge numbers of extra journeys were operated. In this instance, Luton's T 351 stands at Eccleston Bridge, Victoria waiting to work a relief journey on the H2 to Dunstable. A paper label on the bulkhead window has to suffice in the absence of the appropriate display on the destination blind. *J Bonnell*

The contrast between the cosy but dark and slightly claustrophobic interior of the original London Lorries body on T 353 and its new Weymann-built replacement could hardly be greater. The brown and green décor of the lining panels and the moulded window cappings present an ultra-modern appearance and the seats, with their colourful moquette covering on front and back, are spaced well apart to give more than adequate leg room. *London Transport Museum*

In the end, the rebodied Regals never joined the private hire fleet as intended. By the time the first of them was ready for service the summer touring season was over and they were no longer required. The decision was taken, instead, to put them on Green Line work, and they were duly labelled with the GREEN LINE name which was carried below the windscreen. This was the role for which they were probably least well suited, not just because of their low carrying capacity and their rather bus-like seats, but also through the lack of accepted Green Line necessities such as luggage racks, heaters, ash trays and clocks. Being devoid of external brackets to carry route boards, they did not even have provision to carry the route letter which, as a matter of policy, was not shown on destination screens.

The Reigate management decided that the rebodied Regals would take over full operation of Green Line route J (Reigate-Watford), the twelve vehicles being just sufficient to cover the full scheduled requirement when allocated six apiece to the garages at each end of the run, Reigate and Leavesden Road. Reigate was converted first starting with T 349 on 2nd October 1935 with Leavesden Road following on from 25th October until the whole batch was back in service on 6th November. No records are known to survive showing the reaction of the travelling public to these smart but very spartan new 'coaches', but it must be assumed that they were not overwhelmingly popular. Probably as a result of public and/or staff pressure, it was arranged that they would be removed at the earliest possible opportunity which came when the first of the new 9T9 type AEC Regals were placed into service in June 1936.

When first displaced, the 5T4s were dispatched to a variety of garages as far apart as Tunbridge Wells and Tring to continue their Green Line work, which presumably saw them mostly employed as duplicates, but on 27th October 1936 the majority were gathered together at Luton and all but one of the remainder followed soon afterwards. They were now downgraded to bus status and the GREEN LINE name was removed from the front scuttle. Luton received just the right number to cover its bus requirements on routes 356/356A, 360, 364/364A, 376 and 383, allowing one engineering spare. Their arrival relieved a very difficult period of acute vehicle shortage at Luton where a few Gilfords, backed up by standard Ts diverted from Green Line duties, had barely been sufficient to cover the full schedule.

The 5T4s now embarked on the most stable period of their career, although odd ones began to drift away from Luton to other garages from October 1937 onwards, their departure being arranged in numerical order from the highest fleet number downwards. By the start of 1939 only five were still at Luton. A major drawback was their low seating capacity which made them unsuitable for many services, and it is surprising that it took London Transport until January 1939 to rectify this by adding an extra row of seats to bring the total up to a much more respectable 30. All twelve were dealt with between then and the end of March, but time for the class had now run out at Luton and on 1st June 1939 the last five moved to Hertford although, with things seemingly now in a state of flux, three returned later in the same month. At the outbreak of war the twelve vehicles were distributed amongst four garages: Hertford (4), Windsor (3), Luton (3) and St Albans (2). Two from the Windsor allocation (T 354, 356) were conscripted by the army on 1st September and almost immediately placed on 'stand by' at Regents Park, but apart a few trips to the Purfleet rifle ranges on the 18th and 19th September their services were not needed and they were returned to London Transport on 21st September.

The rear aspect of the 5T4 is shown in this official view of ex-Queen Line T 353 taken in June 1937, by which time nine months had elapsed since its removal from Green Line work to cover bus duties at Luton. The curvature of the rear windows is a pleasant design feature and it is interesting to note that, whilst the side panels follow a 'tumble-home' contour at their bottom edge, they sweep outwards at the back of the vehicle. *London Transport Museum*

The early war years found the 5T4s continuing their role as country buses, which kept them fully occupied, although they were subjected to two major bouts of reallocations. The first of these occurred on 4th December 1940 when every one of the twelve changed garage as part of a big upheaval within the Country Bus single deck fleet consequent upon a major reorganisation and extension of the wartime Green Line network. Just prior to this date the twelve vehicles had been based at Luton (5), Hertford (4) and Windsor (3); their new garages were St Albans (4), Staines (4), Leatherhead (3) and Reigate (1). Just a fortnight later the trio at Leatherhead moved away to re-establish the type at Hertford, and the Reigate vehicle was transferred to Staines. More Green Line activity in June 1941, when STLs deposed 10T10s from a number of services on the 13th and 27th of that month, caused a further round of transfers which resulted in the 5T4s being concentrated at two garages, Leavesden Road (7) and Hertford (5). Even this did not mark the end of their wanderings. Leavesden Road's all moved out between December 1941 and February 1942, mostly to Hemel Hempstead but also to Luton with an odd one going to Amersham (and later moving to Luton), while in August 1942 Hemel Hempstead's departed to re-establish the class at St Albans.

In November 1941 T 354, which was allocated to Luton at the time, was used as the test bed for converting 5T4s to perimeter seating, adding 7cwt to its unladen weight and reducing its seating capacity to 27 but allowing it to carry 20 standing. It re-entered service in this form, still at Luton, on 20th December, but several more months then elapsed before any more were dealt with. Six more became standee vehicles in July and August 1942, leaving only T 346, 348, 349, 351, 356 in their earlier form. These five were destined for early withdrawal when many 10T10s became available as a result of the ending of all Green Line operations on 30th September 1942. Thereafter the only work found for them while still in London Transport ownership was as snow ploughs.

The remaining seven soldiered on, latterly at Hertford and Luton, until the beginning of May 1943 when they were gathered together in Chiswick Works. Perhaps because of their modern bodywork, they had been identified as suitable candidates for conversion to gas propulsion, in which form they entered service from Addlestone and Leatherhead garages on route 462 on 1st June 1943, now classified as 13T4/1. The seven carrying this classification were former Blue Belle vehicles T 347, 350, 352 and ex-Queen Line T 353-355, 357. Five out of the seven were still in operation when the gas trailers were removed from 28th August 1944 onwards, after which they continued to run on petrol but with their engines still adjusted for gas, and with their towing eyes still attached, until full conversion back to petrol status could take place during November and December. In fact only two (T 347, 353) remained in service long enough to run in their original condition once again and the last of these, T 347, was de-licensed at Addlestone on 1st February 1945.

It will probably never be known why the 5T4s were selected for disposal in 1945. Logically, with their modern metal-framed bodywork still in good condition, they would have been better vehicles to have held back for further service than careworn 1/7T7/1s when it came to responding to the Ministry of War Transport's call for a fleet of buses to serve with the Allied Control Commission in war ravaged Europe. All 12 5T4s passed out of London Transport ownership in the first few days of May 1945, just before the war in Europe came to an end.

With the declaration of war only a few weeks away, T 354 stands in Hertford bus station alongside Ransomes-bodied ST 1085. T 354 was just a short term resident at Hertford garage but ST 1085 was a feature of the local scene for many years, remaining there all through the war and beyond until the first delivery of new RTs. Both vehicles display the new Lincoln green livery which T 354 received in October 1938 and the ST two months later. *D Evans © Omnibus Society*

T 354 again, this time passing through Slough early in the war with its roof now camouflaged with grey paint and the customary white wartime mudguard markings and headlamp masks. The photograph was taken before it received wartime green and white livery upon overhaul in June 1940. T 354 had arrived on Windsor's allocation in August 1939 and went on to serve at Luton, St Albans, Leavesden Road and Hertford before being converted to gas operation at Leatherhead in June 1943. *Frank Willis*

T 355 was one of seven 5T4s converted for producer gas operation and temporarily reclassified 13T4/1. Displaying the green and white colours which it gained in January 1943, T 355 is seen with trailer in tow heading on route 462 towards its home garage at Leatherhead. Although the rear registration number is not carried on the trailer, it is located in a conspicuous position across the back window of the bus. At the time, most buses serving Weybridge were camouflaged with grey paint because of the strategic importance to the war effort of the Vickers works, but this did not apply to vehicles on route 462 as these did not enter the company's premises. *C F Klapper © Omnibus Society*

# 9 THOMAS TILLING
## T 307-318

The London bus fleet of Thomas Tilling was by far the largest and most high-profile operation in the capital outside of the Underground group and it was run with the same regard for efficiency and cost-cutting as the LGOC. In fact, when it came to vehicle design and specification it probably adopted a more parsimonious approach than General and its associates, struggling hard to keep unit costs down while not benefiting from anything like the same economy of scale. The Tilling operation was kept in the public eye by its large fleet of double deckers many of which were employed on trunk central London services, and comparatively few observers probably realised that it was responsible for one solitary single deck service deep in the southern suburbs on which, from August 1932 onwards, it employed a small fleet of twelve AEC Regals.

Thomas Tilling Ltd was a long-established business with its headquarters at 20 Victoria Street SW1. It could trace its history right back to its jobmaster origins in 1840, with expansion into the bus business following in 1851, the year of the Great Exhibition. Although much of its twentieth century development had been achieved by gaining financial control of established bus operators throughout the British Isles, it continued to maintain its London bus business, and also a branch in Brighton, as a directly controlled operation under

its own name. Outright competition with the LGOC had been eschewed by sharing in the London Omnibus 'Pool', the first written agreement having been signed by the two parties on 15th May 1912. This was updated from time to time, and the most recent agreement signed on 11th November 1929 and valid for ten years stipulated that Tilling would work five per cent of vehicles within the Pool. This meant that the actual number that it ran was adjusted from time to time. In addition to Tilling's own fleet it also worked by agreement a number of LGOC-owned vehicles built and painted to Tilling's own specification and referred to by both operators as "transferred omnibuses". The single deckers employed on route 109 (Penge–Welling) fell within this category.

Brand new, and marking a vast improvement in speed and comfort over the now departed petrol electrics, T 311 terminates outside the Crooked Billet in Penge, having arrived on a Saturdays-only short working from Bromley which, under the Bassom system, was numbered 109A. Its LGOC-allocated fleet number can be seen in neat white lettering on the offside dumbiron. Standing behind T 311 is the LGOC's 'Scooter' LT 1090 providing an alternative albeit slightly longer means of getting to Bromley via route 609. There is a marked difference in height between the two vehicles.

The Tilling operation was unusual in that it employed no inspectors or timekeepers, these services being hired from the LGOC which also provided tickets, waybills and punches. The latter also decided which services Tilling's buses would operate and their frequency, and it also owned the three garages from which the vehicles ran – Bromley, Catford and Croydon. On the engineering side of its affairs, Tilling operated totally independently of the LGOC, both in regard to the vehicles within its ownership and those supplied by the LGOC, which it treated as though they were its own. In 1930 General owned 114 buses out of a Tilling London bus fleet of 364.

By 1932 the time had arrived to replace the small fleet of Tilling Stevens TS7 petrol electrics employed on route 109. These were owned by the LGOC and known as the O-type. As Tilling was now standardising on AECs for its London and Brighton fleets as successors to its famous petrol electrics, it was inevitable that Regals would be chosen to work the 109, and the LGOC duly issued a purchase sanction on its behalf for 12 Regals followed by a separate sanction for a single body to be used as an overhaul float. The LGOC fleet numbers T 307-318 were reserved for them, following on from the last batch of Green Line vehicles delivered at the start of 1931.

The thirteen bodies were designed by Tilling to their own specification and built by them in their coachbuilding factory at High Street, Lewisham, known as the Obelisk Works but sometimes referred to as Salisbury Yard. This was one of three coachbuilding establishments maintained by Tilling in the London area (more details of which can be found in the companion volume on the ST class) in addition to another one at Conway Street, Hove. The Company had found that, by using direct labour to build its own bodies, these could be obtained far cheaper than if they were bought from outside manufacturers, and in fact there was little difference in cost between bodies constructed in Tilling's workshops and those produced by the LGOC at Chiswick.

Although these were the first Regals to join Tilling's London bus fleet, they were not the first that they had operated. The Company had taken delivery of eighteen in January and March 1931 in the form of coaches for their contract and hire operations, but these were unsuitable for bus work and were never used on it. The twelve new chassis were similar to those delivered to the LGOC two years earlier for T 1-50 except that the chassis frame behind the rear axle was shortened by 3½ inches, perhaps to eliminate unnecessary weight. The latest features were fitted such as hydraulic brakes and a Ripault centralised chassis lubrication system, and the engines were of a special low powered type specified by Tilling for most of its London vehicles, Regents as well as Regals, which had sleeved Specialloid pistons but a bore of only 95mm. This specially derated version of the A140 (coded A140E) produced a swept volume of only about 5.5 litres, and though it presumably secured improved fuel economy, it would have produced a less lively performance than could be obtained on a standard Regal. Also presumably as a weight or cost saving economy, or both, Tilling did not require self starters, a most unusual omission as late as 1932. The twelve chassis were 6621134-1145, and at Tilling's request the first two of these (T 307, 308) were fitted with D128 Wilson preselector gearboxes and fluid flywheels; the remainder had standard clutches and D124 crash gearboxes. The preselector vehicles had 6¼:1 axle ratios as did two of the crash gearbox ones; the remainder were 5¾:1.

The Tilling designed bodies would have seemed very conventional in styling had it not been for their exceptionally wide combined destination and route number screens which occupied almost the whole width of the body, front and rear, and projected slightly above the main roof line. There were no glass louvres or metal rail shields even over the opening windows, and all the windows were rounded at their top corners. These vehicles had a firm character of their own and were always instantly recognisable. The thirteen bodies were

Also at Penge, and demonstrating the nearside lines of the Tilling built body, is T 309 awaiting departure on a through trip to Eltham. The driver's door, which has been left swinging open, is a luxury that the LGOC did not consider necessary for its own drivers, but the most prominent feature of these vehicles was their excellent route number and destination display.
*C F Klapper © Omnibus Society*

built alongside a current order for STL double deck bodies and a family resemblance was evident, especially in their internal fittings. Although it may have seemed profligate to build a spare body to provide an overhaul float for only twelve vehicles, which meant that the thirteenth body would remain unused for most of each year, it was in fact very necessary because of the tightness within which Tilling ran its only single deck operation. Route 109 needed eleven buses to operate a full schedule on most days of the week, leaving just one vehicle spare for maintenance and general repair work. On Saturdays all twelve were needed in service. This gave a window of only five working days – Monday to Friday – within which each overhaul could take place, a target which would be unachievable without having a spare body readily available. Chassis and engine overhauls were carried out in Tilling's main workshop at Bull Yard, Peckham, but bodies were overhauled in the Company's other workshops and the spare body was kept at Lewisham when not required for use.

According to one contemporary report the bodies were built as 28-seaters, but this has not been substantiated and they certainly seated 30 by August 1933. Built to a front entrance design, and lacking any enclosing door in compliance with current Metropolitan Police requirements, they looked quite smart in Tilling's dark red and cream livery. Internally they exuded a greater degree of opulence than was apparent in contemporary LGOC bodies through the generous use of mahogany on all the window surrounds and ceiling mouldings, brought to a high gloss finish by being cellulose sprayed to maximise wear resistance. Tubular framed seats were installed, which were a big advance in comfort over the low-backed wooden framed ones that the LGOC was using at the time; they were upholstered in Tilling's own style of moquette and had repp-covered backs. In common with the LGOC, Tilling favoured the use of Numa air-operated bells although these did not turn out to be as satisfactory as hoped and were replaced in early London Transport days by electric bells.

Tilling used the LGOC's fleet numbers for the Regals, which were painted in the Company's usual fashion in discreet white numerals on the offside front dumbiron. By chance, the batch of registration numbers issued for them by London County Council was GY 8408-8419 which meant that

they could be manipulated so that the last two digits matched the fleet number with the exception of T 307 which was GY 8419. The first one to be made available at Bromley garage was T 309 on 25th August 1932 and all twelve were in use by 6th October. The two preselector vehicles, T 307 and T 308, were licensed together on 29th September but presumably driver training had to take place on them before revenue earning could begin as they were the only vehicles in the Tilling fleet with this type of transmission. With the demise of Tilling's London operation on the horizon under the provisions of the London Passenger Transport Act, the new Regals were destined for a very truncated career in the Company's service. Some just managed to achieve a full year while others missed out on doing so by just a few days.

The twelve Regals automatically became the property of the LPTB on 1st July as successor to the LGOC, but they remained part of the Tilling fleet for the time being. Following preliminary discussions between the two parties, it had been fully expected both at 55 Broadway and 20 Victoria Street that the Tilling operations would be handed over to London Transport on 1st August 1933. However this was thwarted, mainly because of an acrimonious disagreement between the two parties over compensation terms, with the result that the Appointed Day was delayed until Sunday 1st October 1933 when the assets were finally transferred. The twelve Regals retained their identities as T 307-318 and the twelve bodies then in use were given new body numbers 13834-13845 in vehicle order with the spare one becoming 13846. These replaced Tilling's own body numbers (X 807, 808, 912-917, 925-928, 942) but not in the same sequence. Their first overhaul programme had already been completed under Tilling's auspices and none of the bodies were still on their original chassis.

T 314 pauses in High Street, Bromley while passengers walk out to board on its westbound run to Penge. Although still bearing Tilling colours and fleet name, standard London Transport features such as the gold fleet number and aluminium running plates indicate that the vehicle is now under new ownership. A further London Transport feature, added just after the takeover, is the offside route number stencil. T 314 was the penultimate one of its class to retain Tilling livery and gained fleet colours in November 1934. *C F Klapper*

Having been overhauled just prior to the London Transport takeover, the Ts found themselves among the last to display the Tilling livery and fleet name which they did until the next overhaul cycle commenced in May 1934, and none are thought to have carried the interim GENERAL fleet name used on a large number of acquired vehicles including many ex-Tilling double deckers. However it was not long after takeover before they received LGOC style fleet numbers, while the Tilling running number and garage code plates were replaced by standard LGOC-type stencils. The last single decker to bear the Tilling name, T 318, went to Chiswick for overhaul on 28th November 1934.

The first Chiswick overhaul cycle saw a number of alterations and improvements initiated on the 'Tilling Ts', as they became universally known. Some improvements had to be made to appease the driving staff who, perfectly justifiably, expected the ex-Tilling vehicles to be brought up to the same standards as the rest of the of the London Transport fleet, of which they were now a part. The biggest complaint was the absence of self starters, and an agreement made between Frank Pick and the Transport & General Workers' Union on 31st October 1933 to fit anti-backfire starting handles as soon as possible did nothing to fulfill the staff's basic requirement. Eventually the provision of self starters began in February 1934 but it progressed very slowly and only speeded

up in October after industrial action had been taken. Improvements to the cabs and windscreens were made on overhaul, and a start was made on replacing the 5.52 litre engines with standard 6.26 litre ones, again largely to satisfy operating staff unhappy with the road performance of the ex-Tilling vehicles. An alteration which changed the appearance of the vehicles to a considerable degree was the reduction in size of the front and rear destination displays to enable the indicator boxes to accept the Board's standard width single deck blinds. As a result, large blank spaces painted in the roof colour of silver were created on either side, and because the depth of the screen was not increased, it was inevitable that not all the lettering on each display could be fully seen. This remained the case on the Tilling Ts throughout the rest of their working career.

T 307-318 were still at Bromley when route 109 was renumbered 227 upon abandonment of the Bassom numbering system on 3rd October 1934. By now it had been decided to convert the two preselector vehicles to ordinary clutch and crash gearbox transmission and T 307 had, in fact, already been dealt with while it was being overhauled in September. T 308 was converted less promptly, and it was still in original condition when it was transferred to Hornchurch garage on 3rd January 1935, the first of the class to leave its native Bromley. It is thought that it may have been sent there to try

Nearly all the Tilling Ts received London Transport colours in September and October 1934, and at the same time they were given modified destination displays as represented here by newly repainted T 315, seen at Eltham church soon after the 109 had been renumbered 227, and out-of-service and possibly broken-down T 309 at Bromley North. The wide expanse of white paint on either side of the destination box of T 315 has been alleviated to an extent by painting the framework of the opening section in black. A minor modification carried out at the same time was the insertion of a grab handle in the panel behind the driver's cab to make climbing into and out of it a little easier.
*J F Higham © A B Cross/ Alan Nightingale collection*

T 309 illustrates the varied uses to which the Tilling Ts were put after being usurped from their original base at Bromley. The first view shows it passing through Addlestone on its way to Woking on route 219. Although officially on the books of Kingston garage, it was actually operating from the Weybridge (WB) outstation on this occasion. The front destination box surround is not picked out in black on this vehicle, and the side lights have been slightly raised so that they now sit above cant rail level. After five weeks off the road in Chiswick Works between March and May 1939, T 309 appeared in the far north of Central Bus territory on the first occasion that an ex-Tilling vehicle had appeared at Enfield garage. A major overhaul had been carried out on the bodywork during which the interior of the saloon had been revamped in a modern, STL-style two-colour scheme, a rare occurrence on this type of vehicle. *C F Klapper © Omnibus Society/D Evans © Omnibus Society*

the transmission out in a different type of operating environment, but T 308 returned to Bromley on 20th March and was converted to crash gearbox at its next overhaul in July 1935. Resulting from this the whole batch was now categorised as 3T3 under the Chiswick coding system, and the 4T3/1 code applied to the preselectors fell into disuse.

All twelve vehicles stayed together at Bromley until March and April 1936 when they were moved out upon the arrival of an equivalent number of LT-type six-wheelers which, being 35-seaters, provided valuable extra carrying capacity that the 227 now needed. Initially they were kept together as a batch and transferred to Kingston garage whose fleet consisted predominantly of single deckers, but they could also regularly be found running from the small outpost at Weybridge which had no regular vehicle allocation of its own and was supplied from Kingston. This situation lasted only a little over a year when a clear change of policy was introduced whereby the Tilling Ts were no longer to be kept together but would henceforth be treated as interchangeable with the 1T1s. The first manifestation of this came in July 1937 when three were transferred to Old Kent Road, and the remaining pre-war years found specimens of the class at garages as widely dispersed as Cricklewood, Enfield, Hornchurch, Hounslow and Uxbridge. However for many years the best place to find 3T3s at work remained Kingston where seven out of the twelve were on books at the outbreak of war, and also at its Weybridge outstation until this closed as a wartime economy on 6th December 1939.

Another policy change to affect the class in 1937 was a decision to stop moving bodies from one chassis to another on overhaul. The last such change took place in March 1937 after which all twelve vehicles retained their existing body for the rest of their London career. Even earlier than this it had been deemed uneconomic to keep a spare body for such a small number of vehicles and in September 1936 body 13841, which had been last used on T 318 up to February 1936, was painted green for country service and placed on the former St Albans & District chassis of T 370. In this form it lasted only until October 1939 when it was the first of the Tilling T bodies to be scrapped.

The Tilling Ts worked solidly throughout the war, during which all of them were fitted with perimeter seating in January and February 1942, giving them the capacity to carry 48 (28 seated and 20 standing). There were no wartime casualties within the batch and on the resumption of peace in May 1945 they could be found at four garages: Kingston (7), Enfield (3), Hounslow (1) and Uxbridge (1). By January 1946 all had been re-converted to transverse seating with the exception of T 307 and T 316 which retained their wartime layout until they went for scrap four years later.

Just before the end of the war and in the months shortly after it the Tilling Ts were given their last real overhaul with the exception of T 313 and T 314 which were dealt with belatedly at Reigate during the first half of 1946. Thereafter, apart from the odd chassis overhaul and some occasional repainting, no major work was carried out on them, but despite the ever more evident sagging of their waistrails they were allowed to continue in service throughout the difficult early post-war years. In common with the 1/7T7/1s drafted in for central area work, they often appeared dowdy and a bit run-down, but they performed a valuable role and none of them was condemned as unfit to continue until T 309 at Sutton and T 318 at Sidcup had to be written off in December 1948.

The post-war years saw the Tilling Ts spreading their wings more widely than ever before although, once again, Kingston remained their main haunt. With its lower Monday to Friday vehicle requirement, Kingston was able to loan vehicles to other garages during the week, and in the late-1946/1947 period it was not unusual to find a Tilling T covering peak-time work from Leatherhead Country Bus garage. There were very few Central Bus garages with single deck allocations from which Tilling Ts did not work at one time or another during the later nineteen-forties, either as part of their official allocation or as temporary loans. They were moved around quite often to meet changing rolling stock requirements and only two – T 311 at Hounslow and T 316 at Kingston – remained at a single garage throughout the post-war era. A snapshot taken on 1st June 1948 would find

During the late wartime years and into the post-war era, the box-like areas on either side of the destination displays were painted in the standard brown roof colour which helped them to merge into the background a little better than they had done in pre-war times. Kingston-based T 308 still displayed its white wartime disc at the back when photographed in January 1948. Deterioration was now setting in fast, and later in the year – in June and July – T 308 founds itself at Chiswick for a chassis overhaul, returning there in August for 'wear and tear' repairs on the body followed by an exterior repaint. T 311, which was a long term resident at Hounslow from November 1942 through to its demise in February 1949, could be readily distinguished from the front by the fact that its destination glass was shallower than usual. It is seen here, near the end of its operating career, running on loan to Uxbridge which was never allocated a Tilling T of its own after 1946. *Alan B Cross*

them at Kingston (5) and Hornchurch (3), plus one each at Dalston, Elmers End, Enfield and Hounslow.

The final year of service operation was 1949. By now the lack of adequate preventative maintenance coupled with advancing old age meant that the vehicles were really beginning to look very tired, and with the class becoming ever more susceptible to the ravages of the Ministry of Transport's unannounced inspections and the fatal PSV71 'stop' certificates that resulted from them, it is surprising that so many lasted in service for as long as they did. However 1949 saw them falling steadily, one by one, to the point that by June all those that remained were concentrated at Kingston where only five were still serviceable by the end of that month. The last of these, T 308, was withdrawn from service on 1st October 1949.

By the end of 1949 all of them had headed for the scrapyard with the exception of T 317 for which other plans existed. Last operated at Tottenham, where it was withdrawn on 2nd May 1949, T 317 was repainted at Chiswick and fitted with a swing door at the top of the entrance steps in preparation

for a new career as an accident demonstration unit. With its external appearance otherwise completely unchanged, it travelled to garages and depots throughout the fleet to demonstrate ways in which accidents could be avoided, particularly during boarding and alighting. Although the requirement for it in this rather specialist role subsequently diminished, T 317 continued to remain active both as a training vehicle for the diminishing number of staff needing to master the intricacies of the crash gearbox, and also as a general runabout for staff at Chiswick. Officially allocated initially to Chiswick itself, it was placed on Hounslow garage's books for maintenance purposes from May 1951 onwards. This extension to its normal life span brought T 317 the accolade of being the very last petrol engined bus in use within the London Transport fleet. The curtain finally closed on its long career when it was delicensed on 1st July 1952, an equally obsolete but diesel powered replacement having become available in the form of T 31. Transferred to the Forest Road yard for storage, T 317 went to the scrap merchant in January 1953.

The survivor. With a door fitted at the top of the entrance steps but otherwise externally unmodified, T 317 could often be found in and around Chiswick Works, and is seen on 19th May 1951 close to the new training school then under construction. It carries a Chiswick (CS) allocation plate, and the notice on the window behind the doorway reads 'Chiswick Accident Demonstration Unit'. *Alan Pearce*

# 10 A GREEN LINE INTERLUDE

In the foregoing chapters the use of T types on Green Line operations has been mentioned on numerous occasions. Such use was widespread; indeed the phenomenal growth of the Green Line network would not have occurred without the ready availability of so many new Regals. Many Ts were dedicated solely to Green Line duties in early years, but such was the flexibility of the overall set-up that many others were employed only on a 'when necessary' basis despite wearing Green Line colours. Viewed after the passage of more than eighty years, the situation can sometimes seem confusing, the confusion being compounded by the various ownerships in which the Ts were vested prior to the formation of the London Passenger Transport Board in 1933.

Today, it is hard to imagine the vibrancy and great spirit of enterprise that must have permeated through the whole Green Line enterprise during its formative period. The sheer scale of work involved in setting up so many new services within a very short time is something that probably could not be replicated in today's much more cautious climate where the mere idea of committing to heavy capital expenditure, often on the basis of little more substantial than intuition

and self-belief, would be an anathema to investors who would wish to commission lengthy and expensive consultants' reports before authorising any move. Back then, the acquisition and commissioning for service of no fewer than 250 purpose-built Regal coaches over a short space of time was a massive achievement in itself, coupled to which were all the logistical problems that had to be solved such as setting-up operating bases, finding and training staff, dealing with a multiplicity of local councils, arranging timetables and publicity, plus all the minutiae of daily operations such as procuring tickets, waybills, uniforms, and much more.

A little puff of exhaust comes from Duple bodied T 270 as it pulls away from the stop at Great Scotland Yard, roughly mid-way on its journey from Ascot to Dartford. A would-be passenger appears to be too engrossed in studying the impressive array of Green Line timetables to notice it go. The vehicle would have been allocated to one or other of the garages at Staines and Crayford, which were responsible for operating the basic Ascot service on non-race days. Coaches on Green Line route A were scheduled to operate alternately to Ascot and Sunningdale and the provision of a reversible slip board on the side information panel reflects this.

The Green Line operation was capable, in its early years, of responding to enormous peaks of demand and none more so than on route A to Ascot on major race days when up to 50 vehicles could be mustered to provide a service of 12 coaches or more per hour from Horse Guards Avenue through to the race course car park. We are fortunate that two recordings, taken at Great Scotland Yard and Grosvenor Road by inspectors W T Robinson and H Olding on Friday 16th June 1933 still survive to this day, and an extract from Mr Olding's Grosvenor Road recordings showing that 35 vehicles passed the point between 9.00am and 12 noon is given (right). With the great majority of coaches full to capacity with passengers paying 3s 6d for a return ticket from central London to Ascot (and more if they had come from further afield), it represented a very lucrative morning's work for the Green Line organisation. The record shows graphically how the use of regular Green Line Ts (in this case T 38, 67, 116, 159, 257, 264 and 287) was augmented within a 3-hour period by no fewer than 28 other coaches including eleven miscellaneous T-types along with various ADCs, Reliances, Gilfords and a solitary Thornycroft. Only the registration numbers of the vehicles were recorded at the time, but an explanation of what each one was has been added in the right hand column.

All the coaches in the list were in Green Line colours but GF 5 still carried the Skylark name. The Reliances were 28-seat 'all-weather' coaches from the private hire fleet, and the six ADC 419s represented a complete batch of all-weather 28-seat touring coaches bought by East Surrey in 1927. The latter were almost at the end of their working lives and were withdrawn from service soon afterwards. The Autocar vehicles would have been performing some of their last duties on Green Line work, being scheduled to pass into Maidstone & District control a fortnight later.

| Time (am) | Coach reg. no. | Passenger loading | and stock no. |
|---|---|---|---|
| 9.00 | UU 6602 | 22 | R 32 |
| 9.13 | UU 6604 | Full | R 30 |
| 9.16 | GH 3820 | Full | T 264 |
| 9.22 | UU 6602 | Full | R 28 |
| 9.28 | UV 4087 | Full | TH 2 (ex-Great Western Railway) |
| 9.35 | PL 6469 | Full | T 317 (LGCS ex-East Surrey) |
| 9.40 | MT 1954 | Full | GF 5 (ex-Skylark) |
| 9.42 | PL 6467 | Full | T 315 (LGCS ex-East Surrey) |
| 9.48 | UU 6653 | 19 | T 38 |
| 9.53 | GC 6351 | Full | GF 30 (ex-Associated (Ongar)) |
| 9.56 | UR 5887 | Full | GF 26 (ex-Bucks Express) |
| 10.07 | UU 6607 | Full | R 33 |
| 10.10 | GJ 8072 | Full | T 350 (ex-Blue Belle) |
| 10.15 | PL 6475 | Full | T 323 (LGCS ex-East Surrey) |
| 10.21 | UV 74 | 18 | GF 20 (ex-Regent Motor Services) |
| 10.28 | KR 3238 | 16 | T 327 (Autocar) |
| 10.36 | PL 6476 | Full | T 324 (LGCS ex-East Surrey) |
| 10.40 | GN 2191 | Full | T 287 |
| 10.45 | PH 1209 | Full | Un-numbered ADC 419 |
| 10.49 | KR 3568 | 18 | T 335 (Autocar) |
| 10.54 | PG 7840 | 22 | T 313 (LGCS ex-East Surrey) |
| 10.57 | PH 1204 | Full | Un-numbered ADC 419 |
| 11.02 | PH 1208 | Full | Un-numbered ADC 419 |
| 11.03 | PH 1206 | Full | Un-numbered ADC 419 |
| 11.10 | UU 6601 | Full | R 27 |
| 11.10 | PH 1205 | Full | Un-numbered ADC 419 |
| 11.14 | PL 6472 | Full | T 320 (LGCS ex-East Surrey) |
| 11.16 | GF 509 | Full | T 116 |
| 11.22 | PG 7682 | Full | T 310 (LGCS ex-East Surrey) |
| 11.26 | GH 3800 | Full | T 257 |
| 11.30 | KR 3237 | 24 | T 326 (Autocar) |
| 11.35 | GF 588 | Full | T 159 |
| 11.40 | PH 1207 | Full | Un-numbered ADC 419 |
| 11.45 | GF 522 | Full | T 67 |
| 11.55 | UR 4879 | Full | GF 25 (ex-Bucks Express) |

One of Green Line's less successful ventures was the opening on Christmas day 1930 of its new Poland Street coach station in a side street near Oxford Circus on a former brewery site. With a contemporary art deco exterior, floodlit at night, and internal waiting room and refreshment facilities, it soon echoed constantly to the sound of 27 coaches an hour, plus duplicates. Most were AEC Regals such as Short-bodied T 144, Guildford based vehicle seen on one of the first services to use the coach station. The building's period of glory was short lived. So many coaches an hour created their own traffic congestion in Soho's narrow streets, and the cross-linking of services greatly reduced the station's usefulness. It closed in October 1933 after less than three years. T 144 was one of many 7T7s to depart from the fleet in the later part of 1938. *London Transport Museum*

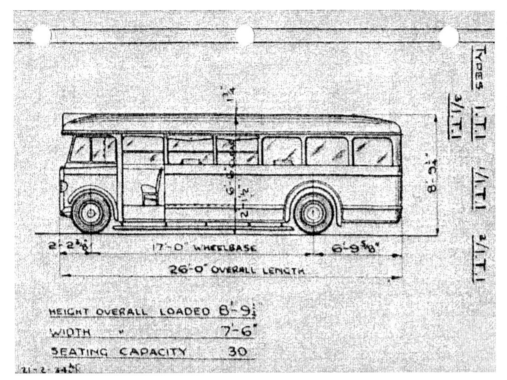

HEIGHT OVERALL LOADED 8'-9¼"
WIDTH  "  7'-6"
SEATING CAPACITY  30

The setting-up of the vehicle coding system occupied several weeks in early 1934. Intended to be implemented in March, some of the detailed work in fact took long than this to complete. To assist staff in the use of the coding system, handy description cards were drawn up bearing basic information and dimensions relating to each code type. Separate chassis and body cards were provided, and this example – dated 21st February 1934 – is the body card relating to the 1T1 and its various sub-categories.

# 11 CHISWICK WORKS AND THE CODING SYSTEM

In the two companion volumes to this one, dealing with the LT and ST classes, we saw how the LGOC's legendary bus overhauling factory at Chiswick tackled with great efficiency the complex task of overhauling the Company's large fleet using industrial style flow-line processes to ensure that each vehicle was accommodated approximately once every year. The system, which required chassis and bodies to be dealt with on completely separate production lines, was best suited to sizeable batches of closely related vehicles where widespread unit interchangeability could be utilised to achieve maximum efficiency. Because bodies almost always took longer to overhaul than chassis, it seldom happened that the same two were married back together after overhaul unless there was a specific reason for doing so, and the Company's laudable aim of extracting maximum financial value from each road fund disc meant that complete vehicle identities were changed at overhaul to avoid any disc being out of use longer than was absolutely necessary. This meant that, theoretically at least, no individual licence was out of use for more than a day or two while, quite frequently, an overhauled vehicle would emerge from Chiswick bearing the identity of another that had arrived for overhaul on that very same day. This same overhauling process persisted into London Transport days although, thanks to improvements in vehicle construction and design, it became possible to widen the period between overhaul from the mid-nineteen thirties onwards, until the whole process was thrown into disarray upon the outbreak of war.

In the case of single deckers, which only ever played a

comparatively minor role within the LGOC fleet, the same economies of scale could not be achieved. It was clearly not economically sound to purchase the spare bodies and chassis necessary to operate a full flow-line system when the overhaul cycle was likely to occupy only a small portion of each year, in effect leaving capital tied up for months on end without being usefully employed. It was only when the 266 strong 10T10 class was purchased in 1938 that spare bodies were obtained for the T class with the intention of setting up an overhaul float, but war broke out before the first overhaul cycle could commence so these were never used as intended.

During the war, and in the early post-war years which followed, bodies continued to be lifted at overhaul but they were almost always re-united with the same chassis and the changing of identities ceased. It was not until 1955 when the ultimately ill-fated Aldenham works came fully into its own that pre-war methods were resumed, but by this time the T class had diminished to a relatively insignificant minority status, and although 26 of the relatively modern 14T12 type were overhauled between September 1955 and February 1957, followed by nine of the even newer 15T13s between May 1957 and March 1958, none of these were dealt with at Aldenham and no body or chassis exchanges occurred.

Two notable exceptions to the principle of retaining original identities for the T class upon overhaul need to be recorded. One took place between October 1931 and January 1932 when, for their second overhaul cycle, a double deck style flow-line system was applied to the bulk of vehicles in the T 1-50 series by temporarily withdrawing two of them from circulation to serve as 'floats' as explained in chapter 1. As a result of this each vehicle concerned adopted a different identity from its original at overhaul; the only occasion on which this occurred within the T class. The other exception was inherited from the Thomas Tilling organisation which habitually maintained spare bodies for its various classes of vehicle, including a spare to cover its twelve Regal buses T 307-318. These had already undergone one body change prior to acquisition by London Transport who continued this process with these twelve vehicles through to 1937 as described in chapter 9.

The coding system for chassis and bodies for which London Transport became renowned was developed soon after the Board's formation. Work on organising the system took place throughout the early months of 1934 in time for it to go live during March, but it covered initially only the Central Bus fleet including the main T class but excluding the three Chiswick-built vehicles T 1000-1002. Country Bus and Green Line vehicles were not brought within the system until responsibility for them was transferred from Reigate to Chiswick in February 1935. The idea was that each principle chassis batch would be allocated a number preceding its class letter, for example 7T was the code given to the first type of Green Line coach in the series T 51-149, 155, 157-206. Bodies were also coded except that in this case the classification number followed the class letter, this same batch of Green Line coaches being coded T7. The two were then put together for record purposes as 7T7. If a difference needed to be indicated, as with the next batch of coaches T 207-306, either on the chassis or the body, it was denoted with a stroke, thus the latter batch became 1/7T7/1. The chassis code for each vehicle was engraved on a brass plate for fixing to the nearside dumbiron, and similarly a brass plate with the body code was attached to the cab side just below the driver's window near the filler cap. A third brass plate, giving the fleet and chassis numbers, was screwed to the offside dumbiron.

The coding system worked well when applied to major classes by enabling compatible categories of chassis and body to be easily recognised when going through overhaul, and it was also beneficial to garage staff when determining and specifying their spare parts requirements. However it proved to be of little value on smaller classes, such as the various batches of Ts, and it did not work at all on the majority of vehicles acquired from other operators which were often lumped together under purely nominal codings despite mechanical and, more notably, body specifications varying greatly. As an example of this, the body code T6 was applied to a miscellany of acquired service buses with various types of bodywork while T8 through to T8/3 denoted a hotch-potch of coach bodies of all sorts of shapes and makes. There was even one glaring error, which was never corrected, whereby the unique short length Regal T 10, which should have been classified 2T2, was wrongly coded 1T1 while, conversely, T 43 which was a perfectly standard vehicle of the 1T1 type, received the erroneous classification 2T2 which it retained until the end of its operating career.

Confusion reigned right from the start over which vehicle should carry the unique classification 2T2 to denote its shorter length than all the others. A non-typical aberration within the normally immaculate record keeping at Chiswick resulted in the classification being awarded to T 43 whereas, from as far back as January 1932, this unique vehicle had been numbered T 10. This photograph, taken when no longer in use, confirms through its short penultimate rear bay that T 10 should really have been coded 2T2. *J H Aston*

Although the application of codes to the T class started off in good faith with the 1T1s, whose mechanical variations were carefully acknowledged through various sub-types, the system became corrupted in 1935 when expanded to cover the country area Ts. A good example of this could be found in the case of the one-time East Surrey saloons such as Hall Lewis bodied T 372 and Weymann bodied T 382 which were clearly not alike and were not even the same length as each other, but were both coded 4/1T6. T 372, with its single servo braking system and rear entrance body was 26ft long whilst triple servo T 382 had front entrance bodywork and was a full 1ft longer. T 372 was photographed after revised external panelling was fitted in January 1938 running from Hertford garage, while T 382, seen heading for the quaintly named destination of Cosy Corner, was a High Wycombe based vehicle when photographed in 1935. *AEC/ J F Higham © A B Cross*

CHASSIS CODES

SS – single servo
TS – triple servo
SH – servo-assisted hydraulic

| | Engine | Brakes | Gearbox | | |
|---|---|---|---|---|---|
| 1T | Petrol A140 | TS | Crash D124 | T 3–5, 9-12, 14, 17, 18, 20, 22-24, 29-32, 37, 41, 42, 44, 46-48, 50, 156 | (note a) |
| | Oil A173 | TS | Crash D124 | T 9, 11, 14, 17, 22-24, 30-32, 37, 41, 42, 44, 46, 156 | (note b) |
| 1/1T | Petrol A140 | SH | Crash D124 | T 1, 2, 6, 7, 28, 33, 34, 39, 40 | |
| | Oil A173 | SH | Crash D124 | T 1, 2, 28, 33, 34, 40 | (note b) |
| 2/1T | Petrol A145 | TS | Crash D124 | T 8, 16, 19, 27, 36, 45, 49 | |
| | Oil A173 | TS | Crash D124 | T 16, 27, 26, 45 | (note b) |
| 3/1T | Petrol A145 | SH | Crash D124 | T 13 | |
| 4/1T | Petrol A140 | SS | Crash D124 | T 369, 371 ex Watford Omnibus Co. | (note p) |
| | Petrol A140 | TS | Crash D124 | T 370 ex St Albans & District | |
| | Petrol A140 | SS | Crash D124 | T 372-379, 383-390 ex East Surrey | |
| | Petrol A140 | TS | Crash D124 | T 380-382 ex East Surrey | |
| 5/1T | Petrol A140 | TS | Crash D124 | T 15, 21, 25, 26, 35 | |
| 2T | Petrol A140 | TS | Crash D124 | T 43 short wheelbase chassis | (note c) |
| 3T | Petrol A140E | SH | Crash D124 | T 307, 309-318 ex Tilling | (note d) |
| 4T | Petrol A140E | SH | Preselect D128 | T 308 ex Tilling | (note e) |
| 5T | Petrol A140 | ? | Crash D124 | T 346-351 ex Blue Belle | (note f) |
| | Petrol A140/145 | TS | Crash D124 | T 346-357 ex Blue Belle and Queen Line | (note g) |
| 6T | Petrol A145 | ? | Crash D124 | T 352-357 ex Queen Line | (note f) |
| 7T | Petrol A140 | SS | Crash D124 | T 38, 51-149, 155 | (note q) |
| | Petrol A140 | TS | Crash D124 | T 157-206 | |
| 1/7T | Petrol A145 | TS | Crash D124 | T 207-306 (except T 216, 268, 274, 305) | (note h) |
| | Petrol A145 | TS | Crash D124 | T 391, 392 ex Bucks Express | (note i) |
| 2/7T | Oil A161 | TS | Crash D124 | T 216, 274, 305 | |
| | Oil A173 | TS | Crash D124 | T 396 | (note j) |
| 8T | Petrol A140 | SS | Crash D124 | T 150-154 | |
| | Petrol A140 | SS | Crash D124 | T 319-324, 399-402 ex East Surrey | |
| | Petrol A140 | TS | Crash D124 | T 393-398 ex East Surrey | |
| 1/8T | Petrol A140 | TS | Crash D124 | T 359, 361, 362, 364-366 ex Amersham & District | (note k) |
| | Petrol A ? | SS | Crash D124 | T 358 ex Aston | |
| | Petrol A140 | SS | Crash D124 | T 360, 363 ex Lewis | |
| | Petrol A140 | TS | Crash D124 | T 367, 368 ex Lewis | |
| 2/8T | Petrol A145 | TS | Crash D124 | T 391, 392 ex Bucks Express | (note l) |
| 9T | Oil A171 | SH | Preselect D132 | T 403-452 | |
| 10T | Oil A180 | SH | Preselect D132 | T 453-577, 603-718 originally | |
| 1/10T | Oil A180 | SH | Preselect D132 | T 578-602 (6¼ :1 rear axle) | (note m) |
| | Oil A180 | SH | Preselect D132T | 19 various (special gearbox) | (note n) |
| 2/10T | Oil A180 | SH | Preselect D132T | 19 various (special gearbox) | (note o) |
| 11T | Oil A 173 | TS | Crash D124 | 31 various | (note p) |
| 12T | Producer gas | TS | Crash D124 | T 273, 288 | |
| 13T | Producer gas | TS | Crash D124 | T 347, 350, 352-355, 357 | |
| 14T | Oil A173 | SH | Crash D124 | T 719-768 | |
| 15T | Oil A208 | Air | Preselect D140 | T 769-798 | |

| Notes: | (a) | T 10 classified as 1T in error for T 43 |
|---|---|---|
| | (b) | From 1950 onwards |
| | (c) | T 43 classified as 2T in error for T 10 |
| | (d) | T 307 originally intended to be coded 4T but modified before coding took place |
| | (e) | Modified to 3T in 1935 |
| | (f) | Code allocated but not used |
| | (g) | Rebuilt and fitted with new Weymann bodies 1935 |
| | (h) | T 120, 369 later also classified 1/7T. 26 rebuilt as 11T in 1938 |
| | (i) | Originally classified 2/8T |
| | (j) | Rebuilt and reclassified 2/7T 1938. Reclassified 11T later in same year |
| | (k) | T 359, 361, 362, 364 later rebuilt to 11T |
| | (l) | Later reclassified 1/7T |
| | (m) | 1938/1939 only |
| | (n) | In service use 1939 only |
| | (o) | In use 1946 onwards |
| | (p) | T 369 later rebuilt as 1/7T |
| | (q) | T 120 later rebuilt as 1/7T |

BODY CODES

| | Entrance Position | | Compatible Chassis | |
|---|---|---|---|---|
| T1 | Front | T 1-14, 16-20, 22-24, 27-34, 36, 37, 39-42, 44-50, 156 | 1T, 1/1T, 2/1T, 3/1T | (note a) |
| T1/1 | Rear | T 15, 21, 25, 26, 35 | 5/1T | (note n) |
| | Front | T 2, 9, 14, 16, 17, 22-24, 27, 28, 32, 36, 37, 40-42, 44, 46 | 1T, 1/1T, 2/1T | (note o) |
| T2 | Front | T 43 | 2T | (note a) |
| T3 | Front | T 307, 309-318 | 3T | (note b) |
| T3/1 | Front | T 308 | 4T | (note c) |
| T4 | Dual swing | T 346-351 | 5T | (note d) |
| | Front | T 346-357 | 5T | (note e) |
| T4/1 | Front | T 396 | 2/7T | (note f) |
| | Front | T 347, 350, 352-355, 357 (gas propulsion) | 13T | |
| T5 | Rear | T 352-357 | 6T | (note d) |
| T6 | Rear | T 369-379, 383-390 | 4/1T | |
| | Front | T 380-382 | 4/1T | |
| T7 | Rear swing | T 38 | 7T | |
| | Rear recessed | T 51-149, 155, 157-206 | 7T | |
| T7/1 | Front | T 207-231, 233-267, 269-306 | 1/7T, 2/7T | |
| | Front | T 391, 392 | 1/7T | (note g) |
| T7/2 | Front | T 232 | 1/7T | (note h) |
| | Front | T 273, 286 (gas propulsion) | 12T | |
| T8 | Dual swing | T 150-154 | 8T | |
| T8/1 | Front swing | T 319-324, 399-402 | 8T | |
| T8/2 | Dual swing | T 393-398 | 8T | |
| T8/3 | Rear | T 359, 361, 362, 364-366 | 1/8T | |
| | Dual swing | T 360, 363 | 1/8T | |
| | Rear | T 358, 367, 368 | 1/8T | |
| T8/4 | Front | T 391, 392 | 2/8T | (note i) |
| T9 | Front | T 403-452 | 9T | |
| T10 | Front | T 453-498, 500-521, 523-564, 566-598, 600, 601, 603-606 | 10T, 1/10T, 2/10T | (note j) |
| T10/1 | Front | T 522, 565, 599, 602, 607-718 | 10T, 1/10T, 2/10T | (note k) |
| T10/2 | Front | T 499 | 10T | |
| T10/3 | Front | Various | 10T | (note l) |
| T11 | Front | Various | 11T | (note m) |
| T12 | Front | T 719-768 | 14T | |
| T13 | Front | T 769-798 | 15T | |

Notes: (a)    T 10 and T 43 erroneously coded; should have been coded T2 and T1 respectively

(b)    T 307 originally intended to be T3/1 but modified before coding took place.
One spare body built; later placed on a 4/1T chassis as T 370

(c)    Modified to T3 standard 1935

(d)    Code allocated but never used

(e)    New Weymann bodies built 1935

(f)    Code used only in 1938; reclassified later in same year as T11

(g)    Formerly coded T8/4

(h)    New Weymann body built 1933

(i)    Later re-coded T7/1

(j)    40 re-coded T10/3 in 1951/52

(k)    3 spare bodies also built

(l)    40 vehicles re-coded from T10 in 1951/52 and repainted red

(m)    31 vehicles. Weymann 1935-built bodies fitted 1938

(n)    up to 1945

(o)    from 1949 onwards

KX 6785, Amersham & District's no. 34, must have looked impressively modern when introduced into service in April 1931, and with its deep, comfortable seats and luxurious dark curtains clearly visible through the low windows, it would certainly have stimulated trade on the company's trunk service to Windsor. In this 1933 view, it is about to depart from the northern terminus at Chesham.

# 12 AMERSHAM & DISTRICT AND LEWIS

**T 359-368**

Serving the country districts to the north west of London and straddling the Hertfordshire/Buckinghamshire border were two medium sized but high profile companies, both of which were notable for the strength of their efficient management, their successful pursuit of expansion and consolidation, and their enviable profitability. The Amersham & District Motor Bus & Haulage Company Ltd and the Lewis Omnibus Company Ltd, based in Amersham and Watford respectively, could both be viewed as examples of independent bus operation at its very best. However, hidden away below the surface in both companies were substantial shareholdings by larger

organisations which, though not quite sufficient to give a controlling interest in either case, proved invaluable in supplying the finance to permit growth, consolidation and essential fleet renewal. And both, independently of each other, turned away from other makes to buy AEC Regals when modernising their single deck fleets.

Amersham & District's origins dated back to 1919 and its strength lay mainly in the abilities of two local businessmen, its Chairman Charles Ivins and its Managing Director William Randall. The latter, in particular, was instrumental in building the business to the extent that, at the time of its

The Strachans bodywork incorporated the curved bulkhead window which was popularised by Wycombe Motor Bodies on Gilford chassis but was copied by a few other coachbuilders at the time. Amersham & District's no. 35 demonstrates the rear sliding door fitted to these vehicles while terminating at Windsor on a journey to the hospital with a vehicle from one of the many small operators which then served the town standing in the background. *Omnibus Society collection*

takeover by London Transport, it had garages at Amersham and High Wycombe and was operating 23 bus services, a London express run, and numerous excursions from Chesham and High Wycombe. In 1929 the LGOC acquired a 50% interest in the business through a nominee company, West Nominees Ltd, but such was its faith in the Amersham & District management that it never even troubled to exercise its option to nominate anyone to serve on the board of directors. Except where its interests immediately coincided with those of the LGOC, such as the London express service, Amersham & District was left to go completely its own way, and this included the purchase of new rolling stock. Under part V of the second schedule of the London Passenger Transport Act, Amersham & District was listed as an independent undertaking and it was finally acquired as such by the LPTB on 29th November 1933, whereupon the Board inherited an extensive inventory of rolling stock which included eleven AEC Regals.

The Lewis Omnibus Company Ltd could trace its entry into the passenger transport field back to 1920 when Frederick Lewis, its founder, purchased a single Ford-T charabanc. An astute businessman in the same mould as William Randall, Lewis made the most of the burgeoning demand for bus services in and around his home town of Watford, and strengthened the business in November 1929 when a substantial financial interest in it was acquired by the Metropolitan Railway. This was when the limited company was formed, and thereafter Lewis and the railway company held equal shares in it, though neither quite owned 50% because of the existence of a few small private shareholdings. The Metropolitan Railway was represented on the Lewis board of directors, and this proved a very harmonious arrangement with the two sides sharing a common distrust of the Combine and its various subsidiaries. Like Amersham & District, the Company operated from two garages, but these were both in Watford, the main one being in Cassiobury Park Avenue close to the Metropolitan Railway's Watford station, and the other right in the town centre at 25 Market Street. Although Lewis's bus operations fringed on those of Amersham & District the two did not compete except over the section between Chalfont St Giles, Gerrards Cross, Slough and Windsor, where traffic was so buoyant that there was plenty of room for all comers. The Lewis company was specifically designated under the London Passenger Transport Act for

acquisition by the Board because of the Metropolitan Railway's holding in it, but largely because of major clashes over compensation the business did not pass into complete London Transport ownership until 1st October 1933, at which time four modern AEC Regals were amongst the mixed fleet taken over.

Amersham & District's first experience in running AEC Regals came in January 1931 with the introduction of the Company's express service from Amersham to London. However this was worked on behalf of the LGOC and used standard Green Line rear-entrance T-type coaches, five of which were purchased by the Company during February 1931 and duly repainted into its own colours. The five vehicles, GF 535, 536, 543, 544, 550, retained their Green Line fleet numbers (T 69, 71, 89, 96 and 104 respectively) and, as far as is known, never intermingled with other vehicles in the Amersham & District fleet. Their story has already been told in chapter 2.

At the time, Amersham & District's first completely new Regal had been purchased from AEC and the chassis was at Strachans' works in Acton where its body was under construction. The Company had enjoyed a close relationship with Strachans over the years and most of its bodies were built by them. When it arrived, the new Regal was quite a striking addition to the fleet where it received the next fleet number in line, 34, and was registered KX 6785 ready to be licensed for service on 9th April 1931. Its long, low lines were enhanced by Amersham & District's very attractive rich shade of green with creamish-yellow upper parts picked out by contrasting mouldings and with prominent gold lining-out on the lower panels. The stylish fleet name, which was an unashamed copy of the one used by the larger Aldershot & District company, was a further attractive embellishment. The passenger entrance was at the rear where a sliding door was provided, the emergency exit being at the offside front. Although the interior was sumptuously furnished with curtains and high-backed moquette covered seats, and there was an external luggage rack on the roof, the principal employment for this new 30-seater was destined to be on bus rather than coach service, and it was on the prestige Windsor run that it could normally be found.

Over the course of the next four months three more Regals were received at Amersham which were identical to no. 34 except that they had 32 seats instead of 30. Nos. 35 and 36

In general appearance the Lewis Omnibus Company's Regals of June 1930 were not unlike the touring coaches added to the East Surrey and Autocar fleets at about the same time. Although Lewis described them as 'Pullman Coaches', and they were no doubt very comfortable to travel in, there was a certain ungainliness about their appearance. UR 8601, which was numbered R6 in the Lewis fleet, was one of a pair used mostly on the company's express services to the coast. *Ken Blacker collection*

(KX 7635, 7634) entered service on 26th October 1931 and no. 37 (KX 7886) on 1st January 1932. Two more joined them on 27th May 1932 which took fleet numbers from older and now withdrawn rolling stock to become nos. 4 (KX 8644) and 7 (KX 8643). This pair differed slightly from the earlier four in having a revised front dome arrangement and being devoid of a luggage rack on the roof. Apart from a solitary Gilford AS6 in May 1933, they were the last new vehicles to enter the Amersham fleet.

Lewis's first two Regals were the same age as the five Green Line style vehicles operated by Amersham & District on the London run, and although both sets of vehicles were classified as coaches they differed considerably from each other both in concept and in general appearance. The Lewis pair were licensed on 4th June 1930 as UR 8601 and 8602 in Lewis's maroon and cream livery with the prime intention of using them on the Company's regular express services to the coastal resorts of Portsmouth and Southsea (for the Isle of Wight) and to Clacton-on-Sea, a type of operation that Amersham & District did not undertake. They were un-ashamedly long distance 32-seater coaches in the then-modern idiom with strongly raked half canopy fronts to create an air of streamlining and speed, comfortable if a little cramped leather seats, and canvas roof centres which could be rolled back on fine days. Bodied by Harrington, they were described by the Company as combining "dignity and luxury". On days when the express services did not operate they were available for a whole host of excursions and tours, and when not required for these either, the Company was not above putting them on ordinary bus service despite the general unsuitability of their bodywork, especially in having two heavy swing doors, one at the front and the other at the rear. Like Amersham & District, Lewis gave its vehicles fleet numbers and UR 6801/6802 were R6 and R7 respectively.

The second pair of Lewis Regals came almost two years later and were registered on 10th May 1932 as JH 1915 and 1916 with fleet numbers R 9 and R 10. (The missing R fleet numbers were double deck AEC Regents which later became part of the ST class). Although once again bodied by Harrington, this time as 31-seaters, they looked nothing like the earlier pair and were much more in the dual purpose mould to better suit them for all facets of the Company's operations. Once again deep leather seats and a canvas roof centre were featured, and there was now a roof-mounted rack for carrying long distance passengers' luggage, but their basic contours were considerably more bus-like and a single sliding door was fitted at the rear to speed boarding and alighting. They were, in fact, ideal and handsome multi-use vehicles which could just as often be found at work on the Watford–Windsor stage carriage service as on the Company's coastal runs.

London Transport's takeover of the Lewis business on 1st October 1933 saw the immediate disposal of the express services, which the LPTB was not allowed to operate, along with most of the excursions and tours. However the remainder of the operation stayed unchanged for the time being. Despite having had ample notice of the takeover, the Country Bus & Coach department was not ready to absorb the extra operations at its Watford High Street garage, so Frederick Lewis was employed to continue running the business as before until it was able to do so. He finally relinquished control on 15th November 1933 although the Lewis schedules continued in operation, albeit from the Board's own premises, through to 31st January 1934.

Although it sold Lewis's non-stage carriage operations, London Transport retained the four Regal coaches, and an immediate start was made on repainting them into the standard country livery of green and black with GENERAL fleet name. Some vehicles appeared in this form even during the interim period in October/November while Frederick Lewis was still managing the operation. They were now, of course, employed solely on bus work, but this was about to change. Once the main rush of enforced acquisitions had ceased, the Board's officials had the opportunity to assess at greater leisure all of its acquired rolling stock to ascertain its mechanical and structural condition and to decide its future use, if any. As a result of this the four ex-Lewis Regals were placed on Green Line work at Grays for the next year or so even though the two older vehicles were not particularly popular there as they were amongst the very few Ts on Green Line with kerbside swing doors (the only others were T 38 and all-weather coaches T 309-324). By the start of the 1935 tours season all four had been selected by virtue of their comfortable seating and their opening roofs for reallocation to the prestigious private hire fleet based at Brixton. Apart from the two older ones having to return to Chiswick for leaking roofs to be attended to, they appear to have given complete satisfaction until new rolling stock became available at the end of 1937,

After takeover on 29th November 1933, the six Strachans bodied Regals stayed at their Amersham base for a number of years along with most of the 7T7s formerly operated by Amersham & District. However instead of being used on bus services, their main employment in London Transport days was as Green Line coaches for which they were suitably liveried and given brackets to support side route boards. Amersham garage – which was duly extended in size by the LPTB – had absorbed extra Green Line work from Leavesden Road following a reorganisation of services in the Watford area, and the Regals were handy to cover this work. Their one drawback was that they lacked saloon heaters, but this omission was rectified in about December 1933.

Perhaps because they were a type already familiar to the engineers, the six ex-Amersham & District and four ex-Lewis Regals were allocated fleet numbers much earlier than most other vehicles absorbed by the new Country Bus & Coach department. As they passed through the Reigate paint shop soon after acquisition they were allocated fleet numbers T 359-368 in the Green Line T series following on from the six Queen Line Regals acquired by Green Line in April 1933 and a solitary Regal taken over from Christopher Aston of Watford in May. At the same time, they were fitted with the old Green Line-style rectangular fleet number plates on their bonnet sides, and were the last to receive these. Because the ten vehicles were numbered upon arrival at Reigate, and their order of arrival was haphazard, the end result was a jumbled mixture from the two fleets as follows:

| T 359 | KX 7886 | ex Amersham |
| T 360 | UR 6801 | ex Lewis |
| T 361 | KX 7634 | ex Amersham |
| T 362 | KX 7635 | ex Amersham |
| T 363 | UR 6802 | ex Lewis |
| T 364 | KX 6785 | ex Amersham |
| T 365 | KX 8643 | ex Amersham |
| T 366 | KX 8644 | ex Amersham |
| T 367 | JH 1915 | ex Lewis |
| T 368 | JH 1916 | ex Lewis |

The second pair of Lewis Regals looked like, and indeed were, ideal and versatile dual purpose vehicles. The incorporation of an inset panel above the windows for promotional or advertisement purposes was a new feature at the time which was subsequently favoured by a number of coachbuilders during the nineteen-thirties. On this occasion JH 1915 (Lewis R 9) is seen working on the company's Watford–Windsor bus service.

The transfer of responsibility from Reigate to Chiswick in 1935 led to the allocation of body numbers to T 359-368 which, because they were issued when the vehicles went into the works for overhaul, ranged between 15377 and 16610. At about the same time they were brought within the coding system, with code 1/8T8/3 being allocated to all ten of them irrespective of the glaring differences in bodywork between the Amersham vehicles and the two pairs of ex-Lewis ones. The whole process seems to have been treated as little more than a paper exercise and the codes were never entered on to the record cards for the four ex-Lewis vehicles, which were now operating in the private hire fleet and may never have had their brass plates attached showing the code details.

The six Strachans Regals stayed true to their Amersham roots until early in 1937 but, in the meantime, changes were made to their external appearance. The first modifications were comparatively minor and involved moving the side lights from the front mudguards to the canopy and the removal of the luggage racks from the four vehicles fitted with them. Much bigger changes followed in 1936 when some, or perhaps all, were rebuilt with more substantial side pillars and square-cornered half-drop windows, together with the fitting of bus-style front indicator boxes which projected angularly above the roof line and completely ruined the frontal appearance of these formerly quite elegant vehicles.

The LPTB lost no time in repainting the Amersham & District and Lewis Regals into its Country Bus & Coach department's livery of green and black with GENERAL fleetnames. Still plying the Watford–Windsor route, JH 1915 is otherwise unaltered from its Lewis condition except that its black on white destination blinds have been replaced by others in a more conventional style. At this stage the vehicle has still to receive its official London Transport identity as T 367. *J F Higham © A B Cross*

The arrival of new 6Q6 coaches at Amersham made most of the Ts redundant there. T 364 was retained as a spare to cover duplicates etc, but the remainder were re-employed, two at Tring and three at Luton. Further changes resulted in the Luton trio moving again, this time to Romford (North Street), in October 1937. Later in that same month T 361 was seconded to the private hire fleet at Brixton, acting as a precursor for the remainder which followed suit early in April 1938 just in time for the start of the summer hiring season. By this time the dedicated private hire department at Brixton had been disbanded (on 22nd December 1937) and the transferred Regals became temporary Central Bus stock for one final summer in the hire fleet. Four were based at Clay Hall and two at Holloway until all six were delicensed on 1st October.

Meanwhile the arrival of the superb new LTC class coaches for private hire work from November 1937 meant that the four ex-Lewis Regals were now without work. London Transport appeared to be reluctant to dispose of them immediately, so between 1st and 4th December they were returned to the Green Line fleet to serve as stand-bys and duplicates. They were quite widely dispersed with T 360 going to High Wycombe and later Epping, T 363 to Staines and then Windsor, T 367 to Windsor, and T 368 to Tring and then Hemel Hempstead. However this arrangement proved short-lived, and in February and March 1938 all except T 367 were finally withdrawn from service pending disposal. The latter returned to private hire duties and was based at Holloway for one final season from 1st August. Like the Amersham & District vehicles, it was finally taken out of service on 1st October 1938.

For four of the Amersham vehicles this was by no means the end of the road. In November 1938 T 359, 361, 362 and 364 emerged from Chiswick with new oil engines and modern metal-framed Weymann bodies removed from older AEC Reliance chassis to form part of the 11T11 class described in chapter 16. Ahead of them stretched up to 14 more years of service, a reprieve twice as long as the time that they had already served.

According to their Chiswick record cards the other three 1st October withdrawals, ex-Amersham T 365 and 366 and ex-Lewis T 367, were also fitted with Weymann bodies at the same time as the others. The record card entries go on to say that these bodies were removed on 7th December 1938 and placed on T 223, 237 and 234 respectively, and that their old bodies were put back on and the vehicles subsequently sold. There is no mention of any of the three chassis being converted to diesel propulsion. The strong suspicion remains that none of the recorded body changes actually took place and that the initial record card entries were made in advance of events that were planned but subsequently amended, requiring the second entries to be made in order to set the record straight prior to the vehicles leaving the fleet.

An early repaint to prepare it for Green Line service was Amersham & District's KR 7634, which has also had its roof luggage rack removed. The Regals were issued with numbers in the T series and given rectangular Green Line style fleet number plates which, in KR 7634's case, denotes that it is now T 361. Behind it, the old company's name is still displayed on the frontage of the office block which had formerly served as Amersham & District's administrative base. *Alan B Cross*

A couple of years later, the location is still the same but the shop front has been repainted and T 366 (the last of the Amersham Regals KX 8644) now carries two tone green livery as well as a full set of Green Line route boards and running number plates. Its bonnet number plate is now also in the correct London Transport style. The side lights have been repositioned from the Amersham company's favoured spot on the front mudguards to either side of the destination box which, on the newest two Regals, was neater in style than on the earlier four. *D W K Jones*

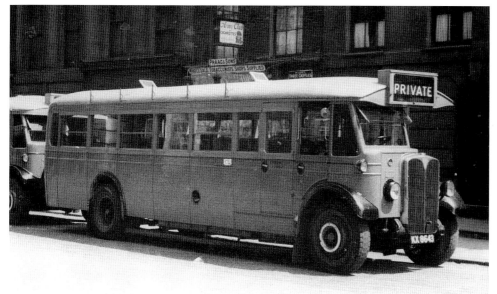

The final ignominy to befall the Amersham Regals was the rebuilding of their Strachans bodywork which, though probably necessary to retain structural integrity, did nothing to help their overall appearance. The square topped indicator boxes are particularly ungainly, and an unusual feature is that several side pillars are now of virtually double width, possibly to give extra strength but, equally likely, to permit the purchase and fitment of proprietary half-drop windows in place of the original full-drop arrangement. In their final days, under Central Bus control as private hire vehicles, a pair of them are seen operating from Clay Hall garage with T 365 in front and T 359 behind. *Dave Jones collection*

Ex-Lewis T 363's final year in the private hire fleet was 1937 during which it is seen standing in the sunshine with its roof rolled fully back during a lull on a hire job for the well-known tour agents Dean & Dawson. It has barely altered in appearance from Lewis days with the obvious exception of its livery; even the outlet for the bulb horn remains in its unusual original location above the bulkhead front window. *D W K Jones*

# 13 FOUR MORE HERTS REGALS

## T 358, 369-371

The pleasant county of Hertfordshire, which in the early nineteen-thirties had still to develop into the bustling commuter belt territory that it is today, was the place to go to find AEC Regals running in the ownership of small independent operators. Some have already featured in earlier chapters: the four Lewis vehicles in chapter 12, Queen Line's six in chapter 8, and the Bucks Express pair in chapter 7. Four others remain to be described, in three different ownerships. T 358 was brought into the main fleet with the purchase of Christopher Aston's business just before the formation of London Transport, as were T 369 and T 371 from the Watford Omnibus Company, while T 370 came from St Albans & District as the result of a compulsory purchase which took place later in 1933.

### ASTON – T 358

Christopher Aston, who had been in the haulage business before the First World War, launched out into coach operation from his premises at Loate's Lane, Watford in 1924, but became better known for the Watford–Aylesbury and Watford–Abbots Langley stage carriage services which he subsequently developed, and for the two Leyland Titan double deckers that he ran from May 1930 onwards. In their striking if somewhat garish livery of orange and white, Aston's buses could hardly fail to be noticed.

In later years Aston operated mainly Dennises and Leylands, but a new AEC Regal was purchased in May 1930 which became 18 in the fleet numbering sequence. Registered UR 6564 on the 8th, just over two weeks ahead of the new

Titans, it was a 30-seater with bodywork manufactured in Romford by Metcalfe. Built in a plain and not particularly inspiring style, the body was fitted out internally as a very comfortable touring coach. From the outside, however, it was distinctly bus-like in appearance, with a high waist line surmounted my narrow, shallow windows, and it had a bus-like front destination screen, fixed roof and sliding rear-entrance door. An unladen weight of only 4tons 15cwt 3qr would tend to indicate a degree of flimsiness in the construction of the bodywork.

Aston purchased UR 6564 primarily for use as a coach, and there is no evidence that it ever ran on bus service although it could easily have done so. It was bought so that Aston could get back into the field of coaching and private hire work which he had largely neglected while building up his bus operations, and it proved useful in the development of a busy summer express service from Watford to Southsea as well as excursions and tours to a host of coastal and other destinations. In fact, so successful were these activities that two more new coaches were bought in 1931, but these were Leylands and UR 6564 remained unique as the only AEC in the fleet. In 1932 Aston quite rightly came to the conclusion that there was no future for his business with the shadow of the London Passenger Transport Board looming on the horizon, and in due course he offered it for sale. It was taken over by London General Country Services on 10th May 1933 whereupon UR 6564 received fleet number T 358 in the Green Line series following on from the latest AEC Regal acquisitions, Queen Line T 352-357.

The ex-Aston Regal was an unremarkable looking vehicle and not at all coach-like in external appearance. Despite this its entire service with London Transport appears to have been spent on Green Line work, hence its designation T 358C. In this rare photograph of it in action, it is seen working on route K1 from Hitchin garage and is passing the Two Brewers at Hadley Highstone, a short way into its journey from Welwyn Garden City to Dorking. *J F Higham © A B Cross*

The change from red livery to green did nothing to disguise the distinctive shape of the Tilling body fitted to T 370 in about September 1936. No notable modifications appear to have been made to suit it for country area service apart from bringing the side lights down from roof to waistrail level. This photograph of it operating from Hemel Hempstead garage during its final days of service emphasises the inability of its shallow front destination screen to show the full particulars of its operation on route 307. *Alan B Cross collection*

If its chassis number was anything to go by, T 371 was the oldest Regal within the London Transport fleet. The great majority of its time under the Board's ownership was spent working from Amersham garage, as it was doing on this occasion when unloading passengers upon arrival at Chesham Broadway. It carries its final livery of two-tone green into which it was repainted upon overhaul in November 1935. Peering through the rear of the saloon, it is just possible to see its oval rear window arrangement in the centre of which was located the emergency door. *J F Higham © A B Cross*

Having examined their newly acquired rolling stock to ascertain its condition and future use, the new owners obviously decided that T 358 was best suited for employment within the Green Line fleet, although the range of its operations in early London Transport days are not confirmed. By 1935 it was operating from Hitchin garage alongside the ex-Queen Line Regals and may well have been there from the time it was taken over. During that year it was coded 1/8T8/3 (the same as the ex-Amersham & District and Lewis Regals) and was allocated body number 15927. T 358 finally departed from Hitchin on 22nd September 1936 with the intention that it would be overhauled and then reallocated to Tunbridge

Wells but this did not happen. Considerable rebuilding of the bodywork must have taken place while it was in Chiswick as almost one ton was added to its weight with the vehicle finally tipping the scales unladen at 5tons 13cwt 0qr. Unfortunately no documents or photographs appear to exist which might give a clue as to what work was carried out on it. Upon its resumption of work on 23rd October 1936 T 358 worked on Romford area Green Line services, firstly from the London Road garage and from 12th December 1936 at North Street. When the new 10T10s came along its demise was inevitable, and it was withdrawn from service on 9th June 1938 and subsequently sold.

## ST ALBANS & DISTRICT T 370

The St Albans & District Motor Services fleet of Charles Russett & Sons shared common ground with Christopher Aston insofar as both only ever ran one solitary AEC, and a Regal at that. However the St Albans fleet was incredible for the mix of vehicle makes that it seemed to operate perfectly efficiently, which at the time of the London Transport take-over included vehicles of BAT, Bean, Commer, Guy, Lancia, Leyland, Reo and W&G manufacture as well as the lone Regal JH 5101.

Charles Russett had come to St Albans from Bristol as recently as 1930 to take over at a rock bottom price the ailing District business of Harry Lintott, and all except two Beans had been bought since then. He adopted a canny purchasing policy of buying some fine and expensive modern vehicles as front line machines, backing them up with a whole miscellany of second rank vehicles presumably obtained as cheaply as possible. The fleet was mainly run from a former army drill hall in Hatfield Road, St Albans although a small garage was also used which was in the town's main thoroughfare, St Peter's Street.

The fifth and final new vehicle purchased was AEC Regal JH 5101, and even this was not strictly speaking new although it had never previously been licensed. Although taxed for service on 16th June 1933 the chassis had been built in about October 1931 and had presumably been retained by AEC for demonstration purposes. Its 32-seat rear entrance bus body was built by Short Brothers but its true origin is not known. It may have been built for AEC when the chassis was a demonstrator for them, Short Brothers often being selected by AEC as their bodybuilder of choice, but it is just as likely to have come from some other source. Like Aston's Regal, it must have been of flimsy construction as the completed vehicle weighed only 4tons 16cwt, a good quarter of a ton less than even the most basic equivalent buses of the time. St Albans & District ran from the town to Kimpton, Harpenden and Shenley as well as a local service in St Albans itself, but some of the fleet – including JH 5101 – were not licensed to run within the Metropolitan Police District which would have prohibited them from running to Shenley.

JH 5101 wore St Albans & District's smart green livery, embellished with prominent gold lining-out and a large arched fleet name contained within a scroll, for only a few months. On 10th November 1933 the undertaking was acquired by London Transport and Charles Russett moved back to Bristol leaving the contentious matter of how much the Board should pay for it to the Arbitration Tribunal. JH 5101 would have been quickly repainted into the Board's green and black colours although it did not receive its fleet number, T 370, until early in 1935, and round about the same year it was allocated body number 16075 and type code 4/1T6.

Following the takeover, the future T 370 possibly remained for a while at the drill hall garage which London Transport adopted as its initial base in St Albans, but by the end of 1934 it was allocated to one of the Ware premises, moving from there to the new Hertford garage upon its opening on 2nd January 1935. November 1935 found T 370 at Tring and August 1936 at Dartford, but a major metamorphosis was about to take place. On a date officially recorded as 26th September 1936 (though events may not have been quite as precise as this), T 370 was in Chiswick Works where its Short Brothers body was removed and soon afterwards scrapped. In its place was mounted Tilling body 13841, an altogether more substantial affair which resulted in a notable increase in overall weight to 5tons 8cwt. This was a typical front entrance 30-seat body of the type familiar on the twelve-strong Tilling batch T 307-318 for which 13 bodies had been built, and it had been lying around unused at Chiswick since the previous February when it was removed from T 318 at overhaul. For those used to seeing the distinctive lines of the Tilling bodies in red livery, T 370 must have looked very unusual in two-tone green. In its rebodied form T 370 was classified 4/1T3.

Now in its new guise, T 370 returned to spend a while longer at Dartford before moving to Hertford in March 1937 and, finally, Hemel Hempstead at the start of November 1938. Withdrawn from service on 1st January 1939 it was still in stock at the start of the war but did not join the numerous other delicensed Ts that were given a new lease of life then. Instead it was taken from storage to Chiswick on 5th October 1939 and is recorded as being broken up there eight days later.

## WATFORD OMNIBUS COMPANY T 369, 371

In common with Charles Russett's St Albans & District, the Watford Omnibus Company Ltd was a comparative newcomer to bus operation within the town that it was named after, having taken over in March 1931 from the grandly named but financially ailing Watford Co-operative Mutual Omnibus & Transport Company Ltd. The Managing Director of the Watford Omnibus Company was Benjamin Holt who, along with his brother Frank, owned much of its shareholding and provided its garaging facilities at his premises in Radlett Road. Benjamin Holt had, in fact, come to the Co-op's assistance in November 1930 by supplying funds to hire an additional bus which it desperately needed but could not afford, and in January 1931 he dug into his pocket again to further update the rolling stock on the Co-op's services.

Although it did not look outdated in anyway, MY 2276 was in fact a very early Regal whose chassis number 662020 marked it as being older than any in the LGOC fleet, and Holt hired it as a demonstrator before finally purchasing it. Nothing is known about its date of first registration or its activities, if any, before arriving with Holt. Its rear entrance body was supplied by Hall Lewis and fitted out as a 30-seat service bus, and it was quite rakish in appearance with sharply angled windscreen, well rounded back end, and an oval window arrangement at the rear in a style that was enjoying a degree of popularity at the time. It carried the standard fleet livery of pale blue which was lined out in gold, although this embellishment barely showed against the light background, and the 'Watford' fleet name was prominent on the sides in gold script letters.

Between July 1931 and August 1932 the Watford fleet doubled in size to meet additional commitments, and along with second-hand ADC and Leyland acquisitions came a second Regal which the Company registered on 27th July 1932 as JH 2701. Although giving the appearance of being a new vehicle it was, in fact, another former demonstrator which no doubt appealed to Holt who clearly had a knack of acquiring vehicles at bargain prices. Its chassis number 662478 suggests that it was built in the late spring or early summer of 1930 with the specific intention of demonstrating it to potential customers in South America where AEC traded under the ACLO banner instead of under its own brand name, a feature which it always adopted in Latin American countries. Although the driving position remained on the right hand side, the cut-away rear entrance to the body was reversed from the normal position to suit the South American

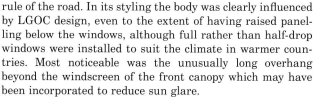

Displaying the very English-sounding destination 'GARAGE', the future T 369 is seen being inspected in Lima by the Prince of Wales – wearing a straw hat – and others in his entourage accompanied by sundry local officials. The vehicle is painted in a light colour – possibly cream or yellow – with silver-painted radiator grille, and carries the fleet name METROPOLITAN. With all eyes on the Prince of Wales as he alights from the rear entrance, many onlookers may possibly have failed to notice the dents on the rear corner panel indicating that the otherwise pristine-looking vehicle has already been involved in a mishap.

Thanks to the royal visit, we are fortunate to have a very rare interior view of the same vehicle. This shows that the seats were basic bus-style ones with LGOC-type grab handles, and that luggage racks were provided as were no fewer than three mirrors on the front bulkhead. Of particular note are the rolled-up sun blinds located beneath the luggage racks and the fare board container on the bulkhead which is exactly like those fitted on the LGOC T class.

rule of the road. In its styling the body was clearly influenced by LGOC design, even to the extent of having raised panelling below the windows, although full rather than half-drop windows were installed to suit the climate in warmer countries. Most noticeable was the unusually long overhang beyond the windscreen of the front canopy which may have been incorporated to reduce sun glare.

Accounts vary as to where the body originated, one theory being that it was a product of the Chiswick body shop and the other that it was built by Park Royal. Both, of course, had produced near-identical bodies in the recent past; the LGOC for its T 1-50 series, and Park Royal – in its former guise as Hall Lewis – for East Surrey and Autocar. The latter can be considered the more likely supplier as the LGOC's manufacturing capacity, although the greater of the two, was fully committed at the time in fulfilling the Company's own requirements for new vehicles.

The new Regal's full exploits abroad remain obscure, but it is well known as having been demonstrated in the Peruvian capital Lima in February 1931 where its presence coincided with a royal visit to South America by the Prince of Wales and his brother Prince George who inspected it as part of a press photo-shoot. Clearly no sale was achieved, for the vehicle returned to Britain in due course whereupon its entrance position was reversed in a mirror image with a view to selling it on the home market as a 31-seater bus.

For service with the Watford Omnibus Company, the rear doorway was moved to the British nearside but little else appears to have changed from its days as a demonstrator. JH 2701 is seen, with its light blue paintwork looking a little faded except on the rear panel, which has possibly been repainted after accident damage, covering a short working to Oxhey Hall Farm on the company's Harebreaks–Hamper Mill service. *J F Higham © A B Cross*

The two Regals worked actively on the Watford Omnibus Company's three scheduled services, a semi-country run from Watford to Abbots Langley and two locals from High Street to Leavesden and Harebreaks to Hamper Mill. The untimely death of his brother and pressure of other business interests caused Benjamin Holt to offer the business to the LGOC in the spring of 1933, and the purchase was completed on 23rd June with London General Country Services nominated as the actual buyer. With the formation of the London Passenger Transport Board looming little more than a week away, the Watford Omnibus Company continued to trade as a separate entity until it was transferred to the LPTB on 1st July along with all the LGCS's other assets.

In common with most other acquired buses administered initially under the Reigate regime, JH 2701 and MY 2276 remained without fleet numbers through to 1935 when they became T 369 and T 371, receiving body numbers 16005 and 16059 as they passed through overhaul at Chiswick in September and October 1935 respectively. Both were coded 4/1T6, the same as ex-St Albans & District T 370, the body codes being nothing more than meaningless paper entries as the three were all completely different from each other. By 1935 T 371 was operating from Amersham garage followed by spells at Hemel Hempstead, Amersham (again) and, lastly, Luton from which it was withdrawn from service on 1st January 1939. It was a victim, like T 370, of a drive to eliminate non-standard vehicles and, again like T 370, it was removed from storage at Chiswick tram depot on 5th October 1939 and dismantled on the 13th.

T 369 was much more fortunate and long lived. Its earliest days in the London Transport era were spent at High Wycombe but from October 1936 it worked short spells at Leavesden Road and Hemel Hempstead before returning to High Wycombe in March 1937. Whilst on Leavesden Road's

Seen in Northwood Road, Harefield during the latter part of 1934, JH 2701 carries full London Transport green and black livery and recently introduced running number stencils, but has yet to gain its official identity as T 369. The HA garage plate indicates that it is working from the small Harefield garage (which closed on 1st January 1936), but this had no T-type allocation of its own and T 369 officially belonged to High Wycombe garage. However the fact that a route 309 destination blind has been specially printed for it tends to indicate that much of its time was spent at the Harefield outstation. *London Transport Museum*

Now displaying its London Transport fleet number, T 369 carries the latest version of country livery gained on overhaul in October 1935. Its open rear platform arrangement is clearly demonstrated as it waits on the stand at High Wycombe in front of a Thames Valley Leyland TD1. It is working the 362B service to Penn post office acquired with the takeover of the Penn Bus Company on 1st August 1935, and the traffic notice carried adjacent to the rear wheel arch proclaims 'Reduced Fares on this Route'. *J H Higham © A B Cross*

allocation its seating capacity was reduced – during overhaul in December 1936 – from 31 to 30. The next overhaul, which commenced on 30th March 1938, was to determine its future. The ex-demonstrator body was removed and placed on the chassis of standard Green Line T 300 which was then disposed of, T 369 receiving in its place T 300's body 16800 newly converted into bus format. It its new guise T 369 re-entered service at Dartford on 14th April 1938, now classified 1/7T7/1. The outbreak of war found it at Amersham after a spell back at High Wycombe, both ideal operating territories as the vehicle was fitted at the time with a 110m engine well suited to local hilly operations.

T 369's pattern of wartime service was similar to that of many other 1/7T7/1s. It continued at Amersham until February 1942 when, upon being converted to standee format, it found its way to Addlestone where it was repainted grey in August of the same year. It was included within the

mass withdrawals of 1st June 1943 and then not used again until it was revived at Kingston, still in grey, on 12th January 1945. A repaint into red followed in March but the standee seating remained in place. Withdrawn once again on 1st May and sent to Chiswick for evaluation, T 369 escaped being sold a few days later along with so many other Ts, perhaps because money had been so recently spent on repainting it.

The post-war era ushered in four more years of service for T 369 with appearances at many of the Central Bus garages with which the 1/7T7/1s became associated, and during overhaul in June 1946 it reverted to its pre-1942 seating layout. Its longest unbroken allocations were at Uxbridge from August 1945 to January 1947 and at Hounslow from April 1947 to February 1949. The end came at Hornchurch on 15th December 1949 when, probably having received a PSV71 'stop' notice, T 369 was delicensed and sold for scrap on the same day.

In post war years T 369 looked like any other 1/7T7/1 – which was how it was now classified – with only its Hertfordshire JH registration plate marking it out from the remainder. Carrying red livery since March 1945, its Ransomes-built body still looks superficially smart even at the very end of its career although a close examination reveals that most of the side pillars have been braced with heavy metal straps to hold the structure together. T 369's final five months' service in 1949 were spent at Hornchurch garage from which it went for scrap on 15th December. *Alan Nightingale collection*

# 14 9T9 COACHES FOR GREEN LINE
## T 403-452

For much of their career with London Transport T 403-452, known collectively as the 9T9 class, tended to be regarded as a less elegant and performance-wise more ponderous poor relation to the spectacularly successful 10T10s which are described in the next chapter. The story of the 9T9s starts, in fact, in an interesting and unusual way because, in stark contrast to London Transport's normally carefully contrived forward planning, it was not originally intended that they would be purchased at all. Instead, they were obtained as a last minute stop-gap to permit urgent modernisation of a section of the Green Line fleet when it became clear that the original replacement plan had become unworkable.

By early 1935 the Board's engineers, who had been examining bus design and forming plans for future development, had arrived at the conclusion that the traditional front-mounted engine was not the best arrangement on a single decker and had determined to break away from it for future deliveries. Their preferred option was to power the vehicle from the rear, and discussions had already taken place with Leyland Motors over the latter's tentative plans to develop designs incorporating either a rear or an underfloor mounted engine. The Board's traditional supplier, AEC, had also indicated that it had a rear-engined chassis at the design stage, but nothing seems to have come of this. Meanwhile, in the absence of any better alternative, the side-engined AEC Q

had been adopted as the Board's preferred single decker for new deliveries, and the Q offered the major design advantage that it could be flexibly configured to suit all of London Transport's varied operating requirements in the Country Bus, Central Bus and Green Line fleets.

A snapshot of the Green Line fleet at 31st March 1935 shows that it consisted of 423 coaches of AEC, Leyland and Gilford manufacture of which 114 were Gilfords. (This excludes the 42-strong private hire fleet which was under Green Line control and comprised at the time a mixture of vehicles of AEC, Albion, Daimler, Dennis and Morris manufacture.) The Gilfords, though perfectly capable of acquitting themselves well at times, were temperamental and expensive to maintain, leading the Board to decide that they should be

The defining feature of the 9T9 class was always its distinctive front end structure which wrapped, slightly unsatisfactorily, around the radiator and headlamp in a heavy-handed attempt to look modern. T 404 appears to have been photographed almost immediately after delivery, before it was licensed for service and before a supply of decorative wheel trims had been received. Not even a fleet name is carried and the lettering on the board listing points on route J is still incomplete. Running under trade plates, it has a measuring device fitted in the doorway and was probably being used on a route survey somewhere. *Alan B Cross collection*

disposed of as quickly as possible. To this end, plans were drawn up for the purchase of 100 Q-type coaches, and AEC was asked to quote for their cost and to start arranging their production with a target date of May 1936 for the first ones to go into service. As the Chiswick body shop was already fully committed, tenders were issued to outside manufacturers for the bodywork. No single manufacturer was able to build all 100 bodies within the timescale envisaged, so it was decided that production would be split 50-50 between Park Royal and Weymann with each factory producing identical 32-seat coach bodies on metal frames.

By the start of January 1936 it had become evident that, because of several novel features in the design of the Q-type coaches, including provision of a high and level floor and a new power ventilation system to heat the coach in the winter and cool it in the summer, it would be impossible to obtain deliveries until August at the very earliest. So great was the urgency to replace the worst of the Gilford coaches that this delay was deemed unacceptable, and on 9th January 1936 a revised plan was authorised by Lord Ashfield. The requirement for Q-type coaches would be halved to 50, all of which would be bodied by Park Royal, and meanwhile AEC would guarantee to provide 50 Regal chassis for delivery at the rate of six per week commencing on 10th March. In fact AEC bettered this already ambitious target by producing chassis from 26th February onwards. These went to Weymann for bodying, arriving at Chiswick as completed vehicles from the end of May with fleet numbers T 403-452 following on from the last of the inherited petrol Regals. This batch was unusual in that the registration numbers (CLX 551-575, CXX 151-174), chassis numbers (06621952-2001) and body numbers (16620-16669) were all applied in strict numerical sequence.

Nothing quite like the 9T9 had been seen before. With its curvaceous lines it was well ahead of most modern trends, but traces of the experimental Weymann body on T 232 could be detected within its overall concept and notably through the raised windows towards the rear. Bits of STL were evident in the windscreen, canopy and mudguards, but a totally one-off feature was the strange bulbous and rather convoluted bonnet design which, combined with the cowling enclosing the nearside front headlamp and the valance below the radiator, gave a front-heavy appearance and remained unique to this batch of vehicles. The polished front bumper was quite an attractive and unusual feature though it probably served no real purpose other than being purely decorative. Even more attractive were the handsome wheel embellishments which were provided on both axles. Made to London Transport's own design and requiring special brackets to hold them in place, they were also tried out in April and May 1936 by Central Buses on a small batch of new STLs, and though not immediately accepted for bus use they were subsequently adopted as a standard feature for new coaches from 1938 onwards.

Viewed from the offside, the heaviness of the front end arrangement is less pronounced, and the pleasant modern lines of the Chiswick-designed body can be better appreciated. Notable features are the lack of separate side lights, the STL-influenced front mudguard design, and the semaphore direction indicator just behind the driver's door. A conspicuous feature is the new style of GREEN LINE fleet name neatly incorporating the legend LONDON TRANSPORT in an elongated box below it. T 405 is fully plated and fitted with blinds and route boards to enter service from Leavesden Road garage on 8th June 1936. *London Transport Museum*

The built-in bonnet structure was unusual in that both it and the front wing were supported from the bodywork, but its reliance on the heavy gaiter, especially where it surrounded the radiator shell, was detrimental to the overall appearance. Another novelty was the omission of separate side lights. These were incorporated as a second bulb inside each of the main headlamps, a feature never repeated in any future vehicle orders and one which probably turned out to be less satisfactory than originally hoped. No official explanation has ever been offered to explain the reasoning behind the 9T9's somewhat unorthodox frontal design, and it can only be conjectured that it came about in a misguided attempt to make the vehicle look as ultra-modern as possible to compensate for the loss of the full front which made the Q-type stand out most noticeably from other designs of the time.

A further innovation was the provision of semaphore type direction indicators built into the front bulkhead just above waist height complemented by repeater arrows mounted in the centre at the rear, just under the centrally placed door which formed the emergency exit. They were clearly not a success and their use, if it occurred at all on a regular basis, appears to have ceased by the end of the decade, although the fitments remained in place long afterwards. However, the rear arrows were painted out and in some cases the semaphore apertures were plated over.

Internally, the new Ts were comfortable 30-seaters with well-padded polished aluminium-framed seats all of which faced forwards, the last four rows being mounted slightly higher than the others on shallow plinths to mitigate the intrusion of the rear wheel arches. The windows, which were mounted in pans, were shrouded on the inside in the same manner as other recent London Transport single deckers, and a winding mechanism was provided for those that opened with the handle mounted at the top. The concept of a forced-air heating and ventilation system was abandoned (although it was present in the 50 Q-type coaches when these were delivered later), and a conventional Clayton Dewandre heater was mounted on the front bulkhead. The clock above it – a feature of all Green Line vehicles – had a rectangular face in the latest idiom instead of a conventional round one. As befitted its role as a coach the interior décor was much more sombre than the two-tone scheme favoured for buses, the overall vista of green given by the upholstery, side lining and floor lino combining with the clean-looking cream rexine underside to the roof and luggage racks to give a calm and reasonably opulent look to these very pleasant vehicles.

Under the eye of a watchful inspector T 452, the highest numbered 9T9, loads at Eccleston Bridge soon after entering service from Hatfield garage on 16th September 1936. It is working a journey on the K1, but Hatfield's coaches also covered the K2, hence the detachable destination slips on the side destination board. A notable feature of the neat rear end design is the panel below the emergency incorporating destination arrows on either side of the central brake light; these worked in conjunction with the semaphore signals at the front.
*London Transport Museum*

The interior décor of the Weymann body was plain but restful, and exuded just about the right air of comfort and opulence for Green Line operation. The square-faced clock and the Clayton heater were conspicuous features, and the simple but stylish roof ventilators combined with the gangway lighting gave a modern touch. Ample additional lights were provided below the luggage racks, but the racks themselves appeared less roomy and capable of accommodating large pieces of luggage than those on the 1/7T7/1s. *London Transport Museum*

Mechanically the new 9T9s held no surprises and would have been very familiar to staff in garages already running STLs to which they were closely related. Based on a 17ft 6ins wheelbase Regal chassis and with an overall length of 27ft, they were powered by 7.7 litre Comet Mark III engines, had D132 preselective gearboxes coupled to fluid flywheels, and servo-assisted Lockheed brakes. A rear axle ratio of 5.2:1 was specified as being best suited to the limited-stop Green Line work for which they were intended.

At 10ft 2ins in height and 27ft 5ins in length the 9T9s would have been impressive vehicles by virtue of their bulk alone, but in their attractive Green Line livery of mid-green with lighter green window areas, and with mudguards and mouldings picked out in dark green, they made quite a resplendent sight when they commenced work on route J (Watford–Reigate) from Watford, Leavesden Road garage in June 1936. The first one licensed for service was T 418 on the 3rd of that month, and Leavesden Road's full complement of seven had been received by the 16th. Although the main reason for buying 9T9s had been to displace Gilfords from Green Line work, an even more urgent task was to oust the twelve recently rebodied but unsuitable 5T4s (T 346-357) which was why route J was chosen first, and along with its 5T4s Leavesden Road also lost its only swing-door coach, the prototype T38. Reigate's share of route J was dealt with next after which the Gilford replacement scheme really began in earnest. No 9T9s directly replaced Gilfords, this purpose being achieved by reallocating 7T7s and 1/7T7/1s from garages in receipt of the new 9T9s. Between 4th July and 1st August route I (Crawley–Abbots Langley) was converted to 9T9 with new vehicles going first to Crawley followed by Leavesden Road's second allocation and then Reigate's. Following on from this were routes K1 (Dorking–Baldock) and K2 (Horsham–Welwyn Garden City/Hitchin at weekends) which were served by four garages, with 9T9s going to Leatherhead, Dorking, Hatfield and Hitchin in that order, after which the remaining four vehicles out of the 50 were sent to Amersham between 16th October and 7th November were they were employed to part-convert route B (Wrotham–Aylesbury). By this time the first deliveries into Green Line service of the new 6Q6s was imminent, and the programme for these included five for Amersham where their performance could be directly compared with that of the 9T9s.

In service, it very quickly became apparent that the 9T9s looked much better than they actually performed. They were generally unpopular with staff who found them slow and hard to keep time with compared to the old petrol Regals which, though theoretically equal in power, were a full ton lighter and much more sprightly. Other complaints were that they were prone to vibration, were heavy on steering, and insufficiently responsive on braking. Undoubtedly many of the shortcomings could be attributed to their unladen weight which, at 6tons 15cwt 0qr, was greater than a double deck STL and almost 2cwt more than the 6Q6 with which their performance was inevitably compared, usually unfavourably. The latter were perceived as being quieter and more lively although they, too, had problems which were peculiar to their side-engined design and were mostly associated with overheating and with lack of adequate cohesion with road surfaces, the latter problem a result of having only single wheels at the back. On 30th August 1937 T 405 and Q 236 were dispatched for comparative skid tests to Fort Dunlop in Birmingham, arriving back in London on 6th September. An outcome of this was that the Qs were fitted with a new design of cross-cut rear tyre which improved their road holding considerably, but it is not known if any modifications were specified for the 9T9s as a result of the tests.

Starting with T 404 on 2nd June 1936, before it had even entered service, a stream of 9T9s began returning to Weymann's factory at Addlestone for bodywork alterations and repairs. These were at their peak between November 1936 and June 1937 but continued through to January 1939. Although some are known to have involved repairs to roof panels, a general requirement to modify the MCW metal frame structure may have arisen as many other buses with similarly constructed bodies – including rebodied R-types, the 5T4s, the 'Godstone' STLs and even double deck Q 5 – were recalled too.

In September 1937, and now almost exactly a year old, Dorking-based T 446 arrives at Victoria heading for Welwyn Garden City on route K1. Close examination reveals an early addition to the original design in the form of an unpainted aluminium kick plate covering the top and outer edge of the front mudguard to disguise the inevitable scuffing caused by fitters climbing on to the structure to gain access to the engine compartment. This modification was carried out on the whole class during its first year of service. G H F Atkins

In placing the 100 9T9s and 6Q6s into service during 1936 London Transport's aim had been to remove all remaining Gilfords from Green Line operation, but this target was not quite achieved. Through a mixture of service revisions and increased requirements for duplicates, the completion of the new coach programme left as many as 27 of them still available for service which, at the start of 1937, were nearly all to be found at garages in the Northern Division. St Albans had 10 and Hertford 9, with two apiece at each of the Romford garages and one at Hemel Hempstead, the balance of three being temporarily seconded to the private hire fleet. With no further new coaches on the immediate horizon 27 4Q4 service buses were delicensed on 1st October 1936 for conversion into temporary Green Line coaches, a task which involved a considerable amount of bodywork alteration to accommodate luggage racks and instal a forced air heating system similar to that on the 6Q6s, a feature detectable from outside by a square-shaped intake grille inserted into the front panel. They were not, however, given new seats to replace the wooden-framed bus type ones already fitted, so they were not very coach-like either in comfort or appearance. Reclassified as 1/4Q4/1, these 27 Qs mostly entered service as coaches on 25th March 1937 although a few did so beforehand where the Gilfords that they were due to replace reached the point of expiry. Even then, the requirements of the 1937 summer programme meant that a few Gilfords lingered on until they were finally withdrawn on 1st October, almost a year later than originally intended.

The first overhaul cycle for the 9T9s commenced in the autumn of 1937, but although it involved the bodies being lifted in the usual way they were all returned to their original chassis and no changes of identity occurred. However a very visible difference on the overhauled vehicles, which undoubtedly improved their appearance even further, was a livery modification pre-empting a new styling planned for introduction on the forthcoming 10T10 class of Green Line coaches. The roof and back dome areas were now painted dark green in sharp contrast to the main body panels, as were the mudguards and the valance below the radiator.

T 449 is heading through North Finchley displaying the cramped and almost illegible destination wording which was a feature on many of the new blinds printed for the 9T9s. It is, in fact, heading for its home garage at Leatherhead. Newly repainted at the start of February 1938, T449's roof and lower front valance panels are now picked out in dark green, producing a very handsome livery styling which was destined to remain in vogue for less than a year. Trams are still in evidence, but overhead wiring for trolleybuses is in place ready for the new mode of transport to take over on 6th March 1938. *A D Packer collection*

First to appear ex-overhaul in three shades of green was Leavesden Road's T 418 on 23rd October 1937 and over the next few months all 50 vehicles were similarly dealt with, ending with Amersham's T 439 which went in for overhaul on 4th July 1938.

For approximately two years, from the time of their introduction in 1936 through to the autumn of 1938, the 9T9s led an uneventful life on Green Line service. By and large they remained faithful to the garages and routes to which they had originally been allocated, the only exception being that Amersham garage and route B were removed from their

Photographed outside Reigate garage before heading off on route J to Watford, and also displaying the new livery – which in this case was applied in December 1937 – is T 420. No explanation can be given as to why its ornamental wheel trims have been removed as it was certainly not the practice at the time to do so. Possibly it was being monitored as part of a study into the incidence of brake overheating with or without the presence of wheel trims, but in the absence of surviving data from the time we will probably never know. *Alan Nightingale collection*

Demotion of the 9T9s to buses was well under way when T 431 was sent to Hertford on 23rd June 1939 to work on rural operations such as the spasmodically timed cross-country 384 between Hertford and Letchworth. It was photographed still carrying full Green Line livery, which it would have lost soon afterwards upon overhaul in August 1939. T 431's pre-war spell on bus work was destined to be short lived; after a little over two months it was converted into an ambulance, still based at Hertford, and did not resume revenue work until December 1945. *D Evans © Omnibus Society*

sphere of operation early in February 1938 when old petrol Regals were drafted back in and Amersham's contingent of four 9T9s was dispersed to other garages which already had vehicles of this type. However their performance, or lack of it, remained a bone of contention with Green Line crews, and on 1st November 1938 London Transport bit the bullet by commencing their demotion to bus status. New 10T10s were now flooding in, and instead of replacing early petrol-engined Ts, some were diverted to displace an initial batch of ten 9T9s taken from the allocations at Crawley, Hatfield, Reigate and Leavesden Road. One more was added to the list in November 1938 after which there was a lull before a more concerted demotion programme resumed in May 1939 which lasted through to August.

Initially the downgraded coaches were little altered from their original condition apart from the substitution of a B (bus) suffix to the fleet number in place of the C (coach) designation, although the clocks were probably removed and, in time, the LONDON TRANSPORT fleet name began to replace the GREEN LINE insignia. The first garages to receive 9T9 buses were Dorking – which was already well versed in running the type as coaches – plus Hertford and Windsor. The subsequent expansion of this operation in 1939 found 9T9 buses at Addlestone, Dartford and Swanley in May, Guildford and Luton in June, and St Albans and Tring in August. By the time that all Green Line services were temporarily suspended at the start of September 1939 as a precursor to the declaration of war, only seven 9T9s are believed to have still been in use as coaches with T 416 operational at Leatherhead, T 424, 443 at Reigate, and T 438, 444, 448, 451

at Leavesden Road. One further change in appearance befell the 9T9s right at the end of the decade as a result of their second overhaul cycle coming into effect. Since the autumn of 1938 the main element of the Country Bus livery had been a fairly dark Lincoln green which was considered more hard wearing than the mid-green shade used previously, and this was used in the overhauling of the 9T9s. A lighter shade of green was still retained around the window areas, but the overall effect was not really beneficial to the 9T9s, giving them a somewhat heavier and more gloomy appearance than hitherto. The first 9T9 to appear ex-overhaul in the revised style was Leavesden Road's T 418 on 14th June 1939, and a further 20 vehicles were dealt with before the onset of war brought the programme to a halt. All the 9T9s in the new livery were officially buses, the seven remaining coaches retaining their old colours right through to the beginning of September 1939 when all 50 vehicles were abruptly taken out of passenger service.

On Friday 1st September 1939 40 9T9s were placed at the disposal of the Ministry of Health followed by the remaining 10 the next day. They were designated for use as ambulances and were joined in this role by all 266 10T10s, 75 TFs newly built for Green Line use (two of which had not yet entered passenger service), the 50 6Q6 coaches and the 24-strong LTC class of private hire coaches. Totalling 465 in all, their use as ambulances under wartime conditions had been negotiated with the Ministry when war began to look inevitable, and an outline of the conversion work necessary to suit them for their new role is given in chapter 15 under the 10T10 heading.

Most of T 408's ambulance career was spent at Grays garage, and throughout the wartime years it retained the late 'thirties Lincoln green and pale green bus livery that it received on overhaul in July 1939. At the start of November 1944 it was transferred to the Central Bus department at Chalk Farm where, being parked along with other bus ambulances in a side street, it was presumably thought prudent to paint the garage code letters directly on to the side of the vehicle in preference to using stencils which could be easily removed. With their side and head lamps combined into a single aperture the 9T9s presented a particular problem when applying blackout masking, and T 408 illustrates one means by which this was tackled. With the war nearing its end, the actual masking had been removed by the time the vehicle was photographed. *Alan Nightingale collection*

Nobody could have known back in September 1939 that a full six years would elapse before any 9T9s would once again carry passengers under the auspices of London Transport; in fact, in the majority of cases, their absence from service would prove to be nearer seven years than six. They were not, however, lost from the London scene in their role as ambulances as they continued to be maintained by London Transport and retained their fleet livery. They could be found stationed at various bus garages, including many Central Bus ones which had never previously seen a 9T9, being sometimes housed inside the premises but more often outside and adjacent to them. Staffed by volunteer drivers from the regular bus fleet, their emergency calls to carry patients between inner London hospitals and special reception centres or railheads were often interspersed with periods of inactivity during which time they would be periodically taken out by engineers on test runs to ensure that they were kept in reliable mechanical condition.

Somewhat belatedly, on 7th June 1940, someone in the Chiswick licensing office remembered that a few 9T9s were still classified as coaches and duly amended their status to 'bus' on the official records. This was, of course, purely a paper exercise as all were in use as ambulances with no prospect of them being returned to passenger service at any time in the near future. The fluctuating fortunes of war, and in particular the ending of the aerial blitz on London, resulted in quite a substantial number of bus ambulances becoming surplus to requirements. This did not herald a return to service for the majority of them; instead 94 ambulances, including six 9T9s, were commandeered by the Ministry of War Transport. After being prepared at Chiswick Works for their revised role, the 94 vehicles were handed over to the US Army. The six 9T9s were T 414-416, 421, 422, 443, and on 30th October 1942 they were dispatched to the US Army's huge motor base at Ashchurch, near Tewkesbury, for general military use, often as troop transports or ambulances. One of the six, T 443, never came back to London Transport and became the only 9T9 casualty of the war, although it did not entirely disappear from view as its body could be found in use as a caravan near Northolt airport in the early post-war years.

With the war at an end, the 9T9s began to be released from their ambulance duties. They were freed in batches starting with a group of 16 on 8th August 1945 and ending with seven on 17th March 1946. After this three still remained as ambulances to cover special requirements, the last two of which – T 403 latterly based at Chelverton Road and T 444 at Hammersmith – returned to the fold as late as 8th March 1947. None were put straight back into passenger service. Each one was initially delicensed and placed into store, and as time permitted they were given a thorough mechanical checkover and, if necessary, repainted. Odd ones, presumably those considered to be in the worst mechanical condition, were subjected to a complete overhaul. Only one 9T9, T 406, had been overhauled during the war and this occurred right at the end of it, in March and April 1945. However, many had been repainted while serving as ambulances into the green and white livery adopted as standard for all country area vehicles in 1940. On these, Lincoln green was retained as the base colour but the pale green shade was replaced by off white except on the windscreen surround which was green, while the three window surrounds at the back were now picked out in white on most but not all repaintings. The roofs were initially in the matt grey camouflage adopted for all vehicles soon after the start of the war, but by 1945 most were in the brown (or, officially, Indian red) introduced later. A few 9T9s were not repainted at all during the war and were beginning to look very shabby indeed by 1945. As if to emphasise their demotion from coach status almost all had lost their ornamental front wheel trims whilst many had lost the back ones too, and in some instances the front bumpers had been mislaid and were never replaced.

A posed scene, photographed at Chiswick Works on 31st March 1946, finds T 406 demonstrating the livery which it was proposed to adopt for the post-war Green Line fleet and carrying destination blinds and side boards for route 715 which had commenced on 6th February using 10T10s in bus colours. The smartness of the Green Line livery is slightly marred in this case by the decision to paint the radiator shell green, although this did not really matter as T 406 had been painted purely for demonstration purposes and was never meant to return to Green Line work. *London Transport Museum*

T 406 contrasts greatly with T 414, the first of the former US Army 9T9s to be returned to Chiswick from storage at Potters Bar and now being assessed prior to the commencement of a full overhaul. At this stage it still carries its wartime colours and its seven digit army number 1824022. T 414 finally re-entered service at Leatherhead on 5th July 1946. *London Transport Museum*

The five 9T9s returned by the American armed forces arrived back in London in dribs and drabs between 26th November 1945 and 30th March 1946, all of them wearing an army livery of khaki and still carrying their American seven-digit service numbers. None was immediately fit for use and they were all placed in store at the side of Potters Bar garage until they could be called into Chiswick for overhaul.

After its late wartime overhaul, which was completed at Chiswick on 27th April 1945, T 406 resumed its ambulance duty at Bromley garage, but this came to an end when it was delicensed on 8th August and returned to Chiswick for more work to be done on it. Chosen, presumably, because of its newly-overhauled status necessitating a minimum of preliminary work, it was now about to be repainted as the guinea pig for the livery in which the post-war Green Line fleet would appear. With the return of peace the resumption of Green Line operations was now high on the agenda, and although the first two services did not start until 6th February 1946 planning for them began well beforehand. The livery applied to T 406 was, in fact, much the same as that used for Green Line coaches just prior to the war, but the blinds and route boards carried the new route numbering in the 700 series soon to be introduced. Although a 9T9 had been used as a mock-up, it was never the intention that this class of vehicle would return to Green Line work after the war, and after being officially photographed and demonstrated to the press in January 1946, T 406 remained unlicensed until it resumed normal bus work six months later.

The standard post-war livery adopted for the 9T9s was the same green and white combination introduced back in 1940 except that the roof was now painted green. Occasional ones deviated from the norm in not having their windscreen surrounds picked out in green, but a body repainting programme ensured that all looked reasonably smart before being put back into public service after their long absence. Complementary to the body repainting programme, a series of full overhauls commenced in January 1946 but it took until as late as April 1948 for the final ones to be called in, the last one of all being T 427 which emerged from Chiswick newly overhauled on 15th June of that year.

The final days of the LPTB were marked by an acute vehicle shortage which was often met by the strangest of inter-garage borrowings, one of which is shown here. T 452, now carrying standard green and white bus livery, makes a surprise appearance at Uxbridge garage on loan from Dorking. The driver is probably pleasantly surprised at having a preselector equipped vehicle to drive in contrast to Uxbridge's normal stock, all of which had crash gearboxes. Although it was not planned at the time, 9T9s later became a regular feature at Uxbridge when they replaced time-expired petrol engined Ts. *LCC Tramways Trust*

No great sense of urgency was exhibited in placing the 9T9s back into service after the war, but to fulfill a special requirement four of them were relicensed on 3rd December 1945 almost three months ahead of any others. The outbreak of war had seen the end of conventional private hire activities, and it was now time to reinstate these starting with a very modest fleet of five vehicles. T 413 and T 417 were relicensed specially for private hire work at Tottenham Central Bus garage along with T 430 and T 431 at West Green; the fifth unit of the embryo private hire fleet was TF 9 – the only one of a batch of twelve vehicles to emerge from the Bull Yard bombing raid – which had been out of use for a while but was now relicensed at Old Kent Road. On 25th March 1946 the very first LTC class private hire coaches were returned to use after serving as ambulances, specifically LTC 13 and LTC 15 at Tottenham and LTC 18 and LTC 20 at West Green, whereupon the four 9T9s ended their brief moment of private hire glory and were sent back to the country area for ordinary bus work.

Resumption by the 9T9s of country area bus operation started in a small way on 1st March 1946 with two at Hertford and one each at Grays and St Albans, but over the ensuing months more flooded back into use. Their employment was seemingly indiscriminate with no clearly defined spheres of operation at this stage, and by the end of 1946 examples could also be found at Amersham, Chelsham, Dorking, East Grinstead, Guildford, Leatherhead, Luton, Reigate, Staines and Windsor. A big surprise, however, came on 15th June 1946 when no fewer than 17 were relicensed to help alleviate a desperate shorting of rolling stock in the central area, with seven appearing overnight at Catford, six at Norwood and three at Victoria. The six at Norwood ran alongside an equivalent number of 1/7T7/1s, constituting an impressive small fleet of green single deckers operating from this officially all-double deck garage. Other garages such as Cricklewood and Elmers End subsequently found them in stock at various times, almost always on trunk services serving central London, until all were returned to the country area on 1st May 1947.

The whole class of 49 was back in use by 27th August 1946 except for the ambulance stragglers T 403 and T 444 which were relicensed at St Albans on 14th May 1947. Over the next couple of years a few areas emerged where 9T9s predominated and where their presence could usually be guaranteed. The operations to which 9T9s were officially allocated (Mondays to Fridays) as at 1st January 1950 were:

| Route | Description | Garage | No. |
|---|---|---|---|
| 304 | Tyttenhanger–Whitwell | SA | 2 |
| 329 | Knebworth–Hertford (Wednesdays) | HG | 1 |
| 386 | Buntingford–Hitchin (Tues/Thurs) | | |
| 356 | Luton–Flamstead | LS | 5 |
| 376 | Luton–Kensworth | | |
| 376A | Kensworth–Dunstable | | |
| 404 | Sevenoaks–Shoreham Village | DG | 1 |
| 413 | Chipstead–Brasted | DG | 2 |
| 413A | Chipstead–Four Elms | | |
| 419 | West Ewell–Langley Vale | LH | 3 |
| 421 | Sevenoaks–Heverham | DG | 2 |
| 422 | Leatherhead–Boxhill Holiday Camp | LH | 1 |
| 427 | Weybridge–Woking via Byfleet/Pyrford | WY | 6 |
| 437 | Weybridge–Woking via Byfleet | | |
| 456 | Weybridge–Woking via Pyrford | | |
| 456B | Addlestone circular via Byfleet | | |
| 435 | Leatherhead–Tadworth | LH | 4 |
| 462 | Leatherhead–Staines | WY | 4 |
| 450 | Dartford–Gravesend | NF | 1 |
| 478 | Swanley–Wrotham | SJ | 2 |
| | Supplementary Schedule | DT | 1 |
| | Supplementary Schedule | WY | 1 |

Route 462 was a well-patronised service on which 9T9s became firmly established in post-war years working from Addlestone and Leatherhead garages. A favourite place to photograph them was the terminal stand outside Staines West station where Leatherhead's T 417 is seen in the company of Twickenham garage's SRT 130 working on route 90. T 417 was one of a number of 9T9s whose front bumpers were lost over the years and never replaced.
*Alan Pearce*

Although this was the theoretical position at the start of 1950, things had begun to change radically shortly beforehand when, between 7th and 13th December 1949, eight 9T9s were culled from various locations to meet an urgent need to replace 11T11s at Uxbridge Central Bus garage. As a result Swanley's route 478 had been temporarily turned over to 4Q4 operation while some of Dunton Green's and Luton's workings were being covered by more modern 10T10s. A similar

process was applied at Hornchurch on 13th January 1950 when six 9T9s were drafted in, depleting the heavy impact that the class had made at Addlestone and Leatherhead. On 6th February 1950 Swanley's requirement for 9T9s ceased when route 478 was turned over to double deck operation using STLs, and at the same time Dartford's 9T9 – which had covered a number of local services while operating its supplementary schedule – was replaced in the same way.

At the same location as the previous photo, but this time with Kingston's newly-rebuilt T 28 in the background, is Addlestone's T 419. Although this vehicle still has its front bumper intact, it has undergone the mudguard modification meted out to the great majority of 9T9s in their later years whereby a plain metal lower section has replaced the STL-style rubber fitment behind the front wheel. It also sports the unflattering green and cream livery received by a few 9T9s, in this instance in November 1948. *D A Jones*

The scene is Leatherhead garage, and despite the prominent LPTB 'No Entry' sign, London Transport is now firmly into the nationalised era as the legal lettering on T 429 confirms. Unusually for a 9T9 at this comparatively late stage of its career, T 429 has managed to retain all its wheel trims, but the bottom section of the front mudguard, which once swept further downwards to match up with a now-removed shroud below the door step, has now been cut to a shorter profile. *D A Jones*

The 'all green' livery adopted from August 1950 onwards is displayed by T 413, which was repainted in this style in October 1950. It was photographed nine months later working as one of the regular 9T9 fleet attached to Uxbridge garage. The bodies on these vehicles were prone to water leaks, which was probably the reason for the untidy makeshift modification at the top of the driver's windscreen. *Alan B Cross*

The use of 9T9s on Central Bus services was only ever intended to be temporary pending the arrival of better rolling stock and no attempt was ever made to repaint them red. However the fact that they were employed at both garages alongside much newer vehicles, together with the rather dilapidated condition into which the 9T9 class as a whole appeared to be falling, meant that they were not accepted with good grace by the local staff. In fact representatives at both garages made strident requests for their early removal, but with nothing available to replace them there was no alternative other than to leave them where they were for the best part of two years. Their demise finally began in October 1951 and was completed on 1st November with the arrival of 10T10s repainted into red livery after being displaced from their Green Line duties following the arrival of new RFs.

The overhauling of 9T9s in the post-war period was spasmodic, and no discernible programme was adopted for dealing with them systematically. They were probably all handled on an individual basis as the need arose, and from 1947 onwards each overhaul took as long as two months, and sometimes three, to complete. This was probably a reflection on their condition, and particularly on the state of the bodywork which had probably deteriorated on most of them as a result of standing outdoors throughout the war with only spasmodic use and very little maintenance. Some received a single post-war overhaul and were not dealt with again after the spring of 1948, but ten were called into Chiswick again in 1949 and another ten in 1950 for further overhauling. From 1948 onwards many had their front mudguards modified upon overhaul to remove the decorative curved rubber extension on the offside and to reduce it in depth on the nearside. In late 1948 a few were repainted with cream window surrounds instead of white, employing a styling also evident on some Leyland Cubs, 4Q4s, and the post-war STLs where the whole of the cab area and the band above it was painted green in a rather unattractive styling. In the case of the 9T9s this was later abandoned in favour of a reversion to the old green and white combination until the introduction to the whole fleet of the 'all green' livery which was subsequently applied to eleven 9T9s between October 1950 and February 1951.

Hornchurch garage was another Central Bus location to find itself with 9T9s where they were not particularly well received by the operating staff unhappy with their rather dilapidated condition, both mechanically and bodily. T 452, which arrived at Hornchurch from Addlestone in January 1950, is seen passing Northern Counties bodied 'utility' G 272 in South Street, Romford. It carries the standard green and white livery into which it was last repainted in December 1948, the month in which the short-lived programme of repainting 9T9s into the more modern colours of green and cream was abandoned. *Alan Nightingale collection*

The final days of 9T9 operation in the country area were marked by the presence of pockets of the class at a few well dispersed locations. In the far north of London Transport's territory, deep in the recesses of Luton garage, Ts 432 (on the left) and 422 await their next call of duty during the closing weeks of the 9T9 regime there. Accompanying them, and typifying the latest generation of London bus, is RT 4034. Both 9T9s were withdrawn from service on 1st January 1952. Far to the south-east, Dunton Green's T 425 was one of the very last 9T9s to be withdrawn from regular service operation on 1st February 1952. Despite their reputation within London Transport for being worn out, a fair number of 9T9s went via dealers to new careers abroad, with T 425 later recorded in Belgium and T 432 in faraway Southern Rhodesia. *Allen T Smith © A B Cross/ Alan B Cross*

The availability of an ample supply of spare 10T10s brought the 9T9 reign in the country area to a swift end later in the same year that the final overhauls on them had been carried out. By the autumn of 1951 all 35 vehicles remaining in country service had been concentrated into seven garages: Leatherhead (with 9), Addlestone (8), Dunton Green (5), Luton and St Albans (4 each), Hertford (3) and Northfleet (2). Addlestone's went first, all being withdrawn overnight on 1st December 1951, with Hertford's and Northfleet's following suit on the first day of 1952. St Albans' 9T9s lasted until 9th January and the last one left Luton on the 21st of that month. By the final withdrawal date, 1st February 1952, Leatherhead still retained five of its contingent (T 409, 410, 415, 429, 448) whilst Dunton Green had managed to keep T 411, 425, 427 and 441 in service until then.

Remarkably, this was not quite the end of the story for a class that had started off life with so much promise but had ended on a downbeat note as a somewhat unloved second best to the very popular and successful 10T10 which had outperformed it in almost every way. At a time when the 9T9s should have all found their way to the yards of dealers or scrap merchants, all-green liveried T 448 was, surprisingly, relicensed on 25th March 1952 at Reigate for conveying staff to and from the overhaul works at Chiswick and Aldenham. However it was only needed for this purpose on Mondays to Fridays, and on Saturdays T 448 was regularly sent on loan to Kingston whose enhanced Saturday single deck schedule meant that vehicles had to be brought in from elsewhere to cover. So, for a few months during the spring and early summer of 1952, T 448 presented a last opportunity to sample the not altogether inspiring experience of a service ride in a 9T9 for one last time. It is not known exactly when it finally ran at Kingston but the last possible opportunity would have been on Saturday 26th July as T 448's licence was surrendered on 1st August 1952.

A totally unexpected event was the return of T 448 to passenger service from Kingston garage on Saturdays, usually on route 213, which occurred between March and July 1952. On Saturday 10th May 1952 T 448 arrives at Kingston with its destination blind already set for a return run to Belmont. It presents an opportunity to study once more – before it finally becomes too late – the unorthodox and ungainly front end of one of London Transport's less satisfactory single deck designs. *Ken Blacker*

# 15 THE UBIQUITOUS 10T10 FAMILY
## T 453-718

Undoubtedly the most successful and widely travelled variant of the T class, and also its largest constituent, was the 266 strong batch numbered between T 453 and T 718. Always referred to generically as 10T10s, irrespective of the various sub-classifications issued from time to time, they proved to be reliable and versatile maids of all work even though their originally designated role was to act purely as units of the Green Line fleet. It would probably be an exaggeration to categorise the 10T10 as a classic design, but nevertheless it was one of the most aesthetically pleasing vehicles of its time. Once its inevitable early teething troubles were ironed out it became universally highly regarded, and certainly made a greater impact on the transport scene in London than any other single decker of the pre-war era.

One of the most pleasing and well balanced designs ever to emerge from the talented team at Chiswick must surely have been the 10T10 which, once a few initial problems were sorted out, proved to be as good as it looked. The vehicle chosen to represent the class for the Board's photographic archive was T 505 which was provided with blinds and boards for the Tunbridge Wells–Chertsey service on which it was due to start work from Addlestone garage on 1st May 1938. The photographs were taken four days beforehand, and even in black and white they give a good indication of how attractive the then current livery using three contrasting shades of green must have looked when new. *London Transport Museum*

Although, by June 1938, all the Gilfords had been eliminated, a high proportion of the Green Line fleet still consisted of petrol-engined machines – mostly AECs but also some Leylands – all of which were scheduled for replacement in pursuit of the Board's goal of having no coaches on regular Green Line work built before 1936. Not only were these older vehicles obsolete in appearance by modern standards, but many of them seated as few as 26 or 27 passengers and were too small to meet current needs. Two separate sanctions authorised the construction of the 10T10s. The first, for 150, covered T 453-602 and was followed quickly by a further 116 (T 603-718), although in reality the two were produced at Southall as a single batch with chassis numbers 06622600-06622865. In contrast to the 9T9s, which had been built on a virtually standard AEC Regal chassis, the new 10T10s were very much bespoke vehicles tailored to suit London Transport's specific requirements. They were the result of a joint design effort between the teams at Chiswick and Southall culminating in a finalised chassis specification dated 23rd June 1937 which was issued in the expectation that delivery would begin at the rate of eight per week from 11th January 1938.

This was an interesting period in the development of the London single decker. The engineering department's initial drive to break away from the use of front-engined vehicles, which had resulted in a short-lived standardisation on the AEC Q, had backfired when these proved less satisfactory than originally expected, particularly in regard to engine overheating and poor road holding. Renewed hopes were now being pinned on the Leyland-designed underfloor engined chassis which London Transport designated the TF class. The first of these entered experimental service from Tunbridge Wells garage on 1st December 1937 and acquitted itself sufficiently well to enable the finalised design for a production batch to be drawn up in February 1938. It was arranged that a batch of 75 (TF 14-88) would follow on from the 10T10s to complete renewal of the Green Line fleet and satisfy its vehicle requirements until 1945/46, but no greater number than this could be obtained because of London Transport's contractual obligation to AEC to provide the bulk of its new vehicle requirement. In fact with an intake of 87 TFs (including 12 private hire coaches) and 79 rear-engined CR-class 20-seat buses (later reduced with Leyland's consent to 48) a real problem arose in this respect in 1939. With the programme for new STLs drawing to a close and the next generation RT fleet coming on stream later than anticipated, the contractual arrangement with AEC was, in fact, infringed during that year and creative accounting had to be employed to cover this up.

Although London Transport had no option, in the interim, other than to revert to the purchase of front-engined single deckers, it had no intention of perpetuating on a wider scale the lacklustre performance of the 9T9s. Foremost among its requirements was the adoption of a much improved power unit, a decision arrived at following operating experience with the 100 strong STD class of Leyland Titan double deckers powered by that Company's standard 8.6 litre oil engine. In terms of smooth running, fuel consumption, reliability, and longevity of its components it proved far superior to the AEC 7.7 unit on which London Transport had, up to now, placed such heavy reliance. Operated from Hendon garage, the STDs covered the whole gamut of operations ranging from slow and congested inner city work to quiet, outer-urban service, and improved results were always achieved whatever the circumstances. The extra power apart, the key strength of the Leyland product lay in its use of direct fuel injection using a flower-pot shaped cavity in the piston crown, a marked step forward compared with AEC whose engineers still preferred to use indirect injection. Now convinced that this was the way forward for the future, London Transport took its evidence of extensive tests on the STD engine to AEC and explained to them that they were expected to produce an engine which could compare with the Leyland product.

AEC took the matter seriously with its Chief Engineer, G J Rackham, himself closely involved in the development of the chassis for the 10T10 including its engine. AEC already had an engine of roughly equal capacity in production in the form of its 8.8 litre A165 which, with bore and stroke of 115mm and 142mm respectively, achieved 130 bhp and was rated at 49.2hp. London Transport was already using more than 300 of these in LT class double deckers. AEC's solution was to modify it with a Leyland style head and, after satisfactory bench trials, it was offered for use on the new batch of Regals under the type code A180.

Although satisfied by the bench tests that the A180 would meet its requirements, London Transport was initially unwilling to enter into a contract for its purchase until certain legal niceties had been sorted out. The Board's technical and legal departments both harboured doubts over possible infringements of Leyland patents due to AEC's use of an injection nozzle exactly like the Leyland type. Indemnity was sought from AEC who disagreed with London Transport and took the view that there was no need for this. It obtained counsel's advice from Sir Stafford Cripps and also from a Mr Mould, an expert in the matter of patent specifications, who were both positive that no infringement existed. Subsequently Leyland themselves indicated that they had no objection provided that the design was not used in conjunction with any patents which they might hold, and this convinced London Transport that no legal liabilities would arise, allowing production to be authorised.

A problem with the A165 engine, and its derivative A180, was its length which, on the LT class, had been accommodated by extending the radiator forwards by almost 5 inches. This could not be permitted on the 10T10 without infringing overall length regulations or, alternatively, shortening the bodywork and thereby incurring an unacceptable penalty in reduced seating capacity. Considerable ingenuity went into squeezing the A180 into the space normally occupied by a smaller engine. The A180, tilted at an angle of 2 degrees, was placed 1¼ inches further back in the chassis than normal, requiring a repositioning of the cross members to take account of this. As London Transport's usual fluid transmission was specified there was no need to make provision for an engine-mounted dynamo, allowing the water pump to be moved to the back of the timing case. The fan, which would normally have been mounted in front of the timing case, was dispensed with entirely as it was considered unnecessary on the cooler-running direct injection engine. It proved possible to locate a specially designed radiator right up against the timing case with the bottom tank located down low in front of the sump, and as a result of all this a deeper radiator cover and grille was designed which was low enough at the bottom for the registration plate to be mounted on instead of below it. With all these modifications a compact front end arrangement was achieved, which was visually more satisfying than the bulbous appearance of the 9T9.

Improvements were effected to the braking and steering systems in the hope of eliminating the complaints received about the 9T9s. In the case of the brakes a larger type of vacuum servo was used to decrease pedal pressures. No change was made to the D132 preselective gearbox which, as usual, was used in conjunction with a fluid flywheel. The wheelbase was 6 inches shorter than the 9T9 at 17ft 0ins with a consequent lengthening of the rear overhang to retain the same overall length of 27ft 6ins. This did not affect the swept turning circle which remained at 63ft 6ins, the same as the 9T9, and when the bodywork was installed the unladen weight remained the same as the 9T9 at 6-15-0. With its greater power the 10T10 was undoubtedly more lively in performance and, with Newton shock absorbers all round, it gave a smoother ride too.

With all the modifications that had to be made to the chassis and its components compared with a standard Regal, and also taking into account the design and development costs, it was not surprising that the price charged for each

chassis at £928 was a substantial £148 (or 9%) more than that for each 9T9 even allowing for the much greater quantity discount on this occasion. Fortunately this was offset by a decision to build all 266 bodies 'in house' at Chiswick where a substantial saving could be made at £775 per body as against the £970 charged by Weymann for each metal-framed 9T9, meaning that the overall cost per vehicle balanced out fairly evenly at £1,740 for a 9T9 and £1703 for a 10T10.

An interesting sideline to all this is that AEC itself still appears to have remained unconvinced by the alleged superiority of the Leyland-style direct injection and still favoured its own Comet Mark III design to the extent that London Transport was persuaded to accept the first three chassis with indirect injection engines for comparative purposes. The fate of these engines is not known, but the rapid way in which similar comparative trials involving ST 1140 (the prototype RT 1) and a few experimental STLs a few months later were rapidly abandoned hints that the three 10T10s may have had only worked in indirect injection mode for a very short time.

The highly organised production line at Chiswick was capable of manufacturing new bodies on a larger scale and in a more modern working environment than most other coachbuilders of the time, and full use was made of pits, lifts and moving belts to make the construction teams' tasks as convenient and speedy as possible. Coachmakers are seen at work here on the partly-clad shell of a new 30-seater with an ST double decker in the background high on a hoist during its routine overhaul. *London Transport Museum*

The contract for building the 10T10 bodies came as a welcome boost for the Chiswick body shop at a time when work on new STL bodies was beginning to slow down. The initial batch of 150 was allocated body numbers 18096-18245 with the ensuing batch of 116 being 18247-18362, but these were not issued to the vehicles in numerical sequence and in practice bodies from the two batches overlapped. The 'missing' body number, 18246, was allocated to the experimental RT 1. At the end came three float bodies, 18363-18365, and these marked the termination of the current numbering series, with the TFs which came next starting a new series from 1 upwards.

The bodies, as specified by the Chiswick design team, constituted an interesting and innovative departure from the normal Chiswick product and marked, in effect, a virtual halfway house between the conventional composite body traditionally produced there and the so-called 'all metal' body (as supplied by Weymann for the 9T9) where timber was used but sparingly and then usually only as a packing on which to

screw mouldings etc., On the 10T10 the pillars and the cross-bars of the floor and roof were of conventional flitched timber, but all the longitudinal rails, such as the waistrail and cantrail, were made of steel. There were no conventional joints of the coachbuilt sort; instead the various parts of the body were joined together by brackets using three bolt recesses in the end of each rail into which were registered similar recesses on the junction bracket, hexagonal bolts being used to fasten the two together. Being bolted, all parts of the framework could be removed, repaired and replaced individually as units. London Transport's publicity machine made great play of the fact that this "metalised" form of composite construction simplified the attachment of various parts and was easier to repair than the conventional steel frame which was normally welded, although in truth very little time saving would have been achieved since cutting and welding in situ had become common practice by then.

The body for the 10T10 was undoubtedly attractive. Although bearing a family resemblance to the 9T9 it differed

An interesting view inside a partly completed body reveals the combination of timber pillars and metal longitudinals which was a feature of the unusual method of construction employed on the 10T10. In this instance the windows have been installed and the luggage racks constructed, and the major task in hand now appears to be the completion of the internal wiring.
*London Transport Museum.*

from it in many respects. The neat and much less fussy front end was an undoubted improvement, and an internal floor line approximately two inches lower than on the 9T9 was reflected in the reduced overall height of the body, giving it a much more sleek appearance. The difference in wheelbase meant that the pillar positions were not the same, and as a result the entrance aperture was narrower on the 10T10 and the rear bay correspondingly longer. The passenger door was hung on a recess in the outside of the bodywork instead of being encased inside an internal pocket, making maintenance easier and reducing the intrusion into the saloon. The doors themselves, which were sourced from two manufacturers for comparison purposes, had a spherical bearing on the top track and ran between Ferodo strips at the bottom set in the step well and its rearward extension. A pair of hinged flaps above the doorway gave access to the door runners and their mechanism which could be easily worked on when the side route board was removed. The mudguards, which were simpler in appearance than those used on the 9T9s, were nevertheless very stylish and were made completely of rubber by Dunlop coloured green to suit the livery. In the three shades of green adopted for the 9T9s in October 1937, and sporting the same handsome wheel trims, the 10T10 was a shining example of London Transport's design accomplishments at their very best.

Internally the 10T10 body closely resembled the 9T9 down to embracing similar décor and the same seating layout for 30 with the four rearmost rows raised higher than the others.

Luggage racks were built integrally with the bodywork and the usual deep-cushioned aluminium framed seats incorporated ash trays which, though not heavily used, were considered by London Transport to be a "psychological necessity" for coaches. The seat supports, which were of steel, were of the cantilever type to facilitate ease of cleaning. Two differences from the 9T9 were immediately apparent. The clock had reverted from a rectangular shape to the normal round format, and the large and intrusive Clayton heater was absent from the front bulkhead. Its replacement was a forced air ventilation system providing warmth in winter and coolness in summer, directed into the saloon at various points through trunking running along the body sides at floor level. Wind tunnel tests had indicated that the best point for gathering in air was at the rear of the vehicle (unlike on the 6Q6 where the air intake was at the front), so the intake grille was mounted fairly inconspicuously at the back of the roof merging neatly into the rear indicator box. The air was piped from the roof through ducts between the rear body panels and then led to a Clayton heater below floor level before finally being let into the saloon by grilles under the seats. Being thermostatically controlled, the heater maintained a constant temperature and could be cut out altogether in the summer with only cool air admitted. The driver was afforded no such luxury as heating, the warmth from the engine being considered adequate for him, but for the first time the lower section of the windscreen was arranged to open as well as the top half to increase airflow on hot days.

London Transport's standard internal décor for coaches was employed inside the saloon with brown at lower levels on the floor lino and the rexine covered side panels. Above this various shades of green rexine were employed along with a pale cream ceiling. The ceiling panels immediately above the luggage racks were also fitted with a length of rubber hose to prevent damage from suitcases. The seat moquette, which was designed to blend with the general décor, consisted basically of a brown and fawn design separated by green stripes. The fabric on the seat backs, and also on the front bulkhead, was initially in a light fawn but this was changed to a darker shade after the first few vehicles had been built because the original colour was found to show scuff marks too easily.

Right from the start there was uncertainty and even controversy between the engineering and operating departments over what seating capacity should be provided on the 10T10s. The latter department was not even sure, at the start, that all of them should be fitted out as Green Line coaches so, as a precaution, the final 28 of the second batch were initially pencilled in to be built as 32-seater service buses minus heaters and luggage racks and with bus-type seats. Under the specification issued in June 1937 the latter would be coded 10T10 while the coaches would be 1/10T11. A rapid change of heart saw the requirement for buses eliminated once the realisation dawned that it would be better to transfer the 9T9s to bus work than to use 10T10s on it. However a general misgiving lingered within the operating department over the fact that the new coaches would seat only 30 when a higher figure was really required, a discontent made stronger by the fact that the TF would be able to accommodate 34 with ease. The Chiswick staff went back to their drawing boards to investigate ways of satisfying the operating department's requirement for more seats.

The first completed chassis (06622601, T 454) arrived at Chiswick from AEC virtually on time on 13th January 1938, and from 2nd February new deliveries began to pour in. Registration number blocks already received for them were ELP 177-289 (T 453-565) and EYK 201-353 (T 566-718), and with bodies now under construction, an entry date into service was anticipated towards the end of March. These were all built as 30-seaters according to the original specification and classified 10T10. However one of the early deliveries, T 499, was set aside on arrival at Chiswick on 26th February while its body (18141) was used for a seating capacity experiment. It had been found that, by making the 10T10 seat back slightly more upright but without otherwise altering the level of comfort that it offered, it was possible to insert one more row of seats into the offside of the saloon. This meant, of course, reducing leg room, but it had the effect of increasing seating capacity to 32. An additional transverse seat could not be fitted into the nearside in the same way because of space limitations, but it was found possible to install a single inward facing seat immediately behind the front doorway partition to further increase the overall total to 33, only one short of the required 34.

The operators appear to have been ambivalent about the proposal, possibly because they had found from experience with the 6Q6s that inward facing seats were not popular with longer distance passengers who liked to face the direction of travel, with the result that these were normally the last seats to be filled. T 499 had still not entered service, and presumably no decision had yet been made on its future, when the engineers revealed in June that the cost of converting the existing 30-seaters to 33 seats upon overhaul would be £34 14s 0d per vehicle if the operators decided to go ahead and adopt the revised arrangement. The operating department's

Internally, the 10T10 did not differ greatly from the 9T9 in regard to décor and general fittings, and although the plain material used on the seat backs gave a slightly more utilitarian look when viewed from behind, the seat moquette itself was more patterned and attractive than that used on the 9T9. The biggest differences, as demonstrated in the forward-facing view inside T 505, were on the front bulkhead where a round-faced clock was now employed, the windows which followed the same level throughout on their bottom ledge, and the absence of a prominent Clayton heater. The view looking rearwards was taken in an unknown vehicle built early in the production run before the light-coloured side lining panels were replaced by a darker brown to overcome the problem of scuff marks. The positioning of the fare board on the emergency door can just about be seen. *London Transport Museum*

T 499 differed from all the others in being built with an inward-facing single seat immediately behind the doorway partition, making it the only 33-seater within the whole 10T10 fleet. Surprisingly, it retained this unique feature right to the end of its working life, the photograph being taken subsequent to the vehicle's second and last overhaul in January 1950. *Alan B Cross*

*Below* 10T10s galore! A line-up of new vehicles taken at Chiswick for publicity purposes shows Ts 540, 517, 507, 512, 548 and 511 fully prepared for service and about to be licensed. All are carrying blinds and boards showing various destinations on routes E and F, augmented by a slip board in the front bulkhead window stating 'VIA LONDON (VICTORIA)'. In fact the use of these on the E and F was aborted when it was realised that these routes would necessitate vehicles specially equipped for steep hill climbing, and all six were used instead on the 1st June 1936 introductions at Luton, St Albans and East Grinstead. *London Transport Museum*

disinclination to do so was probably partly caused by the knowledge that the drawing office had now come up with a plan for a full 34-seater with all seats facing forwards, and though it was not possible to introduce these modifications during the first production run of 150 for which all materials had been obtained, the 151st vehicle onwards could be built on these lines. T 499 was destined to remain unique, and it continued as a 33-seater throughout its operating life, subsequently being given its own coding of 10T10/2.

The designers' subsequent solution to the capacity problem on the 10T10s came with body 18247 upwards and brought about the well-remembered 10T10/1. The key to increased seating capacity lay in projecting the saloon floor forward to occupy part of the former step well whilst, at the same time, eliminating the full-height partition behind the entrance. By

this means an extra transverse seat could be incorporated on the nearside as well as on the offside. It was acknowledged, right from the start, that this revised arrangement had its drawbacks one of which was that wind-flow inside the saloon would be accentuated in the absence of a doorway partition, especially if the vehicle was travelling in summer with the door open. Much more serious, though, was the constriction of the entrance steps which effectively halved their width and was foreseen by some within the operating department as likely to become a major bone of contention amongst both passengers and staff. In this respect they were soon proved right and on 8th August 1938, only a week after the first 10T10/1 had entered service, the operators were informed that it was still not too late to revert to a full width step well for the final 60 bodies which, if they wished, could be built as 33-seaters in the same style as T 499. However this offer was not taken up. Perhaps because of the hurry in which plans for the T10/1 body were prepared, it appears to have been forgotten that a bell push had been located on the now discarded bulkhead partition and no provision was made for a replacement at the very front end of the coach. An outcry was inevitable, and it was not long before a bell push was wired into the main front bulkhead of the 10T10/1s, just above the entrance steps.

Although the entrance steps were narrowed on the 10T10/1, the actual door aperture and the door itself remained unchanged, so it was not possible to view the difference from outside when the door was shut. Without an internal bulkhead, the 10T10/1 was lighter than the 10T10 by almost 4 cwt at 6-11-3 as against 6-15-0 so that, unless filled at or near full passenger capacity, it should theoretically have been a little more sprightly in road performance although in reality there never seemed to be any difference between the two. The 116 vehicles actually constructed as 10T10/1s from new were T 522, 565, 599, 602, 607-718.

Before leaving the subject of seating capacity, it is worth recording that as early as February 1938 serious consideration was given to building 3-axle coaches with a length of 30ft. Sketches were drawn up which showed a T-type capable of taking 34 seats and a TF with 38. It was subsequently decided to go ahead with a single vehicle in the TF version provided permission for its use could be obtained from the Metropolitan Traffic Commissioner, but possibly with the threat of war lying ahead, this option was not pursued.

1st August 1938 saw 34-seater 10T10/1s coming into use for the first time, and those on routes A1 and A2 commenced the process of displacing 4Q4s from Green Line operation. Most vehicles placed into service on that day carried the new Lincoln green livery, and Northfleet's T 619 – seen here speeding past Marble Arch on route for Gravesend – was one of comparatively few 10T10/1s to carry the old colours. Close examination of the curved moulding sweeping down behind the rearmost side window reveals that it projects straight down to the waistrail instead of sweeping backwards at the bottom. This is the only way in which a 10T10/1 body could be distinguished from the earlier 10T10 model when viewed externally.
*P J Jones*

The very first 10T10s were licensed for service at Windsor garage on 26th March 1938 and, for the record, were T 453, 455, 461, 470 and 478. Godstone garage joined in from 31st March, the jointly-operated target being route G (Windsor–Caterham) which had up to then been operated by Leyland Tigers and Titans, almost all of them with a seating capacity of only 26. This was followed in early April by route P (Farnham Common/Burnham Beeches–Horse Guards Ave) worked solely by Windsor from which 7T7s were officially displaced although, in fact, both these and 1/7T7/1s were reallocated elsewhere. The position with these early Regals was very fluid at the time and others were, in fact, subsequently drafted back in to provide summer reliefs.

Next on the list was route D (Staines–Westerham) worked by Staines and Dunton Green, Staines with Leyland Titans and Dunton Green with a mixture of 7T7 and 1/7T7/1s which had replaced Leylands between six months and a year earlier. The main conversion date was 1st May but Staines received a couple of 10T10s earlier than this on 12th April. 1st May 1938 was a very big conversion day when no fewer than 31 new 10T10s were licensed for service, the practice henceforth being to carry out all future conversions on the first day of each month wherever possible. In addition to route D, routes C1 (Tunbridge Wells–Chertsey) and C2 (Tunbridge Wells–Woking) were also dealt with, releasing a mixture of older T types from Tunbridge Wells and Addlestone garages as well as a few Leylands from the latter, and giving 10T10s the opportunity to show their paces alongside TF 1 for a few months until it was transferred from Tunbridge Wells to Romford (London Road) garage on 16th December 1938. The clear-out of old T types was almost complete at Tunbridge Wells, with only one staying on for the summer, but at Addlestone several continued to have a visible presence through to the end of the summer programme. However it marked the end of Leyland Tigers and Titans on Green Line work although a few could still be found in the private hire fleet until their final withdrawal took place on 1st October.

The 1st June conversions exceeded the May total with no fewer than 43 new coaches licensed on this date followed by a further seven over the next three days and three more later in the month. Targets this time included route N (Epping–Windsor), bringing Epping garage its first batch of 10T10s

and Windsor its second. Route B (Wrotham–Aylesbury) introduced 10T10s to Amersham, partly on workings covered earlier by 9T9s but latterly by older Regals, and also to Swanley. Routes H1 (Luton–East Grinstead) and H2 (Dunstable–East Grinstead) brought 10T10s to Luton, St Albans and East Grinstead garages, and route K2 (Dorking–Welwyn Garden City) brought the class to Dorking and Hatfield.

By this time the vast majority of Green Line services were now worked by modern vehicles, the only significant pockets of operation for petrol Ts being those from inner London to Romford, Epping and beyond, and to Grays and Tilbury. Apart from these, the only other routes still scheduled to be worked by the previous generation of coaches were the E (Aylesbury–Chelsham) and F (Hemel Hempstead–Tatsfield/Edenbridge), which were a joint operation covered by Tring, Hemel Hempstead and Chelsham garages. A stumbling block to their conversion was the exceptionally steep Titsey Hill between Chelsham and Oxted on route F which the 10T10 could not manage in its current form if well laden. This problem was first discussed with AEC in May 1938 and there was agreement between the two parties that special reduction gear for the gearbox was needed to overcome the problem. However AEC's design staff were so busy at the time on other projects that the task could not be tackled for at least three months and the Company could only suggest that the problem could be overcome in the short term by adopting a lower ratio axle setting than the existing 5.2:1. Eventually it was arranged that the final 25 chassis in the first sanction would be supplied with 6¼:1 axle ratios even though this meant that, for most of its operating day, each vehicle's performance would be impaired merely for the convenience of climbing one relatively short hill, and then not on every journey. The vehicles concerned, T 578-602, mostly entered service on 1st July 1938 although the Tring allocation was not completed until 1st August. Also on 1st July Epping's routes V (Bishops Stortford–Horse Guards Avenue) and W (Ongar–Eldon Street) received new 10T10s and a start was made on routes Z1 (Tilbury–Aldgate) and Z2 (Grays–Aldgate) worked by Grays garage, part of whose intake included vehicles with revised axle ratio that were surplus to immediate requirements on the E and F.

The modified vehicles, which were classified 1/10T10, were – as expected – not well received by staff who complained vociferously of lack of speed and inflexibility of performance with a consequent inability to run to time. Why, they asked, should drivers consider driving 90 miles with a 6¼ differential just because of Titsey Hill, which was not served by all journeys anyway? Feelings were very strong, and it was probably only through London Transport's firm assurance that a permanent and acceptable solution would be found to the 'Titsey Hill problem' within a year that the staff's goodwill was retained.

The new coach intake of 1st July 1938 included the first two 10T10s to make their appearance at Grays and both were of special interest. One of the pair was the experimental 33-seater T 499 which was now making its service debut, although it did not stay at Grays for long, moving to Leavesden Road in November and Hatfield in January 1939. Prior to entering service both it and its partner at Grays, T 521, had been the subject of a further experiment, this time concerning livery. Dissatisfaction had been felt for some while over the poor wearing quality of the green paint used on the main panels of country area vehicles, leading to an instruction by Frank Pick that much better lasting versions of green must be found. The two new 10T10s were used as the guinea pigs for the trials that subsequently took place. T 499 was repainted in what was recorded as a mid-green shade, which was applied to both the lower panels and the roof, and was in fact the famous Lincoln green subsequently adopted as standard for the whole Country Bus & Coach fleet. The conventional apple green shade was retained around the windows. T 521, on the other hand, was painted in the same general styling but using what was described as a very dark green. It seems likely that this was the same shade used since

1937 on roofs and mudguards but now extended to cover the main panels too, and it would almost certainly have looked too drab and overpowering for general adoption New 10T10s in the Lincoln green livery began to appear in service from 1st August but no record exists of exactly where in the production schedule the changeover occurred. In its original application the new livery was slightly enhanced in its Green Line version by picking out the mouldings above and below the windows with an orange band, but this did not last long and at the insistence of Frank Pick it was changed to chrome yellow from December 1938 onwards.

The Green Line network was now awash with 10T10s and their contribution to the increasing success of the operation cannot be denied, but their introduction had not gone without problems, almost all of which were engine related and were probably a sign that the A180 engine should have been subjected to more testing before being put into production. The early months were, in fact, beset with engine failures, a major cause of which was found to be the use by AEC of defective valve springs. Within a single four week period in April/May no fewer than 52 coaches had suffered breakdowns, representing almost every vehicle licensed at the time. A total of 75 valve springs were found to be faulty. The situation was so serious that G J Rackham himself became involved in seeking a solution which meant sourcing a new, reliable supply and scrapping the whole of the existing stock. Another problem was that the new engines almost immediately began gathering complaints of excessive noise, and Rackham was forced to agree that there was indeed a considerable difference in noise volume between the 10T10 engine and the Leyland one. He was given the loan of an STD for a week to investigate, and it was discovered that by adopting clearances identical to those used by Leyland the problem could be overcome. Yet another source of complaint, excessive smoke, was cured by repositioning the inlet valve. Starter switch failures caused by ineffective springs were remedied by fitting stronger ones, and slowness in pulling away was cured by adjusting the pump settings. This litany of early troubles was finally overcome, after which the 10T10 gained a reputation as an extremely reliable and popular vehicle ideally suited to the work on which it was employed.

The new vehicle intake of 1st August 1938 was significant, not only for introducing the revised livery, but also because 34-seat 10T10/1s were put into service for the first time. Of the 31 new coaches licensed on this date just eight were of the old 30-seat variety, the very last of these to be licensed. As well as finishing the conversion at Tring and continuing the process at Grays, a new emphasis was now placed on eliminating 4Q4s from Green Line work starting with routes A1 (Gravesend–Ascot) and A2 (Gravesend–Sunningdale) worked by Northfleet and Staines garages. The same process continued on 1st September with 10T10/1s going to Leavesden Road for route T (Watford–Golders Green) and Amersham for route R (Chesham–Oxford Circus). In both cases some early T types were also displaced as well as the Qs. A couple of 10T10/1s also went to High Wycombe's route Q (High Wycombe–Oxford Circus). All 4Q4s had now returned to bus work and the elimination of old Regals from Grays was now complete. Now the only garages still left with a scheduled allocation of petrol Regals were the two at Romford, London Road with routes Y1 (Brentwood–Horse Guards Avenue), Y2 (Upminster–Aldgate), Y3 (Brentwood–Windsor Sundays) and seasonal U (Marylebone–Whipsnade), and North Street with route X (Romford–Horse Guards Avenue). It was now time to make inroads into the elderly fleet at Romford (London Road), which received its first nine 10T10/1s on 1st September, but none of the new vehicles were destined ever to run from the North Street premises at which no diesel fuelling facilities were installed. The intake of 34-seaters at London Road in place of former 27-seaters resulted in service reductions which meant that the whole of the Romford fleet could be accommodated there, allowing the North Street premises to be closed on 29th November 1938.

The 1st October batch of 21 new 10T10/1s all went to Romford (London Road) and it might have been expected that when the same number of new coaches was licensed exactly a month later, on 1st November, these would all have done likewise. However it was now time for the first batch of 9T9s to be demoted from coach to bus work at a mixture of locations – Crawley, Hatfield, Leavesden Road and Reigate – for which replacements were required. These were, in the main, obtained by sending new 34-seaters to Epping and Grays which, in turn, dispatched 30-seaters to displace the 9T9s. On the same day the last of the 7T7 27-seaters were withdrawn, and when these manoeuvres were all completed only 20 new 10T10/1s remained unused. Fifteen of these were licensed at Romford on 1st December leaving just five new Ts to begin service in 1939.

On the first day of 1939 four of the remaining five were licensed, leaving just T 691 to enter service belatedly on 25th March. The reason for its lateness is not known but, significantly, on the same day the first twelve of the production series of new TFs made their appearance. With their semi-streamlined fronts they looked far more striking and modern than the 10T10s, and the choice of the slowly-timed Romford routes for their debut was perhaps unfortunate. It was not until after the war that Green Line passengers were able to witness TFs performing at their best and to sample the exhilarating rides that they were able to give. Their arrival at Romford meant that the final petrol engined 1/7T7/1s were removed from Green Line work after which the remaining TFs were used to continue the downgrading of the 9T9s, a task almost but not quite completed by the time war broke out. As recorded in chapter 14. the relocation of the 9T9s was carried out between May and August as almost-new 10T10/1s

were displaced from Romford and sent to Crawley, Hitchin, Leatherhead, Leavesden Road, Luton and Reigate to take up Green Line service where the 9T9s left off.

One final act of significance to record in the pre-war era is that AEC finally came up with a solution to the hill-climbing problem, enabling the 1/10T10s to be removed from routes E and F, although with war intervening by no means all of them were promptly converted to standard 5.2:1 axle ratio. A gearbox with appropriately set ratios for hill climbing which nevertheless allowed normal top speed to be obtained was duly designed and designated D132T (the regular one being the D132QX). Combined with a 6¼ axle ratio, it performed very adequately and eliminated all the previous sources of complaint. As the routes concerned were under pressure from passenger loadings, the straightforward course of adapting the original vehicles was not chosen, and instead a reduced total of 19 10T10/1s were modified. These began work at Chelsham, Hemel Hempstead and Tring between 5th and 23rd May 1939, the vehicles concerned being T 607, 613, 617, 618, 643, 645, 648, 651, 655-660, 662-666. Although it had already been used, the chassis code 1/10T was adopted for them having become obsolete in its original form, their full designation being 1/10T10/1. The onset of war meant that they were destined to run in their revised form for only a few weeks. The service via Titsey Hill was abandoned on 1st September 1939 along with all other Green Line operations and it was not resumed when a limited wartime Green Line network was later reinstated. The decision was subsequently taken to remove and place in store the low ratio gearboxes from all 19 coaches which was done between February 1942 and May 1943, mostly at overhaul, with the exception of T 645 which was dealt with earlier, in November 1940, possibly when its gearbox needed attention.

By the time that war was officially declared on Sunday 3rd September 1939 the 10T10s had already suffered the same major upheaval as the 9T9s in being commandeered for ambulance work. Back in July 1938 the Government had asked London Transport to make plans for the conversion of its entire Green Line fleet at 24 hours notice enabling the vehicles to be put at the disposal of the Ministry of Health for so long as hostilities lasted, their principal perceived use being to transport patients from hospitals in central London to linked establishments in outlying areas. Each vehicle would have to be stripped of its internal fittings and equipped to carry stretchers and, in the first instance, newly built and as yet unlicensed T 661 was sent to the Reigate workshops to ascertain how this could be done. It is thought that further trials subsequently took place at other garages. On 20th September 1938 formal agreement was reached that London Transport would provide 450 Green Line coaches of which 300 would be fitted out and 150 held in reserve. Negotiations over the hire charges were left to be concluded at a later date but it was agreed that any war related losses would be recompensed under the same arrangements outlined in the Compensation (Defence) Act 1939 as if the vehicles had been requisitioned.

It is not clear exactly which 450 Green Line vehicles London Transport had committed itself to converting under the September 1938 agreement, since at the time deliveries of 10T10s were still ongoing and the new TF coaches had yet to be built. Clearly the 50 6Q6s were included as were the 50 9T9s, and the latter continued to be part of the plan even after the majority of them had been reclassified as buses. If war had broken out earlier that it actually did, some 1/7T7/1s

T 539 stands alongside a veteran solid-tyred Associated Daimler lorry outside Reigate garage soon after its conversion to an ambulance. In peace time it had operated from East Grinstead, but most of its wartime service as an ambulance was spent at Reigate apart from a short two-months spell at Guildford in 1944. Despite the camouflaging of its roof in grey, T 539 still looks smart in its original Green Line livery, but it is destined to go almost another six years without being repainted by which time it will far more care-worn. *Alan Nightingale collection*

would inevitably have had to be included within the total. By the summer of 1939 the situation had stabilised at 266 10T10s, 50 6Q6, 50 9T9 and 75 TF, making a total of 441. Added to the list were the 24 LTC private hire coaches, the Central Bus department's only contribution to the ambulance fleet which, when conversion took place mainly on 1st September with just a few more follow-ups on the 2nd, brought the total number dealt with to 465.

The stretcher capacity of the various types of vehicle when converted to ambulances varied according to their design and layout. Each 10T10 (and also the 9T9s and LTCs which were both virtually identical to the 10T10 in internal size and layout) was capable of accommodating nine stretchers. The 6Q6 could accommodate eight stretchers and also six seated patients in the area by the engine, whilst the TF was capable of holding ten stretchers plus two sitting cases in the seat ahead of the doorway which, in peace time, had already proved so popular with passengers because of the splendid view forward from it. Although the coach ambulances were held at the disposal of the Ministry of Health, they remained at London Transport garages and were crewed by service drivers who had volunteered and were suitably trained for the work involved.

In common with the rest of the London Transport fleet, the 10T10s quickly gained wartime white markings, masked headlamps, and matt grey camouflaged roofs. By December 1939 those that remained as ambulances also had the lower halves of their side and rear windows painted green, in addition to which a lattice of tape covered the glass as an anti-blast measure similar to that employed by many people on the

windows of their houses. The latter feature was dispensed with after a while, presumably because it had been found unnecessary or ineffective, and the green paint appears to have been removed from the glass later in the war.

By no means all the 10T10s remained as ambulances. After only a few days 18 of them were returned on 4th September as surplus to requirements and were placed in store, though still licensed, in Romford garage which was one of two that had been closed as an operational base with the cessation of Green Line operation, the other being Hitchin (whose only remaining vehicle, an essential staff bus, was re-housed in the Eastern National premises elsewhere in the town until the London Transport garage reopened). The arrival of the 18 10T10s at Romford did not go unnoticed by the travelling public who asked why. as staff were also present on the site, some sort of Green Line operation could not be re-started. The pressure was removed when the vehicles were transferred away to other garages to run as buses; two to Grays on 6th September and the remainder to Hertford, Leatherhead, Luton, St Albans and Watford High Street on the 26th of the same month. Meanwhile six more surplus ambulances had returned to the fold on 16th September and were put into bus service, three each at Amersham and Windsor. From then onwards 10T10s became a familiar sight on Country Bus operations as well as on their intended Green Line duties for the remainder of their working lives. From early in 1940 repainted vehicles began appearing in the new Country Bus department green and white livery, and repainting into Green Line colours ceased for the duration of the war.

T 499 and another stand outside Hendon garage during the first year of the war, both fully kitted out for their role as ambulances. The green paint on the bottom halves of the windows, and the anti-blast tape above, were applied as a precautionary measure during the latter part of 1939 or perhaps early in 1940 but were discarded later in the war as unnecessary. T 499 was officially allocated to Hendon from 1st December 1939 right through to its release from ambulance duties on 8th August 1945, and for much of its time it would have stood in the same location awaiting calls to action. In peace time T 499 had been notable as the one-off 33-seater, and it had also been the test bed for the Lincoln green livery which contrasts quite strongly with the lighter green vehicle behind. *D W K Jones*

After ending a brief spell as an ambulance on 29th November 1939, 10T10/1 T 714 was converted back to its former condition as a Green Line coach and relicensed on 1st May 1940 ready to commence work from Epping garage on a revived route N. The sun shines on its grey roof camouflage as it stands at its London terminus in Portman Square. *D W K Jones*

Early in the war, the Ministry of Health announced that it was to repatriate a further 164 ambulances, and London Transport selected the 10T10 family for this purpose, preferring to leave the entire 9T9, 6Q6, 2TF2 and LTC fleets on Ministry work. This enormous influx took place on 29th November 1939 and brought 'home' all of the 10T10/1s whose 34-seat capacity rendered them more useful than the pure 10T10s. This large cut-back still left coach ambulances at 20 central and 16 country garages with 10T10s present at nine of the former (Battersea, Cricklewood, Hackney, Hammersmith, Hendon, Muswell Hill, Palmers Green, Tottenham and Twickenham) and at eight country ones (Dunton Green, East Grinstead, Reigate, Staines, Swanley, Tunbridge Wells, Watford High Street and Leavesden Road).

All the coach ambulances received on 29th November were immediately delicensed and placed into store, there being no work readily available for them to do. The first to find employment after only two days of idleness were T 681 and 686 which were dispatched to the Central Bus garage at Old Kent Road to help cover a few essential private hire runs such as the Heinemann contract from Elephant & Castle and Clapham to Kingswood and journeys for the Aliens Office between Marsham Street and Wormwood Scrubs. Meanwhile plans were being prepared for a limited resumption of Green Line services to be carried out subject to staff availability, and the first fruits of this saw the relicensing of 23 10T10/1s at Romford for the reinstatement of route Y2 between Aldgate and Corbets Tey on 13th December 1939. By the turn of the year 49 of the class were back in use. Romford now had 24 and, as recorded above, there were two at Old Kent Road. The remaining 23 were distributed amongst seven garages for use on bus services with eight at Leatherhead, six at Watford High Street, two each at Addlestone, Dorking, Grays and Hertford, and a single example at Luton.

The first quarter of 1940 brought a significant renaissance to the Green Line network with further coaches being relicensed for service almost every month, all of them 34-seaters. On 17th January routes A1 and A2 recommenced, worked as before by Northfleet and Staines, and on the same day the 10T10 family was scheduled for the first time on route Q (High Wycombe–Oxford Circus) worked by High Wycombe and route R (Chesham to Oxford Circus) from Amersham, both of which in pre-war days had been in the hands of 6Q6s. February 7th found the H1 restored but only between Luton and Victoria with Luton as its sole allocation, whilst the M1 was similarly revived at its northern end to run Hertford–Oxford Circus or Shepherds Bush, based on Hertford garage.

This, too, had previously been a mecca for 6Q6s. The next batch resumed on 13th March with route C1 (now re-lettered C) worked, as before, by Tunbridge Wells but with a western allocation at Staines, and the linked routes E and F from Aylesbury and Hemel Hempstead respectively but now running southwards only as far as Victoria and worked by Hemel Hempstead and Tring. On the same day the H1, which had been revived in truncated form in February, returned to its pre-war terminus at East Grinstead and was given an allocation from that end but was now re-lettered H. There was nothing new in April but on 8th May route N was reinstated between Bishops Stortford, Epping and Portman Square bringing Epping back into the Green Line fold. This marked the end of the reintroductions but not before 75 10T10/1s (including spares) had been put back into service during the first half of 1940.

The Green Line fleet at this time was a motley-hued collection of vehicles in three different versions of country area colours, the two original Green Line styles plus the green and white livery which was steadily becoming more widespread. A common factor in all three cases was the wartime grey roof. The repainting of bodies continued on a spasmodic basis even though the pre-war system of overhauling, which was planned with such care and precision, had largely broken down. Despite the wartime conditions a certain amount of chassis overhauling still took place at Chiswick Works, where bodies continued to be lifted from their chassis in traditional fashion, but as far as the 10T10 class was concerned it was only vehicles on active coach or bus service that were called in for overhaul, and then on a far less frequent basis than before the war. Very many 10T10s – principally those employed as ambulances – did not receive their first overhaul until after the war had ended and in some cases not until as late as 1948. From about January 1940 onwards the overhauling of bodies was decentralised to a number of operational garages, the selected ones north of the Thames being Alperton, Chalk Farm, Cricklewood, Hendon, Muswell Hill and Willesden, whilst those in the south were Camberwell, Elmers End, Merton, Mortlake and Reigate. By 1941, with the falling off of air raids and a shortage of skilled labour, the number of decentralised overhaul workshops was reduced initially to nine and ultimately to four. From April 1941 the garages at Alperton, Elmers End and Reigate carried out about 40% of all body overhauls between them, the remaining work being concentrated in the former tram depot at Chiswick which, immediately before this, had been used principally as a vehicle store.

The number of T-types on bus service in the country area was increased with the relicensing on 4th May 1940 of fourteen 30-seat 10T10s to join those which had been employed on this work since September 1939. Distributed amongst a number of garages – Addlestone, Hemel Hempstead, High Wycombe, Luton, St Albans, Tring and Watford Leavesden Road – they brought the number of 30-seaters employed on passenger service during the war to a short-lived maximum of 23. With the sharp deterioration of the war situation in the spring of 1940 it was found necessary to increase the coach ambulance fleet by 50 from 29th May all of which were 30-seaters.

Before this happened, however, there was another big upsurge in Green Line activity towards the end of 1940. All cross-London operation had ceased on 23rd October, but service reintroductions on 4th and 18th December brought the network almost up to its pre-war size although a few notable outer termini were omitted. This coincided with the introduction on 4th December 1940 of service numbers instead of letters on all except Romford's Y2 which was dealt with on the 18th and converted to double deck operation using STLs on the same day. The situation as regards the 10T10/1s can be summarised as follows:

## 4TH DECEMBER 1940

Services already worked by 10T10/1s which continued to be

| New no. | Old no. | Garage |
|---|---|---|
| 2 | A1, A2 | Northfleet |
| 5 | C | Tunbridge Wells |
| 8 | H1 | East Grinstead |
| 20 | C | Addlestone |
| 23A/23B | A1, A2 | Staines |
| 45 | H1 | Luton |
| 52 | N | Epping |

Formerly worked by 10T10/1s and now taken over by 4Q4s

| | | |
|---|---|---|
| 33 | Q | High Wycombe |
| 34 | R | Amersham |
| 49 | M | Hertford |

Services reinstated with 10T10/1 operation

| | |
|---|---|
| 3 (Wrotham–Victoria) | Swanley |
| 18 (Guildford–Oxford Circus) | Guildford |
| 40 (Aylesbury–Victoria) | Tring |
| 40A (Hemel Hempstead–Victoria) | Hemel Hempstead |
| 53 (Bishops Stortford–Aldgate) | Epping |

## 18TH DECEMBER 1940

Services reinstated with 10T10/1 operation

| | |
|---|---|
| 14 (Dorking–Victoria) | Dorking |
| 15 (Dorking–Victoria) | Leatherhead |
| 21 (Staines–Victoria) | Staines |
| 47 (Hitchin–Victoria) | Hitchin |
| 47A (Welwyn Garden City–Victoria) | Hatfield |

Service started on 4/12/40 with 11T11 and now converted to 1/10T10/1

| | |
|---|---|
| 9 (Crawley–Oxford Circus) | Crawley/Reigate |

Service started on 4/12/40 with 7T7 and now converted to 1/10T10/1

| | |
|---|---|
| 10 (Reigate–Oxford Circus) | Reigate |

*Top* With the introduction of route numbers in place of letters for Green Line services on 4th December 1940 route N became the 52. Newly transferred into Epping on that day was T 599 which, though still carrying pre-war Lincoln green coach livery, exhibits a slight variation from normal in that the windscreen surround is in the darker colour. A conventional AEC-type wheel ring has replaced the original decorative trim on the front wheel, a modification which was to become increasingly common as time passed by. Behind T 599 at Oxford Circus stands STL 1150 on route 33, which in 10T10 days had been known as route Q worked from High Wycombe garage. *John L Smith*

*Centre* Although working on Green Line service, T 632 carries the standard wartime green and white colours which, in this instance, were applied when the vehicle was overhauled at Reigate in December 1940. An Addlestone based coach, it is seen laying over outside Victoria garage prior to working to Chertsey on route 20 (the former route C). After Green Line operations ceased on 30th September 1942, T 632 served US troops in this country as a Red Cross Clubmobile. *W J Haynes*

*Bottom* Most of the limited number of 10T10s that remained on bus operation during the war were of the 34-seat variety, such as Dunton Green based T 617 seen here at Sevenoaks. Anti-shatter mesh has been applied to most of the windows on this vehicle which, having been relicensed in March 1940 after a short spell on ambulance work, then remained in continuous service throughout the remainder of the war. *Alan Nightingale collection*

After only two weeks of 10T10/1 operation routes 40/40A were double decked with STLs, and it was through the availability of the displaced single deckers that updating of rolling stock on routes 9 and 10 became possible. Further changes occurred at various dates in June 1941 when, resulting from the double decking of routes 2, 5, 8, 18 and 23/23A, it became possible for 10T10/1s to displace the last remaining 7T7s from route 26 (Windsor–Victoria) and 26A (Farnham Common–Victoria) worked by Windsor garage and also from the 35 (Aylesbury–Victoria) worked by Amersham. In the same sequence of changes Hertford's operation on route 49, which had initially been earmarked for conversion to STL along with the other June double decking, was instead restored back to 10T10/1 operation after six months in the hands of 4Q4s.

These were basically the last wartime Green Line changes to affect the 10T10/1s. A proposal to withdraw routes 9, 35 and 47A with the start of the 1941 winter programme following a request by the Regional Traffic Commissioner to affect fuel economies was not proceeded with, and the only change to occur thereafter was that the rolling stock at Staines garage was swapped around on 8th October 1941 with the 23/23A now being taken back by 10T10/1s with its STLs going to the 21. The position then remained static until a government directive was put into force decreeing that, in common with all other long-distance coach services, the entire Green Line network would cease after operation on Tuesday 29th October 1942.

The great majority of 10T10/1s employed on Green Line work – 84 in all – were delicensed on the morning following the end of operations with just 22 being transferred to various country garages, most of them as replacement for 30-seat 10T10s only three of which (T 479, 535, 540) remained in service on 30th October. A snapshot of the position on that day finds 54 of the class allocated to bus duties at 16 garages as follows:

As a consequence of the cessation of all Green Line operations on 30th September 1942 it was necessary to introduce new 10T10 worked route 359 between Amersham and Aylesbury to avoid leaving sections of road unserved. The 359 was of particular interest in being one of the few instances where London Transport ran a service jointly with another operator, in this case United Counties, an arrangement which lasted for many years. In this instance London Transport's contribution to the service is Amersham based T 596 which, up to the time of the Green Line withdrawal, had been working as a coach at Windsor. *J F Higham © A B Cross*

| | |
|---|---|
| Amersham (11) | T 479, 639, 640, 644, 647, 672, 677-679, 681, 699 |
| St Albans (7) | T 602, 614, 634, 636, 642, 653, 706 |
| Addlestone (6) | T 617, 643, 645, 651, 667, 692 |
| Hertford (6) | T 619, 622-624, 638, 693 |
| Grays (4) | T 610, 611, 618, 716 |
| Hitchin (4) | T 540, 608, 621, 641 |
| Dorking (3) | T 613, 615, 691 |
| Crawley (2) | T 535, 657 |
| Godstone (2) | T 656, 658 |
| Leatherhead (2) | T 629, 700 |
| Reigate (2) | T 663, 664 |
| Epping (1) | T 565 |
| Hemel Hempstead (1) | T 631 |
| Leavesden Road (1) | T 674 |
| Swanley (1) | T 620 |
| Windsor (1) | T 675 |

The most modern class of single decker to be converted to perimeter seating as a wartime measure was the 10T10, and this photograph depicting the first one to be dealt with was taken on 24th December 1941, the day on which its conversion was completed. The lack of a full height partition behind the doorway indicates that this is, in fact, a 10T10/1 whose seating capability under the new arrangement has been reduced from 34 to 30. T 641 re-entered service in this form at Luton soon afterwards and reverted to normal seating in February 1946. *London Transport Museum*

By this time a significant modification was being made to various classes within London Transport's single deck fleet from which the 10T10 family was not immune, as their interior layouts were reconfigured from transverse to perimeter seating as a means of increasing carrying capacity. In August 1941 the Minister of War Transport had issued a significant new directive to the Regional Transport Commissioners permitting single deckers to be modified in this way to carry the same number of standing passengers as there were seats up to a maximum of 30 standees. London Transport was quick to make use of this new facility, though only to the extent that 20 standing passengers would be allowed, which was probably the maximum that could be negotiated with the Transport & General Workers Union. Since up to 12 standees could already be carried under wartime dispensation the extra gain was not enormous, but it was enough to justify the costs involved in rearranging the seats to gain even this small advantage on busy routes where physical obstructions or weight limits prevented the employment of double deckers. Board approval was speedily given to spend £6,580 on converting 188 single deckers and the first conversions to perimeter seating began in December 1941. (Subsequently this initial authorisation was reduced to 176 and the money was underspent by £1,597, partly through more second hand material being used than expected).

Compared with the other classes the 10T10s were slow off the mark with only two conversions being completed initially. T 641 was used as the prototype for the class and was dealt with in November 1941 followed by T 621 in January 1942. The conversions themselves were relatively simple and involved rearranging all except the rear seats around the side of the bus, plus the installation of white-painted upright stanchions for standing passengers to hold on to. Some of these stanchions were full height from floor to ceiling and others reached up only as far as the luggage rack rail. The first two conversions both involved 10T10/1s and over the course of time 48 of these were dealt with. In their revised format the seating capacity was reduced to 30 which, together with 20 standing passengers produced a total capacity of 50. Twelve 10T10s also became standee vehicles. On these it was found that the seats could be shuffled more efficiently within the available space than was possible on the 10T10/1s with the result that only one was lost, leaving them to accommodate 29 in reasonable seated comfort which, along with 20 standees, gave a total capacity of 49. The difference in total carrying capacity between the 10T10 and the 10T10/1 was thus reduced to a mere one, almost eliminating the advantage that the latter type had formerly enjoyed.

The first two began work in their new form at Luton but were subsequently moved to Hitchin, which subsequently became one of the main garages to house standee 10T10s while Luton, on the other hand, barely featured again. Introduction began apace several months later when, between October 1942 and January 1943, many more began work with Amersham, Addlestone and Hertford, as well as Hitchin, prominent amongst the users of them but with lesser allocations also at Dorking, Epping and Leatherhead. April to June 1943 saw another batch of conversions, adding Dunton Green, Hemel Hempstead, Leavesden Road and Tring to the list while, surprisingly, yet another batch of eight was converted just before the war's end in March and April 1945, mainly to augment the number of high capacity single deckers at Addlestone and Leatherhead.

Things were reasonably quiet on the home front in the autumn of 1942 with few calls being made requiring the services of the coach ambulances. It was presumably this lull in their activities that persuaded the Ministry of War Transport to authorise a series of requisitions which resulted in vehicles being handed over to the American military authorities who removed them to their large G25 transport base at Ashchurch, just outside Tewkesbury, for onward transmission to wherever they were required. The first batch of ten was impressed on 16th September (T 488, 492, 524, 566, 572, 578, 582, 586, 592, 594). This was followed on 30th October by five more 10T10s (T 455, 457, 460, 462, 490) along with the six 9T9s detailed in chapter 14, and finally by another batch of ten on 22nd December, of which only nine actually went, these being T 463, 486, 509, 546, 547, 569, 587, 590, 605. Thus by the end of 1942, 24 10T10s had been removed from London Transport's control with no certainty that they would be returned to its ownership when the war ended. The vehicles were repainted in khaki with a white star and given seven-digit army numbers, but records have not survived to show what individual vehicles were used for or where they went. It is known that some of them were dispatched to the Medical Department of the US Army and others may have been used as general staff transport. Eight – exactly one in three – failed to return to London Transport when hostilities ended, the write-offs being T 460, 486, 488, 509, 578, 586, 587, 594.

The next and much larger batch to be impressed consisted of no fewer than 40 10T10s and 10T10/1s that had been made redundant with the September 1942 cuts. These went via the American military authorities to the Red Cross for the purpose of providing recreational services to troops stationed in Great Britain. They became the famous Red Cross 'Clubmobiles' fulfilling a concept by New York banker Harvey D Gibson, the Red Cross Commissioner in the UK, who had the idea of providing a service of "clubs on wheels" which could reach service personnel at their camps or airfields to provide food and refreshments, all free of charge. Between 4th January and 15th February 1943 the 40 coaches left their various storage sites in London to go to two companies contracted to convert them to American Red Cross specification. The main one was Samuel Elliott & Company, a shop-fitting concern at Caversham, Reading, which dealt with 30, while the remaining ten went to a location as yet untraced in Hayes, Middlesex. When complete they were taken to the American Red Cross headquarters for Europe at Duke's Yard, Grosvenor Square, for final commissioning and allocation of a crew.

The conversion involved the complete gutting of the inside of each coach, enabling a kitchen to be installed at the front end which was fitted with an inbuilt doughnut-making machine and a primus stove for heating water for coffee, which was prepared in 50-cup urns. On one side of the kitchen was a counter, and two flaps were also inserted in the offside of the vehicle which opened out for serving the coffee and doughnuts. The back third of the vehicle consisted of a small lounge area with a built-in bench seat on either side, where troops could obtain candy, gum and cigarettes and find a selection of paperbacks to read. A radio and a 'Victrola' phonograph with loudspeakers and a good supply of records was on hand, this equipment being fitted and serviced by R G Jones of Morden to which the Clubmobiles returned periodically when repairs were needed. Each Clubmobile was crewed by three American "donut dollies" – as they were popularly known – who converted the back seats into beds for

Numerous photographs were taken of the 'Clubmobiles', many specifically for publication as post-cards for troops to send to the 'folks back home'. All had to be passed by the US Army Censor and were deliberately vague as to their location which would usually be described as "Somewhere in Great Britain". A platform on the offside was provided to enable servicemen to reach the serving hatch. The photo catches a glimpse of part of the English registration number fortunately retained on the back panel, which traces the Clubmobile as having been T 689 now carrying the name 'Minneapolis'. *Dave Jones collection*

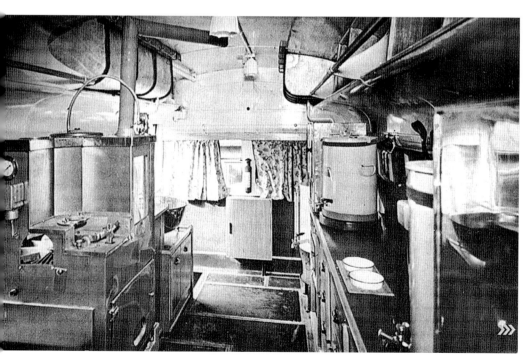

The interior of an unidentified Clubmobile shows the extent of the conversion work carried out to suit these vehicles to their new role. The lack of a doorway partition indicates that this one had been a 10T10/1 in civilian life, but so thorough was the conversion that little else was recognisable. Even the front bulkhead has been ornamented by curtains hanging behind a neatly fitted pelmet to give a homely air. On the left, with the extractor chimney, can be seen the doughnut making machine, while prominent on the right – one on each side of the serving hatch – are two 50-cup coffee urns.

Numbered in a different sequence by the American authorities were the vehicles seconded to the Red Cross. Almost all of these were the famous 'Clubmobiles', but X201123 (alias T 648) retained its bus seating and served from June 1943 onwards as a personnel transporter in which role it was photographed outside the American Red Cross Service Club in central London. Painted in all-over grey, including the radiator, it was probably photographed when the war was drawing to a close as headlamp masks are no longer carried. T 648 finally returned to civilian service at Romford garage in July 1946.

sleeping on board, but the driver was British and had to find his own overnight accommodation. Sprayed in grey and prominently bearing the 'American Red Cross Clubmobile' legend, usually in red outlined in white, the vehicles regularly visited all the American bases throughout the UK, driving around them to serve the men at work, and they also covered docks such as Liverpool, Greenock and Belfast. As a reminder of home, each of the 40 Clubmobiles had the name of an American state painted on it.

By 1943 the 40 original Clubmobiles needed augmenting by a further 15 which left London Transport between 16th and 18th June. They are recorded as having been sent to Hollydale Road, Peckham for conversion, but more than this is not known. There was no perceptible difference between these and the original 40 but the names applied to them were – with one exception – those of major cities and towns in the USA rather than states. The 55 Clubmobiles and their American names are shown below, and all except Rochester (T 665) returned to London Transport after the war, the latter having fallen prey to a flying bomb in Peckham during 1944.

| ARC no. | | Name |
|---|---|---|
| T 465 | X201001 | South Dakota |
| T 652 | X201112 | Seattle |
| T 479 | X201031 | Maryland |
| T 654 | X201028 | Florida |
| T 510 | X201017 | Wisconsin |
| T 656 | X201116 | New Hampshire |
| T 530 | X201032 | Connecticut |
| T 659 | X201025 | Oklahoma |
| T 535 | X201040 | North Dakota |
| T 660 | X201016 | Georgia |
| T 538 | X201021 | Alabama |
| T 662 | X201014 | Indiana |
| T 544 | X201023 | Iowa |
| T 665 | X201110 | Rochester |
| T 549 | X201033 | Washington |
| T 666 | X201020 | Minnesota |
| T 551 | X201002 | Utah |
| T 668 | X201113 | Kansas City |
| T 561 | X201019 | Tennessee |
| T 669 | X201011 | Michigan |
| T 565 | X201015 | North Carolina |
| T 673 | X201109 | Buffalo |
| T 567 | X201035 | Nebraska |
| T 674 | X201117 | Baltimore |
| T 601 | X201003 | Montana |
| T 680 | X201103 | Milwaukee |
| T 603 | X201037 | Oregon |
| T 682 | X201007 | Illinois |
| T 609 | X201029 | South Carolina |
| T 683 | X201114 | Cincinnati |
| T 612 | X201026 | West Virginia |
| T 685 | X201038 | Columbia |
| T 615 | X201012 | Missouri |
| T 686 | X201111 | Indianapolis |
| T 628 | X201024 | Mississippi |
| T 689 | X201107 | Minneapolis |
| T 630 | X201004 | Pennsylvania |
| T 695 | X201005 | New York |
| T 632 | X201027 | Arkansas |
| T 696 | X201018 | Kentucky |
| T 633 | X201034 | Colorado |
| T 701 | X201106 | Newark |
| T 635 | X201039 | Rhode Island |
| T 702 | X201036 | Maine |
| T 637 | X201115 | New Orleans |
| T 703 | X201006 | Ohio |
| T 639 | X201022 | Louisiana |
| T 705 | X201104 | San Francisco |
| T 640 | X201008 | Texas |
| T 708 | X201010 | Massachusetts |
| T 646 | X201013 | New Jersey |
| T 710 | X201105 | Boston |
| T 649 | X201009 | California |
| T 712 | X201108 | Houston |
| T 650 | X201030 | Kansas |

In this view of an unidentified Clubmobile serving a detachment of black troops, one of the 'donut dollies' is seen chatting to a waiting customer. *Dave Jones collection*

After D-Day on 6th June 1944 the American Red Cross wanted to extend Clubmobile operations to the Continent but the converted coaches were not considered sufficiently robust and an alternative was produced in the form of converted 2½ ton GMC trucks. However it is thought that some of the other 10T10s impounded for the American authorities did go abroad, and these could have included some of a further nine coaches removed from London Transport in 1943, bringing the total of 10T10s serving with the US authorities in one form or another to 88. On 16th February T 681 and 688 were taken to the USA Army base which had set itself up in the now-closed Victoria coach station. Subsequent to this T 648 departed on 22nd June to provide transport facilities for the American Red Cross, while between 27th May and 22nd June T 663, 670, 684, 715, 717, 718 were earmarked for the USA Army Special Service headquarters at Cumberland Place, Marble Arch. Once again the exact duties to which these were allocated are not known although T 670 was observed in use as a mobile dental unit. It, together with T 681, never came back, bringing the total of 10T10s lost to London Transport as a result of the war to eleven.

Back in the country area, the sensitive and vital war work being carried out at the Vickers aircraft works in Weybridge led to a government request for camouflage to be employed on buses serving the works. A livery of all-over grey was adopted in August 1942 which was eventually widened to include 47 buses from three garages but predominantly Addlestone. Between 4th June and 16th July 1943 ten Addlestone based Ts were repainted grey (T 534, 620, 657, 667, 675, 692, 700, 704, 709, 711) which they continued to wear until the changing fortunes of war allowed them to revert to standard green and white livery from November 1944 onwards. Only one, T 620, strayed away from Addlestone whilst in grey, spending its final month at Leatherhead before reverting to green, and the last grey one of all was T 709 which was recorded as being repainted green on 27th January 1945.

Service enhancements and other alterations carried out as time went by brought about a modest increase in the number of 10T10/1s in active use. Mostly it was the case of a single extra vehicle here or there but more notable enhancements were the addition of six vehicles at Hemel Hempstead and Leavesden Road on 1st May 1943; three at Addlestone on 7th June of the same year, and six at St Albans and Hertford on 1st July 1944.

On the evening of Tuesday 18th July 1944 the 10T10s suffered their biggest single calamity of the war when a 'doodle-bug' rocket flew through the open doorway of Elmers End garage and exploded, causing extensive damage to the property and the vehicles within it. These included ten 10T10 ambulances the bodies of which were very badly damaged, three of them totally beyond repair. These were bodies 18144 (T 518), 18148 (T 508) and 18209 (T 570) which were all scrapped, but fortunately three spare bodies were in stock at Chiswick to act as replacements. Two were the original float bodies from 1938 which had remained unused up to then; 18363 was placed on to T 518 and 18364 on to T 493, another Elmers End casualty whose original body was placed on to T 508 awaiting repair. T 570 received body 18358 which had been in store at Chiswick since May 1941, having been removed for repair from T 715 which, at the time, had been given the third of the original float bodies 18365.

T 514 was a victim of the Elmers End bombing, and it has been towed to Chiswick Works where it awaits a decision on its future which will be made once an examination has been carried out to determine the full extent of its damage. It was subsequently dispatched to Northern Coachbuilders for repair in August 1944, returning back to Chiswick just over a year later in October 1945. *Alan B Cross collection*

The 10T10s with the least damage were repaired at Chiswick but six were beyond the resources available there. An approach for assistance to the Regional Traffic Commissioner resulted in London Transport being directed to Northern Coachbuilders Ltd of Newcastle-upon-Tyne. This was one of the bus builders under the aegis of the Vehicle Maintenance Repair Division of the Ministry of Supply which was authorised to carry out heavy bodywork repairs and to build new bodies on renovated chassis (although, with Ministry consent, it also built a number of bodies on new chassis on a sub-contract basis). From a London standpoint, Northern Coachbuilders is best remembered for the bodies it supplied on Guy Arabs and on renovated trolleybus chassis. After viewing a sample 10T10 sent to it on 3rd August 1944, the Company agreed to undertake the rebuilding of the six vehicles to pre-war standard, and the remaining five were duly dispatched to its former airship works at Cramlington. The ever-present problem of obtaining materials, aggravated no doubt by the complexity of the work, meant that only one was returned to London Transport within a year whilst others took longer to complete. However when they finally came back the renovated vehicles looked exactly as they had originally been which, considering the extent of work involved, was a tribute to the skill and ingenuity of the craftsmen at Northern Coachbuilders.

The vehicles rebuilt by Northern Coachbuilders were:

| Date out | | Date back |
|---|---|---|
| T 491 | 3/8/44 | 16/4/46 |
| T 502 | 21/8/44 | 25/7/45 |
| T 508 | 29/8/44 | 2/2/46 |
| T 514 | 29/8/44 | 11/10/45 |
| T 515 | 21/8/44 | 22/8/45 |
| T 560 | 23/8/44 | 13/9/45 |

The end of the war in Europe was celebrated on 8th May 1945 on which date 76 10T10s and 10T10/1s were licensed for active bus service distributed amongst fourteen garages as follows: Addlestone (12); Amersham and Hertford (11 each); Dorking, Dunton Green, Hemel Hempstead and Leatherhead (6 each); Grays, Hitchin and St Albans (4 each); Epping and Northfleet (2 each); Guildford and Tring (1 each). This represented almost the entire stock of serviceable 10T10s, but in addition eight former ambulances were theoretically now available having been released from their ambulance duties

in April 1945, although the opportunity had not yet arisen to get them ready for service. The remaining ambulances were mostly released by the Ministry of Health in batches, the biggest of these being on 8th August 1945 and, finally, on 1st March 1946, by which time all of them had been returned.

The Clubmobiles were mostly received back from the American Red Cross during November 1945. Facilities were not available at the time for them to be examined or even stored at Chiswick, so most were taken direct to Potters Bar garage where space was available to accommodate them. Those that could not be housed there were stored at Hemel Hempstead and Tring. A trio of latecomers returned in January and February 1946 to be followed much later, on 2nd May, by T 666. This arrived on the back of a lorry having been damaged beyond repair in an accident at Tidworth in July 1944. After two or three weeks at Chiswick it was taken away for scrap, and was subsequently written off books backdated to the day the American authorities handed it over.

This left the vehicles used directly by the American army. Faced with the massive task of identifying and establishing ownership of the large number of impounded buses of British origin that had been taken under its control, together with the logistics of collecting them into a centralised dispersal base, it was no wonder that the US army faced a greater problem returning the 10T10s to London Transport than had been the case with the Red Cross Clubmobiles. It was equally unsurprising that certain vehicles failed to be correctly identified and ended up with the wrong owners, as happened with some 10T10s (see chapter 19). A start was made in returning the 10T10s in November 1945, a process which went on steadily for the next six months but seemed to peter out after May 1946. A solitary latecomer, T 462, arrived in October 1946, but by this time it was clear that all had returned that were going to do so, and the remainder were retrospectively written off books with effect from the dates that they had first gone to the US military authorities.

In early 1945, in the same line up near Chalk Farm garage as T 408 shown in chapter 14, stands T 504 which not only survived the war unscathed but still exists in preservation to this day. At the time, it had never received an overhaul since the day it was new and so still retained the now-faded original light green livery. It was subsequently repainted before beginning work at Hertford in April 1946 but was not called in for a full overhaul until as late as May 1948 by which time it was just over 10 years old. *Alan Nightingale collection*

A major peace time imperative for London Transport was to get its Green Line operation going once again. Firm proposals for the post-war route network and anticipated frequencies had been lodged with the Metropolitan Traffic Commissioner as early as October 1944, but implementation had of course to wait until the return of peace and the certainty of adequate vehicle and staff availability. With the steady release of former Green Line coaches from their wartime duties a programme was pursued from August 1945 onwards of preparing them for a return to their peace time status. This included, of course, a restoration of all their internal fittings, except that clocks were no longer provided, while the exteriors were repainted to restore a presentable appearance after what, in many cases, had been six years or more of comparative neglect. To start with, the wartime livery of green and white was used with the exception that roofs were now painted green to match the side panels instead of carrying wartime grey or (from December 1941) brown camouflage. As recorded in the last chapter, 9T9 T 406 was demonstrated in post-war two-tone Green Line livery in January 1946, after which all future repaints of 10T10s appeared in this form.

The complex logistics of re-starting the Green Line operation dictated that this could only be done on a staged basis, so a tentative schedule of reintroductions was drawn up with a starting date of Wednesday 6th February 1946. Green Line services were now to be numbered in the 700 series and the first to enter the public view were 715 (Hertford–Guildford) worked by the garages located at each end of the route, and 720 (Bishops Stortford–Aldgate) worked by Epping garage. Both were scheduled as 10T10 operations and the vehicles for

them were taken from a small stockpile that had built up, with sufficient being licensed on 1st February in good time for the scheduled starting date almost a week later. It was hardly any surprise that all were former ambulances, as these required less remedial work than the vehicles returned from the United States authorities.

The next reintroduction, exactly a month later on 6th March, was a more ambitious affair with five services on the agenda. The broad scope of this second phase was made possible only because types of vehicle other than 10T10 were now becoming available to the extent that 6Q6s were reintroduced at Crawley and Godstone, TFs at Grays, and new Daimler double deckers at Romford. The only 10T10 service amongst all this was 704 (Tunbridge Wells–Windsor). The small Tunbridge Wells garage re-opened with an allocation of ex-ambulances licensed on 1st March, and Windsor's vehicle quota was similar except that it included T 628, the first ex-Clubmobile and the first 34-seater to resume Green Line operation. Also among the Windsor contingent was T 499, the experimental 33-seater and the only 10T10/2, which reverted to its unusual pre-war internal layout and remained solely at Windsor for the rest of its operational career.

The resumption of Green Line operation marked a return of sorts to peacetime normality, and it was heartening to see freshly repainted former ambulances returning to these duties. T 581 was one of the inaugural vehicles, having been licensed at Hertford on 1st February 1946 ready for the introduction of route 715 on the 6th. The vehicles carried the green and white bus livery, but although T 581 carries the LONDON TRANSPORT insignia, the GREEN LINE name was shown on others. *AEC*

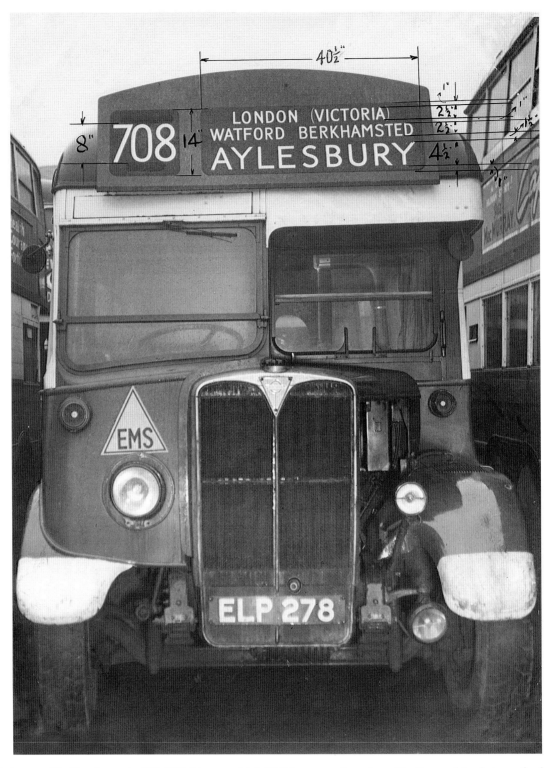

With post-war developments in mind, London Transport set up an internal destination blind committee which issued its first report in April 1946. Much of its work focused on double deckers, but T 554 was fitted with a mock-up display which, had it proved acceptable, would have surpassed anything that had so far appeared on single deckers. T 554 was chosen because it just happened to be in Chiswick Works at the time for conversion back into a Green Line coach having spent the war as an ambulance at Twickenham garage. It duly resumed work at Windsor on 25th March 1946. *Ken Blacker collection*

Only two days later, on 8th March, route 716 (Hitchin–Chertsey) made its debut. It appears that by this time the stockpile of suitably prepared 10T10s was beginning to dry up, and though Addlestone and Hitchin garages both received one each on 20th February for route learning and other preliminary duties, the remainder – all of which were former ambulances – were not available until the actual day of operation.

Almost a month elapsed before the next set of introductions on 3rd April 1946. These, again, were a mixed bunch in which 10T10s were outnumbered by the combined strength of 6Q6s at High Wycombe and Reigate and a further batch of new Daimler double deckers at Romford. Once again one-time ambulances made up the bulk of the 10T10 revivals including all of those licensed on 25th March in readiness for when both Epping and Windsor began running route 718 (Epping–Windsor) nine days later. Swanley, too, received former ambulances for route 703 (Amersham–Wrotham) but the Amersham contingent included the second ex-Clubmobile to be relicensed amongst its newly allocated contingent.

Service introductions on 1st May 1946 were divided almost equally between 10T10s and TFs with the latter class making its debut at Dorking and Luton both of which, in pre-war times, had used 10T10s on their Green Line operations. The former Clubmobiles were now returning to service in quantity and the first of the vehicles formerly used by the US Army drifted back to work too. Route 708 (High Wycombe–East Grinstead) worked by the local garages at each end, and 717 (Welwyn Garden City–Woking) worked from Hatfield and Addlestone garages, both used a mixture of 30 and 34-seaters with the latter predominating. Now past the half-way stage, the next introductions on 29th May saw the final TFs back in service at St Albans and Dorking along with two more 10T10 operations. Route 705 (Sevenoaks–Windsor) increased the size of the coach contingent at both Dunton Green and Windsor, and also new on the same day was route 726, a purely seasonal operation between Marylebone and Whipsnade Zoo. For its first season it was worked from Leavesden Road garage using 10T10s taken off bus work and transferred in from various locations; these were augmented from 19th July by 10T10s from Romford garage – its only single deckers amongst a sea of Daimler double deckers – for the rest of the main summer season.

The final reintroductions came within a few days of each other in June 1946. On 19th June route 702 (Gravesend–Sunningdale) began with 10T10s from Northfleet and Staines, and on the same day Amersham garage began its second Green Line operation but on this occasion the chosen vehicles were 6Q6s, a surprise move since this garage already had an allocation of 10T10s for the 703. Three days later the 702's partner service 701 (Gravesend–Ascot) became operational. Only the 706 (Aylesbury–Westerham) and 707 (Aylesbury–Oxted) now remained for introduction on 26th June, and these had been left to last to ensure that a sufficient number of specially equipped 10T10s was available for them. Jointly operated by Chelsham and Tring garages, they revived the pre-war routeing via Titsey on what had now become the 707 for which extra hill-climbing ability was required. This meant taking the special D132T gearboxes out of store and installing them into eight coaches for use at Chelsham and nine at Tring. The hill-climbing 10T10s were now given the chassis classification 2/10T, and as both types of body were used they became a mixture of 2/10T10 and 2/10T10/1. Most unusually for London Transport, but understandably in the circumstances, the coaches on routes 706 and 707 remained completely unchanged from the time of their introduction through to their replacement by RFs in April and May 1952 except that Tring was supplied with one extra vehicle in November 1946 and another in July 1947. The 2/10T10s which worked the 706 and 707 day in and day out for over five years were Chelsham based T 455, 463, 544, 566, 569, 572, 592 and Tring-based T 453, 457, 461, 496, 519, 547, 597 while Chelsham supplied 2/10T10/1 T 609 and Tring contributed T 615, 676, 705, 710.

Full Green Line livery had been restored by the time that T 702 was sent to East Grinstead for the start of route 708 on 1st May 1946. Unlike many which had served as ambulances, T 702 had not merely been given a cosmetic repaint; it had in fact received a thorough body and chassis overhaul before resuming civilian duty after having been seconded to the US Army authorities from January 1943 through to November 1945. The coaches employed on the 1st May introduction carried a new and very short-lived blind display combining a new layout now adopted as standard but retaining the old white on black lettering, soon to be replaced by black on amber for Green Line work. *Alan Nightingale collection*

Taking into account the speed and magnitude with which the Green Line network had been re-established it was perhaps inevitable that some early changes would become necessary before a settled spell of operation was achieved, and the first of these came about even before the final phase of service reintroductions had taken place. Expediency and vehicle availability had probably dictated that the 6Q6 coaches should be distributed in small numbers amongst four garages (Godstone, Crawley, High Wycombe and Reigate) during the early stages of the reintroduction programme, but these were now the oldest vehicles in the Green Line fleet, and with their operating peculiarities they were not well received at some garages. London Transport's answer was to transfer the majority back to the Hertford–Guildford corridor (now route 715) that they had monopolised before the war, and this move was carried out overnight on 1st June 1946. Hertford received the bulk of Reigate's allocation in exchange for 10T10s which now took over route 711 (Reigate–Baker Street), whilst Guildford was stocked mainly from Crawley (which henceforth ran 10T10s on route 710 (Crawley–Baker Street) and Godstone on route 709 (Caterham–Baker Street). To make up the required numbers, Hertford and Guildford also each received a few newly relicensed 6Q6s. Despite an equal scheduled allocation on the 715, Guildford received twice as many Qs as Hertford, the surplus there being found employment as replacements for 10T10s on local bus operations. This was the first time that 6Q6s had been demoted to such use although they still retained their official status as coaches and vehicles were interchanged haphazardly between coach and bus duties.

The close of the 1946 summer season brought the cessation of route 726, theoretically leaving Leavesden Road's staff without any Green Line work to perform. To relieve the situation its 10T10s were switched to a supplementary operation on route 708 between Watford and Victoria, but this proved unviable and ran for the last time on 16th February 1947. It marked the end of Leavesden Road's involvement in Green Line operation although some 10T10s lingered until November 1947 to cover bus operation, after which the class was not re-established there until February 1952. Route 726 was covered from the summer of 1947 onwards by double deckers from Romford.

When fully implemented, it was clear that the post-war Green Line network was smaller and less ambitious than the pre-war one had been. Quite a lot of unremunerative mileage had been cut out which reduced the road miles over which the vehicles worked from 790 to 646, in the process leaving country destinations such as Ongar, Baldock, Farnham Common, Horsham and Edenbridge unserved. The introduction of double deckers on the Romford services, a slight all-round speeding up, and an efficiency improvement raising the average daily mileage per coach from 204 to 226, all meant that the number of single deck coaches required diminished between October 1938 and October 1947 by 128 on Mondays to Fridays, 148 on Saturdays and 109 on Sundays. This meant that full-time Green Line operation by the whole 10T10 fleet was no longer an option and that many would be employed as country buses, although still retaining their official status as coaches and being available for such use when required.

The first post-war summer programme, introduced on 4th July 1945, found 80 10T10s at work on bus and other special scheduled services in the country area, the majority of them still with their wartime perimeter seating. This included vehicles allocated as engineering spares and others held for unscheduled duplicates etc. A total of 55 was required to cover the basic Monday to Friday schedule, the commitment per garage being: Addlestone 10, Amersham 10, Hertford 8 (9 on Tuesdays, Wednesdays and Thursdays), Dunton Green 5, Dorking 4, Grays 4, Hitchin 3, Leatherhead 3, St Albans 3, Hemel Hempstead 2, Northfleet 1, Tring 1. In the case of Dorking garage, one was regularly outstationed overnight in Holmbury St Mary, a very un-London-like arrangement which persisted throughout the 10T10 era.

One major task which needed to be tackled with a degree of urgency was the implementation of an overhaul programme for the many vehicles which had never been overhauled since new. This omission applied principally to the 30-seater 10T10s, the 34-seater 10T10/1s having mostly been more fortunate in this respect. Even so, the backlog took a long time to clear and it was not until T 500 emerged from Chiswick Works on 1st April 1949 that the whole class could claim to have received at least one overhaul since new, with every vehicle now in Green Line livery. By and large body changes were avoided and most chassis kept their original bodies from start to finish, and although a few swaps took place in 1946 and a couple more in 1948 only eight bodies in total were involved.

An unofficial practice that had arisen during the war was for conductors to remove the fare board, which was mounted at the back of the vehicle on the emergency exit door, and to lean it against the front bulkhead where it was more accessible and easier to read under the much-reduced lighting conditions. Quite sensibly the staff made a request early in 1946 for the front-mounted fare board to become a permanent feature. London Transport prevaricated but eventually, in January 1948, bowed to the inevitable and agreed that retaining clips should be fitted to the front bulkhead as well as to the back door. A bigger and more immediate task, however, was to convert all the standee vehicles back to a conventional seating system but this took a surprisingly long time to carry out. Although a few re-conversions were done towards the end of 1945, the programme dragged on lethargically and there were still fourteen vehicles in service with perimeter seating at the start of 1948. The last of all – now well into the post-war era – was T 657 at Tring which was available for service as a standee vehicle right up to 2nd March 1949, going into Chiswick Works for overhaul the next day.

Some of the re-conversions to normal transverse seating took place during overhaul; others were done when vehicles visited Chiswick for a body repaint. Meanwhile, as part of a programme to relieve pressure on the overhaul shops, London Transport contracted a number of overhauls to outside organisations and as part of this process it was arranged that T 489 and T 505 would go to Tickford Ltd of Newport Pagnell to enable renovation of their bodies to take place. Though not a known name within bus circles, Tickford was an old company with its origins dating back to the 1820s which, in pre-war years, had constructed coachbuilt car bodies on a whole range of different chassis (and whose successors still trade today as powertrain producers in Milton Keynes). The two coaches went to Tickford's on 27th January 1948 and were returned to Chiswick a little under four months later on 18th May. The outcome was deemed sufficiently good for five more vehicles to go to Newport Pagnell: T 471 in June, T 512, 616 in September, and T 591, 647 in December 1948, T 647 being the last to return on 23rd February 1949.

In sharp contrast to the glamorous appeal of smartly painted high-profile 10T10s working on premium Green Line services, a feature of the early post-war era was the run-down and far from premium-looking secondary fleet of the same vehicles relegated to working a miscellany of country bus duties, often with their wartime perimeter seating still in place. This was the case with Ts 677, 678 and 521, lined up outside the garage at Amersham. All three clearly need a fresh coat of paint, the only new paintwork visible being on the mudguards to accompany the recent fitting of shrouds over the offside dumbirons. Black-painted radiators, quite common at the time on shells that had become pitted, do not improve their appearance. The three 10T10s are accompanied by red STL 2220 on loan from Harrow Weald to cover a temporary shortage of available lowbridge rolling stock for route 336, on which T 678 has also recently been employed. The contrast between pristine 10T10s on Green Line work and those used as buses is evidenced by Windsor's T 662 on the 705 standing alongside Dunton Green's T 697 on local route 421 in Sevenoaks bus station. Unlike the Amersham trio, T 697 can at least offer the comfort of transverse seating. The double decker present on this occasion is front entrance STL 1475 on trunk route 402 to Bromley North. *D W K Jones/London Transport Museum*

In the rush to get Green Line services up and running, many 10T10s that had served as ambulances during the war were placed back into service without undergoing any heavy attention, either mechanically or bodily, and as a result the first real overhaul was not carried out on them until they were nine or ten years old. This view, taken in the panelling and glazing section of Chiswick Works, shows the body of Addlestone's T 545 on an accommodation trolley midway through its first overhaul which took from 13th October to 18th November 1947 to complete. Behind is an unidentified 9T9 undergoing similar treatment. *London Transport Museum*

Although conductors and passengers on 10T10s had always enjoyed the benefit of fairly efficient saloon heating, this benefit had never been extended to drivers who were expected to glean whatever warmth was available from the adjacent engine. In the enlightened post-war era London Transport responded to the inevitability of providing both heaters and demisters to the cabs of the 10T10s and achieved a target of having them all fitted before the beginning of the winter of 1949/50. An earlier post-war initiative, dating from 1947, had seen a metal panel introduced at the bottom of the driver's cab between the mudguard and the offside dumbiron – which was now hidden out of sight – as a draught reduction exercise. The usefulness of this modification was presumably not proven, for in many instances these shrouds were later removed resulting in the dumbiron being exposed once again.

The final years of the nineteen-forties witnessed various comings and goings of 10T10s to coincide with changes in schedule or in fleet composition. The first of these occurred as early as March to July 1946 when 10T10s disappeared firstly from bus service in St Albans and then from Luton and Leatherhead as 9T9s were put back into use following the ending of their wartime duties. The only garage to gain a new 10T10 allocation for bus duties at this time was High Wycombe which received a couple on 1st May 1946. The next date of importance was 12th November 1947 when Green Line services were revised to produce 709 (Chesham–Caterham), 710 (Amersham–Crawley) and 711 (High Wycombe–Reigate), which saw the end of routes 724 and 725

and the 6Q6s which had worked them, the latter being mostly demoted to bus work at St Albans. The 10T10s for these revised operations were gathered from a number of sources. Those at High Wycombe included the last three on bus duties at Leavesden Road, and Amersham's contingent comprised the last ones from bus work at Dunton Green for which 9T9s were found as replacements.

Perimeter seating was retained on some 10T10s for a surprisingly long time into the post-war era. The top hand rails of the inward-facing seats can be clearly seen through the windows of T 531 as it stands in the yard at Tring garage on a wet summer day in 1948. It finally went into the Chiswick overhaul shops on 16th September of that year for repainting into Green Line colours and conversion back to a conventional seating arrangement. *D A Jones*

After the war, the interiors of the 10T10s looked just a little more bus-like with the clock having been removed and, in this case, the ash trays too. The fare chart is now carried on the front bulkhead and indicates that this unidentified vehicle is working on Green Line routes 701 and 702. The lack of a full-height partition behind the doorway is evidence that this is a 34-seater 10T10/1. *J M Aldridge*

1948 saw the end of 10T10s at Dorking where 9T9s had superseded them by April, and at Grays where sufficient TFs surplus to Green Line requirements were available to cover all bus duties by July. In the same month 10T10s returned to bus work at Guildford whose 5Q5s were all transferred to the Central Bus department on the 12th, while the same thing happened to restore 10T10s at Dorking after a brief absence on 3rd August. On 12th January 1949 Green Line route 720 worked by Epping garage was changed over from 10T10 to TF operation using spare TFs culled from all the other operating garages of this type of vehicle, Luton, St Albans and Grays but mainly Dorking. This was an astute move as it enabled the running time on the 720 to be speeded up with effect from the summer programme of 18th May allowing one coach to be removed from the schedule. At this time 10T10s were being sent to Windsor to infiltrate the only remaining bastion of 1/7T7/1 operation covering routes 445 and 458 plus a Bucks County Council private hire contract, arriving spasmodically at first as one by one the old petrol vehicles expired, but with a final burst of six vehicles on 29th August on which date the old order was finally eliminated.

A serious delay to passengers involving waits in some cases of up to 2½ hours before there was room for them on a following coach occurred on 19th March 1949 at Hammersmith when a 10T10 broke down on route 716 and no replacement could be found. The repercussions were such that a decision was made to henceforth base two 10T10s permanently in central London to act as breakdown substitutes, one at Hammersmith garage and the other at Victoria. The initial pair which began this arrangement on 8th May 1949 were T 483 at Hammersmith and T 475 at Victoria, but various others took their turn over the course of the next five years. Their employment in this way proved to be a wise move as they were quite often required for action, and the pair were instantly recognisable by their heavily masked destination screens. Special blinds with single line route number and destination displays were printed for them at Chiswick which included details for every Green Line service to ensure complete flexibility of operation.

The new decade dawned with all 254 surviving 10T10s fully employed, although this number was reduced by one in September 1950 when T 638 suffered severe fire damage

A passenger's-eye view of a 10T10 driving cab shows the compact but reasonably comfortable working area provided for drivers on these vehicles. The speedometer is in a prominent position and a bulb horn can be found below the steering wheel even though the button for a modern electric horn is provided on the driver's left. A cab heating system has now been fitted and the trunking for the associated demister can be clearly seen. *J M Aldridge*

whilst on Green Line service from Windsor garage and was subsequently scrapped. As listed below, the total number of 10T10s scheduled for Monday to Friday operation as at 1st January 1950 was 183, the balance being made up of vehicles required to operate Green Line duplicates and to serve as engineering spares. Because of heavy Green Line commitments, the number employed purely on bus work was lower than it had been just after the war with only 50 scheduled as follows:

| | | | | |
|---|---|---|---|---|
| 308 | Hertford–Newgate Street | | | |
| 308A | Hertford–Little Berkhampstead | | | |
| 384 | Hertford–Letchworth | } | EP | 2 |
| 384A | Hertford–Great Munden | | HG | 3 |
| 384B | Letchworth–Walkern | | HN | 3 |
| 399 | Letchworth–Epping | | | |
| 342 | New Barnet–Broxbourne | | HG | 4 |
| 364 | Luton–Hitchin | | LS | 1 |
| | | | HN | 2 |
| 372 | Hertford–Welwyn Garden City | | HG | 2 |
| 373 | Holtspur–Penn | } | MA | 2* |
| 398 | Beaconsfield–Amersham | | | |
| 389 | Hertford–Sawbridgeworth | | HG | 1 |
| 390 | Hertford–Stevenage | | HG | 1 |
| 394 | Great Missenden–Hyde Heath | } | | |
| 394A | Great Missenden–Chesham Moor | | MA | 5 |
| 394B | Great Missenden–Chesham | | | |
| 394C | Amersham–Hyde Heath | | | |
| 412 | Dorking North–Holmbury St Mary | | DS | 2 |
| 425 | Dorking–Guildford | | DS | 4 |
| | | | GF | 4 |
| 428 | East Grinstead–Dormansland | | EG | 1† |
| 445 | Windsor–Datchet Common | | WR | 2 |
| 441 | Staines–High Wycombe | | ST | 1‡ |
| 458 | Slough–Uxbridge | | WR | 8 |
| 469 | Staines–Virginia Water | | ST | 1† |
| P/Hire Berkshire County Council | | | WR | 1 |
| 701 | Gravesend–Ascot | } | NF | 6 |
| 702 | Gravesend–Sunningdale | | ST | 6 |
| 703 | Amersham–Wrotham | | MA | 4 |
| | | | SJ | 3 |
| 704 | Tunbridge Wells–Windsor | | TW | 8 |
| | | | WR | 7 |
| 705 | Sevenoaks–Windsor | | DG | 7 |
| | | | WR | 6 |

| | | | | |
|---|---|---|---|---|
| 706 | Aylesbury–Westerham | } | TG | 8 |
| 707 | Aylesbury–Oxted | } | CM | 8 |
| 708 | Hemel Hempstead–E Grinstead | | HH | 6 |
| | | | EG | 7 |
| 709 | Chesham–Caterham-on-the-Hill | | MA | 3 |
| | | | GD | 4 |
| 710 | Amersham–Crawley | | MA | 4 |
| | | | CY | 4 |
| 711 | High Wycombe–Reigate | | HE | 7 |
| | | | RG | 7 |
| 716 | Hitchin–Chertsey | | HN | 4 |
| | | | WY | 4 |
| 717 | Welwyn Garden City–Woking | | HF | 4 |
| | | | WY | 3 |
| 718 | Epping–Windsor | | EP | 6 |
| | | | WR | 7 |

* Plus one Cub
† Plus one STL
‡ Also Windsor 6 STL + Staines 13 STL

Such was the complexity of Country Bus & Coach scheduling that 10T10s worked from the services listed above to journeys on other routes, or parts of them, as listed below. In the case of Crawley and Dunton Green garages the vehicles concerned were Green Line coaches which continued to display the route boards relevant to their main work whilst carrying out their bus duties.

| | |
|---|---|
| Amersham | 305, 336, 353, 362A |
| Crawley | 405 |
| Dorking | 433 |
| Dunton Green | 413 |
| Epping | 339, 396 |
| Hertford | 331 |
| Hitchin | 303, 303B |

1950 turned out to be a pivotal year for the 10T10s, and indeed for all remaining pre-war single deckers, when in March the London Transport Executive approved a 10-year forward plan for single deck vehicles which would see the phasing-in of the new RF class between 1951 and 1953, for which authority to proceed was duly received from the British Transport Commission which, since nationalisation, had been London Transport's overlord. Crucial to these plans was an agreement that London Transport had made with manufacturer Metro-Cammell in February 1949 whereby the latter would forgo the construction of 550 RTL bodies to which it was already committed in order to produce the 700 single deck bodies needed for the new RF class. This contractual rearrangement enabled London Transport to anticipate the receipt of new single deckers eighteen months earlier than would otherwise have been the case, a fortuitous outcome necessitating a complete revision of the planned withdrawal programme which included an acceptance that an anticipated 18 year life for the 10T10s would now be reduced to 16½ years.

In a surprise move, route 720 lost its 10T10s overnight on 12th January 1949 when TFs were drafted in, providing a more sprightly performance and enabling running times to be speeded up a few months later. Epping's T 712 strikes a typical pose at route 720's inner London terminus at Aldgate during the final months of 10T10 operation. It was one of the vehicles deposed from Epping garage when the TFs arrived, whereupon it was transferred south and placed on bus service at Dorking. *J H Aston*

Although the ubiquitous 10T10 was the quintessential Green Line coach throughout the years immediately following the war, it did not have a monopoly even on its 'own' routes, at least as far as relief workings were concerned, on which vehicles of all sorts could turn up from time to time. On this occasion, in July 1949, 1/7T7/1 T 265 sets out to accompany Epping's T 503 from Windsor on the 718 as far as London. Reminiscent of the adage that 'old soldiers never die', T 265 – which retired from regular Green Line work back in March 1939 – returns to these duties for what may well have been the last time. It left Windsor garage a few weeks later to eke out its final days on Central Bus duties. *Alan B Cross*

T 638 became the first casualty of the nineteen-fifties when it was written-off after suffering fire damage whilst working on Green Line service from Windsor garage, which was where it had been based ever since it was converted back to conventional transverse seating and repainted into Green Line livery in June 1947. Photographed soon after it had been taken into Chiswick for assessment on 12th September 1950, the damage which might have been considered repairable in earlier years was now deemed an unjustified expense with the likelihood of new RFs becoming available only a year hence. *G E Baddeley*

An early priority for the new RFs was to replace the entire Green Line single deck fleet with a hoped-for starting date of May 1951, the immediate outcome of which would be the redeployment of 10T10s as replacements for older vehicles which were fast approaching the end of their useful lives. Although some real old timers such as 'Scooter' LT six-wheelers and a number of equally ancient 1T1s were still active, the greatest urgency was to withdraw the two batches of Weymann-bodied Ts, the 9T9s and 11T11s, which were causing unrest with staff, and particularly with some very vocal elements at certain Central Bus garages, over their perceived poor condition. The Executive was not in a position to deal with their demands immediately but promised that, as soon as some became available, 10T10s would be provided as replacements.

A programme was devised to convert 40 10T10s for use by Central Buses into red livery as replacements for its 9T9s and 11T11s. The vehicles selected for this purpose were all of the 30-seat variety, the 10T10/1s having been deemed unsuitable because of their narrow entrances. It was arranged for the conversions to be carried out at Chiswick as each vehicle went through overhaul with an anticipated starting date of June 1951, but this slipped a little consequent upon the late delivery of new RFs. The first vehicle, T 504, finally went into Chiswick Works on 17th July and a steady stream followed over the course of the next five months. Work carried out on each one included removal of the internal heating system by disabling the heater itself and sealing the intake vents; removing the lino flooring and replacing it with hardwood slats; painting the rexine on the ceilings cream; fixing the saloon door in the open position with a stout leather strap to comply with Metropolitan Police requirements; provision of a used ticket box, and installation of a route number holder above the entrance doorway. The original coach seats were retained (although the ash trays were removed from them), and this caused complaints from some conductors about what

they considered to be the narrowness of the gangway. The red livery, which suited the vehicles quite well, was applied in current styling with a narrow cream band above and below the windows, and for the first time on 10T10s the mudguards and lifeguards were painted black. In their new form the converted vehicles were reclassified 10T10/3.

The conversion of 10T10s into red livery was carried out alongside the normal programme for overhauling 10T10/1s for the Country Bus & Coach department. Despite the arrival of new RFs, these continued to be outshopped in full traditional Green Line livery until January 1952 when the whole 10T10 overhaul programme abruptly ceased. The final vehicle to be dealt with was T 661 which was put back on the road at Hemel Hempstead on 4th February 1952. The curtailment of the programme resulted in only 37 red vehicles being produced out of the planned 40. These were T 456, 458, 459, 470, 473-475, 485, 489, 497, 498, 504, 505, 508, 513, 526, 528, 536, 537, 543, 545, 552, 557, 563, 571, 574-577, 579-581, 584, 588, 589, 598, 606. The outstanding balance of three was made good during February when T 466, 511, 539 were given garage repaints into red livery. Apart from the provision of used ticket boxes, the interiors on these were not touched and they entered Central Bus service still with their Green Line accoutrements such as ash trays and with their country area notices still visible inside them.

The red 10T10s were a real novelty at first, especially when some of them returned temporarily to their old haunts pending replacements becoming available. An early overhaul into red livery was T 498 which returned to its home garage of Dorking after overhaul and made an incongruous sight on the very attractive and rural route 425 between Dorking and Guildford. On this occasion it carries Guildford (GF) garage plates, having overnighted there at the end of the previous day's work, but will return 'home' to Dorking at the end of the current day's duty. *J F Higham © A B Cross*

One of the green 10T10s to work temporarily in the central area during 1951 as a 5Q5 replacement was T 465. Normally a Dunton Green vehicle, it went to Dalston on 31st March 1951, returning home just over a fortnight later on 19th April. The insalubrious East End background is in stark contrast to its normal Kentish surroundings as it stands waiting to take up service on route 208A.
*D A Jones*

The red 10T10s made a big impact for only a comparatively short time, and with the arrival of new RFs they seemed to disappear as quickly as they had come. Typical views of two in service in their later days include Hornchurch's T 576 which is in the process of being overtaken by an even older pre-war AEC, Weymann-bodied Regent JN 4746 of Westcliff-on-Sea Motor Services. State-owned, like T 576, the Westcliff bus carries a very similar red and cream livery and is one of the few out of a once sizeable fleet of such vehicles to retain its roof route number box which, as on London buses at that time, is disused. T 576 spent its entire 'red' career at Hornchurch, whereas T 598 ran from a host of garages starting with Hornchurch but also including Hounslow, Bromley, Merton (at which it was photographed), Sidcup and Kingston. *Alan B Cross/D A Jones*

173

Meanwhile, to show goodwill and to demonstrate to staff the type of vehicle they were going to receive in due course, T 489 was sent to Loughton garage for service in January 1951 and T 508 to Uxbridge, both still in Green Line livery but with LONDON TRANSPORT fleet names. This was an era of extreme and often illogical militancy by workers at certain garages, and London Transport was perplexed and the Union's officers embarrassed by crews at Loughton garage finding, in London Transport's own words, "every objection to working the first 10T10 which had been sent there". The Union's officers agreed to mediate, and 10T10s duly became a feature of the Loughton landscape. In July T 508 left Uxbridge for a month's stay at Kingston to give crews there a foretaste of things to come. An unrelated event, which took place throughout the month of April 1951, was the use of further green 10T10s in the central fleet when single specimens ran from Dalston, Merton, Old Kent Road and Sidcup garages, but these were merely short-term replacements for 5Q5s diverted to temporary driver training duties ahead of the arrival of new private hire RFs and selected for this purpose because of their similar frontal layout. These were all officially organised arrangements, but over the next year or two unofficial short-term loans from country to central garages resulted in numerous cases of green 10T10s appearing on central routes for short periods of time until the chronic shortage of single deckers ceased under the onslaught of new RFs.

The first new Green Line vehicle, RF 26, finally entered service a few months late on 1st October 1951, running from Tunbridge Wells garage amidst a barrage of publicity but in splendid isolation because no others were available at the time. However, steady deliveries eventually got under way and in theory Tunbridge Wells workings on route 704 were all converted to RF by 1st November. In fact no engineering spare was provided either here or at any other garage until the full conversion programme had been completed, which meant that one or two 10T10s were retained at each location until at least August 1952 and their appearances on Green Line service during this interim period remained commonplace. Windsor's fleet for route 704 was dealt with during

November and RFs replaced 10T10s on the remaining routes in the following order:

| 711 | Reigate, High Wycombe | December 1951 |
|---|---|---|
| 710 | Amersham, Crawley | December 1951 |
| 709 | Amersham, Godstone | December 1951 |
| 708 | East Grinstead, Hemel Hempstead | February 1952 |
| 716 | Hitchin, Addlestone | February 1952 |
| 717 | Hatfield, Addlestone | February 1952 |
| 701/702 | Staines | February 1952 |
| 701/702 | Northfleet | March 1952 |
| 718 | Epping | March 1952 |
| 718 | Windsor | April 1952 |
| 706/707 | Chelsham | April 1952 |
| 706/707 | Tring | May 1952 |
| 705 | Dunton Green, Windsor | June 1952 |
| 703 | Swanley, Amersham | June 1952 |

The first priority as regards the 10T10s made redundant from Green Line work was to convert those earmarked for Central Buses as speedily as possible, and an outline programme was drawn up for their future deployment. This envisaged the 9T9s at Loughton and Hornchurch being replaced first, these being the vehicles in the worst condition, after which the 11T11s would be eased out, in some cases by sending in red 10T10s as direct replacements and in others by redeploying post-war TDs from Kingston which would receive red 10T10s to replace them. However this programme was not slavishly followed and the first vehicle to be converted, T 504, went to Kingston on 24th August 1951 in place of a 4Q4 which had to be prematurely taken out of service. The Country Bus department then baulked at the idea of any more going to Central Buses when no immediate replacements for them were available, and as a result most of the next few red repaints were returned temporarily to their original country garages until such time as replacement green ones became available. Eventually ten ran temporarily for Country Buses in red livery, some staying only a few days before they could be released and others somewhat longer.

Green 10T10s made a return to Central Bus operation in May 1952. T 514 was one of very many officially reclassified from coach to bus status on 1st May of that year; it is seen under the wires in Kingston with no trolleybuses in sight but with a pair of RTs trailing along behind. Back in 1944/45 it had been one of the vehicles completely rebuilt by Northern Coachbuilders after war damage, although no evidence of this treatment is apparent. Notable, however, is the addition of a route stencil holder above the doorway, which would have been an unofficial local initiative as there was no official plan to attach these to green 10T10s, which were only regarded as a stop-gap allocation anyway. Like many others of its type, T 514 has now lost the covering over the front dumbiron fitted only a few years beforehand. *Alan B Cross*

Sufficient red 10T10s were received at Loughton and Hornchurch by 14th November 1951 to replace all their 9T9s enabling a start to be made at Uxbridge. However deviations from the programme saw three red 10T10s delivered to Edgware during the last week of November to permit an increase in service on route 240A, while the failure of three 1T1s at Kingston whose bodies were condemned resulted in 10T10s being drafted in as replacements. It is interesting to recall that one of these 1T1s, T 31 which was delicensed on 16th October, had run alongside T 504 at Kingston for a few weeks, and that both still exist to this day, more than sixty years later, in preservation. The other main recipient of red 10T10s was Enfield, but odd ones were also delivered to Leyton, Southall and Tottenham, the last one of all to enter service in its new red guise being T 466 at West Green on 15th February 1952. Although their career with Central Buses was destined to be short – none managed to achieve two years in their new employment – the red 10T10s managed to run from almost every garage which then operated single deckers. A host of inter-garage transfers saw examples of the type running at one time or another from Bromley, Croydon, Dalston, Harrow Weald, Hounslow, Merton, Old Kent Road, Sidcup and Southall. A couple were even allocated to the new garage at Norbiton when it opened on 15th October 1952 and stayed there for just over four weeks.

The great majority of 10T10s were, of course, destined to remain green, although a large number were duly down-graded to bus status with their saloon heaters disabled and with LONDON TRANSPORT instead of GREEN LINE fleet names. The bulk of these demotions was carried out, on paper at least, on 1st May 1952. Although many were redeployed within Country Buses to replace firstly 9T9s and then 11T11s and 4Q4s, direct withdrawals of some 10T10s began to take place as early as April 1952. This was not what the engineers had originally wanted, their preference being to withdraw the TF class ahead of the 10T10s to obviate difficulties they were experiencing in obtaining spare parts for the Leylands which were a non-standard type peculiar to London Transport. Their seating capacity eventually saved the day for the TFs, and a policy was adopted of withdrawing 30-seat 10T10s from service before the higher capacity vehicles could be targeted. However the replacement of TFs from Green Line work at Grays in January 1952 upon arrival of new RFs, mainly for redeployment on bus work at St Albans, was followed by their complete removal from the far eastern area on 1st February 1952 when 10T10s were brought in to cover the few Grays-based bus duties formerly worked by them.

The availability of displaced and demoted 10T10s saw the remaining 9T9s quite swiftly disposed of, the last being from Dunton Green on 1st February 1952, while the final 11T11s in the country area were removed from service at High Wycombe later in the same month, on the 18th. Straight away, withdrawals of 4Q4s commenced starting with Hemel Hempstead and Leavesden Road, in some cases bringing in quite large contingents of 10T10s as replacements such as ten received at Crawley on 16th April and nine at East Grinstead on 1st May. The supply of suitable 10T10s became exhausted on 1st June when Dunton Green lost its last 4Q4, but by that time such a big inroad had been made into the ranks of the Qs that Reigate was the only garage still to hold any, and replacement of these had to wait until April 1953 when new green RFs became available.

Meanwhile the 10T10s had not been totally all-conquering in their quest to dominate country bus operations; at a cluster of northern garages they were usurped by TFs removed from Green Line duties. Hertford lost all its 10T10s in April 1952 followed by Hitchin in May and Hatfield in June, the new arrivals being put to work on Green Line reliefs as well as on local bus services. However, as if to balance this, green 10T10s were sent to Central Bus garages, arriving between May and September 1952 and operated, for the most part, from Kingston although certain of them spent brief spells at Croydon, Edgware and Norbiton.

An interesting but isolated manoeuvre was carried out on 9th June 1952 when a small contingent of eight 10T10s, which had built up in February and March of that year at Leavesden Road garage – its first since 1947 – were sent en bloc to Hemel Hempstead in exchange for post-war 15T13s. Leavesden Road garage was scheduled to close soon after-wards, on 18th June, upon the opening of the large new premises at Garston and the vehicle swap appears to have been carried out so that a uniformly modern fleet could be presented at the opening of the new premises.

A temporary source of new employment occurred unex-pectedly for 10T10s in July 1952 when London Transport faced difficulty in finding sufficient vehicles large enough to meet capacity demands on the airport service which it oper-ated on contract to British European Airways from Victoria garage. The petrol-engined 18-seat Commers traditionally used on this had become totally inadequate, especially since the introduction by BEA of its new de Havilland 'Elizabethan' aircraft, and splendid new 4RF4 37-seater Regal IVs had been ordered to replace them. Although delivery of these had begun in April 1952, the industrial relations problems which engulfed Park Royal Coachworks on and off for much of the post-war era resulted in a complete shut-down between 2nd July and 1st October 1952 and meant that the anticipated supply of new airport coaches was not forthcoming. Starting on 1st July, and building up to a total of ten by the 23rd of that month, London Transport hired 10T10 30-seaters to BEA to cover the peak summer months, mainly on the London–Northolt Airport service. Most were vehicles whose London careers had already ceased but were relicensed specially for this work, and all were placed back on the disposal list as the seasonal requirement for them gradually diminished, the last three being handed back on 27th October.

New RFs flowed into the Central Bus fleet between October 1952 and March 1953, and although none were scheduled to directly replace 10T10s some did so indirectly by displacing TDs, with the result that single red 10T10s held at Harrow Weald, Leyton and Tottenham were withdrawn from service as well as larger allocations at Loughton and Hornchurch, all in February 1953. This left just 23 of the original 40 red 10T10s still in use. One of these was on private hire work at Old Kent Road and the remainder were divided between Enfield with 9 and Kingston with 13. The fate of the Enfield and Kingston vehicles hinged around the conversion of routes 205, 242 and 243 at Enfield to RT operation which, in turn, was dependent upon strengthening work being carried out on the bridge over the railway at Waltham Cross. The arrival of RTs would enable TDs from Enfield to be transferred to Kingston, allowing the 10T10s at both garages to be with-drawn. They were, however, enjoying a temporary stay of execution because the bridge work was held up by cash prob-lems within Essex County Council which had been obliged to divert funds to repair infrastructure damaged by major flooding that had caused havoc along much of the east coast early in 1953. The conversion finally took place on 6th May

1953 and all the red 10T10s were duly withdrawn from service on that day with the exception of T 474 at Kingston which lasted out for just one week longer. This was not quite the end of their story, however. For the remainder of the summer twelve of them, all retrieved from the final Kingston allocation, were used on private hire work in connection with the coronation celebrations from a number of garages – Chalk Farm, Chelverton Road, Merton, Old Kent Road, Putney Bridge and Victoria – the last seven (T 470, 504, 513, 528, 536, 588, 598) being withdrawn on 1st October. The green 10T10s at Kingston had meanwhile been replaced by TDs, the last of them leaving on 24th April 1953. By this time the number of pure 10T10s of the 30-seat variety still in service was fast diminishing although a few managed to remain until September 1953 with a single lone survivor (T 472 at Guildford) going on beyond this to 20th October when it was finally taken out of service.

The final phase of the RF programme began in March 1953 and lasted until December with the focus now being on replacing the country bus fleet which, as far as the pre-war element was concerned, now consisted solely of 4Q4s at Reigate plus 10T10s and TFs at various locations. Reigate was naturally the first recipient of the new vehicles after which the various garages running TFs were treated as the next priority. The displacement of TFs was total and embraced not only the vehicles held as each garage's basic requirement to cover local bus services but also those used for duplicating Green Line workings. The latter were not covered by allocations of new RFs, which meant that during June and July garages such as Hatfield, Hertford, Hitchin and St Albans found themselves with 10T10s once again after a period of absence. The last TF withdrawals from normal scheduled service were on 22nd June 1953, but some were granted a very short reprieve as coronation spares for which seven were sent to Garston where ample space was available to accommodate them. Their relevance to the 10T10 story is that they replaced some of the latter which had been set aside for the same purpose just a week earlier but were more appropriately redeployed at Hatfield, Hertford and Hitchin on Green Line relief work. Whether or not the TFs were used while at Garston in unknown, but the forfeiture of their licences on 1st July marked the end of the class in London Transport service and left a diminishing number of 10T10/1s as the only large pre-war single deckers still active in the fleet.

The time had now come for the bus operations still worked by the remnants of the 10T10 family to be swept away as fast as the incoming surge of new green RFs would allow. Windsor was partly stocked in June; High Wycombe in July; part of Leatherhead and Addlestone in August; part of Dunton Green and Dorking and all of Guildford in September; East Grinstead, Crawley and Epping in October; and part of Northfleet in November. Routes 435 and 462 worked by Addlestone and Leatherhead were left to the end pending confirmation of their suitability for RF operation, but this was duly received and the final delivery of new RFs took over in December 1953. Meanwhile Amersham's route 373 had received new GS 26-seaters, but this still left 10T10/1s in situ at a number of garages at the start of 1954 with no more new vehicles on order with which to replace them. These were the 394 group of routes at Amersham, the 412 at Dorking, 413 at Dunton Green, 329 and 386/386A at Hertford, 489/489A at Northfleet, 441 at Staines, 442 and 445 at Windsor, and various works journeys on a variety of routes at Hitchin.

Going back to 1953, the really big event of the year was the commencement on 1st July of the first orbital Green Line service 725 linking Gravesend with Windsor via Bromley, Croydon and Sutton and operated from Northfleet and Staines garages. Although scheduled to be covered by seven RFs both garages were provided with two 10T10/1s as spares, and such was the instantaneous success of the operation that they were frequently to be found running the service end-to-end fully equipped even with newly made side route boards. When, on 28th April 1954, the operation had to be doubled in frequency between Dartford and Windsor, with Dartford garage receiving its first Green Line work since 1935, a 10T10/1 was also provided as a spare for this.

By May 1953 all red 10T10s had been withdrawn from regular service but twelve survived the summer on private hire work in connection with the coronation celebrations of Queen Elizabeth II. T 504, which had earlier been the first 10T10 to be painted red, was one of the coronation vehicles for which purpose it was based at Chalk Farm garage. They were not intended for use on bus services, but incredibly T 504 was found one day with a full load substituting for a double decker on route 39. This vehicle lives on today in preservation. *Ron Wellings*

The rapidly fading fortunes of the 10T10s were temporarily reversed on 1st July 1953 by the introduction of Green Line route 725. The first orbital Green Line operation, it quickly proved phenomenally successful and 10T10s were a regular sight on it in the early days working alongside nearly new RFs. Although now officially demoted to bus status and carrying LONDON TRANSPORT fleet names, Northfleet's T 680 looks every inch the archetypal Green Line coach, even to the extent of carrying traditional style route boards, as it passes TD 42 on its way through Kingston on its way to Windsor. *G A Rixon*

The final year of public service for the class began with 38 still licensed at 15 garages on 1st January 1954, including the two Green Line reliefs based in central London. Employed on a mixture of local bus services and Green Line relief duties they were still a reasonably common sight albeit very much reduced compared with their ubiquity in days gone by. The actual vehicles in use fluctuated during the year as some were delicensed and others were placed back into service for

temporary Green Line work after lying idle for many months. A few even sported the latest livery of all-over green relieved by a narrow cream band above and below the windows applied during 1953 to freshen the appearance of vehicles on which the regular overhaul programme had ceased in January 1952. Vehicles known to have carried the 'all green' livery are T 617, 669, 685, 688, 696 but there may have been a few others.

Although their end was drawing nigh, a few 10T10s (the exact number is not known) were repainted into the 'all green' livery during 1952/53. This may have made them look a little less jaded but it did nothing to enhance their overall appearance. Displaying the very minimum of cream to relieve the otherwise all-embracing green, T 685 remained available for use on local bus services from Dunton Green garage until the very last day of 1953. *R K Blencowe*

The final scheduled bus operations by 10T10s ceased on 7th July 1954, and Dorking was one of the final five garages to lose them from their roster on this date. This view was taken in 1953 with the photographer looking across the distinctive bonnet of Leyland Cub C 47 (itself withdrawn in December 1953) towards T 599 which is rapidly reaching the end of its operating days. Standing alongside it are RTs, 3124, 3125 and 3516 representing the latest generation of London Transport bus and still very much in their prime. *Michael Dryhurst*

Their use on Dunton Green's bus operations lasted only a month into 1954 with the last three swept away on 1st February. Hertford's ceased on 21st April when new GSs became available, while Amersham's ceased on 1st June when post-war 15T13s were drafted in. This left a few small pockets of operation which all ceased on 7th July when a supply of RFs became available as a consequence of the double decking of Green Line services at Grays. The few remaining 10T10/1 bus operations at Dorking, Hitchin, Northfleet and Staines were wiped out by this means, while Windsor's remaining duties were turned over to GS operation. On the same day the Green Line stand-bys at Riverside and Victoria were also replaced by RFs. With more new vehicles now available to cover Green Line reliefs, the number of Ts needed for this purpose was much reduced and a mere six remained licensed

after the 7th July withdrawals. These were augmented by a further eleven on 4th August for the peak summer season, which found them not only on Green Line relief work but also making a fairly regular return to bus work on route 466 at Staines. However this was destined to be their swan song and soon the melodious tones of 10T10s effortlessly plying London streets would be gone for ever.

As the summer season tailed off various ones were withdrawn to reflect the decline in trade, and the last public service day of all for the 10T10 class was Thursday 30th September 1954. For the record, the final 12 remaining to be delicensed on 1st October had been operating from five garages which were: Dartford (T 714), Hitchin (T 617), St Albans (T 680), Staines (T 607, 671) and Windsor (T 624, 647, 668, 688, 705-707).

As well as ending their days on local bus service on 7th July 1954, the 10T10s also ceased to act as centrally based Green Line stand-bys. Deputising for a Northfleet vehicle on a westbound 702 run to Sunningdale is T 639, the final one of several to be based at Victoria garage over the years, all of which carried the one-line blinds which made them so distinctive when in service. Upon withdrawal, T 639 became one of the strategic reserve fleet stored in New Cross garage whose services were, in the end, never called upon. *P J Jones*

As its final days on Green Line relief work draw to a close, Windsor's T 668 is seen heading home closely followed by one of the all-conquering RFs, in this case RF 281. For one final summer passengers fortunate enough to catch one of the few remaining 10T10s could savour, for the last time, the essence of Green Line travel from a pre-war perspective in one of the most attractive single deck vehicles ever produced by London Transport. T 668 ran right up to the last day of public operation of 10T10s, being withdrawn on 1st October 1954. *G A Rixon*

After withdrawal from public service, 'all green' T 669 helped to make history by accompanying the two prototype Routemasters as the crew bus on their daily trips to the testing ground at Chobham. It was based overnight in Staines garage where it is seen at the garage entrance just after its arrival at the end of a day's work with the two Routemasters, RM 2 in grey primer and RM 1 in full red livery. *J M Aldridge*

Although public service had ceased, the 10T10 story was not quite at an end, and indeed it was destined to continue for the next two years and four months during which six vehicles, which were still in good condition, pursued a new role as staff buses. In addition a further 25 were placed in store at New Cross garage and withheld from the disposal list as a contingency in case of emergencies or for possible use in covering Green Line RFs when these went in for their first overhaul cycle. With just one exception all 25 were vehicles which had operated earlier in 1954 and all were selected because they were still in good order both mechanically and bodily.

The purpose of the staff buses was to ferry employees engaged on bus overhauls from their former work locations to the centralised facility at Chiswick to which they had been redeployed. Four vehicles (T 613, 621, 631, 716) were allocated to Reigate to transport around 90 staff between there and Chiswick over three different routes leaving one vehicle as a spare, while T 697 was based at Plumstead to carry a smaller number of displaced ex-tram staff from Charlton to Chiswick, tasks which most of the vehicles fulfilled through to 1957. More interesting, in historical terms, was the work assigned to T 669 which was officially allocated to Chiswick but was actually based at Staines garage between 17th June and 19th August 1955. It was used to accompany the first two prototype Routemasters between Staines and the Ministry of Supply's Fighting Vehicle Proving Ground at Chobham, Surrey, carrying staff and equipment relevant to the endurance tests being carried out there on the new vehicles. T 669 was subsequently licensed again at Chiswick between 2nd October 1955 and 5th March 1956 after which it was placed in store pending disposal.

By the middle of 1956 it had become clear that the 25 vehicles in store at New Cross would not be needed after all and they were put up for sale. Staff bus T 613 was withdrawn in December 1956 and joined the sales list, leaving just four of the class active at the start of 1957. Their days were now heavily numbered and they ran for the last time on 31st January 1957 with 15T13s taking over their duties the next day. The sale of three of these four – T 621, 631, 697 – had already been agreed and they departed on 13th March as part of a contingent bound for Yugoslavia. T 716 was now the sole remaining 10T10 in the fleet, having been held back in case an example of the class was wanted for the museum collection. As early as August 1953 the proposal had been put forward that one of these vehicles might be kept as a museum piece along with a Q, a TF and an STL but no immediate decision was taken in respect of a 10T10. The ultimate decision was negative and on 29th March the sale of T 716 was approved. When it left the fleet on 30th April 1957 the last link with the pre-war glory days of Green Line was gone.

Even as late as the start of 1957, T 621 could sometimes be spotted on its staff journeys to and from Chiswick Works, looking much like it had always done and helping to keep the memory of the 10T10s alive more than two years after the last of them was withdrawn from public service. Surprisingly, it managed to retain its front wheel discs which had become progressively rarer on 10T10s in their later years, and was the last vehicle in the London Transport fleet to do so.

# 16 THE 11T11 REBODIES

Although only 31-strong, this purposeful-looking small fleet of rebodied vehicles played a valuable and reliable role in maintaining single deck bus operations through some very difficult times and they were a common sight right up to the arrival of the RF era. The 11T11s looked and sounded what they were, an incongruous combination of modern body lines and engine sounds with older chassis sporting old-fashioned spindly back axles and well-outdated two-letter registration numbers.

The story of the 11T11s goes back four years before they were actually created, to July 1934 when a full scale review was undertaken of the Country Bus & Coach fleet which had reached a state of incredible diversity through acquisitions and now needed comprehensive planning to determine its future. Looking at the composition of the crew-operated single deck service bus fleet, which is relevant to the 11T11 story, it was found that 307 were in the department's inventory against a service requirement of only 206. Apart from the 'standard' intake of AECs and Associated Daimlers, no fewer than eighteen other makes were represented including comparative rarities such as AJS, Laffly, Saurer and W&G which would have been difficult and costly to retain in service for long even if the will had been there to do so. In some of the more obscure cases spare parts were virtually impossible to obtain. The decision was taken there and then that, in

reducing the fleet by about one hundred, the only makes to be retained other than AEC and Associated Daimler would be the really reliable ones of Dennis, Leyland and Thornycroft.

At the same time a survey of the combined Green Line and private hire coach fleet revealed the presence of a substantial stock of AEC Reliances, the great majority of which carried now-outdated all-weather bodies. Four had already been sold, but an embargo was placed on selling the remainder in favour of fitting them with new service bus bodies. This would help to speed up replacement of some of the non-standard makes whilst also modernising the bus fleet to a certain extent. It was decided to recommend the purchase of 46 new bodies which would be sufficient to cover the existing fleet of 45 Reliances and also one earlier Associated Daimler chassis now fitted with a Reliance engine and gearbox.

Although no fleet number is displayed on the offside, this AEC Reliance was in fact R 6, and it was typical of the type of vehicle to which new Weymann bodies were fitted in 1935. It was photographed in 1932, with its cape cart hood fixed securely in the closed position, near the Green Line coach station in Poland Street. R 6 was one of a batch of 21 Reliances purchased in 1929 for private hire and touring coach duties, and the front end of its LGOC-built 30-seat body was later rebuilt to incorporate the standard front destination box to enable it to cover Green Line duties, which it was probably doing when the photograph was taken. *J F Higham © A B Cross*

At a meeting on 21st February 1935 Lord Ashfield formally approved the purchase of 43 new bodies at a cost of £24,422 although much of the groundwork had already been done by this time, and it was stipulated that the whole deal was to be completed within five months. Circumstances had dictated a change of plan from that envisaged earlier, brought about by the fact that twelve London Lorries bodies on AEC Regal chassis acquired from the Blue Belle and Queen Line companies (now T 346-357) could not continue in use and would have to be replaced by twelve of the forthcoming new bodies. The only Reliances now to be rebodied would be the 30 redundant all-weather ones which, along with the earlier ADC chassis mentioned above, brought the total new body requirement to the revised figure of 43.

London Transport was keen to widen its experience of operating so-called 'all metal' bodies and 43 of this type were ordered from Weymann employing MCW patented tubular framework of flanged box section made from solid drawn steel tubing. Timber was still employed although to a far lesser degree than on composite bodies and mostly only to provide a suitable base into which screws securing the mouldings could be fixed. The new bodies were built in two separate batches with those for the Reliances dealt with first. Of necessity, these had to differ from the Regal bodies by virtue of the positioning of their wheel arches and mudguards to suit the Reliance's shorter wheelbase of only 16ft 0ins, and while both versions were identical from the waistline upwards, the bodies on the Regals were approximately 2 inches deeper below the waist, making it possible to adopt a very neat, horizontal lower edge to their windscreen. The Reliance bodies, on the other hand, had a sloping line on the foot of the windscreen which, through giving a rather strange appearance when mounted above the low-sited Reliance radiator, was clearly incorporated with the possibility in mind of transferring these bodies to Regal chassis at a later date. The Reliance bodies were fitted out as 30-seaters using the standard type of low and hollow-backed wooden-framed seat then favoured by London Transport and were all painted in standard Country Bus two-tone green livery.

The 30 Reliances destined to receive new Weymann bodies fell into two categories and mostly dated from 1929 although a few were first licensed in 1930 and were, in fact, newer than the oldest Regals. Fourteen of them (R 1-5, 26-34) had been fitted from new with LGOC-built 28-seat dual door canvas-hooded bodies formerly on 1928-built ADC 416A chassis, the latter having been subsequently rebodied for bus use by National. The remainder (R 6-16, 19, 20, 22-24) carried Chiswick-built 31-seat bodies, again of the dual-entrance, canvas-hooded type, which they had had from new. The two types were almost identical in appearance except that the newer batch of bodies had gently sloped rather than vertical windscreens and were built slightly taller; all had subsequently been rebuilt by Strachans with Green Line style front indicator boxes and painted into Green Line livery. The odd man out was an un-numbered open top double decker UC 2265 formerly in the East Surrey fleet which became R 44 when the new Weymann body was fitted. Built on an Associated Daimler 416A chassis, it had been rebuilt to virtually Reliance standard with an A130 6.1 litre engine and Reliance style radiator. This solitary Weymann-bodied ADC ran until August 1937 when the new body was transferred to the standard Reliance chassis of R 40, one of nine such vehicles acquired in December 1933 from the Batten's fleet of Amalgamated Omnibus Services & Supplies Ltd.

On 17th January 1935 a definitive list was circulated showing all 43 vehicles that were to receive new bodies. Most of the Reliances were already in store at various locations and the only ones in use at the time were R 28-31 which were still doing coach duties at Luton and R 34 temporarily employed as a service bus at Hitchin. R 1, T 346 and UU 2265 were already at Chiswick in chassis form, and had been there since 6th October 1934, to ascertain the work required on each type prior to receiving new bodies. On 28th January 1935 the instruction went out listing the dates on which individual vehicles were to be sent to Chiswick for their chassis overhauls to commence which, in the case of the Reliances, stretched from 28th January to 11th March 1935. After being overhauled, each chassis was sent away to Addlestone to receive its new body.

The next time the 31 Weymann bodied Reliances figured in forward planning was in early 1938. Fleet renewal had progressed to the point whereby all Reliance chassis, whether rebodied or not, were to be removed from service during 1938, and it was now time to re-mount the bodies on to Regal chassis made surplus by the Green Line renewal programme. Furthermore they were to be converted to oil operation using new 7.7 litre direct injection engines, and conversion of the 31 vehicles, including the purchase of engines, dynamos and control panels, was authorised by the Chairman on 14th July 1938 at a cost of £12,307. Various modifications were required to the chassis frame, radiator, pedal and brake gear to suit the new engine along with revisions to the fuel supply system and silencer, and the fitting of a 24 volt electrical system in place of the existing 12 volt one. Unlike a much larger number of STLs converted to diesel at the same time, the new engines were given solid rather than flexible rubber mountings. Considerable restructuring of the lower body frame was necessary to move the rear mudguards backwards and the offside front mudguard forwards by a few inches to accommodate the 1ft longer wheelbase of the Regal chassis.

Although the official go-ahead was not authorised until July, work on a trial vehicle commenced as early as January 1938 when one-time East Surrey all-weather coach T 396 was delicensed at Romford, North Street on the first day of the year and sent to Chiswick. By 15th March it had been united with the body formerly on R 15 and it entered service at Reigate on 12th May. Conversion of a second vehicle was commenced ahead of the official authorisation when the distinctive T 232, with its modern semi-streamlined body, was taken out of storage at Chiswick tram depot on 18th June, and although this became the second conversion to enter service, it did not do so until 5th October 1938 at Hemel Hempstead, nearly five months after the first one. The main programme began on 28th September and was completed on 7th December with the last five newly rebodied Regals entering service at a variety of garages on 1st January 1939.

When first rebodied, T 396 was reclassified 2/7T4/1 but this was short lived in favour of the brand new classification 11T11 by which the vehicles were henceforth always known. The majority of the chassis employed in the scheme comprised 1/7T7/1 Green Line vehicles from the T 207-306 batch but four former Amersham & District vehicles were also used. All kept their original registration and fleet numbers so the ancestry of each individual vehicle was easily discernible. As recorded in an earlier chapter, contemporary record cards indicate that the former Amersham & District T 365, 366 and ex-Lewis T 367 were initially partly converted and received Weymann bodies which were then removed again, but this

*Left and right* The old order and the new, photographed at the same location on the 427 Redhill circular. They provide an opportunity to compare the appearance of the 1935 Weymann bodwork as originally fitted to the Reliances – in this case R 8 – and when mounted on the Regal chassis, represented in this instance by T 396. The latter was acting at the time as the prototype from which the successful 11T11 class duly came into being. Without doubt the bodies looked more comfortable in their new guise thanks to the higher positioning and more handsome appearance of the Regal radiator which eliminated the rather mournful expression that they had worn previously. In due course R 8's body reappeared on T 280, making its debut at High Wycombe on 1st November 1938. *R S Turnbull/Alan B Cross collection*

When viewed internally, little structural difference could be detected between the new Weymann bodies as built for the Reliances and those on the 5T4s except in minor matters dictated by the chassis design such as the positioning of the front cowl and the location of floor traps. Obviously different, however, were the seats which, in the Reliances, were of the old wooden framed type topped by curved grab rails, and upholstered in a green moquette to a much less striking design than that used on the 5T4s. In order to attain a higher carrying capacity on the Reliances, four rows of seats were provided on the raised rear section as against three on the Regals. *London Transport Museum*

may never actually have happened. The full list of 31 11T11s, showing the origin of their Weymann body, is as follows:

| | | | | | | | |
|---|---|---|---|---|---|---|---|
| T 208 | R 10 | T 232 | R 3 | T 266 | R 29 | T 296 | R 12 |
| T 212 | R 32 | T 234 | R 4 | T 267 | R 1 | T 298 | R 24 |
| T 213 | R 33 | T 236 | R 11 | T 271 | R 13 | T 359 | R 26 |
| T 214 | R 5 | T 237 | R 6 | T 275 | R 23 | T 361 | R 20 |
| T 215 | R 31 | T 250 | R 7 | T 276 | R 14 | T 362 | R 16 |
| T 216 | R 34 | T 253 | R 2 | T 280 | R 8 | T 364 | R 30 |
| T 223 | R 40 | T 255 | R 19 | T 283 | R 27 | T 396 | R 15 |
| T 226 | R 22 | T 261 | R 28 | T 285 | R 9 | | |

Although, at a quick glance, the 11T11s could easily be confused with the similarly bodied 5T4s (T 346-357), the sloping bottom to the windscreen quickly gave the game away as would, of course, the raucous sound of the diesel engine. With the exception of the first couple of conversions, T 396

and T 232, no attempt was made in most cases to match the nearside front mudguard with the STL-like contours of the offside one, and the fact that the original AEC nearside mudguard had been retained remained another easily recognisable feature. When first placed into service the 11T11s were tried out at a number of garages but the majority allocations quickly settled down at Hemel Hempstead, High Wycombe, Leatherhead, Leavesden Road and Reigate, although as early as 8th February 1939 this picture changed when Leatherhead's were all reallocated elsewhere. An even more drastic event occurred in May 1939 when, over the course of the month, T 208, 213, 216 and 223 (in that order) were repainted into Central Bus red livery and allocated to Hanwell garage to replace small Dennis Darts on route 211 (Ealing–Greenford). The saloon doors were left in position, presumably with an instruction to crews that they were to be left open to satisfy police requirements.

In the case of T 232, the conversion to 11T11 resulted in this particular chassis appearing in its third guise in just over seven years. During this time it graduated from a standard 1/7T7/1 Green Line coach to the striking Weymann one-off metal-bodied experimental coach of 1933, and it was now blending back into the main fleet as one of a batch of 31 identical 11T11s. Photographed in the spring of 1939 working from Addlestone garage, T 232 had already operated in its new guise since October 1938 at Hemel Hempstead, Guildford and Reigate, and it subsequently passed back to Hemel Hempstead where it was still resident when war broke out. *J F Higham © A B Cross*

The four 11T11s repainted into red livery in May 1939 for service at Hanwell would have seemed quite a novelty at first, and no-one could have foreseen at the time that the great majority of the class would finally end up in the Central Bus fleet. Notably, the roof is painted black in preference to the more usual silver, a feature shared with certain other more modern single deck classes in the red fleet. T 208 is seen looking very smart, probably just a few days after being repainted, but nothing is known about the circumstances under which it came to be running from Enfield garage. It may be conjectured that tests were being carried out to ascertain the suitability of 11T11s for possible operation at Central Bus locations other than Hanwell. *Alan Nightingale collection*

Being oil engined, the 11T11s worked solidly throughout the war, government policy being to conserve petrol supplies in preference to diesel. The former was considered more essential to the war effort, in addition to which the greater economy of the diesel engine placed less stress on the hazardous fuel distribution network. A mid-war alteration carried out on the 11T11s was the installation of conventional side lights as a slight aid to driving in blackout conditions, although the original lamps remained, albeit disconnected and painted over, in the front domes of most vehicles.

A major boost to the Green Line network on 4th December 1940 saw the recommencement of a number of services that had been dormant since the start of the war, while at the same time the traditional use of route letters ceased and was replaced by a conventional numbering system. For the first and only time, 11T11s found themselves officially scheduled

for Green Line work when the whole of High Wycombe's contingent was swept away and reallocated to Crawley and Reigate for operation on Green Line route 9 (Crawley–Oxford Circus). Their glory, however, was very short lived, and when conventional 10T10s became available just two weeks later, on 18th December, the 11T11s were returned to bus work.

In common with several other elements of the T class, the 11T11s were earmarked as suitable candidates for the installation of perimeter seating to increase their passenger-carrying capacity, in this instance to 27 seated plus 20 standees. Grays-based T 236 joined the other trial vehicles at Chiswick in November 1941 and entered service in its revised format on 23rd December. Twenty more followed during 1942, and during the course of that year all except ten of the remainder (T 212, 214, 226, 250, 266, 276, 280, 296, 364, 396) were dealt with.

The summer of 1940 finds T 396 operating from Reigate garage, carrying the wartime trappings of masked headlamps and white-tipped mudguards, although the use of anti-shatter mesh on the windows has yet to come. Since March 1940 it has carried the wartime green and white livery with matt grey roof, the latter colour extending at the back right down to waist rail level. *A N Porter*

The 11T11s were not immune from the 1941/42 drive to maximise carrying potential on single deckers, and perimeter seating was installed on 21 out of the 31 vehicles. Three seats were lost, but the overall passenger capacity was increased to 47. Grays-based T 236 was the first to be dealt with, and the rearrangement of the seats inside this vehicle was accompanied by the provision of sundry full-height stanchions along with ample roof-mounted leather grips for straphangers. The rather plain green seat covering perpetuates a style of moquette used in quantity by London Transport during the late nineteen-thirties and was probably installed when the bodies were overhauled and transferred on to the Regal chassis. *London Transport Museum*

With the war at its height, these two photographs were taken of T 216 at Hanwell garage on 26th January 1943. One of the original four red repaints of 1939, it had been allocated to Hanwell ever since then and was, in fact, destined to remain there right through to February 1949. The roof and back window surrounds are now in wartime brown, which was to continue as the standard livery for 11T11s well into the post-war era. Conventionally sited side lights have now been installed, but the original fittings are still in position, albeit unused, in the front dome. *London Transport Museum*

Wartime scheduling requirements saw more of the class painted red for Central Bus service with T 215, 232 and 298 augmenting the existing stock at Hanwell on 14th October 1941 followed by T 214, 226, 250 280 and 296 which adopted red livery ready to start work at Harrow Weald on 1st June 1942. Later in the year, on 11th December 1942, T 213 emerged from overhaul at Chiswick tram depot carrying wartime brown and cream livery, one of the first in the fleet to do so. It was followed on 6th February 1943 by a second brown 11T11, T 223, on the very last day that this temporary colour scheme was used, adequate supplies of conventional red paint having now become available once again. One other 11T11, T 216, was overhauled in between these two but remained red, its overhaul having been carried out at Alperton where, rather than fully repainting vehicles, the normal process was to touch up and varnish. T 250 was returned to country service in April 1945 and became unique in marking the only instance where an 11T11 reverted back from red to green. While the red 11T11s remained solely based at Hanwell and Harrow Weald during the war, the green ones moved about to locations such as Dorking, Dunton Green, Grays and Hertford, but from approximately December 1942 onwards it became clear that they were being assembled at just four locations: High Wycombe, Leavesden Road, Luton and Windsor, and these are where they remained until the war ended.

The return of peace found all 21 vehicles with perimeter seating converted back to their normal condition as 30-seaters during December 1945 and January 1946. These early post-war months found the Country Bus & Coach department holding a surplus of single deck service buses whereas a desperate shortage prevailed on Central Buses, and an obvious course of action to help restore the balance was to paint yet more 11T11s red. Seven were dealt with in January 1946 (T 234, 236, 237, 272, 276, 285, 359) followed by four more in April (T 253, 255, 267, 275), leaving just eight out of the original 31 to work through to the end in green (T 212, 250, 266, 283, 361, 362, 364, 396). The reason for the sudden surfeit of service buses for country service was the return to normal duties of vehicles employed for the past six years as ambulances. The availability of 9T9s after their wartime absence resulted in the displacement of all of Luton's 11T11s in preparation for their red repaints in January 1946 while the April repainting was a result of former ambulance 1/7T7/1s being made available for service at Windsor. This left High Wycombe and Leavesden Road as the only country area garages still with 11T11s, a situation which pertained right to the end. In the central area it was necessary to find garages from which to run the newly won 11T11s, and this resulted in Kingston being chosen for the January intake and Uxbridge in April. Second thoughts soon prevailed, and in May half of the Kingston intake was removed to enhance the fleet at Hanwell while in July most of the remainder departed to fulfill a similar role at Uxbridge. The sole survivor left Kingston in January 1947 to establish a tenuous 11T11 presence at Enfield of one or two vehicles which lasted throughout 1947 and 1948.

The memories of war were still fresh in everyone's mind when T 271 was repainted from green to red and sent to work from Kingston garage in January 1946. At some time during its short stay there, which lasted only until May of the same year, it was photographed on the bus stand at Staines GWR station in the company of T 690, which had been based at Leatherhead since October 1944, and a lowbridge ST on route 436. *Alan Nightingale collection*

11T11s were a regular feature of the Uxbridge scene for several years along with newer, post-war Ts of the 14T12 class. One of these nearly new vehicles is sandwiched between T 280 and ST 465, the latter representing the type of double decker on which the Uxbridge fleet was standardised for many years. Close examination of the front offside mudguard reveals that it has been re-profiled to match the nearside one. In this instance the old sidelights have been removed from the front dome whereas on many 11T11s they were allowed to remain in place, albeit painted over, right to the end. *D A Thompson*

A set pattern was now established for the 11T11s which maintained a stable presence on a limited number of services throughout 1947 and 1948, giving them an unusual degree of stability at a time when the London Transport fleet as a whole was in a state of great flux. The services which they operated during this period, together with the number of 11T11s allocated to each garage at 1st January 1948, is tabulated below.

High Wycombe (5)
363    High Wycombe–Totteridge (plus jnys on 362, 366)

Watford, Leavesden Road (3)
361    Rickmansworth–Chorleywood (plus jnys on 309, 351)

Enfield (1)
205    Chingford–Hammond Street
242    Epping Forest–Potters Bar

Hanwell (12)
211    Ealing Broadway–Ruislip

Harrow Weald (5)
221    North Harrow–Pinner

Uxbridge (5)
222    Uxbridge–Hounslow
224    Uxbridge–Stanwell

The re-profiling of the front offside mudguard on the great majority of 11T11s was carried out at the same time as the STL-type decorative rubber extension piece behind the wheel was removed, a process also carried out on many 9T9s and on a huge number of STLs. Former Amersham & District T 361 was one of the eight 11T11s that remained in green livery and it spent the whole of the post-war period working from Leavesden Road garage, appropriately enough – in view of its fleet number – on route 361. It was photographed subsequent to its final overhaul in June 1948 when it received the 1948 Country Bus livery with green roof and mudguards and cream window surrounds. *F G Reynolds*

The only former Amersham & District 11T11 to receive red livery was T 359 (in January 1946). It stops to pick up a passenger outside Alexandra Palace, the historic site of Britain's first television transmitting station, whilst operating from West Green garage where it was stationed between November 1948 and April 1949. This period marked the start of the redistribution of the 11T11s to all manner of garages as temporary replacements for their regular single deckers which, in the case of route 233, would have been a 5Q5. *A D Packer*

On Central Buses this picture of stability changed completely at the end of 1948 when the 11T11s suddenly adopted the 'maid of all work' role formerly carried out by the unrebodied petrol-engined T-types. The catalyst for this was the availability from October 1948 onwards of new Mann Egerton bodied TDs, but even after their arrival a fall-back fleet of older vehicles was still required and with the petrol Ts now gradually dropping by the wayside the 11T11s served as a handy substitute. Their first appearance in new territory was at West Green in November 1948 but this was extended in 1949 to Edgware, Hornchurch, Hounslow, Leyton and Tottenham, together with a big upsurge in the number present at Enfield. Many of these moves were made possible because of an influx of post-war 14T12s into Hanwell during 1949 (although three 11T11s remained there afterwards), and also at Uxbridge where a big exodus of 11T11s in January 1950 established the class at Loughton which, with a couple more arriving in June, ultimately found itself with seven on the books. Sidcup was added to the list in March 1950 and even Kingston acquired a couple of 11T11s for the first time since 1946, albeit only for a few weeks.

With their future regarded as more long term than other vehicles dating from the 1930/31 period, the 11T11s received regular overhauling throughout the early post-war years to keep them in reasonable condition. From early 1948 this brought about a change of livery for the country ones which, though barely perceptible in black and white photographs, gave them a slightly more cheerful appearance. In common with other country area stock being overhauled at the time, the off-white areas around the window frames became cream and the brown roofs gained the main bodywork colour of Lincoln green, as did the mudguards. The same treatment was not initially meted out to the Central Bus vehicles which continued to be repainted in their wartime-derived livery of red and white with brown roof for another year or so, although a few appeared in red (including the roof) and cream during 1949. From early in 1948 time a programme was introduced for modifying the front offside mudguards from which the

rear STL-like rubber streamlined extension was removed, while on most but not quite all vehicles the front of the mudguard was re-profiled to resemble the older-style near-side one which had remained in situ since pre-Weymann rebodying days. Only one vehicle, T 255, retained its STL-style mudguard to the end. With no immediate demise in sight, overhauling of 11T11s continued into 1950 and from August of that year the so-called 'all red' (or green) colour scheme was adopted with future spray painting in mind, and eight vehicles – six red and two green – emerged in this form before overhauling finally ceased after T 232 had been dealt with in February 1951.

The decision to terminate the overhaul programme was no doubt influenced by the fact that work on the now ageing bodywork was becoming increasingly time consuming and uneconomical, and it was made in the knowledge that new RF coaches would be available within the next nine months which would release the far superior 10T10s to cover a range of bus duties temporarily until the manufacture of purpose-built bus RFs could begin. Furthermore, London Transport had now come under heavy pressure from staff – particularly at Loughton garage – through their union representatives to urgently replace the 11T11s with newer vehicles. An almost inevitable outcome from terminating the overhaul programme was that, by the latter part of 1951, vehicles with the 'oldest' overhaul dates were beginning to attract PSV71 'stop' notices. One of the first to do so was Enfield-based T 253 which had not received any major attention since December 1947, but nine others had also reached the end of the road by the close of 1951. The number of garages with 11T11s on their books had likewise diminished with Edgware, Leyton and Loughton losing their last ones in November 1951 followed by Harrow Weald and Southall (the now-renamed Hanwell) in December. These last two had both ended up with one vehicle apiece, the last of a long line of 11T11s held at both garages. Dalston garage, which had built up a small fleet of six inherited from other locations as recently as October and November 1951, found all of them delicensed on 1st January 1952.

Towards the end, the continued presence of 11T11s on the rolling stock roster at Loughton garage was met with considerable hostility from staff working on route 254. One of the last to leave there was T 255 on 12th November 1951. Still looking reasonably smart despite the dent in its midriff, it was notable for being the only one to retain its STL-style front mudguard right to the end. After leaving Loughton, T 255 spent a brief spell at Dalston before being withdrawn on 1st January 1952. *Ron Wellings*

A few 11T11s received red and cream livery in 1949 including T 285 which was overhauled in February of that year. A tell-tale sign that this has taken place, visible even in a black and white photograph, is the cream painted surround to the first offside window of the driver's cab. T 285 passes Kingston bus station with rebuilt 1T1 T 42 standing just inside. *Allen T Smith © A B Cross*

At the start of 1952, with the end clearly in sight, the 21 remaining serviceable 11T11s were scattered amongst seven garages:

| | |
|---|---|
| Bromley (TB) | T 296 |
| Enfield (E) | T 208, 213, 216, 223, 236, 276 |
| Sidcup (SP) | T 226, 298 |
| Tottenham (AR) | T 271, 285 |
| West Green (WG) | T 214, 215, 234 |
| High Wycombe (HE) | T 212, 250, 266, 364, 396 |
| Watford, Leavesden Rd (WT) | T 361, 362 |

With only a few months to go, this remaining small fleet was still capable of producing re-allocation surprises, and there was much changing around of garages amongst those that were left. Enfield's last ones were cleared out on 1st February 1952 as were Leavesden Road's, and the final country bus location, High Wycombe, succumbed when its 11T11s were withdrawn on 18th February. Tottenham also dropped from the list in February followed by West Green in March. One of the latter's 11T11s went, surprisingly, to Croydon which had never before included one of these vehicles within its allocation and retained it in operation for exactly three weeks.

Hounslow was added briefly back to the list with two vehicles in February, which had both departed by mid-April, while Kingston made a third stab at operating the class from 16th April onwards when three 11T11s were received, one each from Bromley, Hounslow and Sidcup. Two weeks later the end arrived with the withdrawal on 1st May 1952 of T 214 at Bromley, T 215 at Sidcup and T 236, 285 and 298 at Kingston.

While the latter were sent away for storage in Highgate trolleybus depot to await their fate, one member of the class was back in use, albeit in a non-psv role. On 28th January 1952 T 280 was revived from the Forest Road storage yard and dispatched to Sidcup garage to serve officially as a hut or store shed. This appears to have been a rather loose description of its function as it appears to have remained unaltered and was seen on the road on at least one occasion, 16th May, heading for Sidcup, and it seems probable that it was used in a mobile capacity on other occasions too. T 280's reprieve lasted until September 1953 and its stay of execution ensured that it outlasted all the other 11T11s in the London Transport fleet. Its eventual sale to Leeds dealer W North on 9th October 1953 marked the end of an interesting phase in the story of the T class.

By the time that this photograph was taken of T 236 at rest along with a miscellany of other Kingston-based single deckers on 20th April 1952, the operational fleet of 11T11s had shrunk to a mere five vehicles, and these had only a few days left to run. Although T 236 looks far more modern than 1T1s T 14 and T 9 standing alongside, they were both destined to outlast it. It sports the final livery style to appear on the 11T11s. T 236 was one of the final 11T11s withdrawn from service on 1st May. *Alan B Cross*

# 17 EARLY POST-WAR ADDITIONS

## T 719-768

On Saturday morning 20th October 1945 an important meeting was convened at Chiswick Works attended by A A M Durrant, London Transport's Chief Mechanical Engineer, and E C Ottaway, Supplies Officer, who met with W R Black and B Homfray-Davies, the Managing Directors of Park Royal Coachworks and Weymann Motor Bodies respectively. The purpose of the meeting was to secure a supply of bodywork for 352 new chassis which the Board had been given a licence to acquire during the first half of 1946. At the time, allocation of new chassis was still controlled centrally but recipients of them were now required to source their own bodywork, which often proved difficult because of the ongoing prevalence of shortages of material and manpower. To safeguard its position, London Transport had come to an arrangement whereby it would purchase all its new bodywork from the two manufacturers as far as was practicable, hopefully guaranteeing a dependable source of new bodies while at the same time minimising the number of suppliers that it would have to deal with.

Durrant explained to the meeting that the allocation comprised 331 double deckers (100 Daimler CWA6, 65 Leyland PD1 and 166 AEC RT types) but only 21 single deckers (Leyland PS1), and that the single deck element was considered insufficient to meet the Board's immediate needs. To

remedy this, he had contacted a Mr Lovell at the Ministry of War Transport who had indicated that he might be able to make 40 AEC Regals available in addition to the 21 Leylands. On the strength of this civil service equivalent of a nod and a wink, he wished these 40 Regals to also be taken into account when discussing future body orders at that morning's meeting. Homfray-Davies confirmed that, through his own grape vine, he had heard that AEC had approximately 115 Regals still unallocated from its 1945 programme which would presumably now be rescheduled for 1946. Many of these could, in all probability, be made available very quickly.

When they first arrived, the 14T12s looked quite alien to the existing single deck fleet by virtue of their shape and livery. Although unfamiliar non-standard designs had begun to proliferate within the double deck fleet in the form of various 'utility' and early post-war types, these were the first single deckers to break away from the established mould. T 723 was one of the initial delivery of seven vehicles to Uxbridge garage which started work on 1st April 1946 on route 223, and it was photographed whilst still in pristine condition a few days later. Some early deliveries of 14T12s had chromium plated windscreen surrounds which, like the unpainted aluminium kick plate surrounding the driver's step, were painted red at the vehicle's first overhaul. *J F Higham*

Although unable to commit Weymann to the construction of any double deckers in the first half of 1946, Homfray-Davies offered to provide bodywork for all the single deckers as long as London Transport was prepared to accept a body currently being designed for the British Electric Traction group who were placing an order based on the AEC Regal chassis for its Devon General, East Midland, Hebble and Rhondda companies. He said that the general arrangement drawing for this body was almost complete and Mr Ottaway would be able to visit the Addlestone factory on the following Thursday to finalise the Board's specific requirements. The same body could, with suitable modifications, also be used on the Leyland chassis, and production could begin quite soon.

Thus the ground was laid for London Transport's first post-war additions to the T class. When confirmation finally arrived from the Ministry it was for 50 Regal chassis (the allocation of Leyland PS1s was also increased by 10 to 31), and a Special Expenditure Requisition was issued to cover these 50 vehicles on 31st January 1946 at an estimated cost of £2,494 each. Following on from the 10T10s, they were numbered T 719-768 with body numbers 1155-1204.

AEC allocated chassis numbers 06624307-56 to the London Transport order, and Homfrey-Davies's prediction of early delivery of some, at least, of them proved to be correct. On the very first day of 1946 three chassis were made available for the coachbuilders, who had received 18 by the end of January. Thereafter progress was slower as the stock of already-built chassis became exhausted and the manufacturing of the remainder fell prey to the ever-present fluctuations in the availability of materials that beset all of the motor industry at that time. Most chassis had, however, been taken into stock by the end of June 1946 apart from the final three which were delayed until late in August. The chassis themselves were unremarkable and very basic, befitting the austerity of the time with 7.7 litre A173AF 105x146mm

direct injection engines rated at 41hp, crash gearboxes, triple servo braking systems, rear axle ratio of 5.2:1, and a wheelbase of 17ft 6ins. The complete vehicle, with bodywork installed, was shown as weighing exactly 6 ton unladen and was classified 14T12.

The first completed bus to arrive at Chiswick from Weymann's factory was T 726 on 7th March. Like many other first deliveries it was subjected to close examination and various tests, plus the usual official photographs, all of which took time with the result that it was by no means the first to enter service. Seventeen others had already done so before it was licensed at Kingston on 20th May. The new vehicle could best be described as workmanlike but hardly handsome, and there was almost nothing London-like about its general appearance. Weymann influence could be detected in the outswept panels at the rear, and the BET influence was apparent in the provision of an offside emergency door (rather than the rear door layout normally favoured by London Transport) and in the internal décor with its extensive use of dark stained and varnished wooden mouldings. A supply of half-drop windows was not available at the time construction commenced so Rawlings patent sliding ventilators were used instead, the design being such that each ventilator comprised three separate pieces of glass. Sliding ventilators were a new feature for single deckers on London Transport although they had been fitted to a few pre-war and wartime trolleybus bodies and also featured on a fairly recently delivered Guy Arab double decker. The saloon entrance was at the front and was permanently open in compliance with Metropolitan Police regulations, while the emergency exit was behind the offside rear wheel arch where the last transverse double seat was moved forward in relation to its nearside counterpart to give access to it. The 35 seats were all forward facing on tubular steel frames and were upholstered in RT style moquette.

It was when viewed from the rear that the 14T12s perhaps looked at their most un-Londonlike, and the indicator box sat uncomfortably on the rear dome requiring an awkward upward sweep of the panelling to accommodate it above the large single rear window. T 726 was kitted out with Kingston garage blinds for its official photograph session and duly entered service there on 20th May 1946.
*London Transport Museum*

Despite the extensive use of dark woodwork on the window surrounds, the interiors of the 14T12s did not look unduly gloomy. The wooden slatted floor and cream painted ceiling were familiar London Transport requirements included within their specification, and the now standard upholstery, combined with green rexine backs, was used on provincial style seat frames similar to those found on many recent double deck deliveries. *London Transport Museum*

London Transport specified a new red and cream livery, with the relief colour restricted to mouldings about 1 inch deep above and below the windows, and the front and rear destination boxes were of the Board's standard size for single deckers. At the back, the space availability within the rear dome was inadequate to accommodate the box in its entirety so a pronounced and rather odd-looking upward sweep had to be incorporated into the roof line to achieve the necessary height. This would probably have looked better and would have given the body a more balanced appearance if the same process had been applied at the front where space was also limited, but instead the roof line remained steady here and the destination box was projected downwards below the cant rail to give a very squashed-up looking appearance to the area around the windscreen which was not helped by the need to accommodate the rather tall AEC radiator.

Although they were designed primarily to meet BET requirements, the majority of the 14T12s actually preceded the BET Regals off the production line by a fair margin and it was not until July 1946 that the first provincial ones entered service with Devon General and East Midland. By then, three garages had been nominated to receive 14T12s and all had a fair smattering of them in stock. Uxbridge had

been the first recipient starting on 1st April, where their initial task was to displace LT six-wheelers from route 223 (West Drayton–Ruislip). Kingston followed on 9th May with routes 215 (Kingston–Ripley) and 219 (Kingston–Weybridge/ Vickers Works), but numbers gradually built up to include route 206 (Hampton Court–Claygate) and also the Kingston– Walton-on-Thames workings on route 218, the full length of the latter to Staines being out-of-bounds for them because of the weight restriction on Walton-on-Thames bridge. However in typical Kingston fashion, the official version of things was never treated as being cast in tablets of stone, and 14T12s could often be found wandering on to the 201 (Kingston– Feltham) and 213 (Kingston–Belmont), where their seating capacity of 35 was equal to that of the encumbent LTs. The same applied at Muswell Hill which began receiving new Ts on 14th May, ostensibly for route 212 (Muswell Hill–Finsbury Park) although they were equally as likely to be found on the 210 (Finsbury Park–Golders Green). Material supply problems exacerbated by the Board of Trade's drive to prioritise export orders over home ones meant that receipt of the new vehicles was more protracted than originally anticipated and the last of the class to be placed into service, T 767, was not licensed at Uxbridge until 9th November 1946.

Having received the last of its allocation of 20 new Ts as late as 7th November 1946, Muswell Hill began the process of losing them all on 23rd December. The reason for this was that the new Leyland PS1s, designated the TD class, had now started to arrive, and with 31 of these in prospect there would be almost enough to convert all of routes 210 and 212. Although the official order for these had been placed earlier than that for the Ts – reflecting the fact that the Leylands formed part of the Board's official allocation whereas the AECs did not – construction of the TDs had been much slower to the extent that none of them were received within the planned timescale. Carrying Weymann bodies conforming to the same basic design as those on the 14T12s, the new Leylands looked almost identical to them from most angles, the only real difference being at the front where the slightly more spacious, square cornered cab was fitted with a deeper windscreen. The lower edge of this was in line with the side windows, eliminating the old-fashioned looking bulge found on the Ts and reducing the frowning effect which was a feature of the fronts of these bodies. The TDs were a full quarter of a ton heavier than the 14T12s, but a significant difference was that they seated only 33 as against 35 on the Ts. This reduction occurred as a result of replacing the transverse seat on top of each rear wheel arch with a single, inward facing one, and it resulted in a much better and more comfortable arrangement to which all the 14T12s were converted on overhaul between May 1949 and January 1950. It was, in fact, a modification of an experiment carried out on T 757 either from the time it was new or very soon afterwards (but never recorded on its internal record card) whereby the nearside transverse wheel arch seat for two had been replaced by a single inward-facing one, as on the TDs, whilst on the offside the last two sets of forward facing seats had been replaced by a bench seat for three.

The first 14T12 disposals from Muswell Hill made it clear that these almost-new vehicles were destined to go to Sidcup garage where they would work alongside 5Q5s on route 241 (Sidcup–Welling). However, after the first two had made their way south-eastwards, a sudden change of programme in January 1947 saw five diverted to Uxbridge to depose older

Ts from route 222 (Uxbridge–Hounslow), although on most days at least one could also be found on the 224 (Uxbridge–Stanwell). The progress of the remainder towards Sidcup was leisurely thereafter, being dependent upon the protracted delivery of the new TDs, and the last did not go across from Muswell Hill until 25th June 1947. Although 14T12s were destined to be a feature of the Sidcup scene until January 1953 their reign on route 241 was relatively short. During 1948 an influx of Q-types from the country area, including all the green 5Q5s which went to Sidcup itself, produced sufficient to cover the entire 25 bus allocation on route 241, so the Ts were moved across to Sidcup's other single deck service 228 (Eltham–Chislehurst) from which they displaced all of the resident LT six-wheelers between July and September 1948.

Brief mention was made earlier of the 1949 overhaul programme for the 14T12s, their first, and the conversion carried out on them at the time from 35 to 33 seats. This programme began when T 720 went into Chiswick from Uxbridge garage on 10th March 1949 and was completed when T 765, also an Uxbridge bus, emerged from overhaul on 17th January 1950. London Transport saw this as an opportunity to alter the vehicles from their original provincial standard up to its own specification. Much of the work remained unseen to the casual observer although it was quite extensive and involved an almost complete re-wiring, the replacement of electrical control panels in the cab, and the installation of a driver's floor mat. On the bodywork the Rawlings-made window sliders, which were beginning to disintegrate, were strengthened with brass reinforcements

The first major upheaval to affect the 14T12s was when the whole of the Muswell Hill contingent was replaced over a period of several months by new TDs. T 734 stands alongside TD 9 at Golders Green during the transition period, allowing the frontal differences between the two Weymann bodied models to be easily compared and clearly illustrating the difference in height between the top of the standard AEC radiator and that of its Leyland contemporary. T 734 went south to Sidcup garage in June 1947 after spending 13 months at Muswell Hill. *Alan B Cross collection*

T 720 adopts the same pose at Uxbridge station as in an earlier photograph, but the older vehicle behind it on this occasion is 11T11 T 359. T 720 now displays the new bonnet profile and engine cover fitted on its first overhaul in April 1949, and the new piping to carry the wiring into the bodywork is visible above and below the sidelight. T 720 was destined to spend its whole passenger service career at Uxbridge after which it spent three years up to November 1958 in the 'learner' fleet. *Denis Battams*

on their corners. There were, however, a few visible signs of change to look out for. At the very front the hooter, situated below the offside headlamp, was raised to a non-visible location behind the canopy and the redundant aperture was panelled over. The side light on the front bulkhead was henceforth placed on a block to enable a tubular wiring channel which ran from top to bottom of the bulkhead to be located behind it, this channel being necessary because wiring formerly carried on the chassis was now transferred to the body. The most visible difference was the fitting of a standard London Transport bonnet top and side cover which meant raising the bonnet plinth attached to the bulkhead by 1⅜ inches, accompanied by an unseen repositioning beneath the bonnet of the autovac tank.

A further receipt of ex-country area Qs saw them gradually taking over routes 215 and 219 at Kingston during 1950, the result being that by the start of the winter programme on 11th October no 14T12s were scheduled on these services and they could be found instead on the 213. This remained their Kingston-based focus, along with route 206, until 14th May 1952 when the splendid new garage at Norbiton was commissioned. The 206 and Kingston's share of the 213 were amongst the services allotted to the new premises, and as a result all of Kingston's 14T12s – most of which had been there from the start – moved the short distance to the new garage. Norbiton also introduced 14T12s to route 201 (Kingston–Hampton Court) which in Kingston garage days had latterly been worked by TDs.

For the most part, the 14T12s led a fairly predictable existence and it was not common to find them straying away from a few designated garages except for a short period in 1953 at the start of the RF influx. In this instance T 753 makes a rare appearance at Bromley garage on route 227, having presumably been loaned for the day from Sidcup to cover a temporary shortage of LT class six-wheelers such as the one standing behind it. *Alan B Cross*

Route 211 was destined to be one of the last strongholds for the 14T12s and T 734 was one of the ex-Sidcup contingent that introduced them to it in January 1953. Accompanying it in Ealing is STL 1681, representing a fast-fading class of double decker and itself a recent albeit temporary introduction to route 97 in place of wartime B-class Bristols pending the arrival of new RTs in October and November 1953. *Ron Wellings*

New RFs were now coming into service, on Green Line at first but on Central Buses from September 1952, and it was inevitable that their arrival would impact upon the 14T12s, either directly or indirectly. Two separate allocations of 14T12s were affected simultaneously on different parts of the system. Norbiton's allocation on route 213 gave way to the new vehicles in December 1952 and January 1953 although none of the Regals was immediately displaced. Instead they were reallocated to route 264 (Kingston–Hersham Green) which was no longer subjected to a weight limit on Walton-on-Thames bridge. They replaced the venerable 1T1s which had worked it until then, the last of which were withdrawn from service at Norbiton on 16th January 1953. Further to the east, RFs on route 228 heralded the departure from Sidcup garage of all its 14T12s during December and January, most of which moved to pastures new at Southall garage displacing TDs from route 211 (Ealing Broadway–Greenford). The following months brought a short spell of instability for the class when odd vehicles appeared for varying periods of time at garages at which they were not normally seen – Croydon, Hounslow and Old Kent Road – temporarily bolstering the home fleets at these locations. Even Kingston garage got a couple back briefly in March 1954, but by May of that year all such wanderings came to an end. It had now

become apparent that no long term justification could be made for retaining all 50 vehicles and the decision was taken to withdraw T 719-742 from service as soon as it became feasible to do so.

A plan was devised which envisaged the remaining 26 vehicles running only at Southall and Uxbridge, and in the expectation that several more years' service would be required from them two modifications were carried out. The first, which was for the benefit of conductors, was implemented in July and August 1954 when they were converted into 32-seaters by reducing the front offside seat from a double to a single to give more manoeuvring space. The second, this time for the benefit of drivers, saw the fitment of cab heaters during October 1954. Norbiton's Ts were to be replaced by TDs, though not all at once. The first batch of these arrived on 1st September, ostensibly targeting routes 201 and 206 although, in fact, insufficient were received to convert both of these in their entirety. The final clear-out, and the conversion to TD of route 264, came on 1st December 1954 using TDs made surplus at Loughton after the latter had received RFs for route 254. With the exception of T 719, 720 and 724 which became long-term driver trainers, all those numbered below T 743 were placed in store and were ultimately sold for further service in Yugoslavia.

Norbiton garage opened on 14th May 1952 with a strong contingent of 14T12s on its books, all inherited with services transferred from nearby Kingston. Ts 745, 747, 746 and 752 are seen plated-up and ready to enter service. The destination blinds in them are the same ones formerly used at Kingston with that on T 752 being one of the old style which had mostly fallen out of use by this time. All four moved to Uxbridge on 1st December 1954 to replace others of the same type which had been withdrawn from service. *G A Rixon*

From now onwards the plan to concentrate all the remaining 14T12s in west London at Southall and Uxbridge was rigidly adhered to. At the latter, route 223 was omitted from 16th February 1955 when it became entirely RT operated (having been partially covered by double deckers over the Ruislip–West Drayton section since July 1951, initially with STLs), but its loss was compensated by new T-worked 224A (Uxbridge–West Drayton, Mill Road) from the same day. On 23rd January 1957 the 224 group of routes was expanded even further with the new 224B (Uxbridge–West Drayton, Stockley Estate).

The end came suddenly and in a way that the planners had never anticipated. The long and ill-conceived strike by bus crews in May and June 1958 caused many drivers and conductors to seek alternative employment to maintain their income, and once those that were left returned to work it quickly became clear that passenger numbers had fallen substantially and would almost certainly never return to their pre-strike level. London Transport had plunged into a serious downward spiral from which there was no immediate remedy other than to cut frequencies or in some cases discontinue services entirely, and to reduce the number of operational garages. Schedule reductions began in stages on Central Buses starting on 20th August 1958, but the biggest set of cuts came into force on 26th November when, amongst 371 buses withdrawn from service, 54 were single deckers. Being the oldest ones remaining in the fleet, the 14T12s were clearly prime candidates for withdrawal and the whole lot – including the three driver trainers – ran for the last time on Tuesday 25th November 1958. They were replaced by RFs on routes 211 and 222 and TDs on the 224 group of routes.

Not quite all of the batch T 743-768 lasted in service right to the end, accident casualty T 745 having been delicensed at Southall on 1st November 1956 and sold to a London dealer in April 1957. It was the only one of its batch to finish its life on home soil. The remainder were eagerly snapped up by the Ceylon Transport Board and all had set sail by January 1959.

A final brief moment of glory came for the 14T12s when they were used to inaugurate new route 224B on 23rd January 1957, the very last new operation ever to be entrusted to the T class. T 767 stands at the Uxbridge end of the route accompanied by RT 2165. *Fred Ivey*

The final demise of the 14T12s came suddenly. One day they were operating in full force on their scheduled services from Southall and Uxbridge garages and the next day – 26th November 1958 – they had all gone. These typical latter day scenes show T 768 – the highest numbered of the batch – along with others at West Drayton, and T 766 at Ealing Broadway. Less than two months later all were on board ship on their way to Ceylon. *Denis Battams/Ron Wellings*

The huge Sunday bus excursion programme was a popular feature in the days before private car ownership began to reach epic proportions, but whether Sunday excursionists would have appreciated the somewhat spartan nature of a 14T12 for their day out remains a matter for conjecture. T 757 is about to head for the rural delights of Newlands Corner when seen in Uxbridge followed by RT 3007 heading for the more prosaic destination of West Drayton Station on route 223. *Ron Wellings*

# 18 THE MANN EGERTON REGALS

## T 769-798

As befitted the final vehicles to join the T class, T 769-798 were the most powerful and technically advanced of them all. The 30 vehicles were all destined for the Country Bus & Coach department which had submitted a strong case for new rolling stock to allow the development of new services to go forward and also to improve the general condition of its single deck fleet and their purchase was authorised by Lord Ashfield on 3rd April 1947 at a provisional cost of £90,300.

This authorisation marked the culmination of work which had been going on in the background for many months. A promise had been extracted from AEC to provide 30 of its Regal Mark III chassis within six months of the placing of an order, but in common with most operators at that time,

London Transport found acute difficulty in sourcing bodywork to mount on the new chassis. Eight bodybuilders were contacted and the only one able to offer assistance within a reasonable timescale was Mann Egerton & Company Ltd of Norwich. An order was duly placed with this company for the supply of 30 timber framed bodies which would be built to a general specification supplied by London Transport.

The first of the class, T 769, was received at Chiswick on 25th March 1948 and was straight away put through its paces to determine its suitability for service and to check on its build quality. One of the first tasks was to submit it to the tilt test which was undertaken without any problems. *Dave Jones collection*

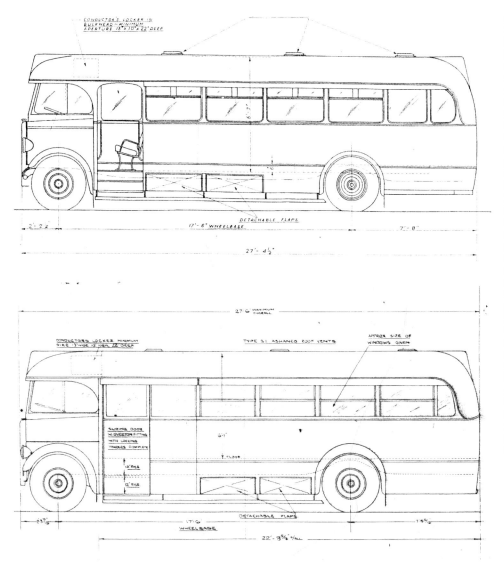

An interesting comparison of the outline drawings for T 769-798 as supplied to Mann Egerton by London Transport, and as adopted as the final design by Mann Egerton, show many differences between the two. The Board's thinking was clearly influenced by the Weymann bodies carried by the 14T12s although a deeper roof line was incorporated to make the indicator boxes fit more neatly and the outswept lower panels were eliminated. It is interesting to note that London Transport initially envisaged an open doorway while Mann Egerton subsequently included a sliding door. Although the two drawings retained exactly the same body outline, major differences included revised pillar spacings, half-drop instead of sliding windows, a higher internal floor line, and a revised positioning for the detachable side flaps to accommodate the sliding door. Mann Egerton finalised their own specification on 26th March 1947 but many months were to elapse before materials became available to allow construction to commence.

Mann Egerton was a well-established company with origins dating back to 1898. It was mostly known as a motor car engineer and dealer although it had amassed considerable experience in constructing car and commercial vehicle body-work and had been a major contractor to the Admiralty and War Office during the recent war. In the past it had even constructed aircraft and its main works were, appropriately, located in an old World War I hanger on Aylesham Road, Norwich. The Company was, in fact, already well known and highly regarded by London Transport for its work on renovating large numbers of the Board's double deckers, initially LTs and STs but latterly STLs, based on a contract signed on 8th August 1945 and subsequently extended on various occasions. This work on behalf of London Transport was a major undertaking, very efficiently carried out, employing in the region of 100 staff and justifying the full-time attendance of a London Transport resident inspector. Such was its major impact in the early post-war years that A A M Durrant was on record as stating that no other company could have provided the level of assistance given by Mann Egerton. However renovating old bodies was one thing; the construction from scratch of a sizeable batch of brand new bus bodies was a different matter altogether.

The drawing office staff at Chiswick set about the task of producing a general arrangement drawing for Mann Egerton to work from which was completed on 18th February 1947. This clearly took the Weymann body on the 14T12s as its inspiration although a deeper roof line was employed to accommodate the Board's standard destination boxes more neatly, and the typical Weymann flared lower rear panels were omitted. Armed with this, Mann Egerton produced just over a month later the detailed specification that it planned to work to. This embodied several differences, including a wider doorway aperture, and it also included the use of half-drop windows with Widney 'Ace' winding gear instead of sliding ventilators, the Company having managed to secure a supply of these. Because London Transport was undecided at the time whether it wanted the vehicles built as 31 or 33 seaters provision was made for both, the difference being that the 33-seat option envisaged longitudinal seats for two over the rear wheel arches instead of for one, with the transverse seats forward of it placed correspondingly closer together. London Transport finally decided to adopt the 31-seat version.

The Mann Egerton specification was for an underframe of oak or ash, side framing of ash and roof hoopsticks of ash or birch, all treated with Cuprinol as a rot resistance measure and strengthened with steel brackets where necessary. As it was hard to obtain seasoned timber, all units would be dried in Mann Egerton's own kilns. Except for the centre and side roof panels which were steel, all panelling would be in aluminium. W Overton provided sliding doors, not only for the saloon but also for the driver's cab, making these the only T-type vehicles fitted with this feature. Deans 'DAPTA' lightweight tubular steel-framed seats were specified with top rails either in stainless steel or chromium plated. A London Transport peculiarity was the provision of a bell cord along the length of the saloon on the offside with a single bell push on the front bulkhead, and another of the Board's requirements, to bring these vehicles into line with RT practice, was the provision on the offside of a battery booster socket. A fixed price was agreed of £1,354 per body.

The chassis for T 769-798 were allocated numbers 0962154-183 and they comprised the most sophisticated version of the Regal Mark III range with 9.6 litre 120x142 direct injection engines rated at 53.5hp, coupled to air-operated preselective gearboxes with fluid flywheels and air braking systems. In fact, in technical specification they were very similar to the RT although the standard AEC front end arrangement was featured which, perhaps surprisingly, retained the use of a tall, high radiator despite the adoption of a far preferable low bonnet line by other manufacturers such as Bristol, Crossley and Guy, and even by AEC itself on the RT. The wheelbase was 17ft 6ins and the rear axle ratio was 5.2:1.

The new chassis began to drift out of the Southall factory very slowly at first, commencing with T 769 on 8th July 1947 but with the total still in a single figure by the end of the year. This did not matter, however, as the allocation of materials to Mann Egerton for construction of the bodywork was lagging seriously behind and very little work could be done on any of them before the closing months of 1947, by which time an order for a further 100 generally similar bodies had been placed for TD 32-131. When the first completed vehicle was delivered to Chiswick on 25th February 1948 it bore the name of the new London Transport Executive, the branch of the state-controlled British Transport Commission which had taken over from the old London Passenger Transport Board on 1st January 1948.

After taking delivery of the tenth chassis (T 778) on 1st January 1948 an enforced break in continuity ensued as AEC was instructed to direct its resources elsewhere. Conflicting decisions by various government departments, or sometimes the lack of them, were interfering seriously with new vehicle deliveries everywhere. As far as the current order was concerned, AEC felt it prudent to warn that production promises could only be given for 22 out of the 30 chassis, and that construction of the rest may have to wait until the second half of 1948. In fact it subsequently proved possible to resume deliveries in the middle of March and to continue them steadily until the whole batch was completed, the final chassis to be delivered being that of T 795 on 4th May. Meanwhile, by the time production resumed, AEC had redesignated its models with the result that the chassis numbers for T 779 upwards carried the new prefix 9621E instead of the familiar 0962.

The first fully completed vehicle, T 769, arrived from Mann Egerton on 25th February 1948 and was almost straight away subjected to the close scrutiny traditionally given to the first of any new class, and its official photographs were taken. Production of the bodies seemed to be hesitant at first, but starting with T 774 on 30th April a steady input of one or two per week was achieved – mostly in strict numerical order – until the last was received from Norwich on 31st August. Classified 15T13, the new vehicles were allocated body numbers 1901-1930. Though they could probably be described as workmanlike rather than handsome in appearance, they were attractive enough except for their rather disappointing rear ends and were a distinct improvement over the fussy-looking 14T12s. The 14T12s, and also the TDs, had introduced a modern red and cream styling and it might have been expected that this would have been replicated on the 15T13s albeit in green. In complete contrast to this, London Transport specified the now outdated livery of green and off-white first introduced in 1940; indeed Chiswick even provided the paint for Mann Egerton to use, dispatching quantities of Lincoln green and synthetic grey (the official title for the off-white shade) to Norwich for this purpose.

T 769 posed for the official photographer at Chiswick on 5th March 1948, the day before it entered service, and this rear view shows the rather untidy way in which the waistrail moulding was raised up at the rear to meet the bottom edge of the back window to spoil an otherwise quite well balanced design. The photograph was taken before the bottom edge of the rear panelling was raised to avoid grounding on inclines. *London Transport Museum*

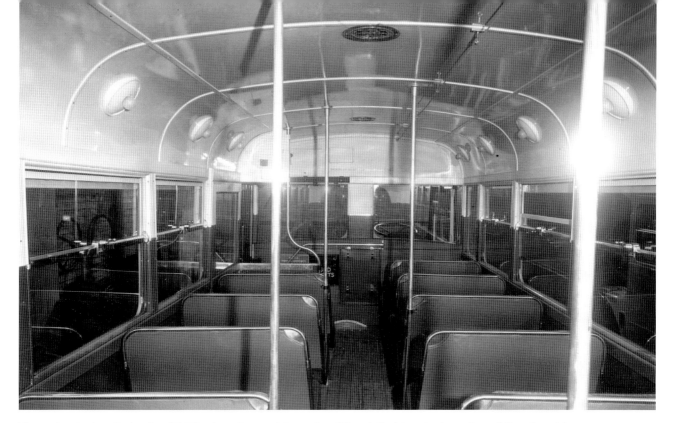

Views taken to show the interior of T 769 prior to its entry into service. Although the internal colour scheme follows that of the contemporary RT design, it omits the thin red band from above the windows, and the general appearance is much more utilitarian especially in the use of very basic looking seats. The quite high ceiling gives a more cavernous air than was apparent on the 14T12s, and although a bell cord is fitted for the first time on the T class, it is positioned at such a high level as to be unreachable by children or passengers of short stature. *London Transport Museum*

Internally the new vehicles presented a much brighter and more modern appearance than the 14T12s. No polished wood was visible, and instead there was an attempt to emulate the colour styling used inside the RTs through the extensive use of rexine, using brown on the lower side panels, green on the lower halves of the window frames and the seat backs, and cream above. Brown lino was used below the windows on the front bulkhead, but the thin red band above the windows, an attractive decorative feature of the RTs, was absent from the 15T13s. With an unladen weight of 6 tons 15cwt these were solidly built vehicles, but the fact that they weighed a full three quarters of a ton more than the 14T12s would inevitably have rendered them less economical to operate. At 9ft 9½ ins unladen, they were 3½ins taller than 14T12s, a factor which helped to accommodate the destination boxes within a flat roof line, and they were an inch longer at 27ft 5½ins.

In preference to scattering the new Ts around its fleet to provide a modicum of modernisation everywhere, the Country Bus & Coach department decided to concentrate them all in the north-west corner of its territory served by Hemel Hempstead and Watford, Leavesden Road garages, with Hemel Hempstead designated as the first recipient. T 769 arrived there ready for service on 6th March 1948, just over a week after delivery and six days before the second of the class was received from Norwich. Before this, the preliminary examination of T 769 upon arrival at Chiswick had revealed that the bottom of the rear bodywork overhang was 2 inches lower than required to guarantee safe operation under all circumstances without grounding and immediate steps were put in hand to modify the production process. This came too late for the bodies on T 770 and 771 which had progressed too far, but these – along with T 769 – were subsequently brought into line.

Between the arrival of T 769 in March and 2nd July 1948 when T 786 entered service, the new deliveries were allocated solely to Hemel Hempstead, for which garage this proved to be a pivotal year. The first new RTs for the country department came on the scene in July and Hemel Hempstead was one of the first recipients of these along with Tring. Its fleet was now by far the most modern in the whole of the Country Bus & Coach department. The final 12 new vehicles, T 787-798, were delivered to Leavesden Road between 7th July and 3rd September 1948. In all cases the new 15T13s had displaced 4Q4s which were redeployed elsewhere, some of them in the Central Bus department repainted red. Hemel Hempstead's entire single deck bus allocation now consisted of new vehicles but there were insufficient to oust all of Leavesden Road's 4Q4s, and a few much older 11T11s were also retained there for routes 309 and 361. Requiring a driving technique virtually identical to that of the RT and with a performance to match, the 15T13s made a favourable impression on every conceivable type of country bus operation ranging from heavily peaked works services, through routes serving rapidly developing housing areas, to sparsely served country village lifelines. A large amount of scheduled interworking together with periodical schedule alterations make it hard to be specific, but their main operations were on the services listed below.

307 Boxmoor–Harpenden
317 Watford–Berkhamsted
318 Watford–Chipperfield
318A Watford–Two Waters
320 Watford–Boxmoor
322 Watford–Hemel Hempstead
337 Hemel Hempstead–Dunstable
352 Berkhamsted–Dunstable

In addition they could also be found, mostly at peak times, working journeys on routes 301, 302, 307A, 318B, 319, 377 and 377A, and a Hemel Hempstead based bus was even scheduled to make a token appearance on route 391 which was theoretically the sole preserve of 4Q4s from St Albans garage.

The first overhaul cycle for the 15T13s began in August 1950 and when the first pair to be completed emerged from Chiswick on 9th October it came as no surprise to find that the original green and white livery had been abandoned in favour of a more modern all-over green relieved by cream mouldings below and above the windows. The revised styling was introduced by T 770 at Hemel Hempstead and T 788 at Leavesden Road, and when Leavesden Road's T 797 went into

*Top* Early in its career, T 770 stands below the gasometer in the yard across the road from Watford High Street garage. Despite showing a destination display, it has, in fact, arrived out of service and has perhaps come from Hemel Hempstead for routine docking. The vehicle carries the partly masked destination screen which some of these had in their very early days, and it happens to show a rare factory working covered by Hemel Hempstead on a service nominally worked solely by St Albans garage. Although provision is made for carrying a route number stencil above the doorway, these were not used in Country Bus service. *V C Jones*

*Centre* The 15T13s sported the Mann Egerton version of London Transport's standard bodybuilder's plate as used – with the appropriate wording – from the first post-war RT deliveries of 1947 onwards. The spaces set aside for patent and UK design numbers remain vacant as there is nothing applicable to put in them. *Owen Phillips*

*Bottom* A regular haunt for the 15T13s was route 337 between Hemel Hempstead and Dunstable on which a new and sparkling T 775 is preparing to depart with what appears to be a full load. Full-sized destination blinds have now been supplied so there is no longer any need for masking on the indicator box glass. These were the last new vehicles to enter London Transport service in the now-outdated green and white livery, and the only vehicles in the T class where drivers were provided with the luxury of sliding doors. *Alan B Cross*

The twelve highest numbered 15T13s spent the first years of their working careers at Leavesden Road garage, and the highest numbered of them all was T 798. Excluding the now long-forgotten T 1000-1002, this was as high as the T series was destined to get. Both T 798 and Windsor-based T 658 which it is just passing have the lower halves of their windscreens open to make the most of the hot weather on a July day in 1949. *Alan B Cross*

overhaul almost eight months later, on 5th June 1951, the old livery was gone for good. In fact the new styling suited the vehicles well and they carried it for the rest of their time with London Transport.

Nothing occurred to disturb the original balance of 15T13s between the two north-western garages until 9th June 1952 when T 779-786 were transferred from Hemel Hempstead to Leavesden Road, leaving eight 10T10s to be moved in the other direction to compensate for their loss. The 10T10s had displaced Leavesden Road's last 4Q4s at the start of March when these were withdrawn from service to await disposal. The reason for the move was to become evident nine days later, on 18th June, when Leavesden Road garage closed and all its single deck workings were moved into the brand new garage at Garston, the first to be opened in the country area in post-war times. This enabled Garston to begin life with a thoroughly modern fleet of 31-seat single deckers to the detriment, of course, of Hemel Hempstead whose average fleet age had risen considerably.

Back in 1951 a detailed review had been carried out into the whole London Transport fleet to determine its composition over the next ten years, one outcome of which was a decision that all non-standard post-war single deckers, Ts and TDs, should remain in service throughout the decade and would all be replaced in 1960. On the strength of this, it was decided in 1953 that it was financially viable to fit cab heaters in the 15T13s and this task was carried out during the year. Clearly no-one had an inkling at the time that, only a year later, the first of them would be withdrawn from service. 1953 was also the year when new green RFs flooded into service with inevitable consequences for the 15T13s whose tidy and close-knit existence in the north-west segment of the country area ceased abruptly from July onwards as the bulk of the large Garston contingent was dispersed elsewhere. From October, only five 15T13s remained at Garston to work on routes 309 and 361, which were not considered busy enough to justify the use of RFs, plus some contract and duplication work.

During their green and white phase the 15T13s were allocated solely to Hemel Hempstead and Leavesden Road garages, so it was a surprise to find T 790 in the unfamiliar setting of Aldgate bus station working from Grays garage on Green Line service 723. The circumstances whereby this came about are not recorded, but presumably a loan to Grays had been arranged to cover a temporary shortage of TFs such as the one standing behind T 790. No-one could have known at the time that, one day in the future, 15T13s would be permanently added to the Grays allocation. *G E Baddeley*

The change of livery in 1950/51 showed the 15T13s off in a different light and somehow managed to give them a more sturdy appearance. Hemel Hempstead's T 780 emerged from overhaul in this guise in May 1951; it was subsequently one of the vehicles transferred to Leavesden Road in June 1952 in readiness for the opening of the new Garston garage later in the same month. *Ron Wellings*

These changes happened to coincide with the start of the second overhaul cycle for the 15T13s during which they were beautified by the fitting of rear wheel discs using the same type of retaining brackets as on RTs. The first to appear adorned in this way, T 788, was one of a number of Ts dispatched to the very southernmost outpost of the country area at Crawley, principally to work on the 426 Crawley circular via Horley but with appearances on route 424 and various works services. The 15T13s also went as far east as they could go, to Grays, which received five in July 1953 as replacements for 10T10s on the local service in Rainham between the town and the ferry with positioning runs to and from Grays on routes 371 and 374.

Two Ts were sent on 13th July to Tring, one of which provided peak hour capacity for commuters heading to and from the town's station on route 387 (Tring–Aldbury). The 387 was primarily the province of CR type one-man operated 20-seaters, although older conventional Cubs replaced these and ran alongside the T for the final two months until new GSs made their debut on the first day of 1954. The spare T had, meanwhile, been removed from Tring in September 1953 as unnecessary. Tring's 15T13 led a fairly leisurely existence, its most active day being on Saturday when it deserted the 387 and appeared on route 352 on the only day of the week when this much reduced service still ran right through from Dunstable to Berkhamsted. One further, short-lived 15T13 reallocation at this time was a single vehicle sent from Garston to Hatfield on 1st October. Its purpose was to cover a long-established working shown in the official allocation book as 'scheduled duplicates'. This was Hatfield's only scheduled single deck bus operation, which had formerly been covered by a 10T10, but it ceased on 13th January 1954 when T 796 was transferred to Grays.

The last few 15T13s at Garston enjoyed less than a year's

The first 15T13 to be dealt with on the second overhaul cycle in July 1953 was T 788. When it started work at Crawley on 1st August it was seen to have been embellished with rear wheel discs. This helped to improve and modernise the vehicle's appearance and seemed to acknowledge that the 15T13s were, indeed, regarded as modern vehicles in the same mould as the famous RT. Gradually every vehicle in the entire batch of 30 was similarly beautified as it went through overhaul. *R K Blencowe*

In the main, the Grays allocation of 15T13s performed a very low key role shuttling around Rainham on the 375 local service. T 796, which served in this capacity from January 1954 to June 1956, stands by a very utilitarian-looking concrete passenger shelter outside Rainham station preparing to carry factory workers down to the ferry. *Ron Wellings*

Amersham garage ran 15T13s briefly on the 394 group of routes, but after their departure T 782 was retained as a spare vehicle. In this role its duties could be very varied, and on this occasion it is about to cover a route 703 Green Line relief duty as far as London. Also in view outside the splendid Amersham garage, which opened alongside the old Amersham & District premises in August 1935, are a mixed bag typical of the time comprising an RT2 'learner', a standard post-war RT and a GS. *Denis Battams*

reprieve before they, too, moved to pastures new. Routes 309 and 361 were converted to one-man operation on 19th May 1954, leaving the five remaining Ts surplus to requirements there until 1st June when they moved to Amersham to herald the end of 10T10s on the 394 group of routes. Soon afterwards, on 13th August when T 795 was relicensed into Amersham, the current overhaul programme came to a close. On 1st September T 774 and 776 were delicensed as surplus to requirements followed by T 772 on 1st October. After just over six years their London careers had come to an end and they were sold for service abroad in March 1956.

One-man operation using RF 39-seaters had now become the norm within the Country Bus & Coach department resulting in further instability for the 15T13s. The 1956 summer programme introduced on 11th July saw a partial

withdrawal from Hemel Hempstead with conversion of the 317 and 317A while the two year tenure of the class at Amersham drew almost to a close with RFs taking over the 394 group. However a single T was allowed to remain there to serve as a spare and for duplication work, remaining active in this role for a couple more years. Of most interest, however, was the transfer of three vehicles to the Central Bus department from 8th August 1956 when they appeared at Kingston garage to work on route 216. As far as Kingston was concerned, this was a short lived arrangement and on 1st December 1956 the three vehicles (T 785, 794, 796) moved the short distance to Norbiton to take up a more permanent role on route 201. Apart from having their saloon doors locked open, they ran unaltered and were never repainted into red livery.

It was always a little surprising that greater use was never made of the 15T13s in the central area in view of the superiority of their technical specification to that of the native 14T12s and TDs. At one time a proposal to overhaul 13 of them into red livery for service at Southall on route 211 was seriously considered as part of a scheme for redeploying RFs and organising an overhaul programme for them, but it came to nothing. The actual 15T13s employed at Norbiton varied from time to time as odd ones arrived and others left, but there were never more than four based there at any one time and often only three. Whilst mostly confined to route 201, Sundays could find them on route 206 and sometimes also on the 213. Apart from the Kingston area vehicles, only one other instance was recorded of a 15T13 working in the central area when T 783 paid a brief visit to Hounslow for route 237 during the last fortnight of September 1957.

At Hemel Hempstead routes 307, 307A and 337 were scheduled for conversion to RF omo on 15th October 1957, but the vehicles for it arrived early and the last two 15T13s drifted away on 1st August. This pair, T 773 and 775, had been at Hemel Hempstead since new in April and May 1948 respectively, and were the longest lived of any of the class at a single location. Crawley, too, gained an official allocation of omo RFs in October 1957 for route 426, but an official requirement remained for 15T13s on works and other services and they could still be found on route 426 and others at peak times.

The summer programme of 1958 found only five 15T13s scheduled in the country area, four at Grays and one at Tring. Crawley, however, retained a single vehicle which continued to find work, albeit unscheduled, mostly on the 426. Amersham lost its scheduled spare on 1st July 1958, but this was more than compensated by the surprise arrival at about the same time of a 15T13 at East Grinstead, a garage whose scheduled operations of large single deckers had been totally dominated by RFs since September 1953. Meanwhile at Norbiton, where the number of licensed 15T13s had fallen to two in November 1958, the final day of T class operation came on 20th January 1959 when T 786 and 794 performed the last runs. RFs officially took over on route 201 the next day.

Conversion of the Grays single deck operations to one-man RFs on 13th May 1959 left just three 15T13s in passenger service, namely the officially scheduled vehicle at Tring and the unofficial ones at Crawley and East Grinstead, and this is how things remained at the start of the nineteen-sixties. A fourth vehicle was, however, in regular use as a staff bus. The withdrawal of the final 10T10s from staff bus duties on 1st February 1957, as recorded in chapter 15, was made possible by the availability of surplus 15T13s to fulfill this role for which purpose two had been based at Reigate and one at Plumstead. The Reigate pair ceased work in December 1957 but the Plumstead vehicle continued in use, ferrying former Charlton works staff to their replacement jobs at Chiswick. This vehicle was later based at Abbey Wood, and for a while at New Cross, reflecting the residential location of its regular driver at the time, before transferring finally back to Abbey Wood in December 1960.

Kingston's brief allegiance to 15T13s lasted only from August to November 1956, and two out of the three vehicles concerned are seen terminating at Staines on the outer end of route 216. The Regals are T 794 (furthest from the camera) and T 785, and also within camera range are Kingston-based TD 15 and Hounslow's RT 1223. *J M Aldridge*

From 1st November 1956 the green 15T13s working for Central Road Services were based at Norbiton garage and could most commonly be found on route 201. Standing at the Hampton Court station terminus on 1st July 1957 was T 794 which stayed at Norbiton until the final day of T operation there in January 1959, always in green livery. The nearside stencil holder, unused in Country Bus days, at last serves the purpose for which it was intended. *Peter J Relf*

1960 was the year in which the master plan of almost ten years earlier had envisaged the demise of the 15T13s. In fact, by the end of 1959, 21 out of the 30 had already been sold and five more left the fleet in April 1960, leaving just four vehicles to represent the T class into the new decade. With the continuation of their operation in mind, it was now time to modernise these by fitting flashing trafficators. This was in accordance with a general fleet policy decided in 1959 that all buses should be equipped with these as soon as possible, and certainly by the end of 1960, to provide effective and essential aids to drivers in worsening traffic conditions. The front indicators, reminiscent of protruding ears, were similar to but more flexibly mounted than a batch tried out experimentally on a number of double deckers in 1956, and they were wired to flash simultaneously with ones at the rear which, in the case of the four 15T13s, were similar to those fitted to RT3 bodies and to the new RMs currently under construction.

East Grinstead's T was removed on 1st September 1960 but the remaining three continued their twilight existence right through 1961 and well into 1962, the specific vehicles being T 787 at Crawley, T 790 at Tring and T 785 at Abbey Wood. In addition, the former East Grinstead vehicle T 792 was relicensed on 3rd January 1961 at Garston where it appears to have served no specific purpose except to be available as a stand-by for the other three whenever they were off the road.

The end came gradually. Crew operation at Tring was scheduled to be replaced by one-man operation with the introduction of the summer programme on 23rd May 1962 and RF 589, newly overhauled and fitted with a saloon heater, was drafted in a few days early on the 18th. It may well have operated in place of T 790, albeit crew worked, before the scheduled changeover day. However T 790 remained licensed at Tring as a spare vehicle until its road fund tax expired at the end of the month, and it will probably never be known exactly when it last ran in public service. A few days later it was relicensed and joined T 792 as a stand-by at Garston, but it is not known if either of them turned a wheel during this period, and both were finally withdrawn on 21st September. Meanwhile T 787 had soldiered on at Crawley until it was finally delicensed on 13th August 1962, but this was a Monday and its final day in use was probably the previous Friday, the 10th. Public operation of the T class had now ceased, but on 1st October T 787 was relicensed at Abbey Wood to replace T 785 on staff bus work, in which role it continued until the start of April 1963. On 1st April GS 50 arrived at Abbey Wood; T 787 was delicensed on Thursday the 4th and at some point during the overlapping period it will have run for the last time.

T 787 was the last of the T class remaining in the fleet, and when it was sold to W North, the Leeds-based dealer, on 21st August 1963 a link going back almost 34 years was finally broken.

The last T of all in public service was T 787 which was used, generally in peak hours, by Crawley garage until August 1962, mostly on route 426. It subsequently served as a staff bus at Abbey Wood until August 1963, and its withdrawal from the latter role gained it the distinction of bringing the T class on London Transport to an honorable end. *Michael Dryhurst*

For the very few 15T13s that were left running after the end of 1960, it was deemed essential that they should be fitted with flashing trafficators. This was not a big task as only four now remained, one of which was T 780 based at Tring. The front view of T 780, taken in the attractive Hertfordshire village of Aldbury, shows the trafficator ears which were of the type familiar on standard London Transport classes such as the RT family and RFs. The rear view illustrates the RT3-type repeaters used on the backs of these vehicles. It also shows the generally untidy aspect of the back end of the 15T13 caused by the off-centre placing of the Daltons Weekly advertisement, and it records a later-day embellishment in the form of a small black and gold bullseye motif. T 780 stayed at Tring until the end of T operation there in May 1962. *N Rayfield/D Pearson*

# 19 AFTERLIFE

Unlike their contemporary LTs and STs, vehicles from the T class enjoyed widespread use in their intended role as passenger carrying vehicles long after leaving London Transport's service, and as well as appearing in the fleets of many small operators in this country their presence also became evident in various countries overseas. The main reasons for this are twofold. Disposals commenced before the war when, with London Transport secure in its monopoly position, it was concerned only with achieving the best price for the vehicles that it was marketing and was unfussy about what subsequent use they were put to. After the war, with the British Transport Commission in command and placing strict controls on the future use of surplus vehicles within Britain because of competition fears, London Transport was fortunate in having many desirable single deckers for disposal, including numbers of quite modern ones, at a time when many overseas operators were clamouring for just that type of rolling stock.

Unsurprisingly, the first Ts selected for disposal in March 1938 were all ones carrying obsolete canvas-hooded bodies. A batch of nine was initially offered for disposal including all five of the private hire coaches T 150-154, which had never been used on Green Line work, along with four of the one-time East Surrey excursion and tours vehicles (T 322, 397, 401, 402). All nine were cannibalised at Chiswick before

disposal by the removal of their head lamps, speedometers, generators and various dials for future use on other vehicles. Their purchaser was G J Dawson Ltd, probably the best known scrap merchant of the time, who cannily made them roadworthy, or passed them to another dealier to do so, with the result that most if not all resumed their life as coaches with a variety of operators. The first to leave the London Transport fleet was T 322 on 9th March 1938 and the other eight departed during the course of the next nine days.

Former East Surrey touring coach T 401 was amongst the very first group of five Ts sold to George Dawson in a dealing capacity in March 1938 with the expectation that they would be re-sold for further service elsewhere. It passed into the fleet of W Wootton & Sons Ltd of Lewisham and was still there when photographed in June 1949. Close examination shows that its original Park Royal body – or parts of it at least – was still intact. The flared sides and attempts at streamlining cannot disguise the fact that the side pillars are still in their original position, and although a new front bulkhead has been installed to permit the provision of a sliding door, the cab structure is still totally unchanged from its original design and the upper half of the front destination box assembly remains in place, as does the opening roof and the glass window louvres. T 401 stayed with Wootton's until 1952 and then managed to struggle on for a little while afterwards with other operators. *Alan B Cross*

After a two month gap disposals began in earnest, not just of canvas-topped vehicles and various acquired oddities but also of standard Green Line 7T7s and country area bus bodied Regals still with their rear entrances. From September 1938 onwards even a few 1/7T7/1s joined the exodus which, between May 1938 and March 1939, saw the departure of no fewer than 142 Ts from the fleet. Four dealers accounted for the bulk of the sales during this period; Arlington Motor Company, R A Jordan of Biggleswade, Lancashire Motor Traders and Steel Breakers of Edgware and Chesterfield, all of which were successful in finding buyers to pass them on to. Their success in doing so can be judged from September 1938's disposals, to take these as a typical example, where out of 19 Ts sold during the month only one has not since been traced to a subsequent operator. Closer to the war, some that were still awaiting buyers were acquired by the Ministries of Supply and Works for war related duties. Many lasted well into the post-war period, usually with new bodies fitted to them or otherwise heavily rebuilt to modernise their appearance and, in some cases, to suggest an element of streamlining.

This was a time of great flux in the fleet, with new 10T10s being delivered in bulk from Southall at the same time as older Regals departed. It was during this period that the fleet of T-types reached its maximum size when, for a few fleeting days between 1st and 4th December 1938 inclusive, it peaked at 631 vehicles. After this, with all 10T10s now on books and disposals continuing at an ever-increasing rate into the start of 1939, the number of Ts plunged steadily downwards. Then, after the departure of former Amersham & District T 365 to Arlington's on 30th March 1939, sales were abruptly cancelled. The prospect of war now looked ever more likely, and it was thought prudent to stockpile any further surplus vehicles as no-one could foresee what contingencies might arise in an uncertain future.

Even before disposals commenced, the usefulness of employing redundant Regal chassis in the Board's miscellaneous fleet had been recognised and arrangements were made for three all-weather Ts to be rebodied as specialist vehicles for the Tram & Trolleybus department. T 319 and 393 were destined to be converted into tramway conduit cleaners in place of a pair of Tilling Stevens petrol electrics which had been doing the work previously, and after being overhauled their chassis were transferred to the Steel Barrel Company at Uxbridge in March 1938 for tanks to be fitted. T

320 was destined to become a much more famous and impressive machine which could be found patrolling the trolleybus system, with twin trolley poles attached, as an overhead wire lubricator in which role it augmented a converted NS bus which could no longer cope alone owing to the rapid spread of the trolleybus network. Conversion of all three was completed in May and June 1938 and they continued to work under their old fleet numbers until a separate numbering system was introduced for the service vehicle fleet in 1939 when T 319, 393 and 320 became 112W-114W respectively.

This was only the start of the lorry conversions and a more ambitious programme covering 22 Ts commenced in January 1939 with the converted vehicles starting work in their new roles between May and July. One single contractor, the Transport Engineering Company based in the Old Kent Road, was responsible for building the bodies on all of them. These were of various styles and had varying floor heights to suit the different types of work for which the chassis were required as 6½ ton stores or towing lorries or, in one case, as an oil barrel lorry. Identical chassis were used in every case, all of them taken from the ranks of former 1/7T7/1 Green Line coaches. Numbered 387W-408W they had previously been T 278, 284, 238, 299, 259, 243, 282, 304, 260, 279, 257, 294, 210, 246, 303, 227, 242, 221, 241, 269, 245, 256.

Next to carry W numbers in the miscellaneous vehicles series were 16 1/7T7/1s set aside for use as staff ambulances at the start of the war to become 423W-438W, but with one exception these were all reconverted for passenger use and regained their original T numbers as described in chapter 3. The exception was 436W whose body was destroyed by bombing in September 1941 and which was rebuilt a year later as a breakdown tender.

The best remembered of the T conversions were those destined for a second life as stores and towing lorries, examples of which could often be seen bustling around - usually under trade plates - in their typical Chiswick green livery carrying out a miscellany of tasks throughout London Transport's widespread territory. Subtle differences in appearance could be detected between individual vehicles, but most stayed virtually unchanged throughout their lives as lorries although odd ones gained full length canvas tilts, while some had their lower panelling removed to alleviate damage caused through their day to day use. Seen in 1949 towing broken-down ST 1 back to its home garage at Alperton is 448W (ex T 169), one of the final Regal conversions carried out in 1940. *D W K Jones*

The next three conversions were done after the creation of the staff ambulances although they were numbered ahead of them. Sent to Chiswick for conversion in November 1939, these were the former T 159 and T 178 which were rebuilt as towing lorries 420W and 421W, along with T 306, formerly the highest numbered of the 1/7T7/1 Green Lines, which emerged as another overhead wire lubricator numbered 422W, all three taking up their new roles in February and March 1940. Following on, between April and October 1940 and dealt with as time and resources permitted, came the final batch of 15 T conversions 439W-453W (the former T 165, 167, 203, 175, 206, 164, 163, 181, 171, 169, 174, 199, 160, 176, 172). Most of these appeared with lorry bodies of various sorts for towing or for the conveyance of stores etc, but 441W-443W were very impressive and well-equipped 7 ton railway break-down tenders which became a familiar sight over many years whilst on stand-by duties at strategic locations such as Baker Street and Euston.

These marked the final conversions of Regal chassis for miscellaneous uses, and when further additions were required after the war former STL Regent chassis were available readily and, for some applications, were preferable. The comparatively long wheelbase of the T chassis, when matched to a short rear overhang, combined under a full load to put excess weight on the front axle and the shorter STL proved better balanced in this respect. Most of the converted Ts lasted within the London Transport fleet much longer than they would have done as buses and coaches, all except 399W (ex T 210) having survived the ravages of war. A few, such as the conduit track cleaners and the overhead wire lubricators, became redundant during the nineteen-fifties and three of the lorries were also declared surplus during that decade, but the great majority were still functioning at the start of the nineteen-sixties. AEC 7.7 oil engines were fitted into 23 of them in 1954 and 1955, and most but not all of those still retaining petrol engines were withdrawn in 1960. By that time modernisation was afoot with a determination to replace them with purpose-built commercial vehicles, and the last of the Regals to leave the fleet were stores lorry 396W (ex T 279) and towing lorry 401W (ex T 303) in June 1964.

Apart from scrapping seven redundant Regals in October and November 1939 and selling the three Chiswick-built vehicles T 1000-1002 in August 1940, London Transport made no further inroads of its own into the T fleet until just before the war ended. Rear entrance T 15 fell victim to the bombing of Bull Yard, Peckham on 7th September 1940 where it had been stored, but the remaining deletions from the fleet were six obsolete petrol engined vehicles commandeered by the Ministry of War Transport in January and February 1940 and, of course, the 9T9s and 10T10s famously handed over to the United States military authorities, not all of which returned after the war. However, dramatic events in Europe were destined to have a big impact on the T class in the days just prior to the cessation of hostilities, leading to the final demise of several variants within it.

With the fall of the Third Reich now inevitable, planning for the future of the devastated European continent was already under way, and to help restore transport services within it the recently formed European Central Inland Transportation Organisation (ECITO) asked to be provided with any surplus British buses that might be available. The War Office, through the Ministry of War Transport, sought urgent help from London Transport which agreed to provide no fewer than 75 vehicles, 55 of which would be petrol-engined Ts and would be dispatched to Germany, with the balance of 20 diesel-engined Leyland Cubs destined for Belgium. Although ill-suited to the continental rule of the road, the Ts could be used by the British Army of Occupation of the Rhine (BAOR) and the Allied Control Commission for various purposes which would reduce the need to requisition other vehicles within Germany itself. The buses were released during the first few days of May 1945, just before the war in Europe came to its official end. Their departure removed from the fleet the last 19 remaining 7T7 coaches (excluding T 120 which survived and had now been converted to a 1/7T7/1); T 21, the last of the original 1929 batch of Ts not converted to front entrance; the last five of the former East Surrey rear entrance buses; T 382, the only remaining ex-East Surrey front entrance Weymann bodied saloon; and all twelve of the Weymann rebodied 5T4s. Also now dispatched was ex-Bucks Express T 392, leaving its sister vehicle T 391 as the only ex-independent T left in the fleet still with original bodywork, and 16 1/7T7/1s many of which had been rebuilt shortly before the war with new destination boxes and other features for bus work.

When no longer required for the movement of troops and as leave transports etc, the ones that survived were sold off through the French 'Service des Surplus', with some finding their way into the hands of local operators, notably around the coal mining town of Douai in northern France where the late John H Price found several in service in September 1948. With continental bus manufacturing plants back in business, it is doubtful whether many of the old London stock will have survived in use much beyond 1950.

The 10T10s that failed to return from their war duties are documented in chapter 15, and though the fate of most is unrecorded there were two that became very well-known during the early post-war years. On a trunk run in South Wales between Swansea and Cardiff, and in rural Berkshire running from towns such as Abingdon and Watlington into Reading, they gave a taste of 10T10 travel that could not be had anywhere else other than in London. Presumably, as in the case of many other commandeered buses, the military authorities had 'lost' their original details and thus failed to ensure their return to the true owner who received compensation instead. After being auctioned, T 460 found itself in May 1946 in the Merthyr Tydfil fleet of D J Davies who re-registered it locally as HB 6138. About five months later it passed more famously to Neath & Cardiff Luxury Coaches. Meanwhile T 594 had become BRD 922 in the ownership of Smith's Coaches of Reading, passing subsequently to Kemp's Motor Services of Woodcote and later to its successor Chiltern Queens. In addition to HB 6138, Neath & Cardiff had a second, similar looking AEC Regal on its Swansea to Cardiff run, having obtained a 10T10 body – presumably also ex the US military – which graced the chassis of AEC Regal EM 3855.

The final withdrawals of petrol-engined Ts in 1949 and 1950 gave little scope for any afterlife as most which went either to the scrapyard of Cox & Danks at Feltham, where bodies were scrapped under contract to London Transport and the chassis returned to them, or subsequently to R L Daniels at Rainham, Essex, were too far gone to warrant much further use, although odd ones escaped from the Rainham yard to end up as living accommodation. Strict controls were now enforced, anyway, by the British Transport Commission on the subsequent use in this country of redundant rolling stock. These restrictions still applied when the

T 35 was one of the five vehicles from the first batch which passed to East Surrey in April 1931 and subsequently retained its rear entrance under London Transport ownership. It was the second of the batch to be sold when it went to Arlington's in March 1939, and as no. 12 in the fleet of Venture Ltd it continued to be employed on stage carriage work based at Basingstoke. Converted to diesel in January 1946, it took on a completely different appearance during its time in Venture ownership, although the retention of its open rear platform denotes that heavy rebuilding rather than a complete rebodying has taken place. Under British Transport Commission control, T 35 subsequently passed to Wilts & Dorset when the Venture operation was broken up. *Dave Jones collection*

The great majority of 1938/39 disposals found subsequent employment as touring and private hire coaches rather than as service buses, but there were a number of exceptions to this general rule including one-time Green Line 7T7 T 130. After passing through Arlington's hands as dealer in January 1939, it served with small operators in Glamorganshire before passing to the more substantial fleet of Ralph's Garages Ltd in Abertillery where it was one of a number of ex-London Ts in stock. Photographed still with Ralph's in 1948, it now carries a Burlingham-built 'utility' body dating from 1942 or 1943. *D A Jones*

Many of the pre-war T disposals were given completely new and totally up-to-date coach bodies before re-entering service, and ex-Green Line T 140 was one of these. Lancashire Motor Traders had it rebodied, it is believed by Plaxton, after acquiring it in August 1938. By 1948 it had arrived in rural Essex and still looked sufficiently modern to serve on the scheduled express service into London operated by S Blackwell of Earls Colne. A fully floating rear axle has been fitted which helps to hide its true age. *D A Jones*

remnants of the 1T1s came on the market in 1952 and 1953 along with the 9T9s and 11T11s. However the mood and the market had now changed and various firms tried to buy the redundant vehicles, mostly with an eye to selling them abroad. Purchasers such as G H Morgan of South Wales Motor Traders, C J Green of Tooting and the Benhill Machinery & Equipment Company were happy to pay £150 (minus tyres) for 11T11s. Green, for instance, claimed to have established a market for eighteen of them in Belgium. T E King & Company was the major buyer of 9T9s at £250 a time (less tyres), taking no fewer than 30 out of the 49, but sometimes there were losers too, such as L W Vass of Ampthill, Bedfordshire, who unwisely offered as much as £325 each for ten and then found difficulty making a profit on them. Having dispatched a couple to New Zealand, most or all of the remainder were eventually broken up at Ampthill. T E King, on the other hand, was much more successful, being in cahoots with established exporter Comberhill Motors, who found markets for many of the 9T9s in Las Palmas (Canary Islands), Colombo (Ceylon) and Salisbury (Southern Rhodesia) where they continued their service career for a few more years.

The biggest player of all in the second hand bus market was W North of Leeds Ltd whose yards full of buses, totalling 40 acres, will never be forgotten by those fortunate enough to have explored the treasures that lay inside. Run by A W Elvins and financed – London Transport suspected – by G J Dawson, North's was set up to deal in used buses on a huge scale and was proving very helpful to London Transport which was faced with the task of disposing of huge numbers of pre-war and wartime buses in a relatively short time. By 1953 North's had taken no fewer than 931 double deckers and 489 single deckers from London Transport. They were prepared to take every one at a scrap price of £35 (without tyres) rising to £150 or more if the vehicle was subsequently exported. This covered all types of bus, even including unpopular ones which other dealers were reluctant to handle such as the AEC Q-type. So well geared up to export markets were the Company's salesmen that they even managed to export Qs to such far-flung destinations as Cyprus, Malta, Libya and Burma even though the cost of shipping vehicles to somewhere as far away as Rangoon could far exceed their purchase price. Their first export success with the Ts was the disposal of 9T9s to the West Indies and to Smedevero in the Serbian province of Yugoslavia, but it was in selling 10T10s that they really excelled.

T 460 was one of the 10T10s that failed to find their way back to London after the war even though its distinctive shape, identical to many other vehicles being repatriated at the same time, could have been expected to give the US military authorities a clue as to its origin. Its best known post-war role, under the Merthyr Tydfil registration number HB 6138, was as a front line vehicle on the trunk Swansea to Cardiff service of Neath & Cardiff Luxury Coaches, a type of work not dissimilar to its pre-war Green Line role. Carrying that company's distinctive brown and red livery, and with a host of places served emblazoned along its side, and its conductor standing expectantly at the doorway, T 460 arrives in Cardiff at the end of its run. After about seven years in this role, T 460 spent a further decade as a caravan. *D A Jones*

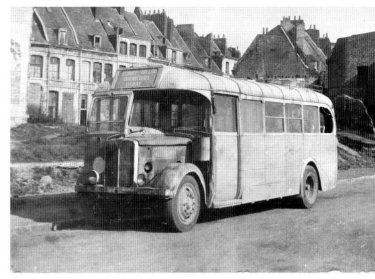

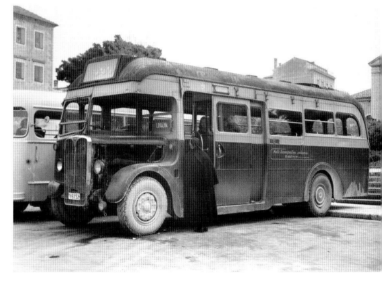

*Top left* A dull coat of army livery cannot disguise the unique shape of this one-time pride of the Bucks Express fleet, T 392, which was amongst the 55 petrol Ts handed over for service in Germany during the first week of May 1945. In pre-war times it had been one of the former Green Line coaches demoted to bus work, and its conversion had employed a rather more curvaceous front indicator box than was fitted to its contemporaries. Totally unmodified to suit the continental rule of the road, and now looking a little the worse for wear, it was found in Hannover serving as a team coach for the combined forces' football team with the British Army of the Rhine. A second T-type had formerly worked alongside it, but had recently been replaced by the locally-built vehicle standing behind. *John H Price*

*Top right* The scene is badly war-damaged Douai in northern France and the vehicle is one of the 5T4s originally sent to Germany and now clearly in the final phase of its operating career. The English headlights have been replaced by ones mounted on the substantial front bumper and the horn now has a novel outlet below the driver's side window. Although the original passenger door remains in place it is now unused and a replacement has been cut out on the other side. Although the glass is missing from one of its windows and the vehicle looks barely roadworthy, this unidentified 5T4 manages to struggle on, its destination box bearing the legend "Ecourt, Arleux, Bognicourt, Douai". *John H Price*

*Above left* Occasional 10T10s were donated by London Transport directly to charitable causes. Famously, T 703 found a new life in Japan carrying Commonwealth servicemen on rest and recuperation leave from the war in Korea. Another of these was T 613 which served as a staff bus until as late as December 1956 and was handed over on the 19th of that month to the British Voluntary Relief Association of London SW7. It was photographed with its new owner after the bodywork below the roof line had been repainted, a Union Jack had been patriotically emblazoned on the side, and a large luggage rack installed on the roof. It was photographed at Chandlers Ford in February 1958 and little is known of its subsequent exploits except that it was rumoured to have departed for Hungary – then behind the Iron Curtain – but failed to arrive there.

*Above right* In the small town of Sibenik on the Adriatic coast of what is today Croatia, a 10T10 still carries Green Line colours and has been put into service with its original entrance door still in use. The legend on the side indicates that it is in the fleet of Auto Transportno Poduzece Sibenik who have removed the bonnet side, presumably to improve cooling in the prevailing warm climate. The presence of a route stencil holder above the doorway denotes that it was one of the green 10T10s operated for a while at Kingston; it was, in fact, T 490. *D W K Jones*

Although the exact total will probably never be known, North's alone exported in the region of 100 10T10s, and their known destinations included Aden, Antigua, Australia, Canary Islands, Cyprus, Uganda and Yugoslavia. At an advertised price of £450 per vehicle they represented a bargain for cash-strapped overseas buyers, and for a small extra fee North's would land them ready for collection at Ostend or Dunkirk for onward driving to European or North African destinations. Yugoslavia proved to be by far North's most important market with at least 33 sent to work in and around the capital, Belgrade, 10 in the coastal city of Split plus various others. In addition ten 10T10s (and a larger number of Guy double deckers) were sold in March and April 1953 direct by London Transport following an approach from the communist state's Yugoslav Timber Exporting Corporation on behalf of the Municipality of Sarajevo. As the vehicles concerned had already been notionally sold to North's, London Transport had to share receipts from the sale with them. Later, in October and November 1954, Lancashire Motor Traders found outlets for 10T10s in Belgium and Gold Coast, and even when the final group of vehicles came up for sale as late as March 1957 a ready market for the last 14 was again secured in Yugoslavia, this time through a London-based trading organisation BSE Ltd.

The first sign of post-war Ts being sold came as early as August 1955, and from then until March 1956 the BSE organisation shipped 21 14T12s along with consignments of STD class Leyland PD1s for service in Yugoslavia. These comparatively new vehicles obviously commanded a higher price, and the 14T12 went at £386 each. When, after the transactions were completed, three 15T13s became available, London Transport let BSE have them for the same price even though they were fully aware in doing so that these were superior in specification to the 14T12s. Finally, between April 1958 and April 1960, came shipments of both 14T12s and 15T13s to the Ceylon Transport Board accompanied by huge numbers of RT family vehicles. The sale price now climbed to its maximum with £800 charged for each 15T13 although this included a complete docking before departure and the provision of new tyres. So great was the overseas demand for post-war Ts that only one out of 50 14T12s remained in this country and six out of 30 15T13s.

One of the 9T9s which escaped to the warmer climes of the Canary Islands was T 423 after it was withdrawn from service at Uxbridge on 1st October 1951. By the middle of 1953 it was in the apple green and cream livery of Transportes Guanarteme serving Las Palmas on Gran Canaria, and was numbered 8 in that fleet. The London indicator boxes have gone and the former doorway has been neatly removed and replaced by a separate entrance and exit on the Spanish nearside. A trio of small maker lights has been installed near the top at the front with a further two much lower down on the mudguards. *Alan B Cross*

T 219 was a fortunate choice when it was selected for preservation way back in 1950, for without it nothing would remain to represent the swashbuckling era of franetic Green Line expansion at the start of the nineteen-thirties. Early features such as the chromium plated cab window surrounds and the tester's tip-up seat – and, of course, the original livery – are all recorded for posterity, and all that is missing, when viewed from the front, is the tinted window above the main windscreen which is currently plated over, as indeed it was for most of T 219's working life. *Owen Phillips*

Another remarkable survivor is T 31, which is generally acknowledged as having marked the start of bus preservation by private individuals when it was acquired from London Transport on 18th October 1956. It was photographed later in the same day upon arrival at the open yard at Swiss Cottage which was to be its first 'home' under private ownership, and although it looked superficially healthy enough, the severe sag in the roof gives a clue to the true condition of the bodywork. A steep learning curve was encountered when, as the outer panels were removed, major chunks of rotted wooden framework came away too. Today T 31 is once again petrol engined, and a superb restoration job completed in 1979 has resulted in a very close approximation to its condition when new at Nunhead garage back in December 1929. *Ken Blacker/Alan Nightingale collection*

Of all London Transport classes originating from the pre-RT era, the Ts are best represented today in preservation. First came Duple-bodied T 219 which London Transport wisely set aside in March 1950 at the end of a spell of service at Hounslow, transferring it on 7th March 1951 to the museum fleet which was then kept in the old East Surrey garage at Reigate. It was probably chosen because it was the last of its type to have received major attention of any sort which had resulted in it being unique as a 1/7T7/1 in carrying green and cream livery. T 219 was repainted into original Green Line colours early in its preservation days, which was a wise move because there were still staff around at the time who could recall the exact shades used and were able to advise on their accuracy. First placed on public display at the excellent Museum of British Transport at Clapham in February 1960 and then at Syon Park after the closure of the Clapham museum on 23rd April 1973, it is now once again out of regular view and stored, in a slightly fragile state, at the Acton offshoot of the London Transport Museum.

Next came T 31 which was purchased for preservation by a group of private individuals in October 1956 after it had been stored out of use in Norbiton garage for a little over four months. At the time, preservation of buses by individuals was a phenomenon unknown to bus companies and which was by no means guaranteed a welcome reception, so the purchase of T 31 was carried out on the group's behalf by Peter Davis who, four years beforehand in 1952, had gained experience in overcoming the hostility of London Transport's officials when purchasing HR2-type tram 1858. Soon after acquisition, the bodywork on T 31 was found to be totally decayed, and great credit goes to Norman Anscombe and LPC Coachworks at Hounslow for its subsequent reconstruction to represent T 31 in its early days. Today it is owned by the London Bus Preservation Trust and is on regular display in the London Bus Museum at Brooklands.

The next oldest to survive, although it is currently still in 'as discovered' condition, is T 357. This real gem is a Weymann-rebodied 5T4 of a type not seen in service with London Transport since 1944, and it is the only ex-independent T to survive, having originated with Queen Line of Baldock. Altered in the war to perimeter seating and producer gas operation, it was one of the 55 Ts which passed to the Allied Control Commission in May 1945. It ended up as a mobile home in France and was discovered in a barn in Dunkirk in 2002, finally landing back in this country in March 2003 after nearly 58 years away. Although owned by the London Bus Preservation Trust, it is not on show at Brooklands at the time of writing.

T 448 was the last 9T9 in the London Transport fleet and it survives as a reminder of what can perhaps be regarded as one of the LPTB's less successful vehicle types. It is extremely fortunate that a very derelict T 448 was rescued from scrap yard oblivion in 1968. A quick repaint followed which allowed it to be rallied, but the post-war Green Line livery which it carries is incorrectly applied at the rear of the vehicle and was never worn by it anyway. Hopefully T 448 will one day be restored to represent in an authentic way one of the stages which the 9T9s passed through during their working lives.
*Robert F Mack*

T 448, the only surviving 9T9, was the vehicle that survived all the others of its class in the service of London Transport, being finally taken out of use on 1st August 1952. It was subsequently sold to Harperbury Hospital at Shenley as a staff transport in March 1953 for £200, and was used by them until 1958 when its engine seized. Discovered almost completely overgrown by foliage in February 1968 and partially restored to an inaccurate version of Green Line livery, it is currently part of the Brooklands collection and is under restoration again.

Two 10T10s have survived one of which, T 499, is of particular interest in being the experimental 33-seater of 1938 and the original vehicle to carry the classic Lincoln green livery. It was the only one to be classified 10T10/2. T 499 was one of the many 10T10s sent abroad by North's, in this case to Australia where it ended up working as a school bus in the Western Australian outback until it was retired in 1962. After a long period out of use, T 499 was retrieved by Ensignbus from Perth and returned back to Britain in December 2004. Its restoration to Green Line condition was interrupted in December 2013 when it was temporarily shown in grey undercoat with wartime 'Clubmobile' lettering for an appearance at the Company's vintage bus running day. Its wartime career had, in fact, been as an ambulance as, indeed, had been that of T 504, the other preserved 10T10

which can today be seen at Brooklands. Historically interesting for having been the first one to be repainted – in August 1951 – into Central Bus red livery, it was found in a dilapidated state in an Oldham scrapyard in 1968 after becoming redundant as a mobile showroom, and it arrived at the former Cobham bus museum for preservation in February 1977. T 504 has subsequently been evocatively returned to Green Line condition with some of the work carried out by apprentices at London Transport's Aldenham overhaul works in 1983.

The earliest type of T survives in the shape of T 31, and it is fitting that the final version should also be represented in preservation by T 792. Dating from July 1948, it recalls the era when London Transport relied heavily on Mann Egerton of Norwich for assistance in keeping the fleet in reasonable order, and is a rare example of bodywork by this manufacturer still in existence. After passing from London Transport to the Ampthill dealer, L W Vass, in February 1963, T 792 served as a contractor's bus in London before being saved for preservation in 1967. Always privately owned, it was initially restored into the original green and white livery but, after extensive rebuilding of the bodywork, it currently carries the later 'all green' styling which is more appropriate to the trafficators and decorative rear wheel trims which vehicles of this type carried in their later days.

The 10T10 represented the public face of the T class far more than any other of the many other sub-types within it, and it also demonstrated London Transport's pre-war design expertise at its very best. It is fitting that two of these handsome vehicles should survive today. First to show its face in fully restored form, back in 1983, was T 504 which is currently on show in the London Bus Museum at Brooklands. Ensignbus were particularly innovative to add wartime decals to the grey restoration undercoat of T 499 in December 2013 and to display it, albeit temporarily, in the guise of a wartime 'Clubmobile'. It returned to Green Line colours in 2014 for the first time in 60 years. *Owen Phillips*

Current owner John Herting has rebuilt and restored Mann Egerton bodied T 792 to a high standard of finish and originality, and it is historically important as the sole survivor of the 211 T and TD class single deckers bought as stop-gap measures by London Transport in the early post-war years. *Laurie Akehurst*